D0296663

PLANTAGENET SOMERSET FRY'S

C·O·M·P·L·E·T·E B·O·O·K

OF

FACTS

PLANTAGENET SOMERSET FRY'S
C·O·M·P·L·E·T·E B·O·O·K
OF
FACTS

Mexican statue on front cover,
reproduced by kind permission
of the Mexican Government
Tourist Office.

Dragon
An imprint of the Children's Division
of the Collins Publishing Group
8 Grafton Street, London W1X 3LA

First published in two volumes; 3,000 QUESTION
AND ANSWER BOOK (1977) and 3,000 MORE QUESTIONS AND
ANSWERS (1984) by William Collins Sons & Co Ltd.
This edition published 1988.
© 1977 Plantagenet Somerset Fry (3,000 QUESTION AND ANSWER
BOOK), © 1984 Plantagenet Somerset Fry (3,000 MORE QUESTION AND ANSWERS).

ISBN 0 00 190093 5

Printed and bound in Great Britain by Mackays of Chatham PLC, Kent

Contents

Who built the first castles?
Castles may have been built by the early Egyptians as fortresses for troops on the borders of their lands. The Romans built stone forts all over their empire. In Europe, the first stone forts, or castles, were built in the 800s AD, but it was the Normans who introduced them on a large scale.

What was a motte-and-bailey?
This was a mound of earth, up to 30 metres (98 feet) high, on which was built a wooden fort. The mound, or motte, stood in a larger area called a bailey, surrounded by a wooden wall. The motte-and-bailey was a type of castle in use all over Europe before stone castles were first built, and for some time afterwards.

What is a keep?
It is the word for the great stone tower of a castle. Usually the tower was the largest and stoutest building in a castle. The word keep was not used until the 16th century.

What is the Krak des Chevaliers?
The famous concentric castle built by the early Crusaders in Syria in the 12th century. It is a huge fortress with square, round and D-end towers along both rings of walls. Much of it stands today.

What was a barbican?
This was a continuation of a castle gateway. It projected outwards and was meant to protect the gate by enclosing the approach to it. It had walls and sometimes a roof. Troops stood on guard along the tops of the walls and from this position had advantage over oncoming attackers.

What is crenellation?
If you see battlements round the top of a castle tower or along the top of a castle

wall, the correct word for these is crenellation. In the Middle Ages in England a licence was needed to put crenellation on a castle tower or along walls.

Who was Master James of St George?
He was one of the leading castle builders of 13th-century Europe. He began working on castles in Italy and France. Edward I of England employed him in Wales to supervise the building of the first big castles there. He also worked in Scotland.

What is a concentric castle?
A castle which has two or more rings of walls, with or without towers along the circumference. The gates were at opposite sides to each other so that if an enemy broke in through the outer gate, he had quite a job getting round to the gates of the next ring, and so on.

Why has Rochester Castle, in England, a rounded corner to a square tower?
Because in 1215 engineers of King John successfully brought down one square corner of the tower by digging a tunnel underneath it and making it collapse (this is called mining). When it was repaired, it was replaced by a rounded corner which is much more difficult to mine.

What is a belfry?
A tall wooden tower on wheels, used by attacking troops. Men stood on the platform at the top, generally covered by a sloping roof. They could fight at the same level as the men defending the top of the castle walls.

Who built Château Gaillard in France?
Richard the Lion Heart, king of England, built it at the end of the 12th century.

It overlooks the river Seine and it was one of the first concentric castles in western Europe. It was thought to be impregnable.

Who brought about its fall?
Troops of Philip Augustus, king of France, who were attempting to take it from forces of King John of England in 1204. They dug a tunnel and got inside under the outer walls. Then they got into the sewers of the middle part and through these to the innermost building and there forced the defenders to surrender.

What is machicolation?
In some castles you can see special holes along the tops of walls or at the top of great towers, through which defenders could drop missiles or liquids on to attackers. This was called machicolation, a stonework feature which came into use in the 14th century.

What is a gun-loop?
An opening in a castle wall, or in a tower, through which to poke a gun barrel.

What were the main weapons for besieging castles?
Mangonels (stone-throwing machines), trebuchets (mechanical slings), arbalests (huge crossbows), battering rams, penthouses (mobile tunnels which were run up to castle walls for men to run along under cover) and scaling ladders.

Where are Z-shaped castles usually found?
In Scotland. They were fortified houses, whose plan was roughly Z-shaped, that is, two round towers were connected by a square building. A good example is Claypotts, near Dundee, which still stands in good condition.

Who built brochs in Scotland?
These were large cylindrical towers of stone built by the Celtic people in Scotland 2000 years ago, chiefly as defences against raids by Roman raiders who landed in Britain to seize slaves for the Italian slave markets. There is a particularly good broch standing in Mousa in Shetland.

What is unusual about Raglan Castle in Wales?
It is a 15th-century structure, of polygonal design. Its great tower, the smaller towers and the gatehouse all have six sides, and not round or square plans.

What is a loophole?
The slit or opening in a castle wall or tower, through which an archer shot arrows. It afforded some protection against retaliation, but of course the range of view was extremely narrow.

Bamburgh Castle, Northumberland

What is yoghurt?

It is milk that is thickened and allowed to ferment by activating it with bacteria. The word is Turkish in origin. Yoghurts can be flavoured with a great variety of fruits such as cherries, raspberries and blackcurrants.

What are coquilles?

As a dish for a meal they are scallop shells filled with a concoction of grilled or baked sea foods.

What is tapioca?

Tapioca is a starchy substance which is obtained by heating cassava roots which are bitter and poisonous. The heat removes the poison and leaves grains which are boiled in water. These swell up into something looking like frog-spawn.

What is rennet used for?

It is used mainly to make junket. It is an enzyme which comes from the lining of a calf's stomach. Put into milk and boiled, it produces junket which sets in a jelly-like state.

What is molasses?

Thick black-brown syrup which is very sweet. Molasses is separated from sugar when raw sugar cane is processed. It is said to be much better for you than refined sugar.

What are chives used for?

Chives are a garden herb very much like thin spring onions to look at and to taste, though not quite so strong on the tongue. They are usually chopped up and used to flavour sauces, soups and so forth.

What is Wiener Schnitzel?

It is cutlet of veal with the bones taken out, coated with breadcrumbs and fried or grilled.

How would you get white rice to look yellow when it is cooked?

One way would be to put a pinch of saffron powder into the pan in which you are boiling or frying the rice. Saffron, a word that comes from the Arabic *za'faran*, is produced in Asia Minor from the dried stigmata of autumn crocus plants.

Why are grapefruit so called?

Grapefruit don't resemble grapes, except of course that they grow in bunches. They grow chiefly in Israel, the West Indies and other hot climates. They were called grapefruit because of their many pips.

What are whitebait?

Very small fish, about two cms (one inch) long, which are like miniature herrings. If you order whitebait in a restaurant you'll get a plate of fifty or so which have been fried whole.

How is meringue made?

You take the whites of several eggs, beat them together, with a very small amount of sugar, until you get a frothy paste. Then put this into the oven in a dish and bake it. Meringues can be coloured by using colourants like cochineal.

What is pâté de foie gras?

It is a rich-tasting paste produced from the livers of geese which are forcibly over-fed to enlarge their livers. It is a great delicacy, but if you reflect on the suffering of the geese whose gross livers eventually become pâté, you probably won't want it at all!

When is a dish flambé?

When it has been sprinkled with warm brandy – or perhaps drenched with it, in some restaurants – and then set alight. The flames burn up very quickly and do not spoil the dish.

What is steak au poivre?
This is steak sprinkled with ground
peppercorns, soaked in brandy and set
alight to produce a distinctly sharp and
rarely-cooked meat.

When would you eat antipasto?
Before you started the meal proper.
Antipasto is the Italian for 'before the
meal' and in an Italian meal it is
generally the first course.

**What does it mean when cauliflower
is served au gratin?**
It means cauliflower that has been
sprinkled with breadcrumbs when
cooked, perhaps also with a little grated
cheese, and put under a grill to brown.
Done well, it really does make
cauliflower appetizing.

What is laitue Colbert?
Strictly speaking it is lettuce prepared
in the way enjoyed by Colbert, minister
of finance to Louis XIV of France.
Actually, it is lettuce cut into shreds,
buttered, rolled up in a mix of egg and
breadcrumbs and fried. Why don't you
try it?

Where does pen oen come from?
It's a Welsh dish, basically lamb's brains,
liver, kidneys and other bits and pieces,
diced up and boiled in a great stew.
Served with mashed potato, it is a grand
filler and has quite a taste. It's very
popular in north Wales.

Who was Escoffier?
Auguste Escoffier (1846–1935) was a
French cook who worked in many noble
houses in France. He was also chef to a
Russian grand duke for a time. Then he
was invited to become *maitre chef* at the
Savoy Hotel in London, and from there
he moved to the Carlton. He was
regarded as the greatest chef of his
generation.

How do you marinade meat or fish?
Well, there are a variety of ways open to
the expert cook, but in principle you
soak the meat or fish in its raw state in a
mixture of red or white wine (or wine
vinegar) with olive oil, mixed herbs and
a rare spice or two (according to what
the experts recommend!). When the
whole lot has been left for some hours,
you cook it in one or other of the ways
suggested in the countless cook-books
available!

Little Quiz 1
What were the dates of the reigns of:
1. William II of England
2. Henry IV of France
3. Kaiser Wilhelm II of Germany
4. Elizabeth I of England
5. Robert Bruce of Scotland
6. Brian Boru of Ireland
7. Philip II of Spain
8. William the Silent of Holland
9. Louis XV of France
10. Peter the Great of Russia
What were the dates of these battles:
11. Balaclava
12. Naval battle of Copenhagen
13. Thapsus
14. Wakefield
15. Mons
16. Naval battle of the River Plate
17. Battle of the Bulge
18. Stalingrad
19. Jutland
20. Talavera
Who was the winning commander at:
21. Lake Trasimene
22. Cynoscephalae
23. Aquae Sextiae
24. Munda
25. Actium
26. Tigranocerta
27. Milvian Bridge
28. Tours

When was the first attempt to propel a ship by water-jet propulsion?

In 1782, on the Potomac River in the United States. This followed a suggestion of Benjamin Franklin's that a ship with a pump mounted at the bows could suck in water and expel it via a tube at the stern, thus propelling it forwards.

Who invented vulcanized rubber?

Charles Goodyear (1800–1860), an American inventor, became interested in the properties of rubber in 1834 and spent the next few years working out how to get rubber into a usable form. His work was successful and by 1844 vulcanized rubber had become a practical possibility.

Who invented the pneumatic tyre?

In 1845 a London engineer, Robert Thomson, invented a rubber tyre which could be filled with air, but the first successful pneumatic tyre was devised by John Dunlop, a Scottish veterinary surgeon living in Ireland, in 1888.

Who first produced a striking match?

Probably the Hon. Robert Boyle, called the father of modern chemistry, and his assistant Godfrey Haukewitz. They had discovered phosphorus and they carried out some experiments using phosphorus and sulphur. The efforts were only partly successful, but the idea was born.

Who first devised the universal joint?

Robert Hooke, the well-known English physicist (1635–1703), when inventing a helioscope (an instrument for examining the sun through a system of reflecting glasses, making it safe to look at it) suggested that it should be operated by means of a 'universal joynt'. This was a metal joint that made it possible to communicate motion in all directions.

14

When was pressure cooking introduced?

Denis Pugin, a French experimentalist who went to London to work for Robert Boyle, demonstrated a steam food 'digester' at the end of the 17th century. It was a container with a tight-fit lid which increased the pressure inside and also raised the boiling point of the water.

Pugin's pressure cooker

Who invented the slide rule?

In 1621 the Reverend William Oughtred made a rectilinear slide rule, with two scales both bearing logarithmic lines, held together in the hand when being used. It was only seven years after Napier had invented logarithms.

When was the first lawn mowing machine invented?

Well, the first to be patented was Edwin

Budding's 51-cm (20-in.) roller-mower which looks much like today's push grass cutter. This was in 1830. He was a Gloucestershire gardener.

Who invented the electrical transformer?
Michael Faraday, in the 1830s. It was but one of his many revolutionary innovations in electricity.

When was the first telegraph operated by electrical current set up?
In 1837, by two people working in cooperation, W. F. Cooke, an amateur engineer, and Charles (later Sir Charles) Wheatstone, professor of experimental philosophy at King's College in London.

When were dentures first made?
It is thought that the ancient Etruscans made sets of teeth bridged with gold, over 2600 years ago. A relatively modern looking set was found in Switzerland some time ago, confidently dated back to about 1500.

Which English monarch was the first to try out a flush water closet?
Elizabeth I, in about 1597. Her godson, John Harington, installed one he devised from an Italian model, and he set it up at her home in Richmond, near London.

Who invented the seed drill?
Jethro Tull, a retired lawyer from Berkshire, near London, who was interested in agricultural improvement. He invented it in about 1700 but did not write about it for a generation. But a few were made in the interval and they began to revolutionize farming.

Who designed the first practical artificial limbs?
Ambrose Paré (c.1517–1590), the French surgeon and physician, devised a number of well-made and practical artificial limbs for injured soldiers. Paré became court physician to four kings of France.

Who invented the knitting machine?
An English cleric, the Reverend William Lee, invented a knitting frame during the reign of Elizabeth I. He had difficulty in interesting anyone in it, but his brother managed to persuade a merchant to back the idea after Lee had died in 1610.

Who devised the Celsius temperature scale?
Anders Celsius (1701–44), a Swedish astronomer. The scale is also known as the Centigrade scale because Celsius divided the difference between the freezing and boiling points of water into 100 degrees, establishing the freezing point at 0 degrees and the boiling point at 100 degrees.

Who invented radar?
Sir Robert Watson-Watt, a British physicist, devised one of the earliest practical systems in the mid 1930s. Radar uses radio waves to detect the position, motion and nature of remote objects, and its name is derived from 'radio detection and ranging'.

Little Quiz 2
What nationality were these composers:
1. Glinka
2. Rossini
3. Franck
4. Dvořák
5. Schubert
6. Berlioz
7. Offenbach
8. Mahler
9. Holst
10. Copland

15

What is the Money Flower?

The Pennywort, sometimes called Creeping Jenny. This is a trailing waterside plant, an evergreen that provides good ground cover, and which bears bright yellow cup-shaped flowers.

What's a moneygrubber?

Someone who is obsessed with the acquisition of money. Generally it applies to people who will go to great lengths to obtain a small sum.

What is a Penny Black?

It is a postage stamp of Great Britain. It was the first stamp to be produced after the introduction of the Penny Postage in 1840, and it bore a portrait of Queen Victoria printed on a black background.

What is pennywise?

It is generally used to describe people who are careful with small sums of money but who at the same time are reckless with large sums. There is an old English adage about being pennywise and poundfoolish.

What do you mean if you describe something as twopenny-halfpenny?

You mean it is unimportant, valueless, and you would generally use the phrase in a derogatory sense.

What is a money spider?

It is a very small garden spider which may crawl over you during the summer. If it does you will have luck with money in the days to follow, according to an old belief.

What is money for jam?

It is a phrase to describe achieving success of some kind with practically no effort. It has a variation, money for old rope. In the US people talk about 'duck soup' to mean the same thing.

What is dollar diplomacy?

It is a phrase applied to a piece of diplomatic negotiation, or perhaps a more general diplomatic policy, undertaken by a country with a specific intention to further that country's financial interests abroad.

What is cash on delivery?

Also known in its abbreviated form, COD, it means ordering goods and not paying until they are delivered.

What is chequebook journalism?

It is a phrase that grew up in the 1960s in Britain when certain people, whose private – or public – lives were questionable, were persuaded to sell their memoirs to newspapers for publication.

What is pennypinching?

It is being mean or stingy.

What was a penny-farthing?

(1) a sum of one old penny and a farthing (both denominations being out of use today) and (2) an early kind of bicycle which had a huge front wheel and a very small rear wheel.

A Penny-farthing bicycle

What were the 3d and 6d Stores?
It was the other name by which Woolworth's stores were known, before the Second World War, because few things cost more than 6d.

What is Bob a Job?
'Bob' was the colloquial word for a shilling in Britain, and Boy Scouts used to call on people offering to do some chore for them in return for a shilling which would go into Scout funds.

If you were handed a 'penny dreadful' what would you get?
A penny dreadful was the phrase used earlier this century for a cheap paper-backed book with stories about crime or horror. They were also known as Shilling Shockers.

Why would someone offer you 'a penny for your thoughts'?
If you were sitting still, your eyes staring out beyond the room, your mind not directly with the things or people around you, someone might say this as a polite way of enquiring what you were thinking about.

What was the value of a Crown?
Five shillings. First minted in the 1550s in England, in silver, it continued as a standard coin of the country until this century. Crowns are still issued now, but only for commemorative purposes, such as one to perpetuate the memory of Winston Churchill.

What was a florin?
It was a two-shilling piece of silver in Britain. It was also, in the Middle Ages, a gold coin struck in Florence in Italy And it is a unit of money in Holland today.

What's a fiver?
Today it means five pounds of British money, in whatever form. Previously it referred more specifically to a five-pound note.

What does the phrase 'a hundred grand' mean?
In Britain it means £100,000 and in the US $100,000.

Little Quiz 3
Who painted these?
1. The Death of Actaeon
2. The Death of Nelson
3. The Death of Chatham
4. The Death of Elizabeth I
5. The Death of the Virgin
6. The Death of Socrates
7. The Death of Mozart
8. The Death of General Wolfe
9. The Death of Rubens
10. The Birth of Venus

Who designed these buildings?
11. Bank of England
12. Chicago Technical Institute – new buildings
13. St Martins-in-the-Fields
14. The Adelphi
15. Viceroy's House, New Delhi
16. Guggenheim Museum of Art, New York
17. Whitehall Banqueting Hall
18. National Theatre, London
19. St Paul's Cathedral
20. Coventry Cathedral
21. Sydney Opera House

Where are these
22. The Cenotaph
23. Shwe Dagon Pagoda
24. The Hermitage
25. Escorial
26. Sacré Coeur
27. Lenin's Tomb
28. Four Courts
29. Mount Vernon
30. The Astrodome
31. Pentagon
32. Topkapi

What happened to Andromeda?
Andromeda, daughter of the king of Ethiopia, said she was more beautiful than the Nereids, the nymphs of the Mediterranean Sea. Because of this she was condemned by the god of the sea, Neptune, to be devoured by a huge sea monster. But she was saved at the last moment by Perseus, who married her.

Why was Prometheus bound to a rock?
Because he stole fire out of Heaven and used it to bring to life a model of a man he had fashioned out of clay.

What was inside Pandora's box?
According to Greek myths Pandora was the first woman. Athene gave her wisdom but Zeus gave her a box in which were all the bad things of life. Although she was told not to open it Pandora's curiosity got the better of her, so she opened the box and its contents – misery – were released.

Who were the Nine Muses?
They were nine goddesses who were in charge of the arts: Terpsichore (dancing), Melpomene (tragic literature), Thalia (comedy), Euterpe (music), Urania (astronomy), Calliope (eloquence), Clio (history), Erato (elegiac poetry) and Polyhymnia (lyric poetry).

How did the Trojan War begin?
Paris, a Trojan prince, son of king Priam, enticed Helen, wife of Menelaus, Greek king of Sparta, away from her husband. Menelaus persuaded allied kings to join him in a war to rescue her.

What was the Procrustean bed?
This was a bed on to which the robber Procrustes lured his victims and chained them down. If they were too long, he lopped off parts of their limbs to fit the bed, and if they were too short he stretched them. In the end Procrustes was killed by Theseus.

Who were the Gorgons?
There were three Gorgons, all sisters, called Medusa, Euryale, and Stheno. People who looked at them were instantly turned to stone. Medusa once annoyed the goddess Minerva who turned her hair into snakes. Perseus cut off Medusa's head and placed it on Minerva's shield, which was then able to petrify Minerva's enemies.

How did Odysseus escape from the Cyclops?
One day Odysseus plied his captor Polyphemus, the Cyclops, with drink. When the Cyclops (one-eyed) got drunk he fell into a heavy sleep. Odysseus and his friends drove a sharp stake into his only eye, and when Polyphemus awoke, he could not see to stop his captives getting away.

What is the origin of the laurel bush?
The nymph Daphne was being chased by Apollo. Zeus could see that Apollo was going to catch her so he changed Daphne into a laurel bush.

What was a phaeton?
It was a horse-driven cab named after Phaethon, the son of the Sun-God. Phaethon was allowed to drive the sun chariot for a day but he failed to control it and Zeus put him to death.

How did the primitive Australian people think the sun was made?
They believed that the emu goddess Dinewan and the crane Bralgah quarrelled one day. Bralgah was so angry that he took one of Dinewan's eggs and smashed it on the ground. The ground caught fire and lit up the world for the best part of the day.

Who was Gilgamesh?
He was king of Erech and is one of the greatest heroes of ancient Babylon. He had many adventures with his friend Enkidu who was half bull, half man. They were written down in an epic called after him.

What was the main characteristic of the Viking gods?
Strength. The Vikings believed that at one time there had been a whole race of giant gods, the Aesir, who were armed with magic and who devoted their lives to fighting. They were not portrayed as attractive people because they were all scarred from their many battles.

Who was the principal god of the North American Indians?
It was Manitou, also known as the Great Spirit, who was regarded as the Great Creator.

Who was the chief god of the ancient Mexicans and Peruvians?
Although they lived in different parts of the American continent, both of these ancient civilizations believed in the same sun god. He had a different name according to the tribe which worshipped him, but he was always portrayed as one who expected daily sacrifices of human beings.

Who was the Aborigine god that filled the earth with good things?
Baiame, the great Spirit, who gave mankind water, mountains and flowers.

What is Valhalla?
Valhalla was a huge hall where the king of the Norse gods, Odin, lived. In this hall wandered the spirits of the dead. There were supposed to be 540 gates, each wide enough to let in 800 men at one time, so that nearly half a million people could enter at once.

Where were the wicked sent after their death, according to Celtic myth?
Evil people go to a hot and fiery place in most mythology, but the ancient Celts believed that their wicked men and women went to Ifurin, where it was always freezing cold.

Ganymede, cup-bearer to Zeus, the supreme god of the ancient Greeks

How was the universe divided in Greek mythology?
It was divided into three parts, the underworld, the sea and the heavens and earth.

Who were the Greek gods who ruled the universe?
They were three brothers, the sons of the god Cronus: Pluto (or Hades) who, with his queen Persephone, ruled the underworld; Poseidon who ruled the sea, and protected all waters; and Zeus who ruled the heavens and earth and became the supreme Greek god.

Who were the Roman equivalents of these Greek gods?
They were the gods Orcus, Neptune and Jupiter.

Who was

The Scourge of God?
The Scourge of God is what history has called Attila, king of the Huns (c.406–453 AD). This ferocious Asian chief brought his hordes of warriors across Europe from Russia in the 5th century, threatened both Constantinople and Rome, and defeated many Christian armies sent against him.

Buffalo Bill?
William Frederick Cody (1846–1917) was an American cowboy from Iowa. His name comes from the feat of killing 5000 buffalo for food for the workers on the Kansas Pacific Railway. He also toured with the famous Wild West Show, and visited many foreign countries where his reputation had spread before him.

Geronimo?
A Red Indian Apache chief who lived to be 80. He successfully fought off all the armies the United States government sent against him until 1886 when he was finally defeated.

The Man in the Iron Mask?
Nobody really knows for certain who was the prisoner in the Bastille in Paris who was kept in a mask of whale-bone and black silk. The most likely candidate was Matteoli, an Italian born diplomat who sometime in the 1670s double-crossed Louis XIV of France and went to prison for his pains. The prisoner became known as the Man in the Iron Mask after a book of that title was written by Alexander Dumas the elder.

Samuel Langhorne Clemens?
When ships went up the shallows of the Mississippi River in the United States in the 19th century, pilots used the call 'by the mark twain' to indicate a depth of two fathoms. Clemens had been a pilot on one of these ships, and he used

20

this cry as a pen-name when he gave up the river to write. He worked for a San Francisco newspaper while making his name as a humorist with a keen social eye. The best known of his extremely popular novels are *Huckleberry Finn* and *The Adventures of Tom Sawyer*. Mark Twain lived from 1835 to 1910.

Stonewall Jackson?
The Civil War in the United States (1861–1865) produced several able generals on both sides. One of the greatest was the Confederate Thomas Jonathan Jackson (1824–1863) who defeated the Unionist army at Bull Run, Fredericksburg and at Chancellorsville. He got his name from his refusal to shift ground backwards in battle.

Marie Henri Beyle?
He was a French diplomat at the time of Napoleon. Later on, he began to write novels under the name Stendhal, and became extremely well-known as a pioneer in new novel-writing techniques. His great work *Le Rouge et le Noir* caused a sensation when it was published in 1831. He died in 1842.

Jeanne Antoinette Poisson?
This humbly born girl met King Louis XV of France in 1744 and became his mistress. He created her Marquise de Pompadour. She dominated the king for twenty years and influenced his policies at home and abroad.

Galen?
Claudius Galenus was a Greek-born physician who lived in Rome in the 2nd century AD. He was doctor to several of the emperors, and he also wrote important works about medicine, as it was known in those days. His books had great influence on the development of medicine for many centuries.

Elizabeth Cleghorn Stevenson?

Elizabeth Cleghorn Stevenson (1810–1865) wrote novels about Victorian English society in the 19th century. She used her married name, Mrs Gaskell, by which she became well known. Among her works is *Cranford* which caused a sensation when it was published in 1853.

Nell Gwynne?

Eleanor Gwynne (1650–1687) was a Welsh-born girl who went to London and served oranges at the King's Theatre in Drury Lane. She was noticed by Charles II and became his mistress, mothering two illegitimate sons. Charles had many mistresses in his time, but Nell was his favourite as she never interfered in politics.

Charles Eduard Jenneret?

This was the real name of the celebrated Swiss architect who liked to be known as Le Corbusier (1887–1965). He was a pioneer in modern architecture, specializing in huge glass facades to his buildings and adding elevated walkways or motor passages beside them. He designed new town centres for Marseilles and Buenos Aires.

Black Tom Tyrant?

Black Tom Tyrant was Thomas Wentworth, Earl of Strafford (1593–1641), the chief minister to Charles I during the eleven years when that king ruled Britain without Parliament (1629–1640). He was able and ruthless but unpopular. When Parliament was eventually summoned in 1640, one of its first demands was the trial of Strafford. He was found guilty and executed.

Edward the Confessor?

Edward was king of England from 1042 to 1066. He was devoted to religion, spent a great deal of time in study and prayer – hence his name.

Mary Ann Evans?

Mary Evans is much better known as George Eliot (1819–1880), the Victorian novelist. Her best-known works are *Adam Bede*, the story of a carpenter who married a simple-minded village lass, and *Middlemarch*, the saga of a typical 19th-century English town.

The Ettrick Shepherd?

This was the nickname of the Scottish poet and novelist James Hogg (1770–1835). The son of a poor farmer, he became a shepherd and taught himself to read and write. He was famous in his own time but is remembered now mainly for *The Private Memoirs and Confessions of a Justified Sinner*, the story of a devout young man's duel with the Devil.

Saki?

This was the nom de plume of Hector Hugh Munro (1870–1916), a skilled English writer whose short stories wittily portray England before the First World War. During the War he sent home descriptions from the front, *The Square Egg and Other Sketches*, and was killed in action in 1916.

Charles XIV of Sweden?

He was born a Frenchman, Jean Baptiste Jules Bernadotte, who, during the French Revolution, rose from the ranks to become a brilliant general, serving under Napoleon Bonaparte. The Swedes, who were governed by an aged and childless king, had been impressed by Bernadotte's conduct and in 1809 invited him to become crown prince. He was formally adopted by the king and succeeded him in 1818. On the whole he was a good ruler and a Bernadotte king still sits on the Swedish throne.

Boz and Phiz?

They were Charles Dickens (Boz) and his illustrator, Hablot Knight Browne.

21

Who founded Rome?
According to Roman legend, Rome was founded by two brothers, Romulus and Remus, in 753 BC. Romulus quarrelled with Remus and killed him, and thus became the first king of Rome.

Who were the seven kings of Rome?
They were, in order, Romulus, Numa Pompilius, Tullus Hostilius, Ancus Marcius, Tarquinius Priscus, Servius Tullius and Tarquinius Superbus.

Why did Rome become a republic?
Tarquinius Superbus (Tarquin the Arrogant), the seventh king, was treacherous, cruel and oppressive. By 510 BC he had so alienated the entire populace of Rome that they drove him out. They promised never to have a king again, and instead began to elect two consuls each year to share the government of the new republic.

Who was the old farmer who led a Roman army to victory in 458 BC?
He was Lucius Quinctius Cincinnatus who had been a leading general but had retired to work his small holding. The Senate, in an emergency situation, elected him Dictator with full powers to raise and lead an army against the Aequi. He did so, defeating the Aequi, and then returned to his farm.

Which were the seven hills of Rome on which the city was built?
They were the Capitoline, the Aventine, the Esquiline, the Caelian, the Palatine, the Viminal and the Quirinal.

What were the twelve tables of the Law?
These were the first Roman laws written down for the Roman people. They were carved on twelve bronze tablets set up in the main market square (the Forum) for all to read.

22

Where did Hannibal come from?
Hannibal was a young military leader from Carthage, a Mediterranean sea power in the 3rd century BC whose capital was in North Africa.

Why did Hannibal make war with Rome?
Because Carthage and Rome were struggling for supremacy in the Mediterranean. Rome had beaten Carthage in the First Carthaginian War in the years 264 to 241 BC, and the Carthaginians wanted revenge.

Did Hannibal really bring elephants across the Alps against Rome?
Yes, he led an army from Spain, in 220 BC, across the Alps, accompanied by a herd of some 50 elephants. Unfortunately, they all died in the crossing.

What happened at the battle of Cannae, in 216 BC?
There, in southern Italy, Hannibal achieved his greatest victory against the Romans when he beat their army in the field. Over 50,000 Romans were left dead on the battlefield. One consul survived to carry the news to Rome.

Who brought about the final defeat of Hannibal?
Hannibal was at war with Rome for eighteen years until 202 BC when he was decisively beaten at Zama, in North Africa, by the Roman general Publius Cornelius Scipio.

What was a trireme?
This was a Roman warship which was propelled by three rows of oarsmen. Most triremes were about 30 metres (100 feet) long, had two masts and a ram. Variations of these ships were quadriremes (with four rows of oarsmen) and quinquiremes (with five rows).

What were the acta diurna?

These were reports on the daily acts of the government of Rome. They were intended to keep the public informed of what was going on, and they were introduced by Julius Caesar.

What was a supplicatio?

If a general won a notable victory or conquered a hitherto unknown land to add to the empire, the Senate might set apart a period of days to celebrate the event. The *supplicatio* was the thanksgiving.

Why did soldiers salute their generals as imperator?

For winning a victory. Julius Caesar won many victories and was created *imperator* for life. From it comes the word 'emperor'.

Who were the Optimates in ancient Rome?

They were the senators and their supporters who liked things to remain as they were, and who fought change.

Who were the Populares?

These were those senators and supporters who welcomed change and often agitated for it.

What were the magistracies in the Roman republic?

Apart from the consuls, there were the praetors who were judges in the law courts, the quaestors who managed the finances of the government, and the aediles who looked after Rome, its corn supplies, public buildings and roads.

What were the fasces?

These were bundles of rods, with an axe in the middle, its blade sticking out. They were emblems carried by the lictors who walked in front of the magistrates in processions.

Who were the publicani?

Businessmen who were given the job of collecting taxes in the provinces. They received generous commission, but it still led to a lot of corruption and much money never reached the state.

Who was Julius Caesar's heir?

Caesar's heir was his great-nephew Octavian, a boy of eighteen when Julius was murdered in 44 BC. As the emperor Augustus he ruled well until his death in 14 AD.

Did an African ever become emperor of Rome?

Yes, Lucius Septimius Severus (193–211). He proved to be a first-rate military leader, a sound statesman and was one of the best of the emperors. He died in Britain in 211 AD.

Did Nero fiddle while Rome burned?

No, of course not. He has been accused of setting fire to the city so that he could make his name immortal by rebuilding it. In fact it was almost certainly set alight by accident, and during the fire Nero opened his royal palace to refugees from the burning streets, and did much to alleviate distress.

Which was the year of the four emperors?

68–69 AD. When Nero (who was not, despite his work in the Fire, a good emperor at all) committed suicide he was succeeded by the general, Servius Sulpicius Galba. Galba was murdered a few months later, and was followed by Marcus Salvius Otho who killed himself. Otho was followed by Vitellius who was deposed and put to death. The army then raised Titus Flavius Sabinus Vespasianus, one of its best generals, to the imperial throne, hardly twelve months after the death of Nero. He ruled well for ten years.

What is wrought iron?
It is iron that contains little carbon. This makes it tough, easy to work and easy to weld, and it is highly suitable for producing decorative work.

What sort of things would a wrought iron craftsman make?
Elaborate fire baskets, firescreens, overthrows for ornamental gates, ornamental gates in singles or pairs, lanterns, weathervanes, figures, door handles, hinges, latches, knobs, knockers and so forth.

Who was Jean Tijou?
He was a French born blacksmith who came to England in the early 18th century to undertake decorative ironwork for several famous architects, including Wren.

What's a farrier?
The farrier's activities have changed over the centuries. At one time he was much the same as a blacksmith who worked iron for tool-making, but he also specialized in making horse-shoes. This led in time to farriers getting to know so much about horses that people who had sick horses took them to their local farrier. Today, farriers shoe horses, occasionally repair farm machinery, but no longer treat horses.

What is dry-stone walling?
This is walling put together with natural stone cut into flattish shapes and laid in layers to whatever height and length is required. As a rule, no mortar is used as the wall is made from stones which will fit well together.

What does a tanner do?
A tanner obtains animal hides and makes leather out of them. There are two main ways to do this. If the hides are heavy they are treated with vegetable salts, if they are light they are dipped in a solution of chromium salts. This makes the hides flexible, elastic and extends their life.

What is a horologist?
He is a clockmaker or clockmender. The word comes from the Greek *hora*, an hour.

What is a shipwright?
A shipwright is a craftsman who is skilled in carpentry and who constructs or repairs small ships and boats, generally made of wood. The term used to cover the person who was responsible for the overall design, building and outfitting of a ship.

What does a cooper do?
A cooper makes or repairs casks or barrels for beers, ales, wines. In some cases he also puts the wine into casks, and even markets it. Nowadays, however, many beer products are put in metal kegs and the need for skilled coopers in woodwork has declined.

What is a cottage industry?
It is a manufacturing business where the workers make the products at home from material given them by a businessman who will sell the products when they are completed. This was widespread in Britain in the 18th century but has declined.

Which are the main areas in Britain where thatching of roofs is carried out?
East Anglia, the West Country and some Midland districts.

How is glass blown?
Today, a typical procedure for glass-blowing is melting down a mixture of sand, lead oxide, powdered glass and potash in a clay furnace until it is

properly molten. A blowing iron is then inserted into a quantity of molten glass and the glass is blown into the form required.

How long has glass in fact been blown?
The ancient Egyptians, who first thought of many things, were blowing glass with some skill 3500 years ago. The Chinese and the Greeks and Romans also practised the art with great skill.

What is welding?
It is joining pieces of metal together by heating the ends of each and rendering them plastic enough to be pressed together. Traditional blacksmiths heated pieces of iron, hammered them as they did so, and when both were very hot indeed, then hammered them together, effecting a weld which set when the metals were cooled.

What are the more modern techniques of welding?
Using a burning gas, such as oxy-acetylene, to heat the metals to be joined, or an electric arc struck between two electrodes, or one electrode and the metal.

How do you electro-plate a metal surface?
Put an object that is to be plated in a bath containing a solution of the salt of the plating metal and pass a current through the solution. Minute deposits of the plating metal will very gradually be built up on the surface of the metal to be plated. Typical plating metals are copper, silver, chromium and nickel.

How was silver-plating done in the days before electro-plating?
Ingots of silver were rolled to the required thickness on to the surface of the metal to be plated. The plating had

to be quite thick, or it would rub off very easily with little wear.

When was the spinning wheel invented?
The spinning wheel operated by a treadle, and very familiar, was said to have been invented in Germany in the 1530s. It arrived in England in the 1540s and quite probably went over the Atlantic to America in the 1620s.

A spinning wheel

What was a saw-pit?
A trench dug by a sawyer for cutting up large timbers. Two sawyers worked at the job as a rule, one holding one end of a long saw and standing at the bottom of the trench and the other at the top holding the other end. These pits were usually near joiners' businesses, for it was they who used the cut wood for making things.

OUI!

What is the Declaration of Human Rights?
Drawn up by the United Nations General Assembly in 1948, it states that all people have the right to life, liberty, education, equality before the law and freedom of religion, association and movement from one place to another.

What was the American Civil Rights Act of 1964?
Pushed through by President Lyndon Johnson, it aimed to guarantee the rights of the black American population in education, employment, housing, elections, public facilities and so forth.

Which language is spoken by the most people in the world?
Chinese, in its Mandarin and Cantonese forms, and other variants: about 750,000,000 speak it. Strangely enough, the next most widely spoken language is English, by some 350,000,000 people followed by Spanish spoken by 145,000,000.

What is Sanskrit?
The language of ancient India, used chiefly in poetry and writing. In its oldest form it is at least 3,500 years old. Many modern Indian languages are descended from it.

What is the Cyrillic alphabet?
It is the Slavonic alphabet which is based on the ancient Greek alphabet. From it the Bulgarian, Serbo-Croat and Russian alphabets are derived. Its name comes from St Cyril, of the 9th century, who is said to have formulated it.

Who spoke Aramaic?
It was a Semitic language in the Near East, and it was probably the tongue spoken by Jesus Christ. It was used by many peoples in the Near East from as early as the 8th century BC.

What is Tamil?
A language spoken in parts of southern India and in Sri Lanka.

Where is Afrikaans spoken?
As one of the two official languages, in South Africa. It is the tongue of the descendants of the Dutch settlers in South Africa and is based on Dutch, with a mixture of such tongues as German, French and some native expressions. It became a written language in the 1870s.

What is Urdu?
One of the principal languages of the Indian sub-continent but which is influenced by Persian. Most people who speak it write it in Persian script.

What are the principal Romance languages and why are they so called?
They are Italian, French, Romanian, Spanish and Portuguese, and they are called Romance languages because they derive from Latin as spoken in the days of the Roman Empire.

What is pidgin English?
A strange kind of English mixed up with words from Chinese and other Eastern languages. It has little sense of grammar or style and it's difficult to understand. One good place to hear it spoken is Hong Kong.

What is restaurant French?
Many English restaurants have menus written in French. When they are on holiday in France, some English people try out their knowledge of it on locals, residents in restaurants and hotels. To most Frenchmen, however, it is something of a mystery!

What is gobbledygook?
The word arose in the US and is now

used in Britain. It refers to heavy official language as used in government service by over-keen staff who hope to impress – or intimidate! It is characterized by the use of very long words and phrases where shorter ones will do.

Who are the Walloons?
They are people living mostly in the south-east of Belgium who speak a kind of French. There are about three million of them. They are descended from ancient Celtic tribes who came under Roman influence.

Who are the Pathans?
They are a fierce tribe of warriors who live in parts of Afghanistan and in north-west Pakistan.

Who are the head-hunters of the Far East?
The Dayaks (or Dyaks) who occupy parts of Borneo. They use blowpipes and poisoned darts to kill animals, and it is not unknown for them to despatch inquisitive humans in the same manner.

Who are the Hottentots?
They are a wandering pastoral people who live in South West Africa. They have over the years mingled here and there with European and other settlers and are not as barbarous as when they were first encountered by Europeans in the 17th century.

What is a Creole?
It is a word to describe a descendant of French, Spanish or Portuguese colonists in the West Indies, parts of the southern United States, Mauritius, Africa and the East Indies.

Who are the Masai?
They are an East African race, distinguished by their splendid physique and their great bravery, who live on the border lands of Kenya and Tanzania. Their diet consists of meat which they wash down with a mixture of milk and cattle blood.

How many black people are there in the United States?
About 24,000,000, or about a ninth of the total population.

What are the six principal Celtic languages?
Welsh, Gaelic (Scots), Erse (Gaelic Irish), Manx, Cornish and Breton. These languages are among the oldest living languages in Europe, and in Wales and Cornwall there is an increasing number of people learning the traditional language of their country.

What is the longest station name in Europe?
LLANFAIRPWLLGWYNGYLLGOGER-YCHWYRNDROBWLLLLANTISILIO-GOGOGOCH! It's in Anglesey in North Wales.

Little Quiz 4

Of which country or countries were these rulers:
1. Alexander the Great
2. Pyrrhus
3. Ivan the Terrible
4. Charles XII
5. Rameses II
6. Malcolm III (Bighead)
7. Roderic O'Connor
8. Zog

How many times were the following prime minister of Great Britain:
9. Winston Churchill
10. George Canning
11. William Gladstone
12. Benjamin Disraeli
13. Lord John Russell

$$2 + 5 \times 3 - 1 \div 2 = 10$$

What is trigonometry?
It is the part of mathematics that is concerned with the sides and angles of triangles, their measurement and the relationship between them.

What was Pythagoras' theorem?
It states that in any right-angled triangle the square on the longest side (the hypotenuse) is equal to the sum of the squares of the other two sides of the triangle.

What is an angle?
When two lines meet at a point they form an angle. It can be a right angle, which means the angle is of 90 degrees, or it can be acute, that is, less than 90 degrees or it can be obtuse, namely, more than 90 degrees.

How are angles measured?
Generally anticlockwise, with the full circle containing 360 degrees.

How do you work out the area of a rectangle?
Multiply the base by the height (or one of the longer two sides by one of the shorter two sides).

How do you calculate the volume of a cylinder?
Multiply the radius at the base squared by π and then by the length.

What is this figure π?
It is the sixteenth letter of the Greek alphabet, called *pi*. In mathematics it is the symbol for the ratio between the circumference of a circle and the diameter. It has a value of 3.14159.

What are the factors of a number?
They are the numbers which, when multiplied together give the number. Therefore 3 and 2 are the factors of 6. One is a factor of any number.

What are a square root and a cube root?
A square root is one of two equal factors of a number, such as the square root of 16 is 4, and a cube root is one of three equal factors of a number, such as the cube root of 125 is 5 ($5 \times 5 \times 5$).

Who was Euclid?
He was a Greek mathematician who lived in Egypt, at Alexandria, in the 300s BC and wrote a number of works on geometry. These became standard works throughout the world. They have remained so, some 2300 years later! He devised most of those theorems you have to learn in geometry classes.

What is an abacus?
A counting machine – you might say, a primitive computer – invented, probably, by the Chinese thousands of years ago. It normally has beads set on horizontal parallel rows of wire or cotton in a frame. A Roman abacus had ten beads on each wire and each wire represented a digital position.

A Chinese abacus

What is Absolute Zero?
It is a temperature of −273.16 degrees centigrade, which is calculated to be the lowest temperature that could exist, a temperature at which atoms and molecules would have no energy.

Who was Charles Babbage?

He was an English mathematician who spent nearly forty years of his life developing calculating machinery, though chiefly on the drawing board rather than in actual machinery. Born in 1792, Babbage also designed an advanced analytical machine which was intended to do any calculation for which instruction could be given.

What is physics?

The science of matter and energy and their interactions. It is divided for convenience into several branches, namely, nuclear physics, solid and liquid state physics, optics, acoustics, thermodynamics, electricity, electronics and magnetism.

What are acoustics?

The science of sound waves and their production, transmission and reception.

What are thermodynamics?

The science that deals with heat and its relations with other forms of energy.

What is a proton?

It is the nucleus of a normal hydrogen atom, and it also happens to be the positive heavy particle of the nucleus of any other atom.

What is an electron microscope?

This microscope uses beams of electrons instead of light beams to produce a greatly magnified image of an object. It is used to look at organisms and other things which are too small to be examined in proper detail under an ordinary microscope.

What is a calorie?

It is a unit of heat, and is the heat required to raise one gram of water through one degree centigrade of temperature.

When did calculating machines really begin?

In the 19th century precision engineering had reached a stage when sophisticated calculating machines were possible, and the first successful machines were made in America by firms like Burroughs. At the beginning of this century electric power enabled calculating machines to be greatly accelerated.

Little Quiz 5

How many sides have these?
1. triangle
2. square
3. tetrahedron
4. prism
5. cuboid
6. pentagon
7. cube
8. right angled triangle
9. duodecagon
10. octagon

How many:
11. inches to the yard?
12. feet to the rod, pole or perch?
13. yards to the mile?
14. square yards to the acre?
15. acres to the square mile?
16. grammes to the kilogramme?
17. pounds to the ton?
18. pounds to a stone?
19. tons in a megaton?
20. pecks to a bushel?

What are the metric equivalents of these:
21. 1 inch
22. 1 yard
23. 1 chain
24. 1 mile
25. 1 international nautical mile
26. 1 pint
27. 1 gallon
28. 1 bushel
29. 1 ounce
30. 1 pound

What is the John Birch Society in the United States?
It is a society of people who believe in the supremacy of white people and who are violently anti-Communist. It was founded in 1958 in memory of an American Baptist missionary, John Birch, who was executed as a spy by the Chinese in 1945.

Who were the Diggers?
A small band of revolutionaries assembled by one Gerald Winstanley in 1649 in England. They believed that ordinary people should not have to pay rent for land and they demonstrated this by digging up the common at Walton-on-Thames and elsewhere in Surrey.

Where did the Jindyworobaks originate?
They were a group of people in Adelaide, in Australia, who in the 1930s championed the individuality of the Aborigines, wrote poetry using Aboriginal words and developed similar legends in narrative form.

Who were the Encyclopaedists?
They were contributors to the massive Encyclopaedia of the French philosophers Diderot and d'Alembert. This great work, produced in the middle of the 18th century, condensed a mass of expression of new ideas about art, science and political thinking, in a word, rationalism. They were an important influence on the movement which led to the French Revolution.

What was an emigré?
It was the name given to someone who fled from France at the time of the Revolution (1789–1794) and sought refuge in Britain.

Who were the Irvingites?
They were a religious sect, known as the Catholic Apostolic Church, founded by Edward Irving (1792–1834) a Church of Scotland minister. They adopted many Roman Catholic rituals and ceremonials and have now declined.

Who were the Mohocks?
A gang of well-born, rich young gentlemen who in the middle of the 18th century molested passers-by in the streets of London – rolling them down the street in a barrel, overturning coaches into refuse dumps and so forth, all just for 'fun'. The name was a corruption of Mohawk, a famous Indian tribe in America.

Where did the beaker folk live?
They lived in Europe and Britain probably in the 1400–1200s BC. They were partly civilized, and are called beaker folk because their culture is distinguished by their large drinking mugs or beakers, ornamented sometimes with shells, lengths of cord, and so forth.

What is a mummer?
The term has really gone out of use now, but in the Middle Ages mummers were actors and actresses who went from house to house, especially at Christmastime, dressed in disguise, performing plays.

Who were the Tolpuddle Martyrs?
A handful of farm labourers who set up their own branch of the Grand National Consolidated Trades Union. In 1834, at Tolpuddle, a village in Dorsetshire, they were tried and sentenced to transportation to Australia for having formed the branch. After a nation-wide campaign of protest, the six farm labourers were pardoned.

What was a Bolshevik?
A member of the Communist Party of Russia, founded secretly in 1903, as an

extreme wing of the Social Democratic Party. The Bolsheviks, led by Lenin, were extremely left-wing. The word means member of the majority.

Who were the Carbonari?
A secret political society operating in the south of Italy in the early part of the 19th century. They campaigned against the monarchy in Naples, and their name comes from the fact that they hid in the hills of the Abruzzi and burned charcoal.

What was the Jacobin Club?
A democratic and republican club born in the French Revolution at Versailles in 1789. It moved to Paris and occupied the Jacobin friary. Jacobin became the name for anyone who supported the revolution, particularly the more extreme side of it.

What were the Janissaries?
The bodyguard of the sultan of the Ottoman (Turkish) Empire. As a body of men it survived from the 14th to the 19th centuries. The Janissaries were noted for their cruelty and repressive activities.

What is the Fabian Society?
A British socialist organization founded in 1884 which provided – and still provides – much of the intellectual and political stimulus for the Labour Party. Called Fabian after the famous Roman dictator Quintus Fabius Maximus Cunctator (the Delayer) who achieved many of his objectives by patiently waiting for the right moment.

Who were the Syndicalists?
They were a revolutionary workers' movement which campaigned for worker ownership and control of industry, each industry to be run by those workers who were in it. The idea began in England but it was in France that it made its special impact at the beginning of this century.

Who were the King's Girls in Canada?
In the early years of the French settlements in Canada, there was a great shortage of women. The French government therefore organized contingents of young and healthy peasant girls and sent them to Canada, with cash endowments, for the men to choose as wives.

Who were the larrikins?
They were 19th-century toughs in Australian towns, identifiable by their broad-brimmed slouch hats and bell-bottom trousers.

Who were the Junkers?
They were landed gentry in Prussia in East Germany. They were reactionary, almost feudal, in outlook, and they were also extremely militaristic. Many leading generals in the Prussian army came from Junkers families.

Who were the Macaronis?
They were young and wealthy men from Britain who, in the 1760s and 1770s, had travelled in Italy on the Grand Tour and sported some of the fashions they had brought back. The name arose from a club they formed, called the Macaroni Club, which introduced macaroni as a regular dish at the well-known London restaurant of Almacks.

Who on earth were the Knownothings?
An American political party in the 1850s, in the eastern states. They resisted immigration from Europe, and they supported slavery. The name came from the fact that when asked what they stood for they always answered 'I know nothing!' However, in 1855 the movement took the title, American party, and lost much of its secrecy. It finally died out about 1860.

What finished the war with Japan?
Dropping the first atomic bombs on the Japanese cities of Hiroshima and Nagasaki in August 1945. The Japanese surrendered unconditionally.

What was Marshall Aid?
It was a magnificent act of generosity devised by General Marshall, American war-time chief of the army staff. America gave $10,000,000,000 in the form of cash and goods to Europe, lying prostrate after the ravages of war. Marshall received the Nobel Prize for Peace in 1953 – and deservedly.

Who was Mohammed Turré?
He was a splendid African ruler, part Moslem Turk, part West African, who built up an empire called the Songhoi Empire in what is now Nigeria, during the 1520s. He introduced up-to-date government and taxation, founded a university at Timbucktoo, and formed a regular police force. Canals were dug for irrigation, and trade was encouraged.

What was the Rump Parliament in England?
In December 1648 about 140 English MPs were prevented by troops from taking their seats at Westminster. Only about 60 pro-army members were allowed to go in. This small remnant became known as the Rump and sat for five years until it was expelled by Cromwell.

**'The Cat, the Rat, and Lovel, our Dog;
Rule all England under the Hog.'
When was this doggerel written and about whom?**
It was written in 1484, allegedly, by a supporter of Henry Tudor, in the time of Richard III (1483–1485). It referred to Sir William Catesby, Sir Richard Ratcliffe and Francis, Viscount Lovell, three friends and advisers of Richard whose badge was a white boar (hence 'the Hog').

32

Why did Edward VIII abdicate in 1936?
Because he wanted to marry a twice-divorced woman. But he was also head of the English church which did not sanction divorce so he could not do so. Nor would the government or country have tolerated it. So he gave up the throne for the woman he loved.

Edward VIII
later Duke of Windsor (1894–1972)

When did the ruler of Great Britain cease to be ruler of Hanover?
In 1837, when Queen Victoria succeeded her uncle William IV. He had a younger brother, Ernest Augustus, Duke of Cumberland, who succeeded to the kingdom of Hanover, while Victoria became queen of Great Britain.

What was a Dreadnought?
A type of battleship, with many big guns, the first being HMS Dreadnought which was built in 1906. It was, as were its followers, the best battleship afloat, and could out-gun and outpace any other in the world. The initiative in getting these ships built was due to Admiral of the Fleet Lord Fisher (1841–1920).

What was the Maginot Line?
A string of fortifications built between 1929 and 1934 along the eastern border of France, from Luxemburg to Switzerland. So called from the then war minister, André Maginot, who masterminded its construction.

What was the siege of Dien Bien Phu?
It was a siege of the town of Dien Bien Phu in what is now Vietnam, held by some 10,000 French and allied troops against forces of the Communists. The siege lasted two months, March to May 1954, and when the town fell, it was the end of French interest in Vietnam.

Who was Alexander Dubcek?
He was a brave but sad Czech statesman who in 1968 as first secretary of the Czech Communist Party attempted to liberalize the Communist regime. The Russians objected, and moved an army into Prague to bring his government down.

On which Christmas Days were seven British sovereigns all living?
Christmas Day 1683 and 1684. Charles II (d.1685), James II (d.1701), William III (d.1702), Mary II (d.1694), Anne (d.1714), George I (d.1727) and George II (d.1760). George II had been born in 1683.

When did the Second World War end in Europe?
May 8th, 1945, when the Germans surrendered unconditionally.

When was the state of Israel created?
1948, after the British forces withdrew from their mandate to govern Palestine on behalf of the United Nations. The first president was Chaim Weizmann a Russian-born scientist who became a British citizen before becoming the Zionist leader in 1920.

What was the Munich Crisis of 1938?
The German dictator Hitler threatened to overrun Czechoslovakia if the Czechs would not join up with Germany voluntarily. Britain and France attempted to moderate Hitler's demands, and at Munich an agreement was reached whereby some Czech territory was handed to Hitler on a plate in return for promises not to take the rest. Of course Hitler broke his promises, and moved into Czechoslovakia in March 1939.

What was Morton's Fork?
A process introduced by Cardinal Morton, one of Henry VII's chief advisers, whereby you paid taxes whatever wealth you had. If you looked rich you could obviously afford to pay; if you looked poor you were obviously hiding the money, and could therefore equally afford to pay!

Why did the clan Campbell massacre the clan MacDonald at Glencoe?
The powerful MacDonald clan had a long-established feud with the clan Campbell. William III used this feud to break the power of the MacDonalds by ordering loyal members of the Campbell clan to attack them without warning one winter's day in 1692.

Which countries formed the Rome-Berlin-Tokyo Axis in 1942?
Germany, Italy, Japan, Hungary, Bulgaria, Romania and Slovakia and Croatia.

What is harmony?
It is a pleasing combination of musical sounds, produced by the formation of a structure of chords and notes that fill out a melody or tune and enhance its meaning.

What is counterpoint?
It is the simultaneous combination of two or more independent melodies, forming a satisfying musical texture. It comes from the Latin phrase *punctus contra punctum*, which means note against note, and was first employed as a musical technique in late medieval plainsong, the unaccompanied chants sung in Christian churches.

How many Brandenburg Concertos did J. S. Bach write?
Six, between the years 1719 to 1721, and these were presented to the Margrave of Brandenburg who had commissioned them.

What is a concerto?
It is an orchestral composition, written in three separate movements, for a single instrument, or for a single instrument as dominant part with other instruments as background or support, or for more than one instrument and orchestra. Mozart wrote more than fifty concertos for a variety of instruments.

What was a concerto grosso?
It was an orchestral composition, especially popular in the 18th century, in which a large group of instrumentalists interplay with a smaller group. The phrase comes from the Italian and means big concerto.

When was the organ invented?
The organ has a long history. There were primitive organs in the 3rd century BC, consisting of simple panpipes in series played by musicians operating bellows on

leather bags to produce the air for all the pipes. The first chromatic keyboard organ was produced in the 14th century.

Who wrote the Enigma Variations?
Sir Edward Elgar Bt, OM, GCVO (1857–1934). He was born in Worcestershire in England and wrote some of the finest music ever to come out of Great Britain. It took nearly 50 years for him to be recognized as a musical genius in Britain, and only then because countries abroad had already acknowledged it. The *Enigma Variations* are a series of orchestral pieces dedicated to, or attempting to describe musically, some of his acquaintances.

What is chamber music?
It is music written for small groups of instruments, not a whole orchestra. It was originally meant to be performed in a room and not in a large concert hall.

When did the violin first appear?
In the 17th century.

What is a Stradivarius?
It is the name given to a violin made by Antonio Stradivari (1644–1737), an Italian violin-maker from Cremona. Violins made by him or by his sons are generally extremely valuable because they were most beautifully made and because of the beautiful tone they produce. He also made violas and cellos, and it is thought he completed about 1000 instruments during his long life although the best date from between 1700 and 1720.

Where did Stradivari learn to make violins?
He learned from Nicolo Amati (1596–1684), one of the Amati family which also lived in Cremona and which was for nearly two centuries among the greatest of all violin-makers.

What is the difference between a violin and a cello?

There are several. A cello is much larger and is played sitting down, held between the knees. It has a range of five octaves, which is more than a violin.

What is an electrophone?

It is a word sometimes used generally to cover musical instruments which are operated electrically or electronically, such as guitars connected up electrically with loud speakers. Electric organs are also electrophones.

What is jazz?

It is syncopated music which is played over dance rhythms. It began in New Orleans in the US in the 1880s, and is particularly notable for the fact that the tunes played were often improvised on the spot from some simple set of chords or a short melody.

What is tempo?

It is the Italian word for the pace at which music is played – or at least, should be played! Most compositions state at the start what the right tempo should be, and elsewhere along the way there are indications where the speed changes.

What are the principal tempi in music?

Adagio: slow and easily; *allegro:* brisk; *andante:* at moderate speed; *grave:* seriously; *lento:* slowly (slower than *adagio*); *moderato:* with moderate speed; *presto:* quickly. All these terms are also Italian.

Is it possible to say who was the greatest composer of all time?

For those who hesitate to commit themselves about who was the greatest this or that, the answer is of course no. But probably the two most generally acknowledged as the greatest were Johann Sebastian Bach (1685–1750) and Wolfgang Amadeus Mozart (1756–1791).

What was the secret of Bach's musical genius?

He developed existing forms of music to an unsurpassed height, and also 'reached forward into the future both with his music and his instruments'. His influence on later musicians would be difficult to overestimate. Several of his children became extremely well-known and gifted composers, especially Karl Philip Emanuel and Johann Christian.

Who is the greatest living violinist?

Few would dispute the supreme virtuosity of Yehudi Menuhin who was born in 1916 and who gave his first public concert at the age of eight.

What is the longest composition for the piano ever written?

It is the *Opus Clavicembalisticum* by the English-born composer, Kaikhosru Shapurji Sorabji, the son of a Parsee father and a Sicilian mother. The *Opus* lasts over 2½ hours and contains twelve movements. It has been performed only once in public, in 1930, and with all the composer's other highly complex works was banned from public performance from then until 1976.

What are Songs without Words?

Songs without Words is the title given by Mendelssohn to eight books of piano pieces which he wrote between 1830 and 1840. He also wrote one for cello and piano.

What is a counter-tenor?

It is the highest male voice, also called the alto. The use of this voice was popular in the 17th century and there has been a revival of interest since the 1950s.

35

What is ashlar?

It is good quality stone cut carefully into rectangular shapes. The sides which are to be the outside and visible parts of the building are then smoothed. Medieval masons used it widely in castle and cathedral construction.

What is a pantile?

It is a tile for a roof, made from heavy clay and shaped like a flat 'S' across its width. They were used widely in Europe and in Britain, East Anglian builders used them a lot.

How do you 'pebble-dash' a wall?

You cover it with cement and sand mixture on the outside and then throw small stones at the covering while it is still wet. Hopefully, the majority of them stick and set in place when the cement dries.

Where does flint come from?

Flint is a hard stone that is generally found in chalky ground, but can also appear in clay-filled soil. It is irregular in shape and can be as small as an apple or as large as a boulder weighing several kilogrammes.

How can brick or stone be 'dressed'?

If the wall of a house is brick but is highlighted with certain stone features such as architraves, courses, balustrades and so on, it is said to be dressed.

What is concrete made of?

Concrete is cement mixed with sand or broken stone and left to set hard. The proportions of the mix depend largely upon the use to which the concrete is to be put. As a building material it was invented by the Romans.

What is terra-cotta?

Basically it is a form of pottery which is very hard and smoother than brick. It was popular for decorative effects on buildings in the Middle Ages but has not been widely used since.

How did medieval builders insulate floors against noise?

By 'pugging', whereby sawdust, bullrushes, cockleshells, odd lumps of cement, earth, sand or bits of rubble lying about were inserted between the floor at one level and the ceiling on the floor below.

What was pargetting?

Strictly speaking, pargetting was another word for plastering a wall. But when the practice of plastering whole areas of outside wall (as opposed to strips between wooden beams) developed, builders would decorate the plaster with patterns, such as bird feet, Tudor roses, 'gridiron' shapes and so on. This has come to be called pargetting.

How is plywood made?

Several very thin sheets of wood are squared off to the shape and size of plywood sheet required. One sheet is glued to the next sheet with the grains at right angles. The third sheet is glued to the second with its grain running the same way as the first sheet and so on. Normally, plywood comes in three, five and seven sheet thicknesses, but there are of course variations.

Why are some roofs thatched?

Possibly because there is a good local supply of reed or straw for thatching or, as in the case of some early civilizations, builders knew no other way to cover a roof.

What are tiles for roofs usually made of?

Clay which is baked and left to harden. Clay tiles are generally reddish in colour, almost always unglazed, and they come in several sizes and shapes. In recent years, some manufacturers of building materials have been making tiles out of concrete.

What is rubble?
Rough and uncut stone, generally the bits and pieces left behind in a quarry after larger and tidier shapes have been cut and removed.

What on earth is wattle and daub?
This charming phrase refers to what medieval builders placed between timber studs (upright beams) in the framework of a building. They made a lacing of willow or hazel sticks between the studs, called wattling, and then covered or daubed this with a mixture of clay and water. Sometimes they used cow-dung and animal hair.

What is stucco?
The Italian word for two kinds of plastering. It is a fine plaster covering for inside walls and ceilings, in which decorative mouldings were impressed or shaped. Or it is a wet mixture of cement, lime and sand plastered on outside walls simply to form a tough coating.

What is a quarry tile?
Quarry tiles are square clay tiles for flooring or paving, of varying sizes. The most general size is 25 cms (10 ins) square, or a half tile 25 cms (10 ins) by 12.5 cms (5 ins). Most quarry tiles are 2 cms (1 in.) or so thick. Older ones were often thicker at one end than at the other and looked like wedges.

Where does slate come from?
It is a laminated rock (a rock built up in layers) which can be easily split to form thin sheets of material for covering. The sheets are cut to size and used as tiles on roofs. Bigger shapes and sizes are used as gravestones, or paving stones. Slate comes chiefly from mountain areas such as North Wales in Britain.

What is mortar?
A mixture of lime (or cement), sand and water which is used to cement bricks together in a wall.

What is cob?
It is a mixture of clay or chalk with gravel, with some straw thrown in for strengthening and binding. Cob was used as a building material for poorer houses.

Little Quiz 6
Which country goes with which capital?

1.	China	A	Cardiff
2.	Ethiopia	B	Madrid
3.	Zaire	C	Nairobi
4.	Brazil	D	Paris
5.	Canada	E	Wellington
6.	India	F	Colombo
7.	Indonesia	G	London
8.	Wales	H	Hima
9.	Haiti	I	Lagos
10.	Poland	J	Washington
11.	Italy	K	Kinshasa
12.	Zambia	L	Dublin
13.	Argentina	M	Moscow
14.	Scotland	N	Ottawa
15.	USSR	O	Peking
16.	Venezuela	P	Canberra
17.	US	Q	Warsaw
18.	New Zealand	R	Addis Ababa
19.	Kenya	S	Port au Prince
20.	Spain	T	Brasilia
21.	Nigeria	U	Edinburgh
22.	England	V	Rome
23.	France	W	Buenos Aires
24.	Australia	X	Delhi
25.	Sri Lanka	Y	Jakarta
26.	Peru	Z	Lusaka
27.	Eire	Aa	Caracas

What is acupuncture?
Acupuncture is a form of medical treatment for various complaints, invented by the Chinese many centuries ago. It consists of inserting small needles into parts of the body and leaving them there for short periods. During this time the body attempts to balance itself and thus helps the complaints to get better. Acupuncture is now being practised in the Western world as well.

Why is penicillin called an antibiotic?
Because it destroys – or at least damages – living and harmful organisms in the body, like bacteria. Penicillin was the first antibiotic and it was discovered by Sir Alexander Fleming, but there have been many others developed since then.

Why is there no cure yet for the common cold?
Chiefly because we still don't know exactly what kind of germ or other organism causes a cold. Much research goes on all the time but the best so far that can be done is to take one or other of many preparations to check the worst symptoms.

What are hiccoughs?
This is when a sudden irritation in the diaphragm of the chest causes the windpipe to close and so interrupt the breathing pattern, which becomes jerky and uneven. Usually, an attack of hiccoughs (pronounced 'hiccups') lasts only a few minutes but there are records of people hiccoughing for hours, even days on end.

What is an allergy?
It is the word describing an unpleasant body reaction to a variety of things like certain foods, pollen, insect stings and so forth.

What is cortisone?
It is one of a group of substances produced by the adrenal gland and it comes from the cortex of the gland. Discovered in Switzerland soon after the Second World War it is used to treat several complaints, among them rheumatoid arthritis and some kidney disorders.

Why do some people have their tonsils taken out?
The tonsils are two glandlike structures at the back of the throat. They can be traps for germs, whereupon they can get inflamed, cause a sore throat and other nasty symptoms.

What is a diet?
A diet is a course of food intake which you may follow for a variety of reasons. There are diets, for example, for people who want to lose weight, and for those who are run down and need to build up their strength. Most diets will do what they are intended to, but the results will of course vary from person to person.

What makes some people snore?
Some people snore when they are asleep because the air they are breathing goes down their throat via their nose and their mouth at the same time. The noise is the result of the two air streams colliding.

What is hay fever?
This is like a mild kind of asthma that some people get in the spring and summer through breathing air in which pollen is floating about, or perhaps it may be caused by fine dust.

What did Cromwell mean when he told the painter Lely to 'paint me as I am, warts and all'?
Cromwell, Lord Protector of England, Scotland and Ireland (1653–58) had a

number of warts, one or two of which were prominent on his face. Lely was about to paint his portrait leaving them out, but the Protector wanted future generations to see him as he really was.

What is a wart?
It is a small hard overgrowth of skin which can appear on the skin in various parts of the body, notably the face and the hands. Warts can often be removed by applying a little caustic (or burning) by means of liquid or a special caustic pencil.

Why do we get holes in the teeth?
Decay begins in the enamel of a tooth. It may be a small crack or chip but germs get in, mix with the fluids in the tooth cavity and finally destroy the enamel so that a hole appears. When this happens the tooth has to be filled by a dentist.

What is asthma?
Asthma is a condition in which the tubes from the windpipe into the lungs get constricted or blocked as a result of an allergy, or perhaps through atmospheric conditions. Sometimes it may be through nerves. The result is wheezing, shortness of breath and watering of the eyes, and while there are things that can be done to alleviate the symptoms, there is not yet a complete cure.

What does a kidney machine do?
A kidney machine separates out the harmful substances from the good ones in the blood. This is the job the kidneys normally do for the body but some people's kidneys cannot function properly so they are connected to the machine for short periods.

Who carried out the first heart transplant operation?
Professor Christiaan Barnard, a distinguished South African surgeon, removed a sound heart from a dead person and grafted it into the chest cavity of a living man, Mr. Louis Washkansky, who had severe heart trouble. This was at Groote Schurr Hospital in Capetown, in South Africa in December 1967. Mr. Washkansky's own heart was disconnected, and he lived with the new heart for nearly three weeks.

What else can be transplanted successfully in human beings?
Up to now, it has been possible to transplant successfully skin, bone, kidneys, heart, hair, liver and parts of the eye. In some cases, such as with skin and bone, the graft is taken from one part of the body and grafted onto another part of the same body.

What is physiotherapy?
This is an applied technique in medicine to help people who have stiff joints, aches and tightness, or immobility after fractures and other accidents, to get moving again. Massage, heat, exercises and electrical stimulation are the chief means employed.

What is traction?
A form of treatment for stretching parts of the body that may have 'seized up', or in the case of some fractures, for holding two ends of the same limb apart while the fractured bone parts get a chance to 'knit' together again.

What is blood transfusion?
If you are injured or lose a lot of blood in a surgical operation, your body cannot always make new blood quickly enough to keep you in good shape. So you can have a pint or two of blood from a blood bank. Blood banks store blood in bottles or packs, according to the blood groups. The fresh blood is allowed to drip into a vein in your arm through a needle.

2, 5, 7...

Who stated the Four Freedoms?
President Franklin Roosevelt of the
US, in 1941, in a message to Congress.
They were freedom of speech, freedom of
worship, freedom from want and freedom
from fear. They formed the basis of the
United Nations charter drafted at San
Francisco in 1945.

**What were the Twelve Labours of
Hercules?**
They were tasks set by the king of
Tiryns to Hercules, a superhuman being
of Greek mythology, and the labours
were: destroying the many-headed
Hydra, slaying the Nemean Lion (with
his hands), capturing the Arcadian stag,
capturing the Erymanthean Boar,
cleaning out the Augean stables,
destroying the Stymphalian birds,
capturing the mad bull of Minos,
capturing the man-eating horses of
Diomedes, stealing the girdle of
Hippolyte the queen of the Amazons,
seizing the oxen of Geryon, a three-
headed monster, taking three golden
apples from the garden of the Hesperides,
and fetching the three-headed dog
Cerberus from its owner Hades, in the
Underworld.

When were the Hundred Days?
1815. This was the time between
Napoleon's return from exile at the
Mediterranean island of Elba and his
defeat at Waterloo on 18th June. The
actual days were from 20th March, when
he entered Paris, to 28th June, when
Louis XVIII returned from exile.

What was the '15?
It is the abbreviated colloquial name for
the Fifteen, the first Jacobite rebellion,
of 1715. This was led, in Scotland, by
James Edward, son of the deposed
James II of England, Scotland and
Ireland (1685–1688) who had died in exile
in 1701.

What, then, was the '45?
This is the abbreviated colloquial name
for the Forty-Five, the second Jacobite
rebellion. The cause of James Edward
Stuart, still living abroad in Italy, was
taken up in Scotland by his son, Bonnie
Prince Charlie. But, like the '15, initial
successes were followed by crushing
defeat, and Prince Charles barely
escaped with his life.

What is a Fifth Column?
A group of people within a country
secretly working for an enemy outside
in time of war. The term arose in the
Spanish Civil War (1936–1939) when the
nationalist General Mola, advancing on
Madrid with four columns, said he had a
fifth column of supporters already within
the city mobilizing to help him take it.

**Why do Americans celebrate the
4th of July?**
Because it is the anniversary date of the
Declaration of Independence, on 4th
July 1776.

Who are the Foursquare Gospellers?
They are a religious movement founded
in 1915 in Ireland by Pastor George
Jeffreys. The movement, called fully the
Elim Foursquare Gospel Alliance,
believes in the literal truth of the Bible,
the effectiveness of divine healing by the
laying-on of hands, and the imminence
of the second coming of Christ.

What was the Thirty Years War?
Possibly the most brutal war in
European history (yes! including the
last two world wars), it lasted from 1618
to 1648 and involved most European
countries. It was the last military
struggle between Catholics and
Protestants to establish once and for all
whether states could individually choose
to be one or the other. It ended with the
Treaty of Westphalia in 1648.

Who were the Fifth Monarchy Men?
They were an English Puritan sect of the
17th century who believed that Christ
was about to found the fifth great
empire. The first four had fallen, namely,
Babylon, Persia, Greece and Rome. They
viewed the downfall of Charles I as the
end of the Roman Empire, because they
included the Papacy in the Roman
Empire and Charles had been pro-
Catholic.

What was 'The Thirty-nine Steps'?
An exciting novel by John Buchan.
Buchan was a diplomat as well as a
novelist and was created Lord
Tweedsmuir. He was Governor-General
of Canada from 1935 to 1940.

What are the Seven Deadly Sins?
According to Roman Catholics, sins are
venial (minor ones) or mortal (serious).
The seven mortal, or deadly sins are
pride, avarice, lust, envy, gluttony, anger
and sloth.

Who were the Minutemen?
An armed militia of American colonists
who, before the War of Independence,
announced that they were ready to join
up and fight 'at a minute's notice' when
called to arms.

What is the Fourth Estate?
It is the phrase, first used by Edmund
Burke – the famous 18th century
statesman, for the press. The other three
estates are the lords temporal (peers),
lords spiritual (archbishops and bishops)
and the commons.

What is Eights' Week?
A period of a week during the summer at
Oxford university which is high-lighted
by a series of bumping races for college
boats on the river. Several college boats
are entered and each boat has eight
oarsmen and one cox.

Who were the Seven Bishops?
The Archbishop of Canterbury, and the
bishops of Ely, Peterborough, Chichester,
St Asaph, Bath and Wells, and Bristol,
who in 1688 refused to order their clergy
to read out in church the Declaration of
Indulgence issued by James II (1685–
1688) which granted considerable
freedoms to Catholics. James arrested
the bishops and had them tried for
sedition, but to the joy of nearly all
England and Wales, they were
acquitted.

What are the 39 Articles?
They are the basis of the doctrine of the
Church of England, and they were
drawn up in the reign of Elizabeth I
(1558–1603) whose ministers were trying
to construct a moderate settlement of
church matters. They were published in
the Anglican Book of Common Prayer.

Who were the Twelve Caesars?
They were rulers of Rome, beginning
with the greatest Roman of them all,
Caius Julius Caesar (102–44 BC). After
his dictatorship and death, there was an
interval, and then his great-nephew
Augustus became the first emperor
(27 BC to 14 AD). The remaining ten were,
in order, Tiberius (14–37), Caius
Caligula (37–41), Claudius (41–54), Nero
(54–68), Galba, Otho, Vitellius (68–69,
the year of the emperors), Vespasian
(69–79), Titus (79–81) and Domitian
(81–96).

**How long did Adolf Hitler promise the
Germans his Third Reich would last?**
1000 years. In fact it lasted but twelve
years, from 1933 to 1945.

Where are the Seven Sisters?
They are a line of white cliffs forming
seven undulating peaks along the south
coast of England between Beachy Head
and Cuckmere Haven in Sussex.

What is a hammer-beam roof?
It is a roof whose timbers are supported by short fat beams that stick out horizontally and inwards from the walls, and which does not need tie beams. Hammer beams are a most attractive architectural feature and if you are ever in London you can see a hammer-beam roof at Westminster Hall.

Where would you expect to find a belvedere?
It is a look-out like a turret or platform on the roof of a house and gives views over the surrounding countryside. It is also the word for a garden hut or small temple such as you can find in some 18th century houses and grounds.

What is a cupola?
Architecturally, it is a rounded roof or ceiling, a small dome-shaped structure on a tower or as part of a roof. Sometimes it may have a weathervane or a clock on top.

Is there any connection between a bargeboard and a barge?
None whatever. A bargeboard is a wide board fitted along the edge of a house gable, which may be plain or decorated. It is there to deflect rain, and the word may have come from 'vergeboard'.

Which are the three main features of stairs?
The tread, the nosing and the riser. The tread is the horizontal plank piece on which you put your foot, the nosing is the rounded edge of the tread and the riser is the vertical plank piece between one tread and the next.

Where is the keystone of an arch?
It is the central wedge-shaped stone at the top, or crown, of the arch, and it sometimes projects below the inner curve line.

42

What are the Five Orders of Architecture?
They are the principal styles of architecture from classical times with special relation to columns – the Doric, the Ionic, the Corinthian, the Tuscan and the Composite. The different orders refer to the capitals and also to the heights of the columns in relation to the widths.

A composite capital

Where would you expect to find the fanlight of a house?
If it has one, it is over the front door (or very occasionally, over a rear door, too). It is a semi-circular light, or window of several panes, or maybe one pane. If it is of several panes, it will be one of many variations of design, some of which look like fans, hence the name.

What's a gargoyle?
It is a water-spout of stone projecting

from a gutter, shaped like a grotesque animal or weird human face. It carries water from the roof of a building clear of the walls, and is a medieval building feature.

Which are the two principal types of window?

They are the casement type and the sash type. The casement type is one which opens outwards – or inwards – on the vertical plane as a rule, and is mounted on hinges. The sash type is generally a pair of glazed frames that slide up and down in front of each other. They used to be suspended on ropes and balanced by weights inside the whole window framework. Today, many sash windows slide up and down on metal tubes.

What would you expect to do in the loggia of a building?

If it had one, you might walk about or sit down and enjoy the sun. It is a covered outdoor area, open on one or two sides, but attached to a building, generally at ground level.

What's tracery?

It is that lovely decorative stone (or wood) pattern in the top part of a Gothic church or building window or opening, formed by interlacing of extensions of the upright posts (or mullions). You can have tracery in wooden or metal screens. A great variety of shapes and designs were employed by medieval craftsmen and are copied today.

What's dado?

It is skirting, but chiefly of the kind that is as much as a metre or so high from the ground. This is generally found in very large rooms or areas with walling.

Where would you find an overthrow?

At the top of an iron gate or pair of gates. It connects the two gate piers across the top of the gate or gates, and in the 17th and 18th century overthrows were frequently most beautifully ornamented.

What is a hip?

The line where adjoining slopes of a pitched roof meet at an external angle of a building.

How do you chamfer a square section pillar?

Cut off one corner all the way down, more or less at 45 degrees, to give a beam or post a bit of distinction. The chamfered surface can later be decorated in a variety of ways. It could be gouged to make it concave, or it could have decorative moulding applied to it.

What's a light, in architectural terms?

It is another word for window or window pane.

What's a dog-tooth arch?

It is a type of ornament on an arch which consists of rows of inverted V-shape mouldings, a style popular with Norman and some early English architects and masons. There is some good dog-tooth arch ornament at Durham Cathedral.

What is a clapboard?

It is the American word for weather-boarding, which is external wall covering of wedge-shaped planks of wood fixed horizontally, one overlapping the next.

What does the lovely word gazebo mean?

It is the word for a summerhouse, or it can be used to mean a belvedere (see above). The origin of the word is not properly known but it may have come from the East.

43

How did the Quakers get their name?
Quakers were nonconformists in England in the 17th century. Their first leader was George Fox, who preached thunderously up and down the country, causing a deal of trouble. When once he was arrested, he said to the magistrate, 'You should quake at the name of the Lord when you mention it.'

What is a chalice?
This is a tallish cup with stem and base, which for centuries has been used for the wine in the communion service in Church. Early chalices were made of wood, glass or tin, but later on they came to be made in more precious metals. Some chalices have two handles.

Who was The Buddha?
The Buddha means the Enlightened One. Gautama Buddha (c.563–483 BC) was a wealthy Nepalese prince who gave up his riches, left home and wandered for several years in great hardship. One day he sat down under a bodhi tree near a town called Buddh Gaya and he became 'enlightened', that is, had a vision about what was the purpose of life. He began to teach and founded an order of monks to spread his word.

What happened at the Council of Trent?
When the Reformation threatened to overthrow the authority of the Roman Church (in the 16th century) its leaders decided to try to reform the Church from within. They held a great conference at Trent, near Venice, and it lasted with intervals for eighteen years.

What is a miracle play?
On the eve of an important saint's day, in medieval Europe, people acted out plays about the saint's life, dressing up in costume and imitating the legendary aspects of the saint's life as well as the realistic parts. Quite often the staging of a miracle play was an excuse for a great feast afterwards.

What is a nonconformist?
The word applies to religion in Britain. In the 17th century many people objected to the way the established Church was run and so they refused to conform. They formed break-away groups, such as Baptists, Presbyterians and, in the 18th century, Methodists.

Who was John Knox?
Knox effectively brought about the conversion of the Scottish people from Roman Catholicism to the Protestant faith. Born in 1505, he was an extremely powerful scholar and preacher, and he thundered against the abuses of the Roman Church up and down Scotland in the 1560s.

Why do we have holidays?
In the Middle Ages, some saints' days were celebrated every year and this usually meant little work was done on those days. They were called holy days from which the word holiday derives. Occasionally there were too many days set aside in a year for celebration and governments tried to cut them down.

When did the Romans officially recognize Christianity?
During the reign of Constantine the Great (306–337 AD). Constantine himself may not have been a believer but he recognized that Christianity was a strong binding force among the peoples of the empire and he encouraged it to spread.

Who was Mithras?
Mithras was a god of the ancient Persians and Indians. He was the sun god, the protector of man. In the middle of the 1st century BC the cult of

worshipping him reached Rome and appealed to many people, especially in the army. Temples were built in his honour.

What did Stoics believe?
The first Stoics were Greeks who based their lives on the pursuit of virtue. Pleasure, according to them, was not a good but an evil thing. They believed that it was not necessary to own or enjoy material possessions, and that happiness was attainable only through being wholly virtuous.

Who were the Vestal Virgins?
Ancient Romans worshipped Vesta, the goddess of the hearth and home. They did so in their own homes and also at temples erected in her honour. At the Temple of Vesta in Rome a sacred fire burned all the time – a symbol of the hearth. This was maintained by six high-born priestesses who served for thirty years before handing the job on. They were bound to remain chaste while they were priestesses.

Who were the Epicureans?
Epicureans were Greeks and Romans who believed that knowledge was obtained through the senses, that it was important in understanding things to be able to feel them, and that pleasure was worth pursuing as an end in itself if it were done in the right way. These ideals were originated by the Greek thinker Epicurus (340–270 BC).

Which ancient civilization worshipped cats?
Cats were worshipped in ancient Egypt, four thousand or more years ago. One of their gods, Bast, was often shown in pictures as having a cat's head. Cats also represented their leading god Ra and their goddess Isis. Many mummies of cats have been found.

What do Hindus believe?
The basis of Hinduism is a belief in the Supreme Spirit, the Brahma, who is the beginning and end of all things. The Brahma works through three gods, Brahma the creator, Vishna the preserver and Siva the destroyer and so creator of new life.

Why do the Jews celebrate the Passover?
During one of the plagues which afflicted Egypt when the Hebrews were in bondage under the pharaohs, Moses suggested that if they wanted to avoid the plague they should sacrifice a lamb to God and daub some of its blood on their front door. This should encourage the plague to 'pass over' the house. Jews celebrate this every year.

Reading the Hebrew Scriptures

What was Telstar?
It was a television satellite put into orbit round the earth in July 1962, by the United States. It enabled 'live' programmes to be transmitted between America and Europe, and it made it much easier, for example, to send television pictures of notable events in one place to audiences which are long distances away.

Which is the oldest broadcasting organization in the world?
The British Broadcasting Corporation (BBC), which grew from a company set up in 1922. Today it broadcasts over the world, in nearly 50 languages.

What are radio waves?
They are vibrations created in the atmosphere by the moving to and fro of electricity between two points. They travel at the same speed as light, that is, 297,600 kms (186,000 miles)/second but vibrate less frequently.

Why do newspapers have advertisements?
To pay for printing, distribution and so forth. Newspapers do not earn enough in sales alone to pay for the now complex business of getting an edition out on the street.

Which was the first successful daily newspaper in the United States?
The *Pennsylvania Packet and General Advertizer*, published in 1784. By now there are some 1800 daily newspapers in the US alone.

What's ticker tape?
It is the paper ribbon that goes through a ticker – a telegraphic instrument which prints up-to-the-minute news as it is received from around the world. It is used like confetti in New York during parades.

What is Reuters?
It's part of an international news agency, known in the UK as Reuters–PA (Press Association), which sends information, generally hot news, round the world for various organs of communication to use if they want.

What does a microphone do?
It converts the sounds you direct into it to electrical vibrations, sends them down a wire and sends them out the other end through a loudspeaker which converts them back into the original sounds.

What is Morse Code?
Named after Colonel Samuel Morse (1791–1872), the US inventor of the magnetic telegraph, it is a code in which the letters of the alphabet and the numbers are represented by dots and dashes.

How did the system of signalling at sea by flags work?
Before telegraph or wireless, ships signalled to one another by using flags which were raised and lowered on the main mast. The flags, differing in colours and patterns, represented numbers which in turn represented words or phrases, single letters, orders, all listed in a special manual.

What is sign language?
It is a way of communicating with people, or between people, who are unable to use their voices or cannot hear. Normally the hands are used to form letters of the alphabet. The five vowels, A E I O U, for example, are indicated by using one hand to point the forefinger to the five fingers of the other hand, in turn. The thumb is A, the forefinger E and so forth.

What is a gondola?
It is a canoe-shaped boat with a square

cabin, which goes up and down the canals of Venice, much like a taxi on the roads in a town. It is about nine metres long and one and a half metres wide, and is navigated by a gondolier who stands in the stern and works an oar over one side.

What is a coracle?

A Celtic (usually Welsh) wickerwork framed boat, oval in shape, covered with a leather skin and rendered watertight with pitch. It is driven with a paddle. In Caermarthenshire in Wales, some craftsmen still make them, much the same as their ancestors did when Caesar visited Britain in 55 and 54 BC.

What is a kayak?

A canoe, but one made particularly by the Eskimos. A framework is covered with stretched seal-skins. The top of the boat is likewise covered in, except for a small well in which the navigator sits.

Where are punts most famously used on the river?

Probably the most famous places where punts are enjoyed on the river are Oxford and Cambridge, in England. No undergraduate can really say he has 'lived' at either university if he has not taken a girl friend out on the river in one of these flat-bottomed boats, manoeuvred by using a long pole.

How many letters are posted every day in Britain?

The Post Office says there were 35 million letters and postcards sent through the post, on average, every day in 1975. This works out at about three-quarters of the population writing one letter each day.

Why are airmail charges more expensive than surface mail charges?

Chiefly because there is very limited space for mail bags on aircraft.

Who runs the post in the United States?

The US Postal Service, an independent government agency set up in 1970. Before that there had been a department of state in charge.

How long did the Penny Postage last?

Introduced in 1840, it lasted for nearly seventy years. In June 1918, the price of a stamp for an inland letter in Britain went up to 1½d minimum.

Who has the most valuable private collection of postage stamps in the world?

HM Queen Elizabeth II of the United Kingdom. She inherited much of it from her father King George VI.

What was a quipu?

A set of coloured strings with knots, used by the ancient Peruvians for counting, about 2000 years ago.

Who invented the telephone?

The telephone was invented by Alexander Graham Bell (1847–1922) at Boston, Mass., USA, in 1876. He and his father were teachers of deaf people, and had emigrated to America from Scotland.

An early telephone

Which country has the most mileage of railway routes?
The US, which has nearly 368,000 kms (230,000 miles). This is about one-third of the world's total of over 1,120,000 kms (700,000 miles).

Which country has the longest individual railways?
Canada. The Canadian National Railways have 37,600 kms (23,500 miles) of line and the Canadian Pacific Railway has 33,600 kms (21,000 miles).

What is the longest railway journey that can be undertaken without changing trains?
The Trans-Siberian Railway journey from Moscow to Vladivostok in the USSR. The journey is almost 9600 kms (6000 miles) long and takes nine days.

Where is the longest stretch of straight railway line in the world?
In Australia, across the Nullarbor Plain, where the line is absolutely straight for 525 kms (325 miles).

Which British railway station has the largest number of platforms?
Waterloo Station in London. It has 21.

What is the largest railway station in the world?
Grand Central railway terminal in New York, US. It covers nearly twelve hectares (30 acres).

How much railway line is in use in Britain for passenger travel?
Over 19,200 kms (12,000 miles), and of this about one-sixth is electrified. This is not, however, the greatest number of kilometres open for passenger traffic in British railway history, for many thousands have been cut in various economy drives to make the railways pay – which they still do not!

What is the busiest railway junction in Britain?
Clapham Junction in London has held this distinction for a long time. Over 2000 trains use the station one way or another in one period of 24 hours.

Which country holds the world speed record for a steam locomotive on the railways?
Great Britain. The Mallard, an LNER engine, pulled a train at 202 kmph (125 mph) average between Peterborough and Stoke in 1938. The Mallard engine has survived and can now be seen at the Railway Museum in York.

Where is the highest station in the world?
In Chile, at 4821 metres (14,463 feet) above sea level. There is also one in Peru at 4818 metres (14,454 feet).

What were the two main railway gauges of the 19th century?
In the early days of railways, some engineers followed the railway gauge of 4 feet 8½ inches (1.43 metres) devised by Stephenson from the width between the two wheels of a family cart. Others, led by Isambard Kingdom Brunel, engineer-in-chief of the Great Western Railway, preferred a wider gauge of 7 feet 0¼ inches (2.13 metres).

What happened to the gauges?
The broad gauge champions fought for a generation to keep their railway gauge, on the grounds that it was safer, ensured greater comfort for travellers and was in the end quicker. But the narrower gauge champions won, and by the end of the 19th century broad gauge had given way completely.

In which country is the entire railway electrified?
Switzerland, because electricity is cheap.

How many different railway lines were there in the hey-day of Britain's railways?
About 120 in the days immediately following the First World War. Then in 1923 they all amalgamated into four groupings, namely, the London, Midland and Scottish (LMS), the London and North Eastern (LNER), the Great Western (GWR) and the Southern (SR).

When were British railway companies nationalized?
In 1948, by the government of Clement Attlee, prime minister from 1945 to 1951.

Which was the first engine-driven passenger railway line in the world?
The Stockton and Darlington Railway, which was opened in 1825. It was built by the pioneer railway engineering genius George Stephenson.

Who was the statesman killed on the Liverpool and Manchester railway line in 1830?
William Huskisson (1770–1830), who had been President of the Board of Trade from 1823 to 1827, and an active pioneer

George Stephenson's pioneer locomotive 'The Rocket'

of free trade. He was accidentally run down at the opening ceremony.

Which was the first engine to have exceeded 100 mph (160 kmph) on a normal journey?
The Great Western Railway's City of Truro claimed to have reached 102 mph (163 kmph) on a normal mail run from Plymouth to London in 1904. But this has since been hotly disputed, and the first accredited run at this speed is now accorded to the Flying Scotsman, an LNER engine, in 1934.

Who were the two great steam engine railway chiefs who competed during the 1920s and 1930s to produce the greatest railway engines in Britain?
Sir Nigel Gresley, of the London and North Eastern Railway and Sir William Stanier, of the London, Midland and Scottish Railway.

How many Crusades were there?

There were nine major Crusades – wars waged by combinations of Western European armies against the Seljuk Turks in or around the Holy Land. The first was in 1095–1099 when Jerusalem was taken.

What was notable about the Han dynasty of China (c.200 BC to c.200 AD)?

Under the Han emperors the Chinese invented paper, gunpowder (which was not used for weapons but only for firework displays), porcelain, and they introduced tea-drinking. They also invented moveable type, nearly 1500 years before it was developed in Europe.

Was there any contact between ancient China and ancient Rome?

Some, mainly through trade. Romans bought Chinese silk from merchants who brought it across the Asian deserts and mountains. It is a pity that the vast distance between the two empires was at the time such an obstacle to their getting to know each other well.

How did the Byzantines discover the secret of silk making?

Two monks from Constantinople set out in the middle of the 6th century AD for China and there found silk cocoons. They hid some in their hollowed-out walking staves and returned with them to Europe. Then they put the eggs on a mulberry tree and waited for them to hatch.

What was Justinian's main contribution to history?

Justinian I, emperor of Byzantium (527–565), codified Roman law which had become very tangled over the centuries. This became the basis of the legal systems of most European countries, but not of England.

50

Where did the Arab people come from?

They were wandering Semites (like Abraham and his fellow farmers in the 2000s BC) from Mesopotamia. They travelled about on camels and horses and never stayed in one place for long. This made them hardy but it also made them aimless. Then, in the 7th century AD they found a leader in Mohammed.

What was Greek Fire?

It was a liquid chemical based on naphtha which could be used as an explosive. It was discovered by Callinicus in about 650 AD and for a time it gave the Byzantines superiority over their Arab enemies.

Who was Charlemagne?

Charlemagne (Charles the Great) was king of the Franks, who occupied most of France and Germany, from 768 to 814 AD. He wanted to unify western Europe and to encourage the spread of learning throughout his domains. By 800 his empire covered France, Germany, the Low Countries, Austria and parts of Italy, and in that year the Pope crowned him first Emperor of what came to be called the Holy Roman Empire.

How long did the Holy Roman Empire last?

After Charlemagne's death the Holy Roman Empire consisted of a collection of states in and around what are now Germany, Austria and Czechoslovakia. It lasted until 1806.

How did the English tell the time in the early Middle Ages?

Among his numerous achievements, Alfred the Great, King of England (871–900 AD), invented the candle clock. It was a tallow candle divided into 12 equal sections, marked by ridges, that burned for one hour each.

Who were the Vikings?

They were an astonishing people who occupied Norway, Denmark, Sweden and parts of Finland. In the 8th century these tough, sea-faring barbarian people began to descend upon the coasts of Britain, France and the Low Countries, and later on attacked Italy and even attempted to attack Constantinople. They were powerful from the 8th to the 11th centuries.

Where was the water-driven mill introduced?

It was introduced in China during the interesting years of the T'ang Dynasty (c.600–c.900 AD). This was an age when the Chinese invented the wheelbarrow, developed porcelain, jade carving, and a host of other fine craft works.

When did civilization begin in the Americas?

Civilization began in North, Central and South America about 4000 years ago. Farmers began to grow corn, pepper, beans and even cotton. People also began to put up buildings of stone. Among the earliest of the South American civilizations were the Inca in what is now Peru and the Maya in what is now Mexico.

Who were the Maya people?

They are thought to have come across the Bering Strait from Asia into Alaska and settled in Mexico, well over 2500 years ago. They knew how to build in stone, but their ordinary houses were more often constructed from timber, with thatched roofs. They paid a great deal of attention to their religious beliefs. They grew maize and made bread from it, and they cultivated tobacco for smoking.

What was the Pyramid of the Sun?

A huge pyramid built in Peru about 1500 years ago by the Mochica people. It was said to contain nearly one hundred million bricks!

Who were the Mauryan kings of India?

They were three great Indian rulers, who reigned between about 316 BC and 226 BC. They were Chandragupta, founder of the Mauryan Empire, his son Bindusari (c.295 to c.275) and his grandson Asoka, probably the greatest of them, who died in 226.

What was so special about Asoka?

He introduced stone buildings. He encouraged the spread of Buddhism as the national faith. He patronized artists, sculptors and architects. He showed how to govern well without repression or excessive force.

Who were the Normans?

They were people of Viking descent who settled in northern France in the 10th century. They fought all over Europe and gave a great deal of trouble. One leader was Duke William of Normandy who invaded England in 1066 and defeated the English under their king, Harold II, at Hastings.

What was Magna Carta?

A document containing a long list of promises made by King John (1199–1216) which were for the most part clauses that gave the barons even more power than they already had.

Did King John sign it willingly?

King John did not sign it at all. He could not write, but his royal seal was affixed to the several copies made. He authorized this under pressure and shortly afterwards the Pope, Innocent III, said he need not abide by its terms, on the grounds that they were extracted under duress.

Why are the Lascaux caves so famous?

The Lascaux caves are in France, about 480 kms (200 miles) south-west of Paris. They contain several coloured wall paintings of animals, and they are estimated to have been painted by prehistoric people about 20,000 years ago. They are the oldest works of art to be found anywhere in the world.

What is a mosaic?

A mosaic is a form of decoration made up by assembling an ordered pattern of tiny cubes of differently coloured pieces of stone. They were developed in Roman and Byzantine times and used to decorate floors, walls and pavements. Mosaics generally depicted people, landscapes or buildings.

Who was Pheidias?

Pheidias was probably the greatest sculptor of ancient Greek times. He worked during the rule of the celebrated Athenian statesman and leader, Pericles, who encouraged artists of all kinds. Pheidias produced many works including a series of figures on the great Parthenon building which stands on the Acropolis in Athens.

Who sculpted the famous statue of the Discus Thrower?

The statue, more correctly called The Discobulos, was sculpted in the 5th century BC in Greece by Myron. He was a sculptor who studied in the same classes as Pheidias.

What is an illuminated manuscript?

Scholars and scribes in the Middle Ages used to write down their works or copy out such famous writings as the Old and New Testaments in fine script in straight lines across pages of vellum, or parchment. They often illustrated these pages with pictures of people and

52

things connected with what they were writing about. It was usual to begin the first word on the page with a highly ornamented letter. Such a work was called an illuminated manuscript, and there are hundreds of these in museums all over the world.

How was enamel decoration produced in the early Middle Ages?

The craftsmen who wanted to produce decorative enamel work first fabricated the design in metal, polishing the surfaces. Then they painted on to them a glassy paste, transparent or cloudy, in one or other of a range of colours. The whole object was heated in an oven to a very high temperature. This was what is what is called 'baking' the enamel on to the metal. The early Irish craftsmen of the 7th, 8th, 9th and 10th centuries were particularly fine enamellers.

Who was Giotto?

Giotto di Bondoni (1267–1337) was a painter from Florence in Italy, who had been found painting animals on rocks in the field when he was a boy. He was sent to art school and before he was fully grown up he astonished his teachers by the natural, three-dimensional style of his painting, and by his amazing use of colours. He set new standards of true representation in painting and is considered the pioneering painter of the Renaissance.

What was the Renaissance?

The Renaissance (or re-birth) is the name given to the three hundred years of the 15th, 16th and 17th centuries in European history when there was a wonderful flowering in painting, sculpture, architecture and literature. This coincided with the re-discovery of the works of Greek and Roman writers and artists, whose fine models deeply influenced the artists of the Renaissance.

They were also fascinated by Christianity and Bible stories and many of the subjects they painted or sculpted had a religious background. Building styles, however, were Greek and Roman in influence.

How is artists' oil paint made?
Artists' oil paint comes in metal-foil tubes. The colour is made by a pigment or dye which is mixed into a stiff paste with linseed or poppy-seed oil. Before it is applied, the surface to be painted is coated with what is called size.

What is size?
Size is thin paste or glue which fills up the tiny pores on a surface. It is made from starch, gum, seaweed and glue. Usually it spreads very easily and dries quickly so that you can get on with painting the surface you have sized.

Where is the Sistine Chapel?
The Sistine Chapel is a private chapel for the popes in the Vatican. It was originally built for the pope, Sixtus IV, hence its name. It contains several wall frescoes by such famous painters as Botticelli and Pinturicchio, and also the marvellous ceiling paintings of Michelangelo.

What are the Sistine ceiling pictures?
Michelangelo painted a series of pictures on the ceiling of the Sistine chapel illustrating scenes from the Old Testament. Among these were representations of the Creation which, according to the Old Testament, took God six days to achieve. To do the work, Michelangelo constructed scaffolding right up to the ceiling and painted lying on his back or crouched on his hands and knees using a mirror. It took him four years, and he is said to have undertaken the work much against his will.

What other works did Michelangelo produce?
Michelangelo Buonarroti (1475–1564) was painter, sculptor, poet and architect. He was one of the two supreme geniuses of the Renaissance (the other was Leonardo da Vinci). Michelangelo was a Florentine orphan whose foster-father was a stone-mason. Little wonder, then, that he grew up to become a sculptor and architect. His sculptures include the marble group of the Pieta and the huge statue of David (king of Israel), both in Florence, and the tomb of Pope Julius II, in Rome. He was one of the architects of St Peter's Cathedral, in Rome, and designed the famous dome. He completed the Farnese Palace in Rome. Among his famous paintings were The Holy Family and The Last Judgment, and, of course, the Sistine ceiling paintings in the Vatican.

Where is Leonardo da Vinci's painting, the Last Supper?
One of Leonardo da Vinci's most famous pictures, the Last Supper, portrays Jesus Christ entertaining his twelve disciples to a last dinner before he was tried and crucified. He is surrounded in the picture by the disciples. The picture is a fresco painted in the church of Santa Maria della Grazie, in Milan in Italy, and was completed in 1498.

Who was the Mona Lisa?
This is the popular name given to the very famous portrait painted by Leonardo da Vinci. The sitter was Lisa di Noldo Gherardini, a Florentine woman who was married to Francesco di Bartolommeo del Giocondo. Painted on a panel at the beginning of the 16th century, it is now in the Louvre Museum in Paris. Leonardo is said to have worked on it for six years between 1498 and 1504 but still did not manage to complete it.

What was the Red River Settlement in Canada?

It was a settlement of Scottish Highland farmers who emigrated to the Red River valley in the early 1800s where the land was good for farming. The settlers endured great hardships and poor harvests to begin with, but persevered and were strengthened when more Britons came out to make new lives in the same valley.

How did the Canadian horse-drawn mower work?

Introduced in the 1840s, the horse-drawn mower consisted of a horizontal bar, two metres long, with widely spaced teeth. One of the wheels of the machine activated a wide blade, also with teeth, back and forwards along the bar, and so cut grain down to the stem. It was a very early harvester.

Where and what was a root-cellar in a Canadian house?

It was part of the kitchen, generally a simple pit with ventilation, deep enough to keep out the frost, where potatoes, turnips and other vegetables were stored.

What was a Canadian pot-belly stove?

It was a metal stove, barrel-shaped with a flat top for the kettle. It had a door at the front, with mica windows.

What is a lumberjack?

Someone who works in a timber-producing forest, cuts down the trees and gets them ready for the sawmills. Although not peculiar to Canada, it is with Canada that one principally associates them.

When was McGill University founded?

In 1813, with money left by an industrialist called James McGill. Its first academic works were in the field of medicine, but by 1855 it was a fully-fledged university with studies in a variety of subjects available to students. Perhaps the best known of the seven major Canadian universities, it is situated in Montreal in the province of Quebec.

What was the Great Drought in Australia?

From about 1894 to 1902 huge areas of Australia were severely affected by a drought that went on for the whole period. 1902 was so bad that it was called 'Sahara Year' because so much of the land looked like desert, and figures show that while there had been over 100,000,000 sheep in Australia in 1891 there were less than 55,000,000 in 1902.

What was the RSL in Australia?

It was the Returned Soldiers and Sailors Imperial League, an organization that looked after the interests of Australian armed forces personnel who came back to their country after the end of the First World War. For a long time the RSL had great influence in Australian politics.

Who or what was Phar Lap?

Phar Lap was a famous race horse in Australia in the 1930s, and was so much followed by the public that when he died his heart was cut out and displayed in Canberra. This was done to convince those that refused to accept the news that he had died.

Who is Sir Donald Bradman?

Donald George Bradman, born in 1908, is the most famous cricketer ever to emerge from Australia, and indeed is one of the greatest players in the history of the game anywhere. He played for Australia from 1928 to 1948 and captained his country's team from 1938 to 1948. His records are unbroken for the highest number of runs in a test series (Australia v England), the fastest double century (214 mins, 1930) and the most runs in a day by one batsman (309, 1930).

What is Waltzing Matilda?
(a) It's a phrase meaning travelling on foot with a pack on one's back and (b) it's the name of the Australian national song.

What is a billabong?
The Australian term for a stagnant backwater.

What is a prickly pear?
It is a kind of cactus plant, and it was introduced in Australia as a popular pot plant in the late 19th century. By the 1900s, however, prickly pear, which some people had used for hedging, had grown right out of control like some creeping plant from a science-fiction story and infested over four million hectares (ten million acres). It was brought under control by infesting it with caterpillars from South America.

What were landsharks in New Zealand?
When British settlers started to buy up land in New Zealand in the 1830s from the Maori native inhabitants, many of them got huge areas for practically no money at all, hoodwinking the Maoris shamelessly. These people were quite understandably described in the history books as landsharks.

Who was Sir George Grey?
Sir George Grey (1812–1898) was a British administrator who became governor of New Zealand in 1845. He served well, obtaining justice for the Maoris and at the same time improving living standards for British settlers. He

left in 1853 for a term in South Africa but returned in 1861 as Governor-General, remaining in office for seven years. He stayed on after his office ended and in 1877 was made prime minister of New Zealand. It was a remarkable career.

Who was New Zealand's greatest scientist?
Ernest Rutherford, 1st Baron Rutherford of Nelson (1871–1937) who before the end of his life had also become the greatest experimental physicist of all time. Rutherford never forgot his New Zealand birth and education, and when his amazing career, during which he split the atom, revolutionized man's ideas about matter, predicted the hydrogen bomb and so many other things, was crowned with a peerage, he chose to be Rutherford of Nelson, the town near which he was born.

Who is Dame Ngaio Marsh?
She is New Zealand's most famous novelist. She specializes in detective stories, which were written with great skill and literary grace. Born in 1899 she was made a Dame of the British Empire in 1966.

Which is the highest mountain in New Zealand?
Mount Cook, which is 3402 metres (11,160 feet) high.

Who was King Dick?
Richard Seddon (1845–1906), prime minister of New Zealand from 1893 to his death. A man with few social graces or intellectual gifts, he was nonetheless a tough, practical politician who understood exactly what New Zealand people wanted and he gave it to them. He was responsible for much of the pioneering social legislation, including state pensions (the first in the world) and national insurance.

What is GMT?
It is Greenwich Mean Time and is the time of day at the Greenwich meridian, registered by a clock which, when the sun is at its maximum height over the meridian, is at 12.00 noon exactly.

How does a sundial work?
It is a flat disc with numbers round a dial. In the centre and projecting outwards and upwards at a slope is a gnomon (a kind of angled bracket) which throws a shadow from the sun on to the dial. Where the shadow alights is the time of day. The gnomon points towards North.

What is an Act of Parliament Clock?
This is a clock with a big dial, unglazed, driven by hanging weights. It is said to have been made for innkeepers to provide the time for customers who would not buy their own watches because of a tax put on them by William Pitt the Younger in the late 18th century. Actually, they were made much earlier and the name came later.

When was the first wrist watch produced?
Towards the end of the last century, when it was better known as a bracelet watch. These were worn by women only, to begin with, but during the First World War both American and British troops were encouraged to use them as they were more easily carried in battle conditions.

What is the origin of Big Ben?
Big Ben is the name of the bell, which weighs over 13 tonnes, in the tower of the Houses of Parliament in London. It was called this after Sir Benjamin Hall, Commissioner of Works in 1858, who arranged for it to be cast at Whitechapel Bell Foundry and positioned in the clock tower.

56

What is a Leap Year?
It's a year that has an extra day in February (the 29th) and it occurs every fourth year.

Who first reformed the Calendar?
Julius Caesar, the great Roman dictator and founder of the Roman Empire. He introduced the year of 365 days with an extra day every fourth year (leap year). He calculated that a solar year was 365 days and six hours, but in fact was slightly out – by eleven minutes and fourteen seconds.

When was this put right?
In 1582 AD, by Pope Gregory XIII who adjusted the calendar.

What is Time and Motion Study?
It is a test to see how long a particular job takes and how much energy is needed to do it, so as to work out whether the task is being done as efficiently as possible.

What are the Six Pips of broadcasting?
In Britain they are six time signals issued at certain hours of the day, exactly on the hour, to indicate the hour. Sometimes they are followed by a news bulletin. They are issued on BBC radio networks.

What is a 'half-hunter'?
It is a kind of watch, usually antique but there are reproductions, which has a cover with a small circle of glass in the centre. The watch is a pocket type, not a wrist type, and through the glass you can see the position of the hands, though not the entire lengths of them.

What is a time signature?
In musical terms it is a sign indicating the tempo of a piece and it is placed after the key signature, expressed generally as a fraction.

What is an hour-glass?
An instrument shaped like two pears whose thinner ends join, made of glass. Mounted in a simple frame, one bulging end contains some thin sand. Turning the glass on one end the sand will run through the narrow bit into the second fat bit, and the narrow bit is fabricated so that the sand runs through at the rate of one bulbful an hour.

What is an astrolabe?
An astronomical instrument which measures the height of the stars above the horizon and thus enables one to tell roughly the time. Invented goodness knows when and used by Arab pilots at sea from very early in their history (perhaps 6th or 7th century AD), it was also used by European navigators.

When was the French calendar radically altered?
During the French Revolution (1789–1794). The revolutionaries changed the names of the months, altered the weeks and so forth, to show how far they believed they had left things of former times behind. But before long France returned to the calendar accepted by most other people.

What were the original names of the months of July and August in Roman times?
Quintilis and Sextilis. The first month in Roman times was March.

How did these months get new names?
Quintilis became July after Julius Caesar and Sextilis became August after his great-nephew Augustus.

When was the coiled spring first devised as a mechanism for timepieces?
In about 1500, in Nuremburg, and it was devised by Peter Henlein. He inserted one into a small clock and thereby made one of the first watches.

What is a grandfather clock?
It is a long-case clock, first introduced in about 1670 when the anchor escapement had been invented, but not called 'grandfather' until the 19th century.

What is a grandmother clock?
The same thing, only a little shorter, and usually about two metres (six feet) tall.

An 18th-century Russian grandfather clock

What were the Druids?
Druids were priests in early Celtic society, in northern France, Britain and Ireland. They were perhaps the only people who had any education and this gave them a lot of power. They made the laws but usually let tougher but less intelligent people enforce them. And they held human sacrifices as part of their religious ceremonies.

What has mistletoe to do with Druids?
Druids regarded the oak as a sacred tree. They held services of worship in groves of oak trees. Mistletoe is a shrub which grows on oak branches as a kind of parasite on the tree. This impressed the Druids who thought that its berries produced good luck.

Who were the Huguenots?
This was the name given to the Protestants in France during the Reformation and the civil wars which followed. France decided to remain Catholic but a great many Frenchmen accepted the newer Protestant doctrines – and were persecuted for it.

Who were the Twelve Apostles?
They were the twelve disciples of Jesus Christ, who accompanied Him on His travels and who promised to spread His word after His death. They were Peter, Andrew, James and John (the sons of Zebedee), Bartholomew, Thomas, Matthew, Philip, James (son of Alphaeus), Thaddeus, Simon the Zealot and Judas Iscariot.

What were the Four Gospels?
The first four books in the New Testament are called the Gospels, according to St Matthew, St Mark, St Luke and St John. They are records of the career and teachings of Christ and were written down between 40 and 70

years after His death in AD 29.

What is the New Testament?
This is a collection of 27 books which cover the story of Christ and His ministry, and the works of the first Christians who came after Him. There are four gospels, the Acts of the Apostles, twenty-one letters from St Paul to various people in the Roman Empire, and the Revelation of St John the Divine.

What was the Sermon on the Mount?
This was a long lecture given by Christ to His disciples, which outlined His teachings. It is recorded in St Matthew's Gospel. It begins with the Beatitudes and includes the Lord's Prayer. It is called the Sermon on the Mount because on this occasion Christ took His disciples on to a mountain to talk to them.

What are the Beatitudes?
The Beatitudes are the first nine sentences in the Sermon on the Mount, where Christ tells which people are blessed in the eyes of the Lord, such as the poor and the meek.

Who was St Paul?
Paul began life as Saul and was born in Tarsus, in Cilicia, a Roman province. He was Jewish and when he grew up he became a tent-maker. Then he went to Jerusalem to study to be a priest. At first his attitude to Christ, who was his contemporary in years, was a hostile one, but a few year's after Christ's crucifixion, Saul was converted. He studied Christ's works and found them the answer to many problems, and he decided to preach these ideas to the Roman world. He changed his name to Paul, made many voyages to lands all round the Roman empire and ended up in prison in Rome where he was put to death.

Who were the Lollards?
They were followers of John Wyclif (1320–1384), the English theologian who questioned the doctrines of the Church and attacked the high living of the bishops and priests. Lollards were persecuted early in the 15th century. One Act of Parliament decreed that they should be burnt at the stake if they were caught.

What was the Ark of the Covenant?
This was a chest in which, in ancient Hebrew times, the tablets of the laws presented to the people by Moses were stored.

Where is the Wailing Wall?
The Wailing Wall is in Jerusalem. It is the last remnant of the famous temple built by Solomon in the 10th century BC. It is sacred to Jews because it is close to the Holy of Holies, the chamber in the original temple in which the Ark of the Covenant rested.

What is the difference between a prior and an abbot?
Not a great deal. An abbot was head of a monastery and a prior was his second in command. Some monasteries were too small to have an abbot and a prior. These were called priories and the prior was the head monk.

Why did Henry VIII dissolve the Monasteries in the 1530s?
Quite simply because he wanted their wealth. He accused abbots, priors and others of running disorderly houses and made that the excuse for closing them down, expelling the inmates, seizing their treasures and letting the buildings be despoiled. Some monasteries *were* lax and even ungodly, but many were not, and their seizure was unjust and cruel.

The Wailing Wall, Jerusalem

£

When was income tax first raised in Britain?
In 1799, by William Pitt the Younger, the prime minister, to help finance the war against France. It was dropped after the Napoleonic Wars and such was the dislike of it that records of its raising were destroyed. It was re-introduced in 1842 and has been with the British ever since!

How does the US raise its income tax?
It is rated by Congress from year to year, on a percentage basis, and individuals have to send in a report of their income for consideration for taxing. Each state also raises an income tax, except for twelve states, viz., Connecticut, Illinois, Florida, Ohio, Nevada, Maine, Pennsylvania, South Dakota, Texas, Wyoming, Washington and Rhode Island.

Is there any income tax in the USSR?
Not directly as there is in so many Western countries. More senior people have their salaries cut by amounts that would ordinarily be raised as tax.

When was there a tax on windows in Britain?
Introduced in 1696, it survived, in various forms until 1851. Scotland, however, was exempted from the time of the Act of Union in 1707. Some houses up and down the country still have windows that have been bricked up. This was probably done during the tax period.

What was poll tax?
This was a tax raised on each person, by the poll or head. It was introduced in 1222 to gather in money for a Crusade, but its most famous imposition was in 1377, with a repeat performance in 1380 (in the reign of Richard II) which led to the Peasants' Revolt of 1381. The revolt
60

came about because the poor paid a percentage that hit them much harder than it did the rich.

When did New Zealand first have a taxation on land values?
Introduced by Sir George Grey in 1877, it provided taxation on unimproved land in the hope that it would get large landowners to break up their land and make it available for the community.

What was the Gabelle?
A tax on salt in France first imposed in the 13th century and still payable in the 18th. Salt was a necessary commodity for all, rich and poor, and the poor could not afford to pay. The retention of the tax in the 18th century was a cause of the French Revolution.

What is VAT?
Value Added Tax. It is charged on the supply of goods and services and on the importation of goods. There are exceptions to its rules for imposition, but basically it is a fixed rate for all.

What is surtax?
It is an additional tax payable by richer people in the UK, dependent upon their income over and above a certain sum. They pay it on top of ordinary income tax, and the richest people can pay as much as up to 80 per cent of income. Surprisingly, however, such people still manage to live extremely well.

What was the Tonnage and Poundage offered to Charles I in 1625 – which he refused?
A tax to help him pursue the war with Spain. Tonnage was 1/6d to 3/- (7½ to 15 pence) on every tun of wine or beer (tun = large barrel) and poundage was a tax between 6d and 1/- (2½ and 5 pence) on every pound of goods imported or exported.

What was scutage?
Shield money, from the Latin *scutum* = shield. This was money you could pay to the king in place of doing your period of annual knight service of 40 days. It was introduced in the late Norman period and became more widely practised in the time of Henry II. It died out in the 13th century.

Who paid tallage?
Under the feudal system a tenant paid it to his immediate lord. It was raised particularly by the kings on their royal lands which they had let, as they were so often short of cash.

What was heriot?
A payment that had to be made, under the feudal system, to the lord of a manor on the death of a villein by his heir. It generally meant handing over an animal.

What are Customs and Excise?
Customs are taxes raised on certain imports, like tobacco, wine, scents, jewellery, and whatever else the government of the day decrees. Excise is the tax raised on things manufactured and sold in a country for consumption in that country.

What was Danegeld?
A tax raised first in 991 AD by Ethelred the Unready, king of England (978–1016) to buy off the raiding Viking Danes. Of course they took the money thus raised, and came back for more: it was as easy as falling off a log!

What were Peter's Pence?
A tax paid by the king to the Pope. It was first imposed in the time of Offa, king of Mercia in England, in the 780s AD. It lapsed about 200 years later but was revived in the time of the Normans.

What are stamp duties?
First thought of in Holland in 1624 it is a tax you pay on having a document of some kind or other stamped, which document is used for some legal purpose.

Little Quiz 7
Which Biblical character
1. had a coat of many colours?
2. built an ark?
3. slew Goliath?
4. saw a bush burst into flames?
5. was cast into a lion's den?
6. went into the belly of a whale?
7. was cured of leprosy by washing in the River Jordan?
8. betrayed Jesus?
9. was a persecutor of Christians until he himself was converted?
10. was stoned to death?
11. doubted the resurrection of Christ?
12. 'cared for none of these things'?
13. went and hanged himself?
14. denied Christ three times?
15. passed by on the other side?

In which books of the Bible do the following occur?
16. The creation
17. The murder of Abel
18. The presentation of the Ten Commandments
19. The collapse of the walls of Jericho after a great shout
20. The murder of Sisera
21. The defeat of an army by Samson, using an ass's jawbone
22. The death of Goliath
23. The succession of Solomon as king of Israel
24. The Moabite rebellion
25. The division of the Red Sea
26. The death of Moses
27. The visit of the Queen of Sheba to Solomon
28. Belshazzar's Feast
29. The dream of Jacob's ladder

In what battle was a British army commanded by a Frenchman defeated by a French army commanded by an Englishman?
This was the battle of Almanza in 1707, where the Duke of Berwick, natural son of King James II and Arabella Churchill (sister of the great Duke of Marlborough) in command of a French army, defeated the Marquis of Ruvigny's British army.

What was the battle of Herrings?
The battle of Herrings was in 1429, during the Hundred Years War, so called because an English convoy carrying fish for troops besieging Orleans was attacked by a French force. The French were driven off.

Why was the victory of the Spartans over the Arcadians in 368 BC called the Tearless Battle?
Because the Spartans defeated the Arcadians without losing a single life.

What was the battle of the Spurs?
This was an engagement between Henry VIII's English force and a French army. The French fled from the field almost without fighting. Their cavalry jabbed their spurs into their horses, turned round and rushed off the field.

What was the battle of the Saints?
A naval action between the French, under Admiral de Grasse, and the British led by Admiral Rodney, it was fought near the Saintes Islands in the West Indies during the American War of Independence. The British won.

When was the battle of the Seven Pines?
During the American Civil War, Unionists under General M'clellan were defeated by Confederates under General Johnston in 1862.

What happened at the battle of Little Big Horn?
This is where the US cavalry commander, General Custer, was ambushed and killed, along with his force, by the Sioux chief, Sitting Bull, at the Red Indian village of Little Big Horn, in 1876.

Why was the battle of Loose Coat Field so called?
Edward IV, king of England, defeated rebels from the north in 1470 at Empingham. The rebels fled so quickly from the field that they took off their jackets first so as to get away more sharply.

Which were Marlborough's four great victories?
They were Blenheim (1704), Ramillies (1706), Oudenarde (1708) and Malplaquet (1709). They were all battles in the War of the Spanish Succession.

What was the battle of the Pyramids?
The French, under General Bonaparte (later Napoleon I, Emperor of the French) defeated the Egyptians under Murad Bey at a fierce battle on the banks of the Nile, under the shadow of the Pyramids, in 1798.

What happened on the Glorious First of June, 1794?
Admiral Howe, the British naval commander, defeated a French fleet off Ushant, in an engagement in which the French lost many ships.

Where was the battle of the Standards?
In northern England, near Northallerton, in 1127, where a Scottish army led by King David I was defeated by an English force led by the archbishop of York and the bishop of Durham. The English carried into the fray the flags of

St Peter of York and St Cuthbert of Durham, hence the battle's name.

At which battle did a king direct the action from a windmill?
At Crecy in 1346. Edward III, king of England, directed his army against the French in the field, while he stood watching progress from a nearby windmill. He is said to have sent his son, the Black Prince, into battle with a troop of cavalry at a critical moment which he could see better than the men on the ground.

Who commanded the French forces at the battle of Quebec?
The French were commanded by the Marquis de Montcalm. He was killed in action, after hearing that the battle was lost. His conqueror, General Wolfe, in charge of the British forces, was also killed. As a result of the battle in 1759, Canada became a British colony.

What is a Pyrrhic victory?
The king of Epirus, Pyrrhus, twice defeated the Romans in battle in the 270s BC but he lost so many troops that he said he could not afford to go on fighting. A Pyrrhic victory, therefore, is one in which the success has been too dearly bought to make it really worth while.

What happened at the battle of Spion Kop?
The Boers drove the British off a ridge called Spion Kop and forced them to give up the attempt to relieve Ladysmith. This was in the first months of the Boer War (1899–1902).

What was the Eureka Stockade in Australia?
It was a rising among diggers in the Ballarat goldfields, in 1854. Rebels built a stockade out of pit slabs and defended it against government troops, but after only a few hours' fighting, the rebels surrendered.

Was there really a battle of the Alamo?
Yes, indeed. In 1836 a Mexican army attacked the Alamo, a fortified mission station in Texas, held by a handful of American troops. The building was fought for, room by room, and it cost the Mexicans several hundred men to win it. Among those killed on the American side was Davy Crockett, the famous frontiersman and politician.

Where was a Turkish fleet almost completely destroyed by an enemy fleet?
At the battle of Navarino Bay, in 1827. In the Greek War of Independence, a Turkish row-boat fired on a British warship. The British commander, supported by ships from France and Russia, turned on the Turkish fleet and destroyed over 60 ships, driving the rest ashore. It was almost the last battl] between wooden ships.

What was notable about the battle of Gettysburg, in 1863?
It was a victory for the Unionists over the Confederates in the American Civil War. Gettysburg is in Pennsylvania, and the success secured an important part of the state for the Union. It was after the battle that President Abraham Lincoln delivered his now famous Gettysburg address, in which he coined the phrase '. . . government of the people, by the people, for the people'.

What was Operation Overlord?
It was the code name for the successful invasion, through the beaches of Normandy, of German-occupied Europe in June 1944 by an Allied army of British, Canadian and American troops.

What is a figure of speech?

It is a variation of the simplest statement made to heighten the effect. Below are questions on some figures of speech.

What is a simile?

This is a clear statement of the resemblance between two things, such as 'the sea lay like a silver mirror beneath the moon'.

What is a metaphor?

It is a simile carried to the point of identity. If the simile above were made into a metaphor, it would read something like 'the sea, a sheet of silver, lay beneath the moon'.

What is a mixed metaphor?

This is using together metaphors that don't in fact match, with unintended comic results. Someone once said 'I smell a rat. I see it floating in the air. I will nip it in the bud,' referring to some political move he did not trust and wished to prevent.

What is metonymy?

Using the name of one thing in place of the word for the thing it symbolizes, such as The Crown, when you mean The Government, or I bought a Shakespeare, when you mean you bought a book of his works.

What does the marvellous word onomatopeia mean?

It means words employed to make the sound echo the sense. These lines from Tennyson are a fine example:
'The moan of doves in immemorial elms
And the murmur of innumerable bees.'

What is alliteration?

Using the same letter or syllable several times in a sentence or line. An example is: 'When fishes flew and forests walked, and figs grew upon thorn'.

64

What is a pun?

It is when a word is used in such a way that it has two meanings in the same expression. 'She was a good cook as cooks go, and as cooks go she went.' It is also a play on the differences between similar sounding words, as in, 'They told the sexton and the sexton tolled the bell'.

What is euphemism?

Strictly speaking, this is to describe something unpleasant in a way that is milder than what is really meant, for example, telling someone that he is putting on weight when he is fat!

What is litotes?

An affirmation expressed by denying its opposite. For example, 'He was not unknown', or 'not a few' when you really mean 'many'.

What is a zeugma?

This is where one word is made to refer to two or more other words, but which has to be understood differently in the different contexts, such as 'She returned in a flood of tears and a sedan chair'.

What is a palindrome?

It is a word or a sentence that reads the same backwards as it does forwards. One well known example is the sentence 'Able was I ere I saw Elba', quite wrongly attributed to Napoleon. It comes from the Greek *palindromos* meaning running back again.

What is oxymoron?

The conjunction of two words in contradiction to each other. There are several examples, such as 'bitter-sweet', 'His honour rooted in dishonour stood', 'cruel only to be kind'.

What is hyperbole?

Another word for exaggeration, and as a

figure of speech a phrase that does this. One famous example of hyperbole is the line of Marlowe's

'Was this the face that launched a thousand ships?'

which referred to the beautiful Helen of Troy.

What is personification?
This is giving life and feeling to inanimate objects or abstract qualities. There are many such figures of speech in Shakespeare, such as 'And pity, like a naked new born babe striding the blast'.

What is antithesis?
It is a phrase using words arranged to emphasize a contrast, such as 'To err is human, to forgive divine'.

What is irony?
This is where what is stated is not what is meant, with the assumption that the reader or listener understands the real meaning. It is often used in plays and perhaps the best known example is in Shakespeare's *Julius Caesar* when, in his funeral oration to Caesar, Mark Antony refers to the assassins as honourable men when he really means the opposite and the audience is well aware of it.

What is synecdoche?
This is a type of metaphor where part of a person or a thing is used to convey the whole. A famous example is the use of 'hands' for crew members, as in 'all hands on deck'.

What is apostrophe?
When an absent person, an abstraction or a personified object is addressed as though present. Two examples are 'Frailty, thy name is woman' from Shakespeare's *Hamlet*, and 'Envy, be silent and attend' from a poem by Alexander Pope.

Little Quiz 8
What do the following abbreviations stand for?

1. RSVP	37. cf.
2. SPQR	38. h and c
3. DBE	39. La.
4. USA	40. LCJ
5. USSR	41. ob.
6. PLO	42. c/o
7. AD	43. eg
8. Fid.Def.	44. viz.
9. BC	45. TD
10. ASC	46. Pp
11. BSA	47. pxt
12. awol	48. OM
13. SEATO	49. JC
14. PRB	50. DHSS
15. RNZN	51. FORTRAN
16. RAAF	52. FRCS
17. USSC	53. FCO
18. UNESCO	54. SBN
19. vtol	55. MEZ
20. FLS	56. UNIDO
21. FRSL	57. MB
22. GCB	58. NCO
23. BA	59. NSW
24. Ph.D.	60. Minn.
25. ICI	61. WHO
26. MIT	62. UDI
27. LSO	63. EEC
28. RCMP	64. IQ
29. RCN	65. IMF
30. NJ	66. EFTA
31. IOM	67. inst.
32. IRA	68. PAS
33. VAT	69. PQ
34. UKAEA	70. Reg. Prof.
35. AMTPI	71. SARAH
36. c and b	72. BIPM

How were the earliest civilized peoples governed?

They were governed by kings who were advised by priests and occasionally by warrior companions. The priests were generally the only people with knowledge or education, and they elected the kings, frequently on the basis of how strong they were.

Who was the first king in the world?

It is impossible to say who was the first king in the world, but a very early king was Menes of Egypt. He reigned in the 35th or 36th century BC, and he united the two kingdoms in the Nile region, Upper and Lower Egypt.

What was a satrap?

Governor of a province in the ancient Persian Empire. In the 6th and 5th centuries BC Persia acquired so many dominions that one man could not effectively rule them all, so the kings delegated power to satraps, that is, local governors who were given extensive powers to raise taxes, run police forces, build roads and so forth. They were responsible to the king, and the system worked well.

What is an assembly?

It is a meeting, and in political terms it is an organized group of people meeting for a purpose. The individuals attending have usually been chosen to do so by others whose views they represent. The assembly was part of the structure of government in many societies, such as the early Celts, the Anglo-Saxons, and it has also been the term used for similar and regular meetings in more recent years, such as in France at the time of the Revolution.

What is a cabal?

It is a clique of ambitious people, generally in politics, who want to run affairs of state between them. The word may have come from an ancient Hebrew word, *qabbala*, but by coincidence, in the years 1667–1672, the first letter of the name of five statesmen who governed England under Charles II happened to spell out Cabal – Clifford, Arlington, Buckingham, Ashley and Lauderdale.

Why was the German Reichstag burned down in 1933?

The National Socialists, under Hitler, wanted an excuse to crush the Communist Party in Germany. So they set fire to the *Reichstag* (parliament) building in Berlin and found a half-witted member of the Communist Party to confess to having started it. He was tried and executed. This gave the Nazis the excuse to ban the Communist Party and round up its members.

What is Dail Eireann?

It is the lower house of the Irish Parliament and was founded in 1918 when in a British general election three-quarters of the members returned to Westminster were members of Sinn Fein, the Irish National Party, who all refused to go to London to take their seats. Instead they set up their own parliament in Dublin. This led to war with Britain, and in 1922 the Irish Free State was created.

What is Plaid Cymru?

It is the Welsh phrase for Welsh National Party. Plaid Cymru wants self-government for Wales. It considers that a nationally-based Welsh government in Wales could hardly do worse for Wales than the British parliament has over the past 700 years.

Who was the first prime minister of Great Britain?

Sir Robert Walpole (1676–1745). He was appointed head of the government in 1721 and held office for 21 years – longer

than any of his successors. He kept
Britain out of many wars in Europe
ensuring a period of stability and
enabling the country to develop
particularly in the agricultural and
industrial areas.

How many prime ministers of Great Britain have there been?

Including Walpole there have been 54
prime ministers, some of whom have held
office for more than one term. Gladstone
is the only one to have been prime
minister for four separate terms.

What is the US State Department?

It is the United States Government
Department for foreign affairs, but with
extra functions. The head is called
simply the Secretary of State, and he is
first in the order of members of the
President's cabinet.

Why does a British MP apply for the Chiltern Hundreds?

Because the law says technically a
Member of Parliament cannot retire
during a Parliamentary session. He can
only leave by applying for the
stewardship of the Chiltern Hundreds.
They used to be districts in
Buckinghamshire, the stewardship of
which once carried with it a fee from the
Crown. MPs are not allowed to have fees
from the Crown, so by applying for – and
receiving – the Chiltern Hundreds a
member can leave Parliament.

What is a government's budget?

It is an annual statement of a nation's
public finances. It covers, in most
countries, income and expenses for the
year just past, and an estimate of the
same for the coming year. And it
suggests changes in taxation which
should produce the money to balance the
books. Unfortunately, as in private life
too, this seldom happens.

Little Quiz 9

How good is your geography?

1. What are the Cinque Ports?
2. How many counties are there in England?
3. How many regions are there in Wales?
4. How many regions are there in Scotland?
5. How many states are there in the United States of America?
6. How many countries are members of the United Nations Organization?
7. What is the highest mountain in the world?
8. Where is the ocean at its deepest?
9. What is its approximate depth there?
10. Which is the largest island in the world?

In which oceans are these islands?

11. The Azores
12. The Philippines
13. The Solomon Islands
14. The Lesser Antilles
15. The Balaeric Islands

What is the approximate population of:

16. Canada
17. Albania
18. Holland
19. Yugoslavia
20. Gibraltar
21. Andorra
22. United States
23. Jamaica
24. Mexico
25. Bolivia
26. Australia
27. Finland
28. France
29. Portugal
30. Iceland
31. Malta and Gozo
32. Turkey in Europe
33. Puerto Rico
34. Brazil
35. Venezuela
36. Tonga Group of Islands

What was feudalism?
Briefly, it was a system in which land was held by a person in return for providing a service to the land-owner who was often, though not necessarily, a king. The service could be one or more of several things, the most important being military service.

How did the feudal system work in England?
It was introduced by William the Conqueror (1066–1087), who took over the ownership of all land in England and parcelled it out among his friends and supporters, gave some to the Church and even let a few defeated Saxon nobles hold on to theirs. The rest he kept for himself. All his tenants, except of course the Church, did knight service of forty days per year or more for the land. Tenants lower down the scale worked the land and had to give up part of the produce to their immediate lords.

Why was Henry I (1100–1135) of England succeeded by his nephew and not by his daughter, as he wanted?
Because the nobles of England did not want a woman ruler, and they did not like the husband of Henry's daughter Matilda, who was Geoffrey Plantagenet, Count of Anjou.

Why was Richard the Lion Heart crowned twice?
Strictly speaking, Richard I (the Lion Heart: 1189–1199), son of Henry II of England, had a 'crown wearing' during his father's lifetime to show who would be the next king, and was then crowned properly after he had succeeded.

What is the origin of the name Plantagenet?
The Latin words for the plant broom (a yellowed flowered bush) are planta

68

genista. The broom plant was the emblem of Geoffrey, Count of Anjou, and father of Henry II (1154–1189), who was the first Plantagenet king.

How long did the Plantagenets rule?
For 331 years (1154–1485). It was the longest ruling dynasty in English history. The Stuarts in Scotland, by the way, ruled for 343 years (from Robert II in 1371 to Anne, queen of England, Scotland and Ireland who died in 1714).

Did Robin Hood really exist?
The story is almost entirely legendary. There were one or two Robertus Hods, described as fugitives or outlaws, but it is impossible to say which if any was the one so popular in legend. Perhaps it was a mixture of them all. One flourished in Richard I's time, another in the time of Henry III, and yet another in Edward II's reign.

What was the Hundred Years War all about?
Briefly, it was a prolonged attempt on the part of English kings to establish a doubtful claim to the throne of France.

How did it begin and end?
At first England was blessed with success. The French fleet was beaten at Sluys in 1340, and the flower of France's army was destroyed at Crecy in 1346 and again at Poitiers in 1356. It ended when in the 1440s England was driven out of all the lands it held in France, except for a few towns such as Calais.

Who were the Mongols?
A fierce, tough and fast-riding race of warriors from central Asia. They spent much of their time on horseback, dashing from one settlement to another, raiding villages, and so forth. At the end of the 12th century they found a magnificent leader in Genghis Khan.

What were the Mongols' homes like?
Some Mongols built circular cottages of thatch and timber on platforms mounted on wheels. These were probably the first mobile homes!

Who was Khubilai Khan?
Grandson of Genghis Khan, he was ruler of China from about 1260 to 1295. Apart from his military skill, he was greatly interested in learning and the arts and he welcomed foreigners to China, especially if they had something to contribute in the way of knowledge or expertise. His empire was prosperous and his court at Peking was sumptuous.

What happened to the Mongol Empire built up by Genghis Khan?
It broke up after his death in 1227, among his sons and grandsons. In the mid-14th century a descendant called Timurlaine attempted to rebuild it as a huge Asian empire.

What was the extent of Timurlaine's empire at his death?
He had captured Delhi which brought him northern India. He was master of Persia, Afghanistan, Syria and much of Asia Minor, as well as parts of Russia in Asia. He had designs on China but died before setting up an expedition, in 1405.

What is the origin of the Ottoman Empire?
Parts of the Byzantine Empire (whose capital was Constantinople) fell to attacks by a tribe of warriors from central Russia in the 1290s. They were led by Othman, a Turk, who began by capturing important areas in Asia Minor. The Empire was named after him.

When was the fall of Constantinople?
In 1453, an event which shocked and frightened all Europe, for the city was reckoned to be impregnable. It was also regarded as the principal bastion against the Turks. It was taken by the army of the Ottoman Sultan, Mohammed II, after a six weeks siege. The last Byzantine emperor, Constantine XI, was killed defending one of the gates.

What was the Big Cannon?
This was a Turkish-made cannon which fired a ball of great weight a distance of well over two kilometres. The cannon had to cool down for about half an hour every time it was fired, and it may not have been an accurate weapon, but despite this its effectiveness as a terror weapon was immense.

Who were the Ming emperors of China?
They ruled China from about 1368 to 1644. The first ruler was Hung Wu and he embarked upon a policy of preserving Chinese civilization and keeping it free from outside influences. Foreigners were discouraged from visiting, let alone working in, China. This was not to the Chinese advantage. Under the Ming rulers some very fine porcelain was produced, and it was also a remarkable age of painting and literature.

When was it forbidden to burn coal in England?
In 1273 the burning of coal was prohibited in and near London because of the danger to the health. Even blacksmiths had to use wood.

Who was the Black Prince?
He was Edward, eldest son of Edward III of England. At barely sixteen years of age he commanded a detachment at the battle of Crecy in 1346 and won his spurs (that is, was decorated for gallantry). Ten years later he beat the French again at Poitiers. The name comes from the suggestion that his armour was black. He was the father of Richard II.

What are these?

Dingo?
Once a domestic dog, which has now gone wild, it is regarded as a dangerous pest in Australia where it will slaughter sheep at the slightest whim.

Platypus?
First seen in Australia about 200 years ago, the platypus is an animal that looks like a dog or wolf but which has a duck's bill. Its front feet are webbed, it has no outer ears and is altogether a very odd-looking creature.

Koala bear?
This is a native Australian bear with a babyish expression. It is about 60 cms (2 feet) tall, with thick fur and prominent snout. It stores food in pouches in its cheeks, and it lives mainly in eucalyptus trees. It is quite harmless.

The Koala Bear

Wombat?
A relation of the koala bear, it is similar to a badger. It has no tail, lives in woodland burrows and it feeds on grass as well as on the bark of trees.

Kangaroo?
The kangaroo is a marsupial. This means that it carries its young in a pouch at the front of its stomach. It leaps about on its two sturdy rear legs and has a dog-like head. Kangaroos are sometimes put into circuses where they are trained to look as if they are boxing their keepers.

Opossum?
An opossum is a marsupial that lives in a tree. There are many different kinds, some as small as mice, some as large as medium sized dogs. It is found in North and South America.

Emu?
This is the Australian ostrich, with a long neck and spindly legs. It has a tiny head and its feathers generally look very untidy. It is very shy and in natural conditions runs away at the slightest provocation.

Kookaburra?
This is a wood kingfisher, sometimes called the 'laughing jackass' because its call sounds like a rude laugh. A kookaburra is about half a metre (18 ins) long with brown plumage, flecked with white and black.

Trumpet-bird?
This is the other name for the brolga, a slim bird with grey plumage, which calls out in a deep trumpet-like voice. It is easily tamed but at the same time it likes to be left alone for long periods. The brolga can dance so convincingly that many native tribal dances have been modelled on its footwork.

Tasmanian devil ?
Found in Tasmania, an island south of Australia, it is a fox-like animal which is a metre (three feet) or so long, with a thicker and fuller head. It attacks other animals to feed or scavenges for dead flesh. It is nearly extinct.

Whistling hare ?
A tailless North American creature, somewhat like a mouse. It has a high-pitched voice which accounts for its name.

Prairie dog ?
It is a rodent, a member of the squirrel family. Prairie dogs have extensive burrow systems in the open prairies of Canada and the US.

Eastern chipmunk?
A squirrel-like animal from south-east Canada that collects and stores food in pouches in its mouth.

Canada lynx?
A Canadian member of the lynx family which chases, kills and eats deer, porcupines and rabbits.

How fast does a coyote travel?
The coyote is something like a wolf, or Alsatian dog, to look at. It lives almost anywhere in North America and can run at nearly 80 kms (50 miles) an hour. It hunts in packs, usually after dark, and its call can be heard over long distances.

What are moose?
They are very large deer with huge antlers. They eat leaves and branches, especially water willows, and they also enjoy water plants. They are not peculiar to North America, however, and in Europe they are known as elk.

What is the biggest bird in the world?
Funnily enough, the biggest bird of them all is one that cannot fly – the ostrich. It is nearly 2.5 metres (8 feet) tall, and can weigh 135 kgs (300 lbs) or more.

How long can an elephant live?
Elephants have been said to live for a century or so, but the most reliable records show that 60 to 70 years are more likely. The only other animal that could beat that age is a tortoise. A few of these are known to have reached as much as 150 years!

When did cats become pets?
The ancient Egyptians domesticated cats and made them pets, over 4000 years ago. Indeed, cats were worshipped as gods.

Are lions really the all-powerful beasts they seem?
The lion has been the symbol of strength for centuries. Certainly he frightens other animals and human beings, but there are in fact several other beasts that can outsmart and defeat him.

What animal does Musquash come from?
A musk rat, which is found in Canada and the US. Musk rats normally live on the banks of streams.

Does a skunk really smell so awful?
When it is irritated or frightened, a skunk turns round on its enemy, lifts its tail and squirts from special glands a jet of very nasty smelling fluid which can burn the eyes of any other animal or human if it touches them.

What is a grizzly bear?
A grizzly bear inhabits parts of Canada and Alaska. It can be over three metres long and weigh over 360 kg (800 lbs). It eats bison and cattle, and tries sometimes to catch salmon. On the whole, however, it does not like human flesh.

71

What is the MCC?
The Marylebone Cricket Club, which is the governing body of English cricket. Founded in 1787, and with its headquarters at Lord's Cricket Ground in London's St John's Wood, it is the authority for drawing up and altering the rules of the game.

Which famous cricketer became a British life peer?
Learie Constantine, the Trinidadian fast bowler who delighted cricket spectators all over the world. Born in 1902 Constantine eventually became Trinidad's High Commissioner in London and was made a life peer.

What are the Ashes?
The team which wins a series of five Test Matches in cricket played between England and Australia is said to have won the Ashes. This comes from the result of the match played at the Oval in 1882 when Australia won and English cricket journalists were so disgusted that one reported 'The body (English cricket) will be cremated and the ashes taken to Australia'.

Cricket – a batsman

72

Where are Test Matches played in England?
There are six grounds from which the five matches may be chosen for playing: Trent Bridge, Nottingham; Lord's; Old Trafford, Manchester; Headingley, Leeds; Edgbaston, Birmingham; and the Oval at Kennington in London.

How long do Test Matches last?
Normally they last five days.

When was cricket first played?
Well, it's impossible to say for sure. People have played an organized game of bat and ball in England for centuries. The first rules for a game of any proportions were drawn up in the 1740s.

How did Rugby football begin?
Legend has it that one William Ellis, an Irishman, playing football in a game in England in the 1850s, broke the rules by picking up the ball and running along the field with it. Before long he was tackled. Boys at Rugby school, were playing a similar game back in 1823.

When was the game formally established on a national basis?
The Rugby Union which governs amateur rugger was founded in 1871.

What are five-a-side and six-a-side football?
In five-a-side, five players on each side play on a field 46 by 29 metres (150 by 96 feet), trying to score goals through hockey-sized goal mouths, being allowed to shoot only from the penalty area. In six-a-side, six players on each side play on a pitch 58 by 34 metres (192 by 110 feet) for ten minutes each way, and the penalty area stretches from one sideline to the other.

What's Australian football?
Difficult to summarize accurately in a

few words, but it could be said to be a mixture of English soccer and rugger. The teams have eighteen men each. The goal posts are six metres (18 feet) high and just more than six metres apart, with two smaller posts on either side. The ball is oval. A goal is worth six points, and there are no scrums.

What's the origin of golf?
Probably Scottish, for there are descriptions of a game like it taking place in the 15th century. James VI (1567–1625), who in 1603 became king of England as well, is said to have imported golf balls from the Netherlands. Golf reached the United States in the 1880s.

What are the three main golf cup matches played between Britain and the US?
The Ryder Cup for professionals (men), the Walker Cup, for amateurs (men) and the Curtis Cup for women golfers.

What is hurling?
An ancient Irish team game with fifteen players a side. Players chase a ball with a hurley, which is a heavy hockey-stick with a much broader blade. The game is played extremely fast and with great skill. It is claimed to be the fastest field game in the world.

What is the American national field game?
Baseball, which may have developed out out of simple English rounders. It is now a sophisticated game with rules. There are nine players a side and they use a round bat more than a metre (three feet) long and not more than 7½ cms (3 ins) in diameter. Baseball was first played in New York in 1839.

What's lacrosse?
It is the national summer game of Canada, and is also played in other countries. It has developed from a centuries-old game played by Red Indians. A ball is chased by two teams of ten or twelve players, using a stick or 'crosse' (the name comes from the French *la croix*) which is hooked at one end like a bishop's crozier. The tip of the hook is connected by a thong to the handle and a loose network of leather straps is stretched across the space.

Who invented basketball?
James Naismith, of Springfield, Massachusetts, US, in 1891.

Which is the best known American basketball team?
It is a New York team with the delightful name of the Harlem Globetrotters.

What is Fives?
It's not unlike squash – but the players use their hands, not racquets. It is played in a court, enclosed on three or four sides. Fives is played in England mostly in public schools, and the three main variations of the game are Eton Fives, Winchester Fives and Rugby Fives.

What is the national sport of Canada?
Ice hockey, which is played almost everywhere there. The game developed from ordinary hockey and is played on a skating rink. There are six players a side and they move extremely quickly. It originated in the 1860s and is now popular in many other countries.

What is the most prestigious event in world tennis?
It is the Wimbledon Tournament, first held in 1877 and organized by the All England Tennis Club. It is open to all comers.

Who invented

The lightning conductor?
Benjamin Franklin (1706–1790) was an American statesman who ran his own newspaper and helped to frame the American Declaration of Independence (1776). He was also a scientist. He ran a strip of copper down from the top of a chimney of a house right to the ground. Lightning flashes were thus deflected away from the house by the copper strip.

The steam engine?
For practical purposes this was invented by James Watt (1736–1819), the Scottish engineer. Other people had developed steam engines of a kind but Watt fitted a special condenser for collecting the steam and re-using it so that the engine would run for long periods without wasting too much of fuel.

The aeroplane?
For centuries men dreamed of flight. Then, in 1903, the American engineers, Wilbur Wright and his brother, Orville, made the first engine-driven aeroplane which got off the ground and flew under power for any distance. It went nearly 260 metres (852 feet), near the coast at Kitty Hawk in North Carolina.

The pendulum clock?
The first clock regulated by pendulum was devised by Christian Huygens in 1656. He was a Dutch mathematician and astronomer who also invented the hair spring for watches.

Television?
TV was invented by the Scottish electrical engineer John Logie Baird (1888–1946). What he did was successfully to transmit images of people and objects along a wire onto a screen.

The hovercraft?
Sir Christopher Cockerell, an English radio engineer, invented the hovercraft in 1955. It is a flat-bottomed craft and uses downward thrusts of air to create a cushion under it. This enables it to float just above the surface, whether land or water. Extra propellers mounted on the craft move it forwards, backwards or sideways, whichever is required.

The barometer?
Evangelista Torricelli (1608–1647) was an Italian physicist who became secretary to the great Galileo in his last days. Torricelli was interested in atmospheric pressure and he devised the mercury barometer to prove its existence. In time the barometer was used to forecast weather.

The jet engine?
The turbo-jet engine was invented by Sir Frank Whittle, who was born in 1907. He devised this efficient form of combustion engine in the late 1930s, and after quite a lot of setbacks got it accepted. The first aircraft to fly under the power of a jet engine was a Gloster E28, in 1941.

Wireless?
Electrical signals were first transmitted across long distances without wiring or cables by the Italian scientist Guglielmo Marconi (1874–1937), towards the end of the 19th century. In 1901 he sent wireless signals across the Atlantic, from Cornwall in England to Newfoundland in Canada.

The motor car?
No one knows who invented the first successfully driven motor car, but Gottlieb Daimler (1834–1900), the German engineer, was the first to make an internal combustion engine, operated on petroleum spirit, run a road vehicle for any length of time and with reliability. This was in 1886.

Photographs?
The first photograph was produced by the French chemist J. N. Niepce (died 1833) in 1822. Niepce worked with Louis Jacques Daguerre, a French painter who had invented his own process of producing permanent images by using sunlight on chemically-treated paper.

The gramophone?
The gramophone was invented in America by Thomas Alva Edison (1847–1931) who called it a phonograph. It was a machine that turned a barrel on which a series of sounds, like music or speech, had been cut by needle, and these sounds emerged out of a trumpet-shaped loudspeaker.

The pencil?
Although there had been several attempts before, the first reliable pencil was invented in 1795 by N. J. Conte. He produced pencils of graphite mixed with clay and fired in a kiln.

Dynamite?
Alfred Nobel (1833–1896), a Swedish chemist, once spilled some nitro-glycerine liquid by mistake, as he was lifting a bottle of it from a box of fine powder called Kieselguhr. It should have exploded, as it is very easily set off. But instead it formed a paste with the powder. Nobel discovered that the mixture was still explosive, but now much safer to handle. He called it dynamite, from the Greek word, *dunamis*, meaning power. He made a fortune which he used to create annual awards including one for peace.

The thermometer?
This was one of the many inventive ideas of the great Italian scientific genius, Galileo Galilei, who experimented with a glass tube to measure temperature, in the 1590s.

The microscope?
It seems that Galileo thought of the microscope as well! But the first standard microscope for examining minute organisms like bacteria was invented by Anton van Leeuwenhoek (1632–1723), the Dutch anatomist.

The typewriter?
The first typewriter was made by C. Sholes, in Milwaukee, Wisconsin, US in 1867. It was a fairly complicated machine which produced the type on the paper in such a way that you could not see it without withdrawing the sheet.

Christopher Latham Sholes using one of his early typewriting machines, 1878

The transistor?
Three American physicists, John Bardeen, Walter Brattain and William Shockley, in 1948 while working at the Bell Telephone Laboratories. The three were awarded the Nobel Prize for Physics in 1956.

Why do some countries put symbols as well as names on ballot papers?

For those who cannot read or write, some nations print the colourful emblems or other designs representing political parties on the voting slips.

What is a secret ballot?

Secret ballot means being able to vote for whom you like, of whatever party, without anyone else seeing your choice or knowing what it was. Not all countries have this procedure.

Who is the Speaker?

In parliamentary terms the Speaker is the officer who presides over meetings of the elected representatives in whatever legislative assembly a country may have. In the UK the Speaker presides over the House of Commons, and in the House of Lords the Lord Chancellor acts as Speaker.

Why was Mao Tse-tung known as Chairman Mao?

When the Chinese people drove out the government of Chiang Kai-shek in 1949 and elected a Communist government, the man who had led the Communists to victory, Mao Tse-tung, was chosen as Chairman of the Government of the People's Republic of China. He remained in office until he resigned in 1958, and from then until his death in 1976 he was chairman of the Chinese Communist Party.

What is a president?

Most countries that do not have sovereigns have a president. As head of the state, he is usually elected by the people and holds office for a specified number of years. In some countries he may be head of the government as well.

What is a diet?

A diet is an assembly of people elected or appointed to govern a country. It is very much like a parliament. One famous diet was the assembly under the Emperor of the Holy Roman Empire. Other countries which had a diet as its main seat of government were Poland, the Scandinavian countries and Japan.

What does it mean when one says parliament is dissolved?

This means breaking up the parliament. When the fixed term for a parliament expires, parliament should dissolve itself and fresh elections should be held for a new one. Sometimes a monarch may, on the advice of his ministers, dissolve Parliament.

In which country were old age pensions first introduced?

It was in New Zealand, in 1898. New Zealand, a young nation which had only become a separate colony in 1841 and won self-government in 1852, was a pioneer in many kinds of social legislation and service.

When did National Insurance begin in Britain?

In 1911 the Insurance Act gave free medical attention and sick pay of ten shillings (50 pence) a week for 26 weeks, followed by five shillings (25 pence) a week, to people earning less than £3 a week. The same act also instituted the scheme of contributory insurance against unemployment in certain trades, which provided seven shillings (35 pence) a week for fifteen weeks in the year.

Who was Simon de Montfort?

Simon de Montfort, Earl of Leicester, was brother-in-law to Henry III of England (1216–1272). In 1264, he led a revolt against his brother-in-law because of the king's incompetence as a ruler at home and in foreign affairs. He then summoned a parliament of barons, bishops, some knights, and a few citizens representing towns and counties to discuss future policies for the country. It was the first such parliament in British history and was held in 1265.

When was there a parliament in Wales?

In the early years of the 15th century, Owain Glyndŵr, a Welsh patriot leader, drove the English out of much of Wales and set up a parliament at Machynlleth, which is in mid-Wales. This met several times. Glyndŵr also captured Harlech Castle.

What is the Privy Council?

It is a body which advises the Crown on government matters in the UK and it comprises all ministers and former ministers, together with a variety of other eminent people in public life in the UK and the Commonwealth. It has a long history, stemming from the king's Great Council of Norman times. In the 18th century its more direct executive work was taken over by the cabinet. Members are entitled to the letters PC after their names.

What then is the Cabinet?

A body of the chief members of the government of the day in the UK – and in some other countries, including the US – chaired by the prime minister. Its decisions are translated into decisions of the Crown and the government. It advises the sovereign and determines the policy of the government. Collectively the members take responsibility for all the decisions made and they aim to maintain a united front in public. It has developed from the time of Charles I who formed a cabinet from the members of his Privy Council, possibly to get support for his attempts to override the advice of the Privy Council – and the wishes of Parliament.

Little Quiz 10

Which teams were English Football League Champions in these years?

1. 1905
2. 1947
3. 1953
4. 1956
5. 1957
6. 1965
7. 1971

Which teams won the FA Challenge Cup in these years?

8. 1932
9. 1951
10. 1956
11. 1960
12. 1966
13. 1972

Some sporting questions

14. How many times has Celtic won the Scottish FA Cup since 1947?
15. How many times has Rangers won the Scottish FA Cup since 1947?
16. How often has England won the World Cup for Football?
17. How many times has London been the meeting place for the Olympic Games?
18. Where were the Olympic Games held in 1976?
19. Where were the Olympic Games held in 1916?
20. When were the Winter Olympic Games inaugurated?
21. Who is the only heavyweight boxer to have won the world title since 1949 who was not an American?
22. When was the first of the famous Boat Races between Oxford and Cambridge rowed?
23. What length should there be between the wickets of a cricket pitch?
24. How tall should the stumps be?
25. How wide should the three stumps be together?
26. What is the right length for the bowling crease?
27. What is the correct maximum width of a cricket bat?
28. What should a cricket ball weigh and what should its diameter be?

What furniture did Hepplewhite make?

There is no record of any furniture made by George Hepplewhite, the north-England-born cabinet-maker. He did, however, leave a large number of splendid furniture designs, which were published a few years after his death in 1786. As a result his name has become associated with a vast number of pieces which resemble the designs.

A Hepplewhite walnut chair from the late 18th century

What is a cabriole leg?

Usually on chairs and tables, this kind of leg curves out on the downward path and then curves inwards again, tapering at the same time.

What is fretwork?

Woodcarving in patterns of straight lines, either open or as raised moulding

78

on a surface, when it is called blind fretwork. The style originated in China.

Where did gesso work originate?

This form of decoration in relief came from Italy. The motif is modelled in a mixture of plaster and size and then surfaced with gold leaf or gold paint.

What is linenfold carving?

One of the most popular patterns of late medieval woodcarving in Europe, linenfold actually looks like folded linen. It was employed on panels for chests, wardrobes and walls.

When is a pediment said to be a broken one?

When a pediment is constructed on a piece of furniture, with its apex missing. This was a favourite feature of Baroque design, in furniture and architecture.

What is patina?

When a piece of furniture has a polished surface that has some depth to it and looks as if it has been waxed and rubbed for years and years, it is said to have a patina.

When is wood said to be 'swash turned'?

This is another phrase for 'barley sugar' twisting, and it relates to the twist turning of wood for chair legs, stretchers, members of chair backs and so forth. It became popular in the 17th century and has been reproduced ever since.

What is a splat?

A splat is a panel of wood slotted between the top rail and the seat rail of a chair back. It lent itself to enormous scope for design and decoration and both Chippendale and Hepplewhite produced hundreds of variations in the splats they designed for their chairs.

How are woods joined by mortise and tenon?
The end of one member of wood has a rectangular section slot into which a similar rectangular section recessed projection fits. The two are glued or fastened by means of wooden dowels, and the joint is normally a very strong one.

What is scagliola work?
Another Italian idea, scagliola is imitation marble made from fine quality plaster and decorated. It can be highly polished and at first will fool you into thinking it is marble.

What is veneer?
A thin layer of wood, once cut by hand using a sharp knife but since the beginning of the 19th century more usually cut by a veneering machine. The layer is used to surface a piece of wood, perhaps to decorate it. Walnut veneer, for example, was often stuck down on oak or pine.

When is a surface said to be 'serpentine'?
It's a nice description of shaping to the front or surface edges of some pieces of furniture, like chests of drawers, where the ends curve inwards to meet the middle which is curving outwards.

What is Chinoiserie?
Applied to furniture it means decorative artwork which has Chinese characteristics, such as pagodas, fretwork, mandarin figures and so forth. Many 18th-century European cabinet makers liked fashioning pieces with Chinoiserie decoration, and the furniture-buying public went on asking for it for many years.

When is a piece of furniture said to be 'crossbanded'?
The term applies to the flat surface of a piece of furniture like a desk, table or chest of drawers. The band is strip wood along the edges, whose grain is usually at right angles to the direction of the grain of the main wood surface. The banding is sometimes of wood different from the rest of the piece.

What's grain?
In wood, the lines of the fibres which produce a pattern. Each kind of wood has a distinctive grain, and so you can see how much variety there must have been in making furniture, considering that over 40 different woods were available even in the 18th century.

When is a chair leg said to be reeded?
When the decoration on it consists of rows of convex mouldings running one beside the other round and down the leg. Flat surfaces can also have reed decoration, such as canted corners to chests.

Who was Chippendale?
Thomas Chippendale (1718–1779) was another north-England-born furniture designer and maker. He went to London to make his fortune and he made numerous pieces of furniture for famous homes, often to designs by architects. Then he produced his own catalogue of furniture designs and this was so successful that it ran to three editions.

Who were the best of the American furniture makers of the 18th century?
They were Duncan Phyfe (1768–1854), Thomas Affleck, and Samuel MacIntire (1757–1811). The first two were emigrants from Scotland.

What is a tallboy?
It is a chest of drawers which looks like one chest on top of another. The American version is more highly decorated and is called a high-boy.

What did Adolf Hitler do?
He rose from almost nothing to become leader of the German people, from 1933 to 1945. In those twelve years he made Germany the strongest military power the world had seen, and he bullied smaller nations into joining with him. He then overran most of Europe, attacked Russia and nearly overcame her, and tried also to bring Britain to her knees. He alienated most of the civilized world which joined in the ultimately successful effort to crush him, in 1945. By that time his warlike activities had brought about the deaths of over fifty million people, the destruction of numerous towns and cities and the obliteration of many industries.

What was the Risorgimento?
After the collapse of the Western Roman Empire in the 5th century AD, Italy was not united as one country again until the 1870s. She was broken up into states which warred much of the time between each other, and so became easy prey to ambitious rulers outside. Then in the 19th century, championed by the great Italian statesman Cavour and others, gradually the states threw off their former rulers and opted to build a new Italy. This movement was called the *Risorgimento*, and the first king of all Italy was Victor Emanuel of Sardinia and Piedmont.

Who was Mussolini?
Benito Mussolini was a journalist who, after the First World War, formed the Italian Fascist Party with the aim of seizing power. In 1921 he persuaded the king to let him form a government and for the next twenty-one years he ruled as a dictator, with the king's silent consent. Despite some worthwhile achievements Mussolini became power drunk and organized military expeditions to

conquer foreign lands – mostly unsuccessfully. More than once his ally Hitler, ruler of Nazi Germany, had to help get him out of trouble. Finally, in 1943, Mussolini was dismissed after a power struggle and in May 1945 he was shot by anti-fascists.

What was the Monroe Doctrine?
A declaration by President James Monroe (1758–1831) of the US, in 1823, to the effect that America resented interference in her affairs by Europeans. Henceforth, any interference would be considered an act of war.

When was Australia first colonized?
Although part of the Australian continent was discovered in the 17th century, it was not until Captain James Cook's voyages that any settlements were made. The first was at Botany Bay, so called because of the interesting plant life that Cook found there. The British government decided to use the area as a convict colony, a place where criminals could be sent instead of being hanged.

Who was Charles XII of Sweden?
King of Sweden from 1697 to 1718, Charles had dreams of building a huge military empire in northern Europe. He was successful in aggressive expeditions against Denmark and Poland, and he even defeated Peter the Great of Russia although he failed to capture Moscow, in 1709. He escaped to Turkey and then returned to Sweden. He turned to domestic matters, but in 1718 he tried to invade Norway but was killed by a stray bullet at a siege.

What caused the Russian Revolution of 1917–1918?
Like the French Revolution, the causes had been building up for a long time. Chiefly, they were grievances against the czar, Nicholas II, and his family,

court and government. Féudalism still existed, everything was inefficiently run, prices were high and food was scarce. The czar went to war on the side of France in 1914 but heavy losses caused military morale to collapse, and unrest began to spread at home. Nicholas was forced to abdicate and a moderate republican government was established. Extreme communist elements led by the great Lenin ousted the moderates and was the beginning of what is now called the Union of Soviet Socialist Republics (USSR).

What brought about the Indian Mutiny of 1857–1858?

Indian soldiers in the British Indian army were from time to time subjected to unnecessary humiliations by their British officers. One was to bite off the pellet stuck into a cartridge before loading it into a rifle. The pellet was smeared in cow grease, and cows are sacred animals to many Indians. This was the final straw and the soldiers mutinied. The revolt was crushed after much fighting.

What caused the Great Depression in the US in the late 1920s?

A general falling off in world trade led to many Americans withdrawing investments in Europe. The value of money was upset, confidence in the future of industry and in the demand for production sank, share prices on Wall Street (the US financial centre) slumped and fortunes were lost overnight. So too were the savings of many small investors. The depression lasted until President Roosevelt introduced recovery measures.

When did Japan become an industrial power?

A little over a century ago. In 1853 an American sea-captain led a fleet into Japanese waters and asked for leave to fish. This was the start of American influence in Japan and some of the great industrial progress of the US rubbed off. The Japanese people seemed to wake up, suddenly, and industrialization swept through the country like a whirlwind.

What happened at Pearl Harbor in December 1941?

On 7th December, waves of Japanese aircraft suddenly swooped down from the sky and attacked the US naval base at Pearl Harbor, in Hawaii. There was no warning, the Americans were not prepared, and they lost five battleships and a good deal else besides. It was a declaration of war, and for three and a half years Japan and the US and her allies were locked in a death struggle, which ended with the complete defeat of Japan in 1945.

What happened in the Hungarian Rising of 1956?

The people of Budapest, Hungary's capital, rose against their Russian-dominated masters and fought them in the streets for several weeks. They appealed to the world for help, but none came. In the end the Russians cruelly suppressed the revolt.

What was the Six-Day War of 1967?

This was when the Israelis and the Arabs went to war in June of that year. In six days Israeli forces conquered the Sinai peninsula, Jordan west of the river Jordan and advanced to within 65 kilometres of Damascus in Syria. Both sides then settled for peace on uneasy terms.

What brought about the collapse of Germany in 1945?

The death by suicide of Adolf Hitler, their leader, in his underground bunker in Berlin, on 30th April.

Who invented the macintosh?

Charles Macintosh (1766–1843), a Scottish chemist who made a coat of waterproofed material which was built up from rubber stuck together with naphtha.

What are Wellington boots?

Rubber knee-length boots, named after the first Duke of Wellington (1769–1852).

What was the hat that Sherlock Holmes was often described as wearing?

Sherlock Holmes, the famous fictional detective, sometimes wore a deer-stalker, which is a cap with earflaps and a peak at both front and back.

What is a Norfolk jacket?

A single-breasted tweedy jacket, loose-fitting, with pleats and belt. It was originally designed for people to wear when out shooting.

What do galoshes mean in Britain and in the US?

In Britain, a rubber shoe stretched over an ordinary shoe for protection when it is wet, and in the US an overboot for the same purpose. The word comes from the French *galoche*, meaning clog, and the British galosh does look a little like a clog.

What are sneakers?

They are American rubber-soled shoes with canvas tops, worn for sports.

Who was Amelia Bloomer?

An American woman who in 1850 designed a short skirt and loose trouser costume, tied at the ankles, which came to be called a bloomer. She was a keen reformer and supporter of women's rights. Bloomers now mean loose trousers or knickers tied or elasticated at the knees.

What is a topee?

A cloth-covered helmet specially made for protection against the sun. It was popular with British service people in very hot countries.

A topee worn with the full 19th-century colonial uniform

What's a bib?
Something a baby wears tied round its neck to cover its chest and to catch food and drink dribbled out of the mouth when feeding.

Who were the Sansculottes?
They were revolutionaries from the lower classes in Paris who during the Revolution abandoned their breeches and started wearing trousers. The Jacobins identified themselves with the Sansculottes.

What is a stovepipe hat?
Not worn now, it was a tall silk top hat. It was popular in Victorian days, on both sides of the Atlantic.

Why is an evening dress jacket sometimes called a Tuxedo?
Because it was invented at a country club in Tuxedo, New York. It is a dinner jacket, which is more comfortable to wear than a more formal tail coat.

What is a brass hat?
In British service terms it is a high-ranking officer. If you reach a rank where you are entitled to a row of gilt oak-leaves or similar decoration around the peak of your cap, you are said to have won a brass hat!

What's a cashmere pullover?
A lovely, soft woolly jumper made from the fleece of a goat from Kashmir.

Who was Blackshirt?
He was an adventurer in a series of novels by Bruce Graeme, who always wore a silk black shirt when out on his nocturnal expeditions.

What are moccasins?
Soft deerskin slippers worn by Red Indians, and now used to describe ordinary slippers that resemble them.

When would you wear a sou'wester?
When it is very wet and blustery. It is an oilskin hat with a large flap down the back to keep the rain off.

When were Balaclava helmets first introduced in Britain?
Soon after the Crimean War (1854–1856). They were – and still are – close-fitting woollen headgear which cover the head and neck, with a slit for the eyes. They were knitted for British troops in the Crimea who were somewhat taken unawares by the extreme cold.

What's an Astrakhan hat?
A fur hat, whose sides can be turned down to cover the ears. It comes from an Astrakhan sheep's wool if it's a genuine article, but the style can be imitated in several materials.

Why are Homburg hats so called?
Homburg is a town in Hesse, in Germany, and the Homburg hat is said to have originated there. It is usually a soft, black felt hat and is associated with civil servants.

Little Quiz 11

What is the female equivalent of these male animals?

1. boar
2. bull
3. bullock
4. colt
5. dog
6. horse
7. ram
8. stag
9. lion

And what is the male of these?

10. ewe-lamb
11. nanny-goat
12. tigress
13. tabby-cat
14. peahen

What is magnetic North?
It is the direction towards which the north-seeking point (or pole) of a compass swings to. It is slightly distant from true north, and its position varies fractionally every year. There is a South magnetic Pole in Antarctica.

Where are the prairies?
These flat grasslands are found in Canada and US. Similar areas are called the steppes in Russia, the veldt in South Africa and in Argentina they are known as the pampas.

What is an oasis?
It is an area in the desert where the ground is fertile through the presence of water.

What are the Roaring Forties?
They are the north-west anti-trade winds which blow steadily between latitudes 40 degrees and 50 degrees south. Anti-trade winds blow in the opposite direction to trade winds.

What are trade winds, then?
These are winds from the north east in the northern hemisphere and from the south-east in the southern hemisphere, both blowing towards the equator. They are tropical winds, and are on the whole steady.

In which direction does a sirocco blow?
It is a dusty hot wind from the Sahara desert region blowing north-easterly towards Italy and Sicily, across North Africa.

Has a coral reef anything to do with corals?
Yes, it is a sort of barrier just below the water, made from millions and millions of broken coral skeletons. Coral reefs can be a hazard to shipping. The most

84

famous coral reef is the Great Barrier Reef, north east of Australia, which is about 1600 kms (1000 miles) long.

What's the difference between a glacier and an iceberg?
A glacier is a mass of ice formed on land in a valley which glides millimetre by millimetre towards the sea, forcing rocks and stones in its path along with it. An iceberg is a chunk of a glacier that breaks off when the glacier enters the sea. Most icebergs sink below the water level, leaving only about a tenth of their bulk above. They are very treacherous things for ships at sea.

Can you have glaciers on land which don't go near the sea?
Yes, in mountainous areas, particularly the Himalayas and the Alps.

What is a crevasse?
It is a deep crack or split in a glacier. They are often hidden under piles of snow and are very dangerous for mountaineers.

What do we mean by a meridian?
A meridian relates to the position of the sun at noon or midday. In geographical language it means an imaginary ring or circle round the earth passing through the two poles (north and south). This means that it is midday at every place on this ring at the same time.

Why do we need to have this imaginary line?
Because latitudes and longitudes are calculated on it, and they are required for navigation, geographical location and many other reasons. A latitude is the the distance of a spot north or south of the Equator, measured in degrees of a circle from the meridian. A longitude is the distance east or west of a spot similarly measured from the meridian.

Why do some maps have contour lines?

They are lines joining areas of the same height above sea-level and they show the approximate shape of the land. In particular they can indicate the shapes of hills, mountains and downs.

What is an archipelago?

It is a sea which has lots of islands in it, but it has now come to mean the islands themselves.

What is a delta?

It is a triangular-shaped mass of land at the mouth of a river, composed of silt and other things shifted there over the years from the river upstream. Generally the land is very fertile, as it was at the mouth of the Nile in ancient Egyptian days. It is so called as it is the same shape as the Greek letter delta.

What is an isthmus?

It is a narrow piece of land that joins two other larger areas of land. Good examples are the isthmus of Panama in Central America and the isthmus of Corinth in Greece.

What is a cataract, in geographical terms?

It is a waterfall, or a series of waterfalls. There are several cataracts on the Nile in Egypt and the Sudan.

Which country is famous for its geysers?

New Zealand, though of course there are geysers in other countries such as Iceland. A geyser is a hot spring which discharges jets of very hot water and steam upwards into the air at intervals.

Are straits always straight?

Well, straits are narrow strips of water connecting one sea to another, such as the Straits of Magellan which are at the bottom of South America and which connect the Pacific to the Atlantic. The strait is not straight but follows the shape of the land on both sides.

What is a sand dune?

It is a heap of sand that is piled up by the wind, and occurs either on or near a beach or in the desert.

What is the Sierra Madre?

It is a mountain range in Mexico. A sierra generally contains many high and sharp peaks.

What is a col?

It is a feature in mountains, a pass between two peaks.

Where are fjords generally found?

In Scandinavia and North America, though there are others. A fjord is a narrow inlet of the sea, generally with steep sides, forming a kind of lake.

Which is the biggest canyon in the world?

The Grand Canyon in Arizona, US. It is along the Colorado river and is about 347 kms (215 miles) long. It is 1600 metres (5250 feet) deep and anything from six to 29 kms (four to 18 miles) wide.

What are the monsoons?

A system of winds which blow almost in the opposite direction to which the prevailing winds blow. Monsoons are prevalent in south-east Asia in the months April to September, and they are accompanied by vast amounts of rain.

Little Quiz 12
   What are these heraldic colours in ordinary terms?

1. Azure
2. Gules
3. Sable

4. Purpure
5. Vert
6. Argent

What is Gothic architecture?

It is the phrase used to describe the
architectural styles of the Middle Ages,
between about 1150 and about 1450. We
can't be too precise about dates because
while a style might have been abandoned
for a new one in one area, it would go on
being used for years in another.
Basically, the Gothic feature is the
pointed arch. There were three periods
of design within the Gothic period, in
Britain.

What are the three Gothic styles of architecture in Britain?

Early English (about 1150 to about
1300); Decorated (about 1300 to about
1375–1385), which was more ornate than
the Early English and featured tracery
in windows and floral decorations; and
Perpendicular (about 1350 to about 1500),
characterized by straight vertical lines,
large windows often with a grid-like
arrangement of lights.

Why do these Gothic features occur also in 18th and 19th century buildings?

Because there was a revival of interest
in the Gothic styles, partly because of
their association with the Middle Ages.
In Europe and in North America this
revival appeared in municipal buildings,
railway stations, monuments, as well as
new cathedrals and churches.

What does Baroque mean?

It relates to a period of art, architecture,
furniture, etc. of the late 16th and the
17th centuries, the main characteristics
of which were rich, decorative effects,
much foliage, rounded shapes, heavy
scrolls, and a general feeling of
exuberance.

Who was Palladio?

He was an Italian architect (1518–1580)
who revolutionized architecture by
86

returning to the principles of the ancient
Roman architect-engineer Vitruvius (1st
century AD). His book *Quattro Libri
dell'Architettura* greatly influenced
designers throughout Europe, and
though it covered buildings of all kinds,
it is remembered for its effects on the
design of great mansions.

A Palladian window

What does mullion mean?

A mullion is an upright post dividing a
window into two or more lights. It is
sometimes the companion feature to a

transom which is a horizontal bar in a window, also dividing a window into lights.

What is a course of bricks?
A row of bricks, extending the whole length of a wall or pillar. Courses of bricks are laid in a variety of ways, called brick bonds.

What are the principal brick bonds in use in British building?
Stretcher bond, Flemish bond and English bond. The first is where the course is laid with all bricks showing their long sides (stretchers). The second is where the stretchers and the headers (bricks showing their short sides) alternate. The third is where the courses alternate, all headers followed by all stretchers followed by all headers, and so on.

What's ogee?
This interesting word describes a moulding or shape, S-shaped in cross-section. It can be seen in many arches, and on a variety of pieces of furniture.

What is a louvre?
A slatted panel whose inclined slats overlap so as to exclude rain or light when fitted into a door or window.

What is a finial?
The architectural term for the ornament at the top of a spire or roof gable, but it can also mean more generally any finishing feature on a projection.

What is fan vaulting?
It is a particular kind of vaulting (arched roofing or ceiling) which spreads like a fan across a roof, the ribs coming out of the pillar or shaft in the same curve.

What is a lintel?
It is a piece of wood or stone which is put horizontally above a window or door frame. Lintels are today also made of concrete or sometimes steel.

What is a pitched roof?
Simply, a roof which slopes.

What was the solar in a medieval or Tudor house?
It was a private room for the owner and his family, positioned usually next to the main hall, at first floor level, and often at the end of the hall.

What was rococo?
Although the word is used with respect to architecture, it is really applied more to interior decoration and furniture. It is a very ornamental style, characterized by curved lines and profuse scrollwork, generally asymmetrical, with much foliage, flowers, and a variety of shapes based on rocks and sea shells. The name rococo comes from the French word *rocaille* meaning pebble-work.

Where did rococo designs originate?
Almost certainly in France, in the 18th century, and they were certainly more widespread and popular there than anywhere else. The concept all began with the artist Jean Bérain, at the very end of the 17th century, and lasted in France until the 1750s.

What's an arcade?
It's a row of arches on columns. It can also mean a covered way whose roof is carried on two rows of arches, and a covered way lined with shops, not necessarily graced with arches or other architectural features.

What is a corbel?
It is an architectural term for a bracket. It is a strong supporting projection built into a wall to support a heavy load like a roof truss or beam.

What is an epidiascope?
It is an old form of slide projector. It projects on a screen the reflected and magnified image of an opaque or a transparent object.

When did comics first appear in Britain?
Ally Sloper's Half Holiday, which first appeared in 1884, was probably the earliest comic. Sloper was a down-and-out who was continually rude about his fellow men and constantly knocking back gin. Famous comics like *Rainbow* (1914), *Tiger Tim's Weekly* (1920) ran on into the 1950s.

What are samplers?
They are embroidered panels which were first made as reference sheets of different embroidery stitches, patterns and colours. Then they became children's exercises in stitchery and usually included an alphabet, some verses and perhaps an instruction or two, together with the name of the worker, all done in embroidery. They were particularly popular in the 19th century.

What is collage?
It's pasting down cut-out pictures, items from newspapers, pieces of coloured cloth and what-not, on a board, screen or even lampshade, to produce a picture or a design.

What is solitaire?
A board game played by one person. The board is round. It has a pattern of holes in which glass balls are placed. One space is vacant. You can take a ball off the board by jumping over it with another, and the object is to get the whole lot off except the last one.

What's patience?
As a form of self-entertainment it is a

game for one using a pack of playing cards. The cards have to be taken as they come and be arranged in set patterns or disposed of according to rules. The objective is usually to get all four suits (spades, hearts, clubs, diamonds) into separate piles, in numerical order. In America it's called – solitaire!

What is prestidigitation?
It's playing tricks with your hands so swiftly that unless people watching are really aware they do not know what you have done. It is particularly applicable to card tricks and some conjuring tricks.

What are cosmetics?
They are preparations designed to beautify the skin and to improve the appearance, particularly the facial appearance of women although their use by men is on the increase.

What is the origin of cosmetics?
Roman women used all kinds of preparations to smear on their cheeks, eyelids and eyebrows. The practice went on into the Middle Ages. In many cases women wore cosmetics to hide the tell-tale lines which might give away their age! Elizabeth I of England used cowslip cream, while one of her male friends was said to have darkened his eyelids so that they might not be so noticeable as hers!

Do cosmetics do any harm?
Not really, but the best remedy for keeping a healthy and attractive skin is proper diet and plenty of fresh air at the right time.

How long have dress-making patterns been produced?
For more than 200 years, though in the 18th century they were in the form of engravings of people wearing certain costumes, which were then coloured by hand and sold as design sheets. These

appeared in the first ladies' magazines in the last years of the 18th century.

What is St Valentine's Day?
February 14th, the day when men and women send greetings cards (usually unsigned) to each other as tokens of affection. This date is the day of the feast of St Valentine, a Christian martyr who died in Rome in 273 AD. In fact, it has no connection with this saint: it was an earlier custom in pagan Rome on or about this day, the feast of the Lupercalia, to exchange love greetings.

Who invented the Christmas Card?
The first card was designed by the artist John Horsley RA – brother-in-law of Isambard Kingdom Brunel – for Sir Henry Cole, in 1843.

What's Monopoly?
It is a board game invented in the 1930s. The aim of the game is for players to move round the board and as they do so they buy cards representing properties on which they build houses or hotels. They are given a sum of money to begin with, and they can increase this by collecting rents from people who land on their properties.

What is a stereoscope?
This is a bar with a grip at one end which holds a card, and an eye-piece for both eyes at the other. Move the latter along a bit and eventually the picture you see appears to be three-dimensional. If you've seen in a junk shop a box with some cards bearing what look like two identical photographs side by side on each card, then these are for use with a stereoscope.

What happens when a photograph is taken using a simple camera?
Light comes in through the lens and strikes a film which is made of a plastic material covered with gelatine on one side. The gelatine contains silver iodide or bromide which is very sensitive to light. The silver compound is changed to metallic silver which appears as tiny specks that are not normally visible to the naked eye. The image of the thing taken is produced on the film which later on has to be developed.

How is the film developed?
A simple film is soaked in a chemical solution that makes the silver specks grow into bigger ones. This is done in a dark room so that the silver is not affected by light. Over a period of minutes a visible image appears. When the process is complete, the film is washed to remove the chemicals and then is 'fixed' in another solution so that it will no longer be sensitive to light.

What is a Polaroid camera?
It is a camera which can develop finished photographs within a minute. The developing and printing process is incorporated at the back of the camera and it will produce a black and white print in about twelve seconds, and a colour print in about 50 seconds. Companies other than Polaroid now make similar cameras.

What is a zoom lens?
It is a lens system that enables an object that is being photographed to be brought nearer or taken further away swiftly without altering the focus. It is used with moving pictures, TV and still photography.

What is composition in photography?
It is the artistic arrangement of colour, shapes and lines in a picture that you are taking with a camera. It is a skilled technique to do it well and takes a lot of practice.

What are teeth made of?
They're made of a bony substance called dentine, and they are capped or crowned with what is called enamel. The hollow part of a tooth contains a pulpy substance that has many highly sensitive nerves and minute blood vessels. If the tooth becomes decayed the blood vessels swell and press against the nerves and this causes toothache.

How do finger and toe nails grow?
They grow from a bed of skin containing keratin – a horn-like substance. This bed lies beneath the top skin and as the nail grows it becomes hard and smooth. There is a similarity between human nails and animal claws and hooves.

What's a taste bud?
The tongue is full of lots of gatherings of cells. These gatherings react to different flavours and allow us to taste the things we eat and drink. Therefore we call them taste buds.

Why do some people have their appendix removed?
The appendix is a small extension of the large intestine that has no function at all. But if it becomes damaged or infected it gets inflamed, and causes excruciating pain. If this happens it should be removed by a surgeon.

What are bones made of?
They're made of a complex network of fibres of animal tissue which are impregnated with salts of lime.

How many bones are there in the human body?
About 200, including the small ones in the wrist, ankles and the lower end of the spine.

Is cartilage the same as bone?
In some respects cartilage performs much the same function as bone, that is, it supports parts of the body and enables muscles to work. But it is tough, elastic tissue. Bones are not elastic.

What is the nasal septum?
It is the piece of cartilage and its protective coating that separates the two nostrils in the nose. In some people it can get bent and thus irritate the nose linings. It can be removed by simple surgery.

What is skin?
It is the protective covering of the body and is in two principal layers. The outer layer, called the epidermis, has no sensitivity and is often scratched or rubbed away. The inner layer, or corium, has blood-vessels and nerves which are sensitive to heat, touch and movement.

How many bones are there in the human skull?
Normally there are twenty-two. They are all flat and irregularly shaped and they form the face and protect the delicate brain. The brain case is called the cranium, the back of the head is called the occipital plate and the front part between the eyebrows and where the hair line begins is the forehead.

What are the principal parts of the brain?
The cerebrum, which is the largest part and has two hemispheres. In it are the controls for the voluntary movements and actions; the cerebellum, which lies just below the cerebrum, also has two hemispheres, and coordinates the muscles; and the brainstem which is the top part of the spinal cord.

What are the sinuses?
They are air-filled pockets within the skull and face bones and they are lined with mucous membrane. They open into

the nose or mouth, chiefly, and they can quite easily get irritated or infected, which can be painful.

What are the endocrine glands?
They are a set of glands that manufacture hormones and introduce them into the body system. They differ from other glands in that they have no pipes for carrying away their productions, and are sometimes also known as ductless glands. They include the thyroid, the adrenal, the parathyroid, the pituitary, the pancreas, and the sex glands in both men and women.

What, then, are hormones?
Briefly – and so, roughly – they are substances produced in the endocrine glands which regulate many of the functions of the body, like growth, metabolism, reproduction. They are very complex chemical substances.

How do the kidneys work?
They have long tubules and these filter impurities in the blood and get rid of them as urine. They also keep the acidity of the blood and other important characteristics of its chemistry at the right levels.

What is pain?
Some people claim that pain is simply imaginary. But in fact it is a nasty sensation which is caused by stimulation of certain nerves by an injury arising from an accident, or the effects of an illness, or even something emotional that sets off the nerves in the diaphragm area or the stomach or perhaps the head.

What is blood pressure?
It's the pressure exerted by the blood on the walls of blood vessels while on its journey round the body, pumped along by the heart. It can vary and is a good indicator of one's general health.

What is saliva?
A colourless fluid which is secreted into the mouth by the salivary glands, which helps to break down the food before it goes along the oesophagus to the digestive system. It is also necessary to enable one to swallow without effort.

What does the spleen do?
It purifies blood, and it also manufactures some of the blood cells for the body. Despite these valuable jobs, it is quite possible to live without a spleen.

What does the knee cap do?
It protects the hinged joint between the thigh bone and the shin bone.

Little Quiz 13
How good are you on the correct plurals for these words?

1. ass
2. box
3. cargo
4. potato
5. folio
6. piano
7. calf
8. chief
9. gulf
10. roof
11. wharf
12. turf
13. ally
14. alley
15. brother
16. ox
17. cod
18. gross
19. score (twenty)
20. species
21. brace (pair)
22. deer
23. toy
24. halo
25. cliff

Who was Bernini?

Giovanni Lorenzo Bernini (1598–1680) was one of the greatest of all the Italian Renaissance sculptors. He produced a variety of very fine works including the fountains of the Piazza Navona in Rome, numerous busts of well-known people, and he designed the great colonnade for St Peter's Cathedral. He is probably best known for his exquisite group of figures, the Apollo and Daphne, which was executed when he was a teenager.

Why did the sculptor Rodin excite such anger over his works?

Rodin was a French Impressionist sculptor. This may sound odd as the word is more often applied to painters, but he believed in their ideas about light and shade, and tried to demonstrate them in his early work. When he entered a figure L'Age d'airain at the Paris Salon in 1879 he was greeted with a storm of criticism. He was accused of taking the cast of the man from a living person. His next few works were similarly greeted, but in time Frenchmen came to see they had in their midst one of the most powerful and exciting sculptors of all time, and in the end they opened a museum to house his works.

Which Rodin work was rejected by those who commissioned it?

One of the most famous of Rodin's sculptures was his statue to the novelist Balzac, unveiled in 1898. It had been commissioned by the Société des Gens de Lettres, to be a memorial of a giant of literature. So Rodin made a giant of a statue, huge in the pronouncement of its features. The Société rejected it and it earned a great deal of insult. But it has since come to be accepted as one of the most astonishing portraits in Europe.

Who were the Preraphaelites?

The Preraphaelite Brotherhood was a group of artists of Britain who in the later 1840s broke away from the popular artistic styles and returned to the ideas of the Renaissance, in particular those of the time of Leonardo, Raphael and their contemporaries. These Preraphaelites were also moved by religion. The leading painters were Millais, Holman Hunt, Dante Gabriel Rossetti, Ford Madox Brown and they were championed by well known artists and critics like William Morris and John Ruskin.

Why was Veronese tried before the Inquisition for a painting?

Paolo Cagliari, who called himself Veronese because he came from Verona, was a painter in Venice who, in 1573, produced a splendid picture called The Feast in the House of the Levi, a Biblical scene. Among the figures in the picture were dwarfs, court jesters and dancers, quite appropriate to a grand dinner party. The church, however, regarded these as offensive in a religious subject and Veronese was brought before the Inquisition.

Which American painter became President of the British Royal Academy?

One of the early presidents of the British Royal Academy of Art was an American painter, Benjamin West, who was born in Pennsylvania in 1738. He came to England in the 1760s and specialized in historical pictures. One was of the death of General Wolfe at Quebec. West taught many visiting American students in England as well as British ones, and in 1792 he was elected President of the RA.

Why did Epstein's sculptures arouse so much feeling?

Jacob Epstein (1880–1959) was one of the most forceful sculptors of all time. His work expressed his ideas with no care for convention, and sometimes his marble figures, such as Jesus Christ in *Ecce Home* (1934) and the figure in alabaster of *Adam* (1938) were gross at first sight. Many people thought them insulting, but in fact they are moving and sensitive. As a sculptor of portraits cast in bronze, Epstein was supreme. You can see his statue of Field Marshal Smuts opposite the House of Commons in London, and there are many busts of other famous people in museums in the United States, France and other places.

What is action painting?

Normally, a painting is produced by applying paint to a canvas or other flat surface with a brush or a palette knife. But Jackson Pollock (1912–1956), an American-born painter of Scots and Irish descent, pioneered a new form of art produced by throwing or pouring paint onto the surface. At first sight this produces messy looking works but they were meant to convey what was going on in his subconscious. This style came to be called 'action painting' and is still done today.

Were there any American Impressionists?

There were several, the two best known being James McNeill Whistler (1834–1903) and Mary Cassatt (1845–1926). Whistler began his career as a soldier, but gave it up to study art in Paris where he was influenced by the then new Impressionism. From France he moved to England and set up a studio in Chelsea. Before long he became a leading painter, much in demand. He was witty and aggressive, and seemed to spend more time cultivating enemies than making friends. Mary Cassatt was born in Pittsburgh, studied art in Spain and Holland and worked in France where she became a pupil of the Impressionist painter Degas. Mary Cassatt's work is of consistently high standard, and the best known is probably *Woman and Child Driving*, now Philadelphia.

What is Pop Art?

Pop is short for popular, and pop art is the name covering an international attitude to art, heavily influenced by American ideas. Pop artists take things like machinery, science fiction, popular advertising material, film star photographs and bits from comics, and lump them together in pictures. In this way they hope to express their feelings about their environment.

Who are the leading Pop artists?

There are many good ones, but perhaps the most sensational is Andy Warhol who was born in 1929. He had a sound art training and worked for a time as a commercial artist. Then he broke out and started to shock people with his pictures and also some blunt films he made. One of his pictures is called *Marilyn* and is made up from ten versions in colour of Marilyn Monroe, the famous film star. He also put together a picture largely made up of photographs of Campbell's soup tins which was hailed as a great work. Other pop artists include Claes Oldenburg, Roy Liechtenstein and Eduardo Paolozzi.

What is Expressionist Art?

Expressionist artists and sculptors paint and model what they feel when they see something. The result may not actually be the thing they saw. Some Expressionists put colours and forms down on canvas or paper simply to express their moods. It is not always easy to understand what these artists are trying to say, but certainly the variety and colour enlivens the artistic scene. One of the leading Expressionist painters was the Russian Vassili Kandinsky (1866–1944).

Who was . . .
Atahualpa?
This great ruler of the famous Inca empire in Peru was captured by the Spanish invaders of South America, under Francisco Pizarro, in 1532. He was promised his freedom if he would give the Spaniards a room full of gold treasure, but when he did so, he was cheated. They had intended to put him to death all the time and he was strangled. The Inca empire collapsed and Peru became a Spanish dominion.

Solyman the Magnificent?
Solyman I (also spelt Suleiman) was emperor, or Sultan, of the Ottoman Turkish Empire from 1520 to 1566. In that time he expanded the empire to almost its greatest extent, from Morocco to the Tigris, from the Nile to the Black Sea, and he also introduced many reforms in government.

Eric the Red?
A Norwegian sailor and tribal chief, Eric the Red set out from his native land in about 985 AD in a long ship on a voyage of discovery in the west. He found Greenland and established the Viking colony there.

John Scotus?
John Scotus is better known as John Duns Scotus (1265–1308), a Scottish-born teacher who had a huge following of students when he lectured at Oxford University. His principal subject was theology, about which he had controversial opinions.

Peter the Hermit?
Peter the Hermit (1050–1115) was a French monk who led a detachment of crusaders to join the First Crusade against the Turks in 1096. His force was overwhelmed and he returned somewhat humiliated to France.

Sir Henry Morgan?
Morgan came from Wales. He was sold as a slave to a plantation owner in the West Indies. He became a buccaneer and eventually captained his own pirate ship in West Indian waters where he caused havoc among the Spanish treasure fleets. He was appointed governor of Jamaica by Charles II, probably as a reward for his gallantry.

Cyrano de Bergerac?
Savinien Cyrano de Bergerac was a French poet who also served in the army. He was an expert swordsman and his romantic nature caused him to fight many duels – usually successfully. But one day he was defeated and maimed so badly that he had to abandon fighting. He wrote poetry thereafter, and died, aged only 35 in 1655.

Nefertiti?
Nefertiti was the queen consort of the Egyptian pharaoh Amenhotep, of the 18th dynasty, in the 14th century BC. She was very beautiful, by all accounts, but she was also wise. Her son-in-law was Tutankhamun.

Nadir Shah?
The Conqueror, as Nadir Shah (1688–1747), king of Persia, was called, greatly enlarged the Persian empire by successful wars against the Turks and the Afghans. He even captured Delhi, then the capital of the Moghul Empire in India.

Farmer George?
This was the popular name for George III (1760–1820) of Great Britain. George was very interested in the industrial and agricultural revolutions in Britain and he ran a model farm at Windsor. He was despised by his sons and by many statesmen but he remained popular with the ordinary people right up to his death.

St Louis?
King of France from 1226 to 1270, Louis IX went on the Ninth Crusade against the Turks, in 1248, but was captured and spent six years in prison until a huge ransom was paid by France for his release. When he came home he introduced many domestic reforms, improved relations between the French Church and the Vatican, and earned the veneration of his people. He was canonized in 1297.

John Wilkes?
Wilkes founded a newspaper in England called *The North Briton*. In it he attacked the government and its leading personalities. He stood for Parliament, won a seat but was arrested when he went to the Commons to take it, because of his press attacks. He stood again, won again and was expelled again. Then in 1774 he got elected Lord Mayor of London. The Commons now had to accept him. He fought unceasingly for the freedom of the press.

The Tichborne Claimant?
In what was one of the longest law cases heard in England, 102 days in 1872, Thomas Castro, a butcher from Wagga Wagga in Australia, claimed to be the heir to Sir Alfred Tichborne, a rich baronet who had died in 1866. Castro, otherwise known as Orton, said he was the elder brother who was thought to have died in an accident at sea. His case collapsed, however, and he was tried for perjury and sent to prison.

Robespierre?
Maximilien François Robespierre (1758–1794) was a sincere but fanatical French lawyer who in 1792 became leader of the extremists in the French Revolution. He called for the execution of Louis XVI (in 1793) and then set up a Reign of Terror in which many people, including leaders, were put to death. But in 1794 he too went to the guillotine.

The Kaiser?
Emperor Wilhelm II of Germany (1888–1918) was called Kaiser, a German word for Caesar. He ruled the German empire extremely badly, dismissing the great Bismarck in 1890, supporting the Boers in their war against Britain in 1899, and finally plunging all Europe into the First World War in 1914 by invading Belgium and France. His forces were eventually defeated and he abdicated.

Colonel Blood?
Blood was an Irish-born adventurer who fought for various rebel causes in Ireland and Scotland. Then, in 1671, he broke into the Tower of London in disguise and tried to steal the Crown Jewels. He was caught, but Charles II pardoned him.

Messalina?
Valeria Messalina was the third wife of the Roman emperor, Claudius. She was good-looking, sly, intelligent and apparently utterly without morals. She had many lovers while she was empress, but when she went through a form of marriage service with one of them, Claudius decided that was enough and he had her put to death (AD 48).

Bonnie Prince Charlie?
In 1745, Prince Charles Edward Stuart, grandson of James II of England, Scotland and Ireland, raised rebellion in Scotland against the English government and the king, George II, claiming that his father Prince James Edward Stuart should be James III. The revolt was successful at first, but Charles, a romantic and dashing leader, overreached himself, and was eventually defeated at Culloden Moor in 1746. His cause collapsed and he fled to Europe.

What are the Doldrums?

The Doldrums are the parts of the ocean near the equator where calm waters and baffling winds prevail and where the atmosphere is very sultry and depressing. The phrase 'to be in the doldrums' means being depressed or in low spirits.

What were the Horse latitudes?

Another area of calm weather and quiet winds, between latitudes 25 degrees and 40 degrees north and south. In the days of sailing ships crews were kept idling in the waters as there was little wind and the ships made little progress. Food ran low and they threw what horses they might have had on board into the sea. Hence they were called the Horse latitudes.

What is the aurora borealis?

The proper name for the Northern Lights. They form a coloured glow of light in the shape of an arch whose apex points in the direction of magnetic North. They are seen only in the northern hemisphere. The colours vary from red to smoky black. They are caused by electrical discharge.

What is a mirage?

It is an optical illusion, that is, something you think you see but which is not really there. Remote objects look as if they are mirrored in water or hanging in mid-air. The closer you get to them, however, the further they fade away, until they disappear altogether. A typical mirage is the imagined appearance of water in the desert.

What is a tidal wave?

This is a huge wave of water created, probably, by an earthquake of major strength. It can sweep over considerable areas for some distance until it plays itself out.

96

What is rain?

When the water drops that constitute a cloud become too heavy for the air underneath to keep the cloud up, they fall as rain.

Why does it snow?

Snow is the result of the temperature at the level of the clouds being lower than the freezing point of water. The water droplets fall as snowflakes which are a number of ice crystals joined together, or as individual ice crystals.

What is sleet, then?

Well, it is really a mixture of rain and snow. The snow falls but the temperature nearer the earth is warmer than it is higher up and so many of the flakes melt into very cold rain.

Why do we suffer from fogs?

Fog is water vapour that is condensed on very fine suspended particles of dust and smoke. When this happens at or near ground level it forms a dense and opaque cloud, making it difficult, if not impossible, to see more than a few metres. Fogs vary in their intensity and in the amount of space they affect.

Is mist the same as fog?

Almost. It is a less dense version of fog, and although it is still hazardous for driving vehicles along the road, it is less frustrating. It is somewhat damper.

How is frost formed?

It is the crystallization of water in the air which falls as dew on the ground when the ground is colder than the freezing point of water which is 0 degrees Centigrade or 32 degrees Fahrenheit.

What is smog?

It is partly naturally created fog which contains a quantity of smoke and gas emitted from factory chimneys and domestic coal fires. It was an all-too-regular and unpleasant occurrence in many industrial cities in the 1940s and 1950s, but has since been greatly reduced in many countries by clean air legislation.

How does an earthquake occur?
It is a movement of the earth in a region, that is caused by volcanic activity underground or by major subsidence of earth which surrounds the region but which is weaker. Earthquakes can occur in most areas but are more frequent in the East Mediterranean, Japan, parts of China, the Pacific. Half of Lisbon in Portugal was destroyed by an earthquake in 1755.

What is a tornado?
A violent whirling wind which carries with it a funnel-shaped cloud that spins at great speed. A tornado can reach 800 kms (500 miles) an hour and can cause destruction over a wide area.

Is a typhoon like a tornado?
Yes. It is a whirlwind of considerable violence which blows in the China Seas and near the Philippine Islands in the summer and autumn.

What is a hurricane?
It is a really severe wind, accompanied usually by thunder and lightning and quite a lot of rain. A hurricane blows at between 128 and 160 kms (80 and 100 miles) per hour, sometimes more.

What is a whirlpool?
It is a circular current in the sea, or a river, brought about by the clash of two or more currents, and its form is determined by the shape of the channel.

What is a waterspout?
It is in effect a tornado that happens at sea. Small ships and boats that get caught up in a waterspout are liable to be destroyed or at least badly knocked about.

What is hail?
Small lumps of ice, anything from the size of an aniseed ball to an egg, which are created during a storm when wet air is drawn upwards very quickly. These lumps get larger as they attract more water vapour to them on their way down towards the earth. They vary in size from 13 mm ($\frac{1}{2}$ in.) to as large as 130 mm (5 ins) but regardless of their size they can do a lot of damage to agriculture.

What causes thunder?
It is the noise created when lightning, an electrical discharge in the atmosphere, expands the air through which it passes. Quite often you will hear the thunder first, in a thunderstorm, but it will always have been the lightning that came first.

Where do avalanches generally occur?
Usually in mountain ranges. They are vast chunks of snow, ice and earth – and whatever else comes down with them – which break away on the side of a mountain and rush down the slope with gathering speed. They are caused by partial melting of ice at the base or by sudden shocks, such as earth tremors.

What is a landslide?
Much the same as an avalanche, except that it does not necessarily contain snow or ice, and can occur from wet or dry hills or cliffs.

What is quicksand?
This is a most frightening thing. It is a mass of sand or mud saturated with water which sucks down into its bulk anything – or any person – that may come on to it.

What have Red Indians to do with India?

Nothing at all, except that centuries and centuries ago it is thought the various Red Indian peoples came from Asia across the Bering Strait into North America. They are called red because of their colouring.

An American Indian

On whose side would you have been in the American War of Independence if you were called a Redcoat?

On the British side. Most British regiments wore red coats, with varying amounts of decoration according to regiment and rank.

Why are some people called red-blooded?

It means vigorous and full of energy.

What is a redcap?

It is the nickname for a military police officer, because of the red band or red

98

cover on his official cap. In the US, red-caps can also refer to railway station porters.

What does it mean if you are caught red-handed?

It means you are caught in the act of doing something unlawful or shifty. It came from being caught with blood on the hands after committing violence to a person.

What is a white-collar worker?

Someone who has a job in an office. Once it meant civil servant but the growth of the complexities of industry and commerce has brought about an increase in the number of office staff needed in many walks of life, and so the term is more widely applied.

When is a woman said to be a white slave?

When she is forcibly taken from her own land and brought to another for purposes of prostitution. It was scandalously widespread in the 19th century, but on the whole it has died out today.

When would a friar be called a Whitefriar?

If he was a Carmelite friar, that is, a member of the Order of Our Lady of Mount Carmel, a monastic organization founded in the 12th century. Carmelite friars wore white habits.

What is a whitesmith?

Strictly speaking, a whitesmith is a craftsman who works with the metal tin, but the term has over the years come to embrace anyone who specializes in finishing metalwork of many kinds.

Would you feel insulted if someone called you a 'whited sepulchre'?

You should do. It means a hypocrite, or

someone who is covering a defective moral character by pretending to be righteous.

What does it mean if someone says you are blue-blooded?
It means that you have a distinguished and aristocratic family tree, that is, you are descended from an ancient and noble or gentle family. Once upon a time these things mattered, but they do not count for much now.

Who was Bluebeard?
He was a legendary character who married several women in quick succession. The point was that he murdered each one in turn. So, you might call a man a bluebeard who had been married and divorced more than once or twice.

Is it complimentary to be called a 'blue-eyed' boy?
Well, it depends! It means being a special favourite with someone. In the United States such people are sometimes called 'fair-haired boys'.

What is the blues?
It is a type of song which developed from the work songs and spirituals sung by the African slaves taken to the United States, and became the basis of American jazz. Although, as the name would suggest, blues songs are often melancholy, they can also be joyful and exuberant.

Why are some girls called blue-stockings?
It is a slightly offensive term applied by men – and perhaps by some women, too – to women who are particularly bright or intellectual. Today, the term seems to suggest that intellectual women are also unattractive to look at, but this is of course nonsense.

What is a blue-jacket?
It is the nickname of an ordinary seaman in the British or the American navy, and comes from the colour of the uniform.

What people are called Bluenoses?
Nationals of the Island of Nova Scotia in Canada. But, if you use the word with a small 'b', it can also mean a religiously bigoted person.

What is a blueprint?
A term – from a type of print – for a sketch or plan of work to be done.

Little Quiz 14

What are the manufacturing nations of these motor cars?
1. Mercedes-Benz
2. Renault
3. Volvo
4. Lancia
5. Lagonda
6. Volga
7. Honda
8. Panhard
9. Jensen

Do you know which countries have these registration letters for their vehicles?
10. SYR
11. YV
12. GB
13. L
14. MC
15. CDN
16. U
17. ET
18. EIR
19. BUR
20. RNR
21. EAK

Which American companies now own the manufacturing of these cars?
22. British Hillman
23. British Ford
24. Vauxhall

What is a suspension bridge?

It is a bridge that is hung from cables which pass over supporting towers and which are firmly anchored on the ground at each end. A fine example is the Clifton Suspension Bridge at Bristol, England, designed by I. K. Brunel and erected as his memorial after his death. The Golden Gate Bridge at San Francisco is a suspension bridge and so is the bridge at Sydney Harbour in Australia.

Sydney Harbour Bridge

What is the St Louis Municipal Bridge in Mississippi, US?

It is a huge girder type bridge with three spans, each nearly 217 metres (712 feet) long. This bridge carries a double deck with two railway lines and a road.

What is a pontoon bridge?

It is generally a temporary bridge made by using flat bottomed boats across which a metal structure roadway lies, connecting two banks of a river. Some pontoons give such good service that they stay in place for a long time.

What kind of bridge is the Forth Railway Bridge near Edinburgh in Scotland?

It is a cantilever bridge, built in the 1890s. A cantilever bridge is one whose span is supported by cantilevers projecting from piers on which it rests.

What is a bascule bridge?

It is a type of drawbridge, but instead of

100

the arm lifting on a hinge it is raised by means of counter-balancing apparatus, rather like a see-saw, which is what bascule means in French.

Why is steel generally used for long-span bridges?

Chiefly because its strength to weight ratio is very high. On the other hand, it is more expensive to maintain steel bridges than reinforced concrete ones of the same size.

What are the two famous bridges over the Menai Strait in Wales?

They are the Menai Suspension Road Bridge built by Thomas Telford in the 1820s, the first suspension bridge of any great size in the world, and the Britannia Railway Bridge, a tubular construction built by Robert Stephenson, in the 1850s, which is a little way to the west of the Telford Bridge.

Which is the most famous drawbridge in the world?

Undoubtedly Tower Bridge at the Tower of London. It is in fact a double drawbridge. Hinged at one end on each side it can be raised to let ships through and when its two halves are down it makes a road for traffic.

Where is the Simplon Tunnel?

It is in Switzerland by the Swiss–Italian border and runs under part of the Simplon road from Brig in Switzerland to Domodossola in Italy. The tunnel is 20 kms (12.4 miles) long.

What is the Box Tunnel?

It is a remarkable railway tunnel on the Great Western Railway route from Paddington, London, England to Bath and beyond. It was constructed by engineers under the direction of Isambard Kingdom Brunel (1806–1859) who designed it.

Is there a tunnel under the Alps?
Yes, under Mont Blanc, the most famous of the Alps mountains. It is about 11 kms (seven miles) long, and it links France with Italy.

Who built the Thames Tunnel in London?
It was designed and the first works were supervised by Sir Marc Isambard Brunel, between 1824 and 1843. Brunel was the father of Isambard Kingdom Brunel. The Thames Tunnel was the first construction of its kind in the world. It is still in use today as a post office transport tunnel.

How many miles of London's Underground system are actually underground?
Nearly 160 kms (100 miles), and there are further lengths planned, including the new Fleet Line.

Which is the longest tunnel in the world?
Unless you include the London Underground railway tunnelling, the longest is the Chesapeake Bay Bridge-Tunnel in Virginia, which links Chesapeake Beach and Wise Point. It is over 27 kms (16.5 miles) long.

What is a canal?
It is an artificial waterway cut through the land to irrigate fields or for transport. Canals have been cut since the earliest days of civilization, notably in ancient Egypt. The Romans were great canal engineers and left vast canal works in many of the provinces they governed.

Are there many canals still in use for irrigation purposes?
Yes. In the State of Victoria in Australia, the Murray Basin district is irrigated by a canal system, and there is also a system in the Great Valley of California in the United States.

Did the ancient Chinese construct canals?
Yes, they built the Grand Canal which connects the Hwai Ho and the Hai Ho rivers, running from Hangchow to Tientsin. The work was started in the 5th century BC, continued over the centuries and was probably completed by the 13th century AD. Its navigable length is over 1280 kms (800 miles).

Which was the first canal built in England in recent times?
This was the Manchester to Worsley Canal, built by James Brindley, to the order of the then Duke of Bridgewater. The Duke wanted to move the coal supplies from his minefields to Manchester quicker than was possible by road. It was constructed in 1761–1772.

What is the Suez Canal?
It is a canal cut between Port Said and Suez in Egypt, which joins the Mediterranean Sea and the Red Sea. It was engineered by Ferdinand de Lesseps, a French engineer and diplomat, and the work lasted from 1859 to 1869. Suez is over 160 kms (100 miles) long.

Who built the Panama Canal?
This was started by de Lesseps, after the successful opening of the Suez Canal, but his efforts did not completely materialize. The US government took over the project at the beginning of the present century and finished the 80-km (50-mile) canal in 1914.

Whose plan to cut a canal in the Isthmus of Corinth, in Greece, was eventually undertaken in 1893?
Julius Caesar's, drawn up two thousand years ago!

Where did the first motor-car race take place?

In France in 1894, and it was won by a de Dion steam car which was driven by the owner-builder, Count de Dion, from Paris to Rouen. He averaged just over 20 kms (12 miles) an hour.

Who was the first man to land on the moon?

Neil Armstrong, the American astronaut, who stepped out of the lunar module *Eagle*, fired towards the moon's surface by the command craft *Apollo XI*. He did so on 20th July 1969. He was followed by his colleague Edwin 'Buzz' Aldrin.

What was the first talking film in cinema history?

The Jazz Singer, which starred Al Jolson and which was made in 1928.

Who was the first European to see the Pacific Ocean?

Vasco Nunez de Balboa (1475–1519), the Spanish explorer who was governor of the new province of Darien at the time. He is recorded as having sighted it on or about 25th September 1513.

Who was the first emperor of Rome?

Caius Julius Caesar Octavianus, who became known as Augustus. He was emperor from 27 BC to 14 AD, and was the great nephew of Julius Caesar, founder of the imperial system.

Who was the first Briton to fly an aeroplane?

John Moore-Brabazon (1884–1964) who became Lord Brabazon of Tara. He was also the first British aviator to hold a pilot's licence.

Who was the first man to conquer the summit of Mount Everest?

Sir Edmund Hillary, the New Zealand mountaineer, who reached the top, accompanied by the Nepalese Sherpa Tenzing, in June 1953. Hillary, by the way, also went to the South Pole in 1958, on Sir Vivian Fuch's overland expedition, and was the first person to reach the Pole by land since Scott in 1912.

Who was the first man to break the sound barrier in the air?

Air Commodore Donaldson, in a Meteor jet in 1946.

Who was the first Marshal of the Royal Air Force?

Sir Hugh Montague Trenchard, Viscount Trenchard, OM (1873–1956), known as 'Boom' Trenchard because of his deep resonant voice. He founded the Royal Air Force, became its first chief of the air staff, and then went on to be Commissioner of the Metropolitan Police.

Who was the first to fly solo from England to Australia?

An Australian aviator, Herbert John Louis Hinkler (1892–1933), who made the trip in 1927. His diary of the flight is now at the Royal Air Force Museum in Hendon, London.

When was the first manned flight into space?

In 1961, when the Soviet Russian astronaut Yuri Gagarin piloted a space craft that orbited the earth, reaching a top speed of nearly 32,000 kms (20,000 miles) an hour.

Who first climbed the Matterhorn?

This 4119 metre (13,515-foot) peak in the Alps was first climbed by Edward Whymper (1840–1911), in 1865. Whymper climbed several other high mountains, wrote about his experiences, and also pursued a career as a wood-engraver.

Who was the first English sea-captain to sail round the world?
Sir Francis Drake (1540–1596), who sailed via the Straits of Magellan and across the Pacific back to England, 1577–1580.

Who were the first members of the Order of Merit (1902)?
Admiral Sir Edward Seymour, Field Marshal Earl Roberts, Field Marshal Viscount Wolseley, General (later Field Marshal) Lord Kitchener, Lord Lister, Lord Kelvin, Lord Rayleigh, Sir William Huggins, W. E. H. Lecky, G. F. Watts, Admiral Sir Henry Keppel and John Morley.

Who was the first man to run a mile in less than four minutes?
Sir Roger Bannister, an English doctor and athlete who, in 1954, covered a mile in 3 mins 59.4 seconds. Since that time many people have managed to do a mile in under four minutes, but for a long time the target had seemed impossible.

Who was the first woman to fly from England to Australia and back?
Jean Batten, a New Zealand aviatrix, who flew to Australia in 1934 and back the next year.

Who first flew across the English Channel?
Louis Blériot (1872–1936), the French aviation pioneer who built his own aircraft and flew from Baraques to Dover in July 1909.

Who was the first man to swim the English Channel?
Captain Matthew Webb (1848–1883), who set out from Dover and reached Calais, in 21¾ hours. This was in August 1875. Webb was killed later on attempting to swim the rapids at Niagara Falls, encased in a barrel.

Who was the first British comedian to receive a knighthood?
Sir Harry Lauder (1870–1950), a Scottish comic singer. Lauder was enormously popular for years, particularly during the First World War with the troops in the battle lines. He wrote many of his own songs, some of which are memorable, including *Keep Right On To The End of The Road*.

Who were the first consuls in Rome?
In 509 BC, the Romans, fed up with the king, Tarquinius the Arrogant whom they expelled, elected two consuls to govern for a year. They were Lucius Junius Brutus and Gaius Collatinus.

Little Quiz 15

Of what countries, arts or trades are these the patron saints?

1. St George
2. St Cecilia
3. St Crispin
4. St Christopher
5. St Peter
6. St Patrick
7. St Luke
8. St Andrew
9. St David
10. St Jude

These ten foods and drinks are well known when they are associated with a particular country. Which country?

11. Sausage
12. Onion
13. Coffee
14. Salad
15. Pastry
16. Bread
17. Delight
18. Tea
19. Butter
20. Rarebit

This is not to say that such foods don't come from other lands; they do.

What was the Roman Senate?

It was a body of Romans who made laws, appointed governors and supervised the running of the state. At first, members of the Senate belonged to the upper class; then some middle class people were elected, and finally distinguished people from Roman provinces were admitted. It was on the whole a conservative body.

Who were the equites?

Often referred to as 'the gentlemen outside the Senate', equites were middle class businessmen, merchants and so forth who owned a lot of the wealth of Rome and who could afford to arm and equip themselves for war service.

What did the Tribune of the People do?

He had wide powers to veto or block bills that were passed by the Senate. He was elected by the people through the Popular Assembly or at elections to protect their interests. At first there were two, then five and finally ten.

What was a proconsul?

This was a consul who, at the end of his term of office, took up a post as governor of a Roman province.

What was a gladiator?

A professional fighter who fought other warriors or wild beasts in the arena in ancient Rome or in any of the other cities. Gladiatorial contests were very popular and attracted all classes. Contestants were generally criminals, slaves or foreign captives.

Where was the Circus Maximus?

On the outskirts of Rome. It was a huge horseshoe-shaped stadium and race-course. Games and contests of all kinds were held here, as well as chariot races. It was started by the fifth king of Rome, Tarquinius Priscus.

What was a toga?

A toga was the main garment of Roman men. It was made of wool and was wrapped round the body in such a way as to allow ease of movement.

What was a stylus?

A metal-pointed pen with which words and numbers were cut on wax tablets.

What was the Suburra?

The most notorious part of the Roman slums, near the Forum and the Esquiline Hill.

What was the Rostra?

Magistrates and officials had to address crowds to pass on news, canvass for votes, announce new laws, holidays, war reports and so forth. One place they did this often was the Rostra, a raised platform in the Forum.

Who were the Parthians?

The Parthians were an Asian race that for about 400 years (*c*.200 BC–*c*.200 AD) occupied part of Persia and expanded their territories to embrace the old Persian empire and more besides. They were a major source of trouble to the Romans with whom they fought for large areas in the Middle East.

Why did Cato the Elder keep on saying 'Carthage must be destroyed'?

Despite the defeat of Hannibal in 202 BC, Carthaginian power was not destroyed, and as the 2nd century went on, its power remained a threat to Rome, though not a very severe one. Marcus Porcius Cato, a senator of good family, who was greatly respected, kept warning the Romans that they would never be safe until Carthage was destroyed. Eventually, in the third Carthaginian War, 149–146 BC, the Carthaginians were defeated and their city was literally razed to the ground.

What was a Parthian shot?

If a battle seemed to be going against the Parthians, their archers, mounted on horseback, would pretend to gallop off the field. Their opponents would chase them, but suddenly the Parthians would turn round in their saddles and shoot deadly accurately, throwing their opponents into confusion. The phrase has come to mean throwing a last decisive remark back into a discussion when one appears to be losing an argument.

How many times was Gaius Marius consul at Rome?

Gaius Marius (156–86 BC) was consul seven times, five of them in succession, from 104 to 100 when he saved Rome from the Teutones and Cimbri who threatened to engulf the whole of Italy.

What were the Sullan proscriptions?

When Sulla seized power in Rome in 83 BC he decided to crush opposition for all time. He published lists of all those he considered his enemies, and those who did not get away were put to death. It was a precedent followed several times in later Roman history.

Who were the members of the first Triumvirate?

They were the three most important men in Rome, Marcus Licinius Crassus, Gnaeus Pompeius Magnus and Caius Julius Caesar. They formed an alliance in 60 BC to bring order after years of civil unrest and sloppy government.

Why did Caesar invade Britain?

Caesar was attracted by stories of British wealth, especially pearls. He also wanted to punish the British for helping their cousins, the Gauls, in his wars against Gaul. Britain did not prove to be anything like as wealthy as he had heard.

What was the Board of Emperors?

In 284 AD, Diocletian became emperor of Rome. But he soon saw that the empire was too big for one man to manage properly, so he created a board of four, each with a quarter of the empire. The board consisted of Diocletian, Maximian, Constantius and Galerius.

Where did Constantine the Great build a new capital for the Roman Empire?

He picked the small Greek fishing port of Byzantium, on the extreme eastern point of Greece. Work began in 324 and six years later he declared the city open. It was called Constantinople after him. Exactly 1600 years later the name was changed again, this time to Istanbul.

Who was Julian the Apostate?

Julian was Constantine's nephew and he became emperor in 361. He ruled well. One of his aims was to curb the growth of Christianity, but he was killed in 363, probably by Christian sympathizers.

Where is Pompeii?

It is a ruined city in Italy, about 24 kms (15 miles) south of Naples, very near to the volcano Vesuvius which erupted in 79 AD with fearful force and engulfed the town. The lava and dust covered Pompeii, and when it was excavated in the 1740s, a great deal of it was found preserved in good condition.

How big was the Roman Empire in Trajan's time?

Trajan ruled as emperor from 98 to 117 AD. The empire stretched from Scotland to south Mesopotamia, from the Black Sea to the Lower Nile.

Who was the last emperor of Rome in the West?

Romulus Augustulus and he was deposed by the barbarians in 476 AD.

What are these?

Lincoln rocker
It is an upholstered rocking chair, with a low seat, tall back and a curved frame, popular in the years 1860 to about 1890.

Roundabout chair
A seat built on the diagonal so that your legs straddle the corner and the leg under the corner. The back is low, with splats on both sides.

Pennsylvania dry sink
It is a kitchen piece for washing dishes, with a hole in the horizontal surface which held a copper bowl. Nowadays these pieces are used for displaying plates, bowls and bottles, sometimes plants, especially in the copper bowl.

Pie cupboard
A wooden box on legs, with the front panel having a central door, and the panels pierced for ventilating the food kept inside.

Hunt table
Popular in the South, the hunt table was a chest on legs, with a table top surface. The chest contained two or three quite deep drawers. So-called because food was laid out for eating after a hunt.

Shaker furniture
A range of pieces made in the early 19th century by the Shakers, a strange religious sect. The pieces are simple, well proportioned and soundly made, in a variety of woods, such as maple, pine, cherry, birch and butternut.

Stiegel glass
Glassware produced at the Mannheim glassworks of William Henry Stiegel, the German immigrant who set up his factory in 1763. He produced tumblers, moulded glass, with ribbed and quilted patterns, and so forth.

Cranberry glass
A clear, pinkish-red glass popular in the US in the 1880s. Jugs usually had handles of clear glass.

Mary Gregory ware
Imitated from a Bohemian glass style in the 1880s by Mary Gregory who worked in the American factory that made it. Clear pieces, usually green, were handpainted with white enamel decoration, like flowers or figures of children. Vases were popular, and often came in pairs.

Tiffany Favrile glass
A style of glassmaking noted for strange and remarkable shapes, like flower petals, generally in the Art Nouveau manner. The colours were deep and iridescent. Sometimes called art glass, it was made by L. C. Tiffany, son of the famous jewel firm founder.

Peachblow vase
Simple glassware in reddish colours, produced by copper-red porcelain glazing.

Redware pottery
Name given to the earliest American pottery made from red clay or clay which went red on firing. It was porous and so was lead-glazed. Designs were often cut into the clay. It was the pottery also of the American Indians.

Deldare
An olive-green pottery produced in Buffalo, New York State, at the beginning of the present century. The decorations were painted under the glaze and pieces of Deldare are avidly collected in the US today.

Rookwood ware
Rookwood pottery made the first Art Nouveau designs in America, in the

1880s, at Cincinnati in Ohio. Pieces were hand-painted under a double glaze, which produced the effect of the design appearing to be under water.

Tucker ware
William Tucker was one of the earliest craftsmen to make fine quality porcelain in America, in the late 1820s. He used kaolin which he dug from a pit not far from his workshop in Philadelphia. His pieces were exceptionally good, and he specialized in jugs and pitchers.

Betty lamp
A very crude form of oil lamp from the earliest days of the settlements in America. The reservoir was oval and the wick came out at the narrow end. The lamp hung from a long hook, and it burned oil or grease.

Montanari doll
Baby doll whose head was extremely life-like, achieved by embedding individual hairs into the wax with hot needles.

Steeple clock
A development of the shelf clock, appearing first in about 1825, often in a Gothic style wooden frame with finials rising on either side of the pointed arch.

'Gone with the Wind' lamp
Made first in the 1880s, this has a globe as a lower reservoir and a globe of similar shape and size to enclose the wick. Named after 1939 from the film in which some of these lamps figured in some of the houses, they were previously known simply as kerosene lamps.

Eli Terry shelf clock
The earliest form of mass-produced clock in America, often made with wooden parts, was the Eli Terry shelf clock, first made in about 1810. It was a crude box,

upright, with clock face in the top half and a picture of some kind in the lower half. The top of the box might have a decorated pediment.

Low-boy
A low-boy is a two-drawer chest of drawers on legs. It was popular in the late 17th and 18th centuries.

High-boy
A high-boy is a tall chest which looks rather as if a chest of drawers has been put on top of a low-boy. Very popular in the 17th and 18th centuries, the high-boy is known as a tallboy in parts of New England and in the UK.

An 18th-century high-boy from Philadelphia

What is a contact lens?
It's a plastic lens, of the correct magnification and shape required, which is worn inside the eyelid on the actual eyeball to improve one's eyesight. They came into general use in the 1930s.

What are varicose veins?
They are veins, usually though not exclusively in the legs, which become stretched or widened through strain of some kind. Varicose leg veins are often the result of prolonged periods of standing over many years.

Why do doctors take your pulse if you are ill?
The pulse is an indicator of the rate at which the heart is beating, and also the strength of the heart beat. It can be taken at various points in the body where an artery is near the surface, such as the wrist, the groin and the neck. The average pulse rate is about 70 beats a minute.

Why are Yoga exercises becoming so popular in western Europe?
Because they are an encouragement to good relaxation and release of tension in muscles and nerves. They are exercises developed over many centuries among certain Hindus in India.

What is an 'iron lung'?
An 'iron lung' is a metal case in which a person who cannot breathe properly can be placed, quite comfortably. It contains mechanical equipment that helps them to breathe.

How do people go bald?
The hair needs nourishment like any other part of the body. If it is starved, the hair dies and falls out, and it is not replaced. Some infections of the skin on the scalp, some fevers, shock, and some nervous complaints can cause baldness.

108

What is First Aid?
It is immediate action taken to help someone who has been injured in an accident. One of the most important things to do is to try to keep the patient as still as possible until a doctor or an ambulance arrives.

What is a third degree burn?
This is where the skin is practically destroyed by the flames and the muscles and tissues beneath are also damaged.

What was the Spanish 'flu epidemic of 1918?
A particularly violent kind of influenza which killed over one million people in Europe towards and after the end of the First World War.

Why do some people suffer from indigestion?
Unless there is some serious medical reason, people suffer from indigestion mainly because they eat too much of the wrong food too quickly. A sudden shock or disturbance can cause indigestion.

What is diabetes?
It is a disease affecting the pancreas gland whose job it is to balance the sugars in the body. The pancreas secretes the hormone insulin for this purpose. Diabetes, which to a lesser or greater degree affects a fair proportion of the population, can lead to unconsciousness, even death, if it is not treated. Nowadays, people with diabetes generally manage to live for years and years quite normally by taking regular doses of insulin.

How do we get insulin?
Insulin given to human beings for diabetic conditions comes either from the pancreas glands of animals, or it can be made synthetically, that is, in a chemical laboratory.

Why do children have diphtheria inoculations?
Because they are particularly vulnerable to the disease. It is an infection in which a membrane forms in the throat and if it is not dealt with, it can choke the patient. Diphtheria can now be prevented by inoculation.

What is arteriosclerosis?
This is the medical term for hardening of the arteries. Arteries are normally quite elastic. This allows them to cope with the pressure of the blood as it goes through them. As one gets older, however, this elasticity deteriorates and the artery walls can become thick and harden.

Is it true that you can have an artificial hip joint?
Yes, certainly. If you break a hip joint and the consultant feels it won't heal properly, you can have the top of the leg bone removed and a metal leg top replacement put in. This should last for many years.

What does an osteopath do?
Principally, he can manipulate a displaced joint in such a way as to get it back into its right position. Osteopaths are very good for things like slipped discs in the spine, dislocated shoulders and so forth.

Why is tetanus known as lockjaw?
Because it is an acute infection, one of whose symptoms sometimes has the effect of fixing your jaw in a closed or open position. Tetanus is an infection picked up generally from soil.

Can you get sunstroke anywhere in the world?
Yes, but you are more likely to get it in hotter countries. It is the effect of the sun on the back of the head and also on the eyes, and you can avoid it by wearing a hat and sun-glasses in the hot sun.

What was the Black Death?
This was a frightful disease which ravaged Europe in the 1340s and 1350s. It killed a third of the population in England when it struck there in 1348–1349. It was bubonic plague, and it was thought to have come to Europe from China. It was called Black Death because among the earliest signs of it were black boils on the skin.

What is rheumatism?
It is a word rather loosely applied to a variety of aches and pains in the joints and muscles of the body. Quite often these are due to dampness in the air, or wearing wet clothing, or standing about in the rain.

Is rheumatic fever anything to do with rheumatism?
Not exactly. It is a disease, probably caused by bacteria, whose symptoms are high temperature and fever, inflamed joints and a general feeling of sickness. The heart can also be affected.

What is psychiatry?
Strictly speaking, it is the science that deals with the illnesses of the mind. This does not, however, mean that everyone who goes to a psychiatrist is necessarily mad. Indeed, most are not. They are generally disturbed by some deep-seated problems, probably going back to their childhood, and psychiatrists are trained to help them sort them out.

What is puberty?
It is the period of development in a human being, usually in the early teens, when what are called the secondary sex characteristics begin to appear, and both sexes become fertile.

What happened to John Hus?
John Hus (1369–1415) was a Bohemian religious reformer who in 1402 became rector of Prague University. He attacked the established Church for high living and for inconsistencies in its teachings. In 1415 he was arrested, tried for heresy and burnt at the stake.

What was the Reformation?
From time to time religions have to examine their doctrines and sort out inconsistencies. If the leaders of the faith do not do this, others will. This is what happened to Christianity in the 16th century. The leaders were living too well. They had forgotten the simplicity of Christ's teachings and they were using Christianity as a means to wield power on a political basis. The number of people who wanted to put an end to this began to grow and in 1517 the German monk Martin Luther voiced his objections in a document which he pinned to the door at Wittenburg Cathedral. He started off a movement to reform the Church that went far beyond his own expectations.

Why was the Welsh translation of the Bible so important to Wales?
Because the Welsh language had been threatened with extinction by Henry VIII, king of England, who ordered that no one should speak it again. In his daughter Elizabeth I's time, a Welsh bishop, Gwilym Morgan, translated the English version of the Bible into Welsh and published it in 1588. This made it available to many Welsh people. It saved the language and brought great comfort to those who felt very oppressed by English dominion in Wales.

What is the Koran?
The Koran, or Qur'an, which means 'that which is to be read' is the sacred book of the Mohammedan faith. It is in Arabic
110

and has 114 chapters which sum up what was revealed to Mohammed, the prophet, when he went into the deserts of Arabia to meditate before launching his new religion in the early 600s AD.

Who was Mohammed?
Mohammed (also spelt Mahomet) was a merchant who lived in Mecca in what is now Saudi Arabia. Born in 570, he spent the first twenty or so years of adult life in business. Then in 610 he suddenly decided to give it all up. He went off alone to study and meditate. He believed that Allah, or God, spoke directly to him, and he wrote down what Allah had told him. Then he began to preach a new religion to the people of Mecca. His success disturbed the authorities who drove him out in 622. He fled to Medina where he organized his supporters into an army to bring the new faith to the peoples of all Arabia. By 630 he was ready to return to Mecca and he was triumphantly received there. He died two years later at Medina.

Is it true that Mohammedans can have four wives?
Yes. It also allows Moslems to divorce wives, and the process in most Moslem communities is quite simple.

How many people in the world are Moslems?
Today there are estimated to be over 450 million, in Asia, Europe and Africa. There are some in America as well, but the number is probably less than five million. Among the nations that are predominantly Moslem are Turkey, Pakistan, Indonesia and all the Arab States in the Middle East.

What is mythology?
Mythology is the study of the various beliefs that ancient peoples had to explain their beginnings, how the world

was made, who were the first leaders and so forth. These beliefs are called myths, and many ancient peoples, such as Egyptians, Greeks and Persians, had their own special collection of myths which formed a basis for their particular religious beliefs.

Who was the principal god and who was his Roman equivalent?
The king of the Greek gods was Zeus and his wife was Hera. To the Romans the king of the gods was Jupiter and his wife was Juno.

Who were the children of Zeus?
There were many, some not by his wife at all but by other women. The best known of his children became gods and goddesses who became associated with certain aspects of life such as Athene (wisdom), Artemis (hunting), Hephaestus (fire), Ares (war), Apollo (music, song, poetry), Aphrodite (love).

What is a mosque?
It is a building for Moslem worship. Usually it has a domed roof and a minaret tower or two. There are no seats, and worshippers kneel on carpets. Every mosque has a niche that points in the direction of Mecca, the Holy City of the Moslems.

What are the Seventh Day Adventists?
This is a religious group of people, chiefly in the USA, who believe that the proper day for the Holy Sabbath is Saturday and not Sunday. They are not alone in this as the Jews also celebrate the Sabbath from sunset on Friday to sunset on Saturday.

Who was Moses?
Moses lived in the 13th century BC. He was leader of the Hebrew people who lived as slaves in the Egypt of pharaoh

Rameses II. Moses quarrelled endlessly with Rameses, constantly begging the pharaoh to let the Hebrews go back to Canaan (in Palestine). The Bible tells of many natural disasters that overtook Rameses and his Egyptians because he would not give Moses his wish, including a plague of frogs, a plague of locusts and a terrible disease that carried off the first born child in every Egyptian family. This was enough for Rameses and he did let the Hebrews go. Moses died before his people reached Canaan.

What are the Apocrypha?
The Apocrypha (the Greek word for secret things) are books of the Bible not included in standard editions because they were not in the Hebrew version of the Old Testament. They include two books of Esdras, Tobit, Judith, the Wisdom of Solomon, Ecclesiasticus, Baruch and the two books of the Maccabees.

Little Quiz 16
Who said the following?
1. 'Am I my brother's keeper?'
2. 'The serpent beguiled me, and I did eat.'
3. 'Behold, this dreamer cometh.'
4. 'Be sure your sin will find you out.'
5. 'The Philistines be upon thee, Samson.'
6. 'Here am I. Speak, Lord, for thy servant heareth.'
7. 'Am I a dog, that thou comest to me with staves?'
8. 'O Absalom, my son, my son.'
9. 'My father has chastised you with whips, but I will chastise you with scorpions.'
10. 'Whence comest thou, Gehazi?'
11. 'I know that my redeemer liveth.'
12. 'Though your sins be as scarlet, they shall be as white as snow.'
13. 'Blessed are the pure in heart, for they shall see God.'
14. 'I am innocent of the blood of this just person.'
15. 'Almost thou persuadest me to be a Christian.'

OUI!

What did the cry of the Roman populace, 'panem et circenses', mean?
It meant 'bread and circuses'. By the early days of the Roman Empire the majority of the Roman people, if not in the army, government service or business, had little to do all day as the more menial work was done by slaves. The cry is said to have been uttered from time to time by crowds when they were bored.

Who said 'Veni, Vidi, Vici', when and where?
It was said by Julius Caesar. It means 'I came, I saw, I conquered' and it referred to the swiftness with which he and his army overcame the army of Pharnaces at the battle of Zela in 48 BC.

What does 'ad nauseam' mean?
It means 'to the point where one becomes bored or disgusted' with something that is going on and on.

What is an ex gratia payment?
A payment given to someone for services rendered, or because they are in need, for which payment would not normally be made.

What is the origin of the phrase 'O tempora! O mores!', which means 'Oh! the times! the manners!'
It was an exclamation of the great Roman orator Marcus Tullius Cicero who was attacking the patrician renegade L. Sergius Catilina for his part in a planned revolt against the state.

Why is anyone called an 'ex officio' member of a committee?
If he is not elected or appointed a member but nevertheless ought to be on the committee because his job or his position makes it desirable, then he may be asked to be an *ex-officio* (by virtue of

112

his office) member of that particular committee.

What does 'annus mirabilis' mean?
It means 'wonderful year', and is a phrase used occasionally in history to describe a particular year in which a lot of good things happened.

Who were or are 'hoi polloi'?
This is the Greek for 'the many', which really meant 'the rabble'. It has come to be an offensive phrase for the masses of ordinary people.

What do the letters RIP stand for?
They stand for *Requiescat in Pace*, which is Latin for May he (or she) rest in peace. They are sometimes carved in a gravestone.

What does 'caveat emptor' mean?
It is the Latin for 'let the buyer beware'. If you buy something it is your responsibility to see that you have got what you are being asked to pay for before you complete the deal. After the money has been handed over it may be too late. Since the Middle Ages, however, when the phrase came into use, there have been several acts of legislation that enable one to get out of a deal if it is unsatisfactory, though this depends upon the nature of the deal, and many other factors.

What is a 'de iure' king?
A king who is entitled to the throne by right of descent, though he may in fact not be actual king because of a number of more practical factors.

What does 'de profundis' mean?
It means 'out of the depths'. Oscar Wilde wrote a poem called 'De Profundis' as an essay of reproach against Lord Alfred Douglas who, Wilde considered, had been the cause of his disgrace. He called

it that because it came from out of the depths of his soul.

Who jumped out of his bath and ran down the streets crying 'Eureka!'?
The celebrated Greek mathematician Archimedes (3rd century BC) who showed that the weight of a body placed in water is equal to the weight of the water displaced. He worked it out suddenly while bathing, and leaped out crying *'Eureka'*, which is the Greek for 'I have found it'.

What is the Latin phrase for someone who arrives at a critical moment in a bad situation and puts it right?
A *deus ex machina*, which means 'a god out of the machine'.

What were Julius Caesar's last words supposed to have been?
They are supposed to have been *'Et tu, Brute!'*, which means 'You also, Brutus!' When he was assassinated in 44 BC by a number of anxious and jealous senators, one of the leaders was Marcus Brutus, whom Caesar had previously regarded as a friend.

What does it mean to be 'in flagrante delicto'?
It is the Latin for being caught in the very act!

What does 'ex libris' mean?
The phrase means 'from the books'. Some people stick labels inside their books with their names written below the phrase. It then means 'from the library'.

What would you mean if you said that such and such a job was 'infra dig'?
It would mean that you considered the job too menial for you to do, or in other words, that it was *infra dignitatem* or beneath your dignity.

When is a person said to be 'non compos mentis'?
When he, or she, is not of sound mind. It can refer to a temporary condition as well as a permanent state of insanity.

What does 'festina lente' mean?
It means hurry slowly, that is, take things easily. It is the motto of the famous English family of Onslow. Can you see the pun there?

Little Quiz 17
What is the singular of the following?
1. scissors
2. spectacles (glasses)
3. measles
4. bellows (for fire)
5. tongs

What is the correct feminine equivalent for the following?
6. proprietor
7. bachelor
8. earl
9. friar
10. governor
11. tutor
12. patron
13. songster
14. traitor
15. executor

And what is the correct masculine equivalent of these?
16. heroine
17. vixen
18. negress
19. witch
20. marchioness
21. lass
22. bride
23. madam
24. sultana
25. abbess

How do you play Broken Bottles?

Form a ring of people. Throw a ball to one person who throws it to someone else, and so on. Whoever drops the ball has 'broken the bottle' and so has to pay a forfeit by being allowed the next time to catch the ball with the right hand only. If he drops it then, his next forfeit is catching with the left hand, the next down on one knee and the next down on both knees. He can remove the forfeit by catching three balls successively in one forfeit position. If he drops the ball a third time while on two knees, he's out!

What are the rules for Hit the Bucket?

One player stands on an upturned bucket in the centre of a ring of other people. He has a stick with which to parry a ball thrown at the pail by one of the ring. If the ball hits the pail, the thrower takes the place of the person who failed to parry it.

What's Russian Hole Ball?

Generally played in the snow, form a pattern of holes in some thick snow. Mark a line about three metres away from the nearest hole. Players should throw a ball and try to get it in the holes. Holes can be numbered in some way for scoring. First person to score 25 or 50 wins a game.

What's sack ball?

There are no rules at all, except that you are trying to play rugger or soccer standing or attempting to move along while in a sack.

What's Bull in the Ring?

Form two teams, of anything from six to twelve a side. Link arms and form two circles. Put one person from each team into the middle of his opposing ring, arms folded. Call out 'bastinado', whereupon he must try to barge his way

out of the ring. Everyone has a 'go' and the team with more break-outs than the other wins.

How do you play Japanese Tag?

One player is 'he', and the rest try to keep out of his way. If one is tagged, he has to clap his hand on the spot where he was touched and then he becomes the pursuer.

What is Bogey?

A tag game. One player walks away and is pursued by the rest of the players. He swings round, whereupon they must rush back to where the game began and he has to try to tag as many as he can. These drop out.

How do you play conkers?

This is played with chestnuts. Bore a hole through the middle of a chestnut (or conker) and thread a string about half a metre (18 ins) or so, with a knot at one end. Hang the conker and challenge a friend with a similar conker on string to a match. You have to strike the friend's conker and break it. If you do, you add to your score the number of other conkers his conker has smashed.

What's Jingle Bonnet?

Take an old hat, get a group of players to put in some coins and then in turn shake the hat about and tip the contents on the ground. The shaker who gets the most coins landing head first wins. Probably not to be played if you are short of money!

What is marbles?

One of the oldest games of all, played probably by the Egyptians and certainly by the Roman emperor Augustus (27 BC to 14 AD). It was played with anything that was vaguely round – stones, nuts, fruit stones, and eventually with chips of marble rounded. The striped glass marble was introduced about a century ago, though clear glass balls were used some time before that.

What's Shuffleboard?
Played generally on board ship on a deck, it's a kind of monster shove-halfpenny. Use wooden discs and big brooms. Push the discs along from a line towards a target marked out about eight metres (24 feet) away. This should have marked out squares big enough to contain the discs with a small amount to spare. Only discs inside the squares and not touching any of the sides can score.

What on earth is backgammon?
A board game, played by two people, using fifteen pieces each and a pair of dice. The pieces are moved about the board according to the dice throw. It is a gambling game that has been played for many centuries.

What is a diabolo?
It is a wooden reel which is spun on a cord stretched between two sticks that you hold one in each hand. The purpose of the game is to throw the diabolo into the air and catch it in the string as many times as you can without dropping it.

When did billiards first become a game in England?
Probably in the reign of Elizabeth I (billiards is mentioned in a Shakespeare play). To begin with it was played with a kind of mace, but in the 19th century the cue was invented.

How is dominoes played?
Dominoes is played with flat pieces of wood, rectangular shaped, with their top sides divided into two equal halves by a line. The two halves carry varying numbers of white dots (or some halves are quite blank) up to six each. The game is played by players placing, in turn, one piece end to end, or at right angles, with the proviso that the end has to have the same number of dots on it as the end on which it is being placed.

What's snooker?
It's a variation of billiards played on a billiards table. While billiards is played with red and white balls only, snooker has a variety of coloured balls which have differing values.

Who was the most famous snooker player of them all?
Probably Joe Davis, born in 1901, who was also a record-breaking billiards player.

How old is chess?
It seems that chess was played in India about 1300 years ago, and from there it gradually drifted westwards until it reached Britain about nine hundred years ago. Some chessmen, possibly of Viking origin, were found on Lewes – off the coast of Scotland, dating from the 11th century, and these are now in the British museum.

Was chess always played the same way as it is now?
No, the rules and procedures have varied over the centuries. The game as it is played today stems from the very late Middle Ages.

How many squares are there on a chessboard?
Eight rows of eight, that is sixty-four, alternately black and white.

What are draughts?
It's a game using a chessboard and a handful of 'men', which are flat discs of wood or some other material. The men are black or white, and the two players have twelve each. The object of the game is to capture all your opponents' men.

Can you eat seaweed?

In some instances, yes, though not necessarily in the raw state. Seaweed is a form of alga, and it contains iodine, a vital requirement for the human body.

Why is an antirrhinum called a 'snapdragon'?

Largely because its flower resembles the head of a monster of some kind. The petals are lipped and they remain almost shut. Humans can squeeze them open by pinching them on the sides, but bees are just about the only other creatures that can get them to open.

Why do some fruits have stones inside?

Simply, to protect the seeds which in the right conditions will produce new plants.

The cherry contains a stone to protect the seed

Why do plants have leaves?

Plants have leaves for manufacturing the chemical foods they need. Food making is done during spring and summer when the leaves absorb water which comes up from the roots through the stem. This water has the chemicals that come from the earth and they are built up so that when autumn arrives there are enough stored in the plant to enable it to survive the winter.

How is maple syrup made?

Maple syrup comes from sugar-maple trees. In the spring maple sap begins to flow through the tree. It contains sugar and to collect it for use you drill a hole about ten cms (four ins) into the trunk and put in a pipe with a tap. If you hang a bucket on the pipe and turn on the tap, the sugary liquid will drip slowly into it. The proper syrup is the liquid boiled to evaporate the water.

What is moss?

Moss is really a collection of hundreds of tiny green plants which make a sort of carpet under a tree, or sometimes in open grass. There are many kinds of moss none of which have roots or flowers. They grow by spreading thin moisture-absorbing threads across the ground. They need lots of water, which explains why they flourish in damp places.

Why is a shrub not a tree?

A shrub has branches like a tree but these grow out of the roots and not out of the stem. If they do have a stem the branches come out at ground level, like a rhododendron. Most shrubs are small, but there are some that are as big as medium-sized trees, such as witch-hazel.

Where does cork come from?

Cork is the spongy bark of a cork oak tree. Cork trees usually grow in Spain and Portugal and they produce a thick bark which is generally stripped off every ten years or so. This is boiled and pressed to make up the material used for bottle stops, mats, and so forth. Cork is very light, floats better than most materials, and so is good for making life-belts and safety jackets.

What is mistletoe?
It is a parasitic shrub, with white berries, that grows on the branches of trees, especially oaks, poplars, hawthorns and apple trees. Its seeds nourish themselves on the bark of the tree branch and in doing so they take a lot of food away from the tree itself.

What is bamboo?
It is a tropical plant, of which there are many kinds. Bamboo is in fact a form of grass, and it grows extremely fast, some types shooting up by half a metre (18 ins) or more a day.

How many kinds of grass are there?
Seeing that a lot of the earth's land area is covered with grass of one kind or another, it is not surprising that there are over 4000 kinds of grass. These include well-known varieties like wheat, barley, rice and oats, as well as bamboo and sugar cane. In some form or other they are eaten by the great majority of human beings and animals.

Where do rhododendrons come from?
Rhododendrons, those lovely red, purple or white flowers on rambling stretches of green bushes in many forests and gardens, came from Asia. They are now established as European plants and are very popular in Britain. Rhododendron comes from the Greek, meaning red tree.

What is a tuber?
It is a plant whose roots are covered with buds which grow underground. The buds may become new plants. Potatoes are typical tubers.

What is the medical use for eucalyptus oil?
If you distil the leaves of some kinds of eucalyptus tree you get an oil that is good for rubbing into the skin around a sprained joint. The oil certainly brings relief, which allows the sprain to heal. Eucalyptus trees grow in North Africa, parts of South America and in most parts of Australia where some can reach as high as 90 metres (300 feet).

What is a lichen?
A lichen is really two plants that grow together. One is an alga and the other a fungus. They grow side by side on soil or on rock, on roof tops or even on walls. They look like mould.

What is a teasel?
This is the prickly thistle-like plant you often find in the fields. It has a scrubbly stem and very sharp and stiff leaves around the flower head, which is shaped like an acorn.

What is a root crop?
A root crop is one whose fruit or edible root grows underground and which has branches and flowers above ground. Best known root crops are potatoes, parsnips, swedes, turnips and beet.

Who first classified plants?
Carl Linnaeus (1707–1778), the Swedish botanist, revolutionized plant and animal biology by classifying both by their genus and species. This enabled easier differentiation. He gave each plant and animal two Latin names. The first, the genus, was to indicate a general class, and the species, the second name, was a much more exact identification. His system has of course been developed and improved over the years.

How does a diesel engine work?

It is an internal combustion engine, as a petrol engine is, but its air is compressed in the cylinder in such a way that its temperature is high enough to explode the fuel which is injected directly into the cylinder. Diesel engines are noisier, slower and generally larger than petrol engines, but they are on the whole more economical.

What was the earliest form of omnibus?

The earliest 'bus was a horse-drawn affair, and one appeared in Paris in 1815. In 1829 George Shillibeer, an English businessman, introduced a horse-drawn bus service in London. The fare was one shilling – expensive for those days.

What's a rickshaw and where is it used?

It's a two-wheeled vehicle pulled by a man running between two shafts. The cabin rests on the axle which holds the wheels and is made of some light material like cane. Some are fitted with hoods for wet days. The rickshaw was originally made in Japan about a century ago and is still in use all over South East Asia.

What is a catamaran?

It is a boat with twin hulls, and when fitted with mast and sail can get up very high speeds, in excess of twenty knots. Originally, it was a raft with a centre log and a balancing hull on either side. Catamaran sailing boats are relatively modern; the rafts have been in use in the East Indies and off South America for thousands of years.

How did steam-driven cars give way to petrol and diesel cars?

Steam cars were quite fast, reasonably quiet and often very powerful – indeed, one American steam car reached 200

118

kms (125 miles) an hour as early as 1906! But they were unreliable, used masses of water, very dirty and it took a long time to start them. In the end the petrol driven car proved its superiority in many ways and manufacturers abandoned steam car-making.

Which is the oldest underground railway in the world?

The Inner Circle and Metropolitan Line on London's Underground. This was begun in 1860 and the first stretch opened in 1863.

What is monorail?

Monorail is a train running on a single rail generally suspended several metres above the ground. The first practical monorail, the Alweg, was built in Cologne in West Germany in 1953. There are monorails now in several other countries, including Canada and Japan.

What were the three types of airship in use in the earlier years of the present century?

The rigid type, with a framework covered with sheet metal and filled with gas lighter than air; the semi-rigid variety which had similar framework and also framework of balloon material; and the non-rigid kind which was almost entirely balloon material. They were all involved in serious disasters and were abandoned as a form of transport before the Second World War.

How does a helicopter work?

It is an aircraft driven by an engine which takes off, rises into the air, travels forward and returns to ground, all by using a rotating spindle and a set of blades on top of the fuselage. The blades are fitted in the spindle so that their angles can be altered by the pilot according to what movement he wants the craft to make.

What was a clipper ship?
It was a swift sailing ship with three or four masts rigged with square-shaped sails. Under full canvas it could move in a good wind at a very considerable speed. The clippers were generally employed on the tea trade runs between America or Europe and the China Sea, in the middle of the 19th century.

What's a dhow?
An Arab sailing ship, with triangular sail or sails. Dhows generally plied the routes from the East African coast up to the Red Sea or the Persian Gulf and back.

Where did trams originate?
Trams were devised first in the United States, in the mid 19th century. They were originally horse-drawn on rails set along the main road in towns, though the rails were not at first sunk into the road surface. Trams were introduced into Britain in 1861 when the first route was laid from Marble Arch down the Bayswater Road in London.

What was the Model T Ford car?
It was a small family car introduced in the USA by the motor-car manufacturer Henry Ford I (1863–1947). It was the first mass-produced car in the world, and between 1908 and 1927 over 15,000,000 of them were made and sold at home and abroad.

What was the USS 'Nautilus?
It was the first nuclear-powered submarine in the world, designed and built in the US. It achieved fame by sailing right underneath the North Pole.

When was the Sedan chair first used for carrying people about?
In Britain in the early 17th century. James I's son, Charles (later Charles I) gave one to the Duke of Buckingham as a present. The Sedan chair seems, however, to have been used in Europe before that time, and probably originated from the French frontier town of Sedan.

What was the Conestoga wagon?
A square-ended and outwards-inclined sided wagon on four wheels, specially designed to cope with bad roads and also to go through deep fords, invented in Pennsylvania and introduced into Canada where it became very popular. The canvas cover was supported by widely curving hoops.

What was the York boat?
It was a keeled boat, about 14 metres (45 feet) long, capable of carrying a square sail even in bad weather. Introduced by the Hudson's Bay Company in the 1820s in Canada for use on the Great Lakes.

What is the London to Brighton run for veteran cars all about?
Every year a number of people enter veteran cars (cars built before 1914) in a race from London to Brighton to celebrate the date in 1896 of the abolition of the law making it compulsory for any road vehicle, other than a horse-drawn one, to be preceded by a man walking with a red flag.

A Lancia Lambda of 1922

Who was Aesop, the composer of the Fables?

A Greek slave, later freed, who lived on the island of Samos. He is reputed to have been put to death by the citizens of Delphi in 564 BC for rivalling Apollo, the god of poetry. His fables are very short metaphorical stories about animals, each illustrating a moral, or a truth, such as: Pride goes before a fall. He never wrote any of them down, but they have been collected and set down by others many times since the 4th century BC.

Who is the greatest writer of fables in modern times?

The French poet Jean de la Fontaine (1621–1695) who drew freely from the works of Aesop and such very different writers as the earthy Rabelais in forming his own collection of fables for children and adult readers.

Why is there a statue of a mermaid in Copenhagen harbour?

The Danes built it to commemorate Hans Andersen (1805–1875), the Danish poet and children's story-teller. One of his highly popular stories was called *The Little Mermaid*.

Who cried 'A horse, a horse, My kingdom for a horse'?

Richard III at the Battle of Bosworth, according to William Shakespeare. Most unusually, Shakespeare considered this stirring line worth using twice – once at the beginning and again at the end of the battle scene. Many other contemporary Elizabethan dramatists paid it the compliment of imitation.

Who was Scrooge?

Charles Dickens wrote about Scrooge in *A Christmas Carol*. He was incredibly mean and cruel until, on Christmas Eve, a terrifying dream led him to change his ways.

. . . and Uriah Heep?

Another Dickens' character – the fawning, mock-humble clerk who doublecrossed the good Mr Wickfield in *David Copperfield*. This great Victorian novel was the nearest thing Dickens wrote to an autobiography.

Who was Mrs Grundy?

A symbol of convention and the British sense of propriety. Dame Ashfield, a character in a play called *Speed the Plough* (first staged in 1798), was constantly wondering – and fearing – what her neighbour Mrs Grundy might say or think. Mrs Grundy herself never appeared.

. . . and Mrs Malaprop?

The original perpetrator of malapropisms – the substitution of one long word for another, similar in sound but not in meaning. An example is: 'headstrong as an *allegory* on the banks of the Nile'. Mrs Malaprop was the heroine's foolish aunt in Sheridan's great comedy *The Rivals*, which was first produced in 1775.

Who believed 'All's for the Best in the Best of all Possible Worlds?'

Dr Pangloss, the aged mentor of the young hero in *Candide*, a satiric novel by the great Frenchman Voltaire. He expresses this view on all occasions – whatever scenes of devastation and injustice may surround him.

How many plays did Shakespeare write?

Thirty-seven. Many people think the greatest are the tragedies *Hamlet*, *Othello*, *King Lear* and *Macbeth*, which were written late in Shakespeare's life. Other very famous plays are the brilliant comedies *A Midsummer Night's Dream*, *Much Ado About Nothing*, *As You Like It* and *Twelfth Night*. Everyone knows the romantic and tragic story of *Romeo* and *Juliet*, and how Shylock in *The Merchant of Venice*, wanted his pound of flesh. Shakespeare also wrote many historical plays about English kings and leading figures in the ancient world such as *Julius Caesar* and *Antony and Cleopatra*. He also wrote two long poems, *Venus and Adonis* and *The Rape of Lucrece* and a collection of 154 sonnets. His first play, *Henry VI* (Part 1) appeared in 1590, when he was 26, and he died in 1616, aged 52.

Where did Shakespeare get his stories from?

Many of his plays, such as *Macbeth, Henry V, Richard II* and *Richard III*, were based on the reigns of British kings. *Julius Caesar* and *Antony and Cleopatra* come, of course, from Roman history, and *Troilus and Cressida* is an old Greek tale of the fall of Troy, as retold by Chaucer. *Hamlet* and *King Lear* were real historical personages, too. Some of the plays we remember best come from Italian stories, or novella. *Romeo and Juliet* is one – also the *Merchant of Venice*, *Othello* and *Twelfth Night*. The comedy *As You Like It* was based on a contemporary English romance, called *Rosalynde*, and *The Tempest* on a German play. It was not considered bad, in Shakespeare's day, for one author to copy another, so long as he improved on the original. And Shakespeare certainly managed to do that!

What is a sonnet?

One of the tightest, and most regular, poetic forms. A sonnet is fourteen lines long with (in English) ten syllables to a line. Different rhyming patterns have been followed at different times. Shakespeare, who wrote 153 sonnets, generally ended with a rhyming couplet. A sonnet is nearly always a complete poem and not one that can, like a ballad or a lyric, be set to music. A very unusual use of the sonnet is in *Romeo and Juliet*: when the lovers meet for the first time, Shakespeare divides a sonnet between them.

What is blank verse?

Poetry that doesn't rhyme and has each line of much the same length. It is based on the iambic pentameter, a Greek and Latin verse form with five feet, or long syllables, to a line, interspersed with five short ones. Marlowe's line about Helen of Troy.

'Was this the face that launched a thousand ships?'

is a typical line of blank verse. Almost all Elizabethan drama was written in blank verse, including the plays of Shakespeare.

And what is free verse?

Again, poetry that doesn't rhyme – but this time the poet may use lines of whatever length and form he likes. It may seem easier to write than rhyming or even blank verse, but it is not. The poet must invent his own rhythms as he goes along. Much modern poetry is free verse.

Who wrote the first limericks?

Nobody actually knows, but the poet who popularized them was Edward Lear (1812–1888). The limerick is a five-lined verse, generally of nonsense, in which the first and second lines rhyme with the fifth and the shorter third rhymes with the shorter fourth. It is thought to have come from an old Irish song in which there is a line 'Will you come up to Limerick?' One famous example is this anonymous limerick:

There was a young lady of Niger
Who smiled as she rode on a tiger:
They came back from the ride
With the lady inside
And the smile on the face of the tiger.

What is caulking a hull?
It is making a hull (usually wooden) watertight by covering the seams between the planks with pitch or oakum. With metal ships the term refers to hitting the edges of the plates with a cold chisel to get the same effect.

What is buffing?
Polishing up a metal, using a wooden block or a wheel covered with leather of some kind to get a shine.

What's chip-carving?
It is decoration of the surface of wood done lightly with tools. It does not require much skill. Chip-carving can be done on most woods, but it was a favourite with oak in the late Middle Ages and beyond in some districts.

What's petit-point embroidery?
Embroidery done on a woven canvas using a diagonal stitch. It was very popular for chair and settee coverings in the 17th and 18th centuries, and is still done today.

What did the Corporation des Fondeurs do in 18th century Paris?
They were a guild of craft metalworkers whose skill was casting and chasing metal for sculpture or furniture mounts.

What did the Corporation des Doreurs do?
They were a craft guild that had the monopoly of gilding in all forms. Principally, they gilded the metal products of the *fondeurs* with whom they worked closely.

What is an adze?
It is a tool not much used today. It has a handle with a slightly curved blade set at right angles at the top. It is for cutting and shaping wood. For centuries it was the next best thing to a plane.

What is a hallmark?
It is, in Britain, an official stamp on a piece of silver or gold put on after the piece has been tested for genuineness of metal and purity. Hallmarks, which were introduced in the very early 1300s, were issued from a number of Assay Offices in Britain, and these included London, Birmingham, Exeter, Edinburgh, Norwich, Carlisle, Sheffield.

What are the usual hallmarks on silver today?
They are usually, though not necessarily always, stamped in a row on the piece of silver, and they are a mark for the maker's name, the date (indicated by a letter), a mark indicating where the piece was assayed (tested) and a mark signifying the purity of the metal.

What is a spokeshave?
It is a plane with handles on either side of the blade which you can pull or push along a piece of wood to make its surface curved. Now used for curving wood for most purposes, it originated as a tool specifically for wheelwrights to shape spokes.

What's a potter's wheel?
A flat disc which revolves by means of a shaft connected to a flywheel of a motor, on which a potter throws clay into round shapes. The original potter's wheel was worked by hand, operated by a treadle, and it is difficult to say when it was first introduced.

What is wattle fencing?
It is fencing made of a network of sticks and/or twigs interwoven in panels. Hazel is the most commonly used wood and the sticks are usually split.

What is creosote?
It is a liquid made from coal-tar and wood-tar and is dark, sticky when it's

drying, and smells richly antiseptic. It stains wood, and it preserves wood that is used on the outside of buildings, and on things like huts, sheds and fences.

What is distemper?
A kind of paint made up from size, colouring and perhaps a little plaster, mixed in water, that was used to paint the inside of houses. It is not so often used today in houses, but it is still put on the walls of barns and outhouses.

How were walls decorated before wallpaper was introduced?
Thin sheets of canvas were stretched on wooden frames, painted and affixed to walls. No one knows for sure when wallpaper was introduced, but Elizabethan house designers knew how to hang decorated paper on walls.

How was lace made?
Hand-made lace was made in one or other of two methods. Needlepoint lace was built up from button-hole stitches and was made widely in Europe. Bobbin (or pillow) lace was made by marking out the pattern on a sheet of parchment laid on a pillow, sticking pins in at key points in the pattern, and anchoring the threads on the pins to make the completed lace pattern.

What is copper-plate handwriting?
It is a phrase to describe the fine, sloping and rounded style of handwriting used in lawyers offices in the 18th and 19th centuries and set for children to learn in many schools and homes. The name comes from the exercise and instruction books on this type of writing which were printed from copper plates engraved with it.

What is embroidery?
It is the skill of decorating by using needle and coloured threads. It is almost as old as civilization itself and has always been done by women and occasionally by men.

What is the Bayeux Tapestry?
It is a long wool and linen embroidered roll, some 64 metres (210 feet) in length, in which the story of the Conquest of England by William of Normandy is pictorially told in 72 scenes. It is in the museum at Bayeux in Normandy and is in remarkably good condition.

How do you make stained glass?
Originally, it was made by cutting pieces of coloured glass to the shapes of the parts of a whole that you wanted to make, joining them together appropriately between lead strips and enclosing the whole in a window or panel. There was an enormous quantity of very fine stained glass decoration and art-work done in Europe in the Middle Ages, particularly in France and England.

A stained-glass Romanesque medallion from Chartres Cathedral

What was unique about President Franklin Roosevelt of the US?

To begin with he won the Presidential election four times running and so master-minded United States domestic and foreign activities for the best part of a generation (1933 to 1945). He did so, greatly disabled by poliomyelitis which kept him frequently confined to a wheelchair. He gave the American people back their national pride and their will to justify the belief that they were the greatest people in the world, by dealing effectively with the mess that followed the Great Depression of the late 1920s. When the Japanese attacked Pearl Harbor in 1941 he led the American people into total war against Japan, and joined with the British and their allies against Germany and Italy. He died, suddenly, a few weeks before the end of the war, but he would certainly have known that it was really all over, bar the shouting.

Why did Napoleon reach such heights and then fall away to nothing?

Chiefly because, like so many great men who acquire vast power, he let this power get out of hand, thus smothering his original and more worthy aims. Napoleon, a young and brilliant general in the French revolutionary army at the end of the 18th century, worked his way via victories on land against France's enemies and by skilful political in-fighting at home, to the topmost position of state. In 1800 he was First Consul, then Sole Consul and then in 1804 he was made Emperor of the French. But even at his coronation by the Pope he snatched the crown and put it on his own head, which was a sign that power for its own sake had begun to eat into his system. He won a further succession of amazing military victories, against Prussia, Austria, and Russia and by 1809

124

was virtual master of Europe. But he had not crushed Britain. Nor had he neutralized the Russians, and his invasion of that nation ended in total failure. In the meanwhile, his armies in Spain were defeated by Britain's Wellington, and in 1815, Napoleon was decisively defeated by Wellington at the battle of Waterloo. It was the end of his career and he went into exile, dying in 1821. He had been born in 1769, the same year as Wellington. Despite this turn of events, it should not be forgotten that Napoleon carried out many crucial reforms in the domestic affairs of France, the effects of some of which have lasted up to today.

What was the secret of Churchill's unique greatness in British history?

Probably his unshakeable belief in the supremacy of the British people and their capacity to endure anything to ensure that justice is done in the world. His career spans sixty years of British history, from a period of eventful service in the army, then as a journalist in which he showed that he could write as well as anyone in the English language, then in politics where at first he championed the cause of reform. Sent to the Admiralty in 1911 as First Lord he entered this work with glee, seeing an opportunity of furthering Lord Fisher's work of making the navy the best in the world. During the First World War he was in the highest levels of government, suggested the Dardanelles enterprise but was blamed when it failed, spent months in the trenches in France, and then took office again in the government. Jumping twenty years, in the late 1930s he warned the nation about the dangers of trusting the word of Hitler, and when war did break out in 1939 he went again to the Admiralty. Within nine months, however, his time arrived and he was called upon to succeed Chamberlain as prime minister. As war leader, he invoked the best qualities of the British and in practical form directed the war effort through to ultimate victory. After the war he spent some years on the opposition benches in Parliament and wrote his famous history of the war which won him a Nobel Prize for literature. He was prime minister again from 1951 to 1955 and then retired from public life. At his death in 1965 when he was 90 he was accorded a state funeral. Only one other commoner had had that before: Gladstone.

Who was the greatest of them all?
If you ask that question of many people, they say they cannot answer. Yet if you say it was Julius Caesar, they hesitate, then say, well, perhaps, there was no one else with such a combination of talents and achievements. And indeed this is the point. If you look at his career and the magnitude of his achievements – he gave the Roman republic a system of imperial government that became the forerunner of Western Europe as we know it today – it is easy to see how Caesar has become the best known man of history. Command in battle, oratory, statesmanship, writing, law, politics, friendship with his fellow men, conversation, appreciation of the arts, he excelled in every one. He was witty, handsome, kind and forgiving. He had immense will power, great personal courage, and a total absence of hatred for anyone. Caius Julius Caesar (c.102–44 BC) was of high birth, went through the normal paths into politics, enjoyed an adventurous if dangerous youth resisting authority, incurred huge debts with people who lent him money because they believed in his ultimate greatness and therefore his ultimate ability to repay it! At nearly forty he took life a little more seriously and commanded an army of Rome's in Spain with distinction.

Then he stood for the consulship and won it, and combining with the two most powerful men in Rome, Pompey and Crassus, he formed the first Triumvirate in 60 BC. From there he went to Gaul as governor and commander and in ten years brought that huge district, as far as the coast of Belgium, into Roman control. He defeated the Germans, visited Britain, and crushed a serious revolt in Gaul. On his return to Rome he struggled to get recognition of his successes and also for his men. This led him to declare war against the state and he eventually won, because he had justice on his side. He hated this civil war, however, and longed to reconstruct the state so that such things could not occur again. His efforts were ultimately successful, though his own life was at risk, and in 44 BC he was murdered by a gang of greedy and small-minded senators, some of whom he thought were friends, many of whom had once wronged him but had been pardoned and given high office. They wanted to keep the republic; he intended to replace it with an imperial monarchy. They killed him, but the republic also died and his monarchy was vested, first, in his great-nephew Octavian who became Augustus in 27 BC.

Little Quiz 18
What were the dates of these treaties?
1. Campo Formio
2. Westphalia
3. Troyes
4. Utrecht
5. Nanking
6. Ryswick
7. Cateau-Cambresis
8. Amiens
9. Adrianople
10. Tientsin

What are, or were, the following buildings?

The Alhambra
A Moorish-Spanish complex of buildings in Granada, Spain, started by Mahomed I, Moorish king of Granada, in the 13th century and finished a century or so later by a Spanish architect. It is surrounded by a wall more than 450 metres (1500 feet) in circumference.

Gateway to the Sun
A large doorway cut out of a block of stone, about three metres (ten feet) in height, with a decorated frieze. It stands in the ruins of the ancient Peruvian city of Tiahuanaco and is over 1000 years old.

Chichen Itza
The remains of an ancient city of the Maya civilization in Mexico, including temples, an observatory and palaces. The city is thought to be at least 1000 years old.

The Colosseum
An amphitheatre for games and gladiatorial contests built in Rome by the Emperor Vespasian (69–79 AD) and finished by his second son Domitian (81–96). The great part of it is still there and is one of the largest buildings in the world.

The Parthenon
The Temple of Athene, built on the Acropolis in Athens between about 447 and 436 BC. It is largely constructed of marble, and it is nearly 61 metres (200 feet) long, with 17 columns on each of its longer sides and eight outer and six inner columns on each of its two shorter sides.

The Roman Aqueduct at Nimes in France
Roman engineers built many aqueducts in the empire, to carry water from lakes and rivers into cities. One which is still standing and is very impressive is the Pont du Gard aqueduct at Nimes. It is over 30 metres (100 feet) high and has three levels of arches.

The Capitol in Washington
The seat of the US Congress, and containing the buildings of the various state legislatures. It was begun in 1793, shortly after the Americans had won their independence of Britain.

The Great Sphinx at Gizeh in Egypt
A huge figure of a mythical being, half-lion with a human head and headdress, about 56 metres (186 feet) long and standing 20 metres (66 feet) high, carved out of rock near the Pyramids at Gizeh on the banks of the Nile.

Anuradhapura
Now a ruined city, in Sri Lanka (Ceylon), it was the principal city of the Ceylonese culture of the 5th century BC to the 8th century AD. In its time it was considered to be as important as Babylon.

Hadrian's Wall
This is the great Roman wall in Britain, stretching from the Solway Firth in Cumberland to Wallsend, near Newcastle on Tyne, some 117 kms (73 miles) long. It is built of stone blocks, stands about six metres (18 feet) high in places and is between two and three metres (6 and 9 feet) thick. At intervals of a Roman mile were placed towers, and in between there were, at regular intervals, some 160 recessed watchtowers.

Angkor Vat
The ruins of a temple in the ancient city of Angkor in Cambodia (south east Asia). It was a place of Buddhist worship and was built over 1300 years ago.

Hagia Sophia
The name of one of the most remarkable cathedrals anywhere. Built by Justinian I, emperor of the Byzantine empire from 527 to 565 AD, in Constantinople (now Istanbul), it is over 45 metres (150 feet) high and the main dome is possibly the largest ever made. The cathedral took 10,000 or more workers working full time six years to build, which is very short indeed. Today it is a mosque.

The Louvre
Once the palace of the French kings, in Paris, it was started by Francis I (1515–1547) and added to by later kings. Today it houses one of the greatest museums and art collections in the world.

Chartres Cathedral, France
There are of course many beautiful cathedrals in France, but that at Chartres, some 88 kms (55 miles) south of Paris, is the finest of them all. It is a supreme example of medieval Gothic architecture, and it has 160 windows filled with beautiful stained glass.

Winter Palace at Leningrad, USSR
Leningrad used to be called St Petersburg in Czarist Russian times. The Winter Palace was the palace of the Czars, started by Peter the Great in the early 18th century and finished by Catherine the Great (1762–1796). It is now the Museum of the Revolution.

The Kremlin, Moscow
We hear a lot about the Kremlin, and perhaps imagine it as some huge prison fortress. Actually, it's the citadel of Moscow, triangular in plan, on a hill, surrounded by a wall two kilometres long, 22 metres high. It was built in the 15th and 16th centuries, though it has of course been added to, and it encloses government buildings, offices, residences, and even two cathedrals.

St Peter's, Rome
This is the principal cathedral church of the Roman Catholics. It is in the Vatican, in Rome. It was built over nearly two centuries, from about 1450 to about 1660. The dome was designed by Michelangelo and the height to the top of the cross on its summit is 151 metres (495 feet). Popes are crowned in St Peter's which is also a place of pilgrimage for all Catholics.

The Pantheon in Rome
This was started by Marcus Vipsanius Agrippa, right-hand man of the first Roman emperor Augustus (27 BC to 14 AD). It was dedicated to all the gods, hence its name Pantheon. Its dome is of solid concrete and is over 42 metres (140 feet) in diameter. It was finished by the emperor Hadrian (117–138 AD).

Post Office Tower, London
One of the highest structures in Britain, a radio communications centre. It is a tall, thin, cylindrical building over 176 metres (580 feet) high, built in 1966–1968.

Sydney Harbour Bridge, Australia
The natural harbour at Sydney is spanned by a suspension bridge over 4½ kms (2.7 miles) long. Its central arch is 503 metres (1650 feet) long, and was opened in 1932.

Little Quiz 19
What is the French for:
1. seven?
2. twenty?
3. eighty?
4. one thousand?
and the German for:
5. two?
6. ten?
7. fifty?
8. one hundred?

What is a blackjack?

One meaning is a pirate flag. It also means a short leather-covered club with lead in the head and a flexible handle.

When would you be in someone's black books?

If you had fallen out with them and they remembered some grievance they had against you.

What is a Blackfriar?

A friar of the Dominican order, founded in the 13th century by St Dominic. The friars wore dark habit.

Where would you be going in a Black Maria?

Probably to a police station, to a criminal court, or even to prison. It is the popular name for a van in which police forces in Britain take criminals from one place to another.

Where would you be living if you were a Blackfoot?

You would be in a reservation, probably, in the USA, as you would be a member of the Blackfoot tribe of the Algonquin Indians.

Who were the Black and Tans?

They were specially recruited British forces, generally drawn from ex-criminals and out-of-work layabouts, who were formed into a kind of 'army' to fight the Irish patriots in the war between Britain and Ireland, 1918–1921. The Black and Tans were so-called because of the colour of their uniforms.

Could you have a house built in the Greenbelt in Britain?

Almost certainly not. It is a term describing an area of trees, fields and countryside near to a town which the authorities wish to preserve unspoiled by additional buildings. Originally, it

more specifically applied to a 'belt' of green area around London.

What would you be doing in a brown study?

Probably you would be sitting or lying down, your mind far away, as it were, from your surroundings.

Who are the Brownies?

They are junior members of the Girl Guide Movement, and are called Brownies because their uniform is a brown blouse and brown skirt, or a brown tunic.

What is a purple passage?

It is a passage of prose or verse which is heavy with sentimental expression.

What does it mean being given the green light?

It means permission to get on with a project you have planned. It comes of course from the green light in the traffic lights set – the signal for 'Go!'

What sort of people would you expect to meet in a green room?

Stage actors and actresses, producers, and possibly critics as well. It is a room in or attached to a theatre where performers gather after a performance.

What is a greybeard?

Quite simply, another term for an old man.

If someone says to you, use your grey matter, what do they mean?

It means use your brains. The term has come from the colour of the active part of the human brain and spinal cord.

What is the meaning of the French phrase eminence grise?

It means 'grey eminence' and refers to someone who wields power quietly in the background through the more public front of a figurehead. It originates from the time of the brilliant French statesman Richelieu who always appeared to be very much in command of any situation. His secretary was said to have wielded the real power in France, but in fact what he did was to shield the Cardinal from those whom he considered unimportant and insignificant.

Why would anyone call you greenfingered?
If you were successful with the work you did in a garden, such as getting plants to grow that many others seem to fail to do, then you might be called greenfingered.

Why were Roman emperors said to have assumed the purple when they came to the imperial throne?
Because they took on the purple toga of their office. Actually, the colour was red-purple, and not the mauve one thinks of today.

What is a yellowjack?
This is a flag flown at sea which indicates that there is disease on board and that the ship regards itself as being in quarantine. It derives from the common nautical disease, yellow fever.

What is a yellow dog contract?
This interesting phrase applies to a contract between a worker and an employer in the US, by which the worker lapses his membership of a trade union while he is employed.

What would be wrong with you if you had pinkeye?
You would have conjunctivitis – an inflammation of the eyeball or the eyelid which causes a discharge of fluid, itchiness and a general redness, hence the name.

Little Quiz 20
In which countries are these mountains?
1. Everest
2. Mont Blanc
3. Eiger
4. Kanchenjunga
5. Kilimanjaro
6. Aconcagua
7. McKinley
8. Popocatépetl
9. Communism Peak
10. Annapurna

Where are these famous volcanoes?
11. Vesuvius
12. Krakatoa
13. Guntur
14. Elbruz
15. Fujiyama
16. Ngauruhoe
17. Stromboli
18. Mauna Loa
19. Hecla
20. Tongariro

In which continents are these deserts?
21. Gobi
22. Kalahari
23. Sahara
24. Kara Kum
25. Nubian
26. Great Victoria

Where are these lakes?
27. Superior
28. Eyre
29. Erie
30. Baikal
31. Ladoga
32. Chad
33. Nettiling
34. Maracaibo
35. Vyrnwy
36. Linnhe
37. Huron
38. Victoria Nyanza
39. Michigan
40. Neagh

How many people are Buddhists today?

There are more than 500,000,000 people who follow Buddha's teachings or versions of them. Most of them live in Ceylon, Burma, South-East Asia, Korea, Japan, Tibet and of course in China itself.

Who was Confucius?

Confucius is the Westernized name for the Chinese philosopher Kung Fu Tsu. (550–478 BC). He was a government servant who sought to find improvements in his own way of life and that of others. He gave up his job, began to teach his philosophy and built up a large following. Later, he was appointed governor of a small district and there he put many of his ideas into practice. Confucianism is still an influence in present day China although played down by the authorities.

What is a totem pole?

A totem is the American Indian word for guardian spirit, and a totem pole is an intricately carved pole showing imaginary figures and animals, which the Indians honoured. Many primitive people believed themselves to be descended from weird animals and they carved these poles in much the same way as other civilizations sculpted statues of their gods in stone or marble.

Who began the conversion of the heathen Anglo-Saxons in England to Christianity?

The first missionary from Italy to bring Christianity to England was the Benedictine monk, Augustine (6th century AD). He was sent there by Pope Gregory I and he landed in Kent in 597. Setting up headquarters at Canterbury he was much helped by the fact that the queen of King Ethelbert of Kent had already become a Christian.

What happened at Iona in the 6th century AD?

Iona is an island off the West Coast of Scotland. There, in about 560 AD the Irish missionary, Columba, settled with a band of helpers to found a religious colony, with the aim of going to the mainland and spreading Christianity among the heathen Picts. By his death, in 597, much of Scotland had been converted.

What is a choir?

A choir is a group of singers who lead the congregation in singing hymns and psalms. They also sing anthems and other compositions while the congregation remains silent. Although one associates choirs with Christianity, the idea actually began with the Hebrews, centuries before Jesus Christ.

What was a priest hole?

In the 16th and 17th centuries in Europe, outlawed priests were often hidden in private houses by sympathizers. Some people had special nooks built into their homes in which these priests were secreted, so that they could escape arrest if the authorities were conducting searches in the neighbourhood.

What is a Jesuit?

He is a member of the Society of Jesus, a strict religious order in the Roman Catholic Church, founded by Ignatius Loyola in 1534. It was formed to set good examples of devotion and simple living and to teach religious principles. Today, Jesuits are as devoted in their work of trying to bring Catholic Christianity to people as they ever were.

What happened to John the Baptist?

John was a cousin of Jesus Christ. He went into the wilderness to meditate because he felt there was important work for him to do. It came to him that he was to prepare the ground for the teaching of Christ, and he actually baptized Jesus in the river Jordan. Later he was imprisoned by Herod Antipas, ruler of Galilee, and put to death.

Who were the principal Roman gods?
Jupiter was King of the gods, and his wife was Juno. Jupiter's brothers were Neptune (god of the sea) and Pluto (god of the underworld). Among Jupiter's children were Minerva (goddess of wisdom), Diana (goddess of hunting), Mars (god of war), Vulcan (god of fire), Ceres (goddess of agriculture).

What are relics?
Parts of the bodies of saints or holy men, or articles connected with them, are called relics. They have been collected and treasured in many religions. One relic much sought after in the Middle Ages was a portion of the True Cross, the wooden cross on which Christ was crucified. There cannot have been more than a few genuine relics of this, though there were thousands of imitations.

Who brought Christianity to Ireland?
Saint Patrick (c.389–461 AD) was a Welsh-born scholar who studied for years in Europe. He had been captured in Wales by Irish pirates and spent some years in northern Ireland before going on to Europe. He was sent to Ireland by Pope Celestine I, landed at Wicklow and was later welcomed by King Laoghaire who protected him.

What is a lectern?
A lectern in a Christian church is a reading desk. The main part is a sloping surface on which a Bible is rested. Quite often below the table part is a brass eagle, the symbol of the carrying of the gospels to the four corners of the earth.

In Moslem mosques, the Koran is supported on a special Koran desk, which is often highly decorated with ebony and pearl inlays.

What is a cathedral?
It is usually a large church which is the principal church of a bishop or archbishop. It has the bishop's throne. There are cathedrals in most major towns where Christianity is, or was, the established religion. Some are quite small but others are massive, like St Peter's in Rome and St Sophia in Constantinople.

What is the Talmud?
The Talmud is an assemblage of writings incorporating the works of Jewish scholars and records of their discussions, especially over legal matters. There were two versions, both of which contained the Mishnah which is the spoken law handed down from generation to generation since the time of Moses.

The Great God Siva,
the four-armed Hindu God

What is a cartoon?

A cartoon is a preliminary drawing on strong paper made as a sketch before actually producing the finished work of art in whatever medium is intended. It is drawn to the size eventually planned. Raphael's cartoons of Biblical scenes for the tapestries in the Sistine Chapel are now in London's Victoria and Albert Museum.

But isn't a cartoon a funny picture?

Well, that is one meaning of the word. In the 1840s an exhibition was held of cartoons for frescoes which would be considered for the new Houses of Parliament buildings to be erected in London. These frescoes produced strong reactions, and the humorous magazine *Punch* imitated some of them in joke fashion, applying them to political issues and personalities of the day. As a result, a cartoon came to mean a pictorial comment, generally humorous, on current events.

Why was Jacobo Robusti called Tintoretto?

Tintoretto is Italian for little dyer. Jacobo Robusti (1518–1594) was born in Venice the son of a dyer. He studied painting under Titian, and before his death had produced a vast amount of very high quality work. His greatest picture was *The Paradise*, which is in the Doge's Palace in Venice.

Who was Spain's leading Renaissance artist?

Probably the most outstanding painter of the Renaissance in Spain was Diego Rodriguez de Silva y Velasquez (1599–1660). He is renowned for the exactness of his representations of the things he saw. His attention to detail, especially to light and shade, was always sharp and accurate. While he produced many portraits of members of Spain's royal

132

family, he was very skilled in his group pictures, such as *The Surrender of Breda* and *The Tapestry Weavers*.

Was El Greco anything to do with Greece?

Yes, El Greco (1548–1614) was a Greek born painter called Domenikos Theotocopoulos. He left his native country which was then ruled by the oppressive Turkish Empire, and travelled to Italy to study under Titian. Then he moved to Spain, set up house at Toledo, and stayed there. Over the next years, almost to his death, he produced a splendid variety of fine pictures. One was *The Burial of the Count of Orgaz*, which is made hauntingly sombre by virtue of his contrasting use of colours. *El Greco* is the Spanish for The Greek.

Who was Goya?

Francisco Jose de Goya y Lucientes (1746–1828) was Spain's leading painter of his age. Like his fellow countryman Velasquez he produced strong realistic pictures, though his attention to light and shade was less accurate. He was also the leading engraver in Spain for many years, and through this medium he expressed more personal views of things going on round him.

What is engraving?

Engraving is the art of drawing on metal or wood using a tool to cut lines to make up the picture. An engraving is the impression produced in ink on paper or cloth from such a drawing. There are several processes, and it is an art form which has been in use for at least five centuries.

What are the engraving processes?

The main engraving processes are line-engraving, etching, mezzotinting, aquatinting and stipple-engraving. In line-engraving the picture is cut directly in lines with a special tool on a copper or zinc plate (or a wood block). The plate is inked, put in a press on paper and copies are run off. Variety of shading and depth are produced by cutting the lines closely or not so closely, as required. Line-engraving was the major process used in the 15th, 16th and 17th centuries.

How does an artist etch an engraving?

The artist takes a copper plate which is coated with wax and cuts the picture into the wax with fine needles. This is a very delicate job and possibly several attempts may be made before he is satisfied with the result. Then the plate is dipped into hydrochloric (or nitric) acid which follows the cut lines in the wax and 'bites' into the metal, tracing them out. Ink is applied to fill up the etched lines and shapes, and the plate is pressed onto paper. The shading is determined by how long the acid is left on the plate.

Who started etching?

We do not know exactly who first used etching, but Wenceslaus Hollar (1607–1677), a Bohemian artist of the 17th century, was probably one of the first. In his time he produced over 2000 different etchings. One was of London actually during the Great Fire of 1666.

Were there any great English Renaissance painters?

Not in the same class as the Italian and other European masters. But in Elizabeth I's time and for nearly a century thereafter, English miniaturists were among the finest artists in this field.

What is a miniature?

A miniature has come to mean a very small picture, usually though not always a portrait. Originally, the word derived from the Latin 'minium' meaning red-lead, the dye used for small decoration in illuminated manuscripts. Miniature painting became popular in the late 16th century. It was done on parchment mounted on card, on polished card, and later on ivory sheet, copper, silver and even stone. Sometimes the pictures were square, sometimes they were round or oval.

What is a mezzotint?

A mezzotint is a development of line-engraving. You take your engraved plate, make it rough all over by scraping across it, and then smooth over those parts you want to be printed in light shades. The lines of the line-engraving almost disappear and you should be left with what looks much like an oil painting when you have printed out on paper.

What were the 'Cries of London'?

These were a set of thirteen prints engraved from original paintings by Francis Wheatley, RA, at the end of the 18th century. The pictures were of street sellers shouting their wares, like 'Two bunches a penny, primroses, two bunches a penny', and they were engraved by two artists, Schiavonetti and Cardon. They proved immensely popular and before long there were many imitations of the prints. It is difficult to assemble a genuine first edition set by the original engravers.

What other material can you engrave on?

Most artists used metal plates, but some liked wooden plates, or blocks. Thomas Bewick (1753–1828) specialized in natural subjects like birds and plants. He reintroduced wood engravings after they had been out of use for a long time. Dürer and Rembrandt had used wood plates for engraving.

How do you make Cock-a-Leekie soup?

This great Scottish soup is made by taking a boiling fowl and a dozen chopped leeks and putting these into water. Simmer it for about four hours adding some rice, pepper, salt and seasoning if you like. Take the fowl out before serving!

What is porridge?

Porridge is fine or coarse oatmeal boiled with a little salt in water, stirred most of the time to make it nice and thick. You eat it with cold milk or cream, and also white or brown sugar.

What is poteen?

It's a highly alcoholic Irish drink. It is a whiskey made illegally in Ireland, which has a much higher alcohol content than normal whiskey. It is pronounced Pocheen.

What is champagne?

A white effervescent wine made in France from specially fine grapes grown in a strictly limited area of the river Marne region near Rheims and Epernay in the district of Champagne. It ferments in the bottle after sealing, unlike other wines. That's why it bubbles out all over the place when you open it, unless you do so with skill!

What is tea?

It is a shrub originally grown in China (and still grown there) whose dried leaves were cut up and infused with hot water to produce a drink by the Chinese two thousand years ago. The idea spread to India, Ceylon, Japan and other parts of South and East Asia.

How many types of tea are there?

Three basic types, and many more varieties. The three are black, green and oolong.

When did tea first arrive in Britain?

In about 1660, whence it came from Holland. Samuel Pepys, the famous Navy Secretary and diarist, recorded one day in 1660 that he had ordered a 'cup of tea (a China drink) of which I had never drank before'. In those days it was only grown in China.

What is the origin of coffee?

It was first grown and crushed to make a drink in the Near East in the 14th century, where, interestingly, it is still a popular beverage. Coffee is grown mainly in Africa, Brazil, Colombia, Mexico and Indonesia.

When did coffee drinking reach Europe?

Not until the late 16th century, and not until the 1630s in Britain. A Cretan merchant, Nathaniel Canopus, is believed to have made coffee popular while he was at Oxford in 1640–1641.

Where does cocoa come from?

It comes from cacao beans which are grown in West Africa, parts of South America, the West Indies, the East Indies, and Ceylon. It was also grown in Mexico and was discovered there by Cortes who in the 1520s destroyed the Aztec empire.

What is malted milk?

In America it is a drink made from dried milk and malted cereal mixed with fresh milk, ice cream and flavouring, and is very delicious. In Europe, malted milk (dried milk and malted cereal) is more generally served hot, stirred into hot milk or hot water.

What's Haggis?

It's the national dish of the Scots and is very tasty if properly made. Chopped sheep's heart, liver and lungs mixed with oatmeal, suet, onions and some spices are put into a bag made from the lining of a sheep's stomach! It's boiled and when it's ready for eating it's normally served with mashed potatoes and turnips.

What is Lancashire Hot Pot?
It is a splendid stew made from lamb chops, onions, mushrooms, kidneys and some oysters. The ingredients are put in an open dish and covered with a layer of sliced potatoes. It's cooked for about two hours until the potatoes are nice and brown. It was a popular dish for shooting parties in Lancashire years ago.

How is jam made?
If you're making it at home – and many people think the home variety is better than the shop stuff – take the fruit you want to use, simmer it with a lot of sugar in a pan for several hours, and then pour it out into jars or pots. That's all basically but there are of course variations.

How do you make marmalade?
In much the same way, except that there is some preparation first. Cut up some oranges and soak them overnight. Then next day add sugar and boil the lot very slowly until it's very thick and sticky. Put it into jars and let it set – it's much nicer than bought marmalade.

What is chutney?
It is a kind of jam, really, but made from mangoes and spices – if it's the proper Indian variety. Eat it with curries. In Western countries, some chutneys can be made from green tomatoes.

What are pickles?
They are a kind of sauce with solid bits and pieces in it, used to add flavour to some main courses like cold meat and salad, or to have with bread and cheese as a quick snack lunch.

What are pickled onions?
They are onions specially treated so that they are tasty enough to eat raw, with salads, bread and cheese, or just on their own. It's best to use silverskin onions. They are left raw after being peeled, overnight, with some salt sprinkled on them. The next day they are boiled with a mixture of spices, some sugar and some vinegar for a short while, about ten minutes or so. They are then taken out and put into a jar. You can then cover them with the liquid when it is cold.

What is ketchup?
It is a sauce which is made with tomatoes, spices and salt and pepper, and is good to have with fish and chips, sausages and chips and things of that kind. The word may come from the Chinese *ketsiap* meaning sauce of pickled fish.

What is Kosher meat?
It is meat used as food that has been killed properly in accordance with Jewish law.

What's tripe and onions?
Tripe is part of the lining of the stomach of certain animals like cows, and cooked with flour, seasoning, onions, a pinch of garlic, a drop or two of lemon juice, preferably by frying it, it is a tasty dish, very popular in the northern half of England.

How is butter made?
Butter is milk that has been churned. It is generally made from cow's milk, but other animal milk has been tried for butter, like goat, ass and even camel.

What's margarine?
It is a butter substitute and is made from a mixture of butter, purified animal and vegetable oils and with extra chemicals.

Which was the first civilization in the world?

The first civilization was that of Sumer. This began in about 4500 BC in the fertile area (as it then was) between the Tigris and the Euphrates rivers, in the Middle East. Each city in the country governed itself, like Ur which was excavated in 1922–34.

How did the Sumerians build houses?

The Sumerians used clay for bricks which they moulded and left in the hot sun to bake. A few bricks were heated in crude ovens. The clay was dug from the banks of the rivers.

When did the Egyptians become civilized?

The Egyptians became civilized in about 4000 BC. They flourished on the banks of the river Nile. At first there were two kingdoms, Upper and Lower Egypt, but in about 3500 the two were united.

How did ancient Egyptian farmers irrigate their fields?

They used the waters of the Nile. They cut dykes at right angles to the river bank and by using wooden gates they were able to control the amount of water flooding over their fields.

How long did ancient Egyptian civilization last?

The Egyptian civilization flourished almost uninterrupted until the time of Alexander the Great, king of Macedonia (336–323 BC) who conquered Egypt and brought it into his empire. Even then he encouraged the Egyptians to continue their own customs and way of life.

Who was Tutankhamun?

Tutankhamun was a boy pharaoh of ancient Egypt and he reigned from about 1360 to about 1350 BC. His achievements
were few and he died before he was twenty. His tomb, however, is famous. It was discovered – intact – in 1922. It contained all kinds of treasures, furniture and ornaments.

What was Hammurabi's Code?

Hammurabi was a great king of ancient Babylon who ruled from about 1710 to about 1670 BC. He drew up a code of laws that he expected his people to obey. It was a harsh code in parts but it was also just, on the whole. He had it carved in brief on a huge pillar of black basalt rock. This was discovered in the 19th century and is now in the Louvre in Paris.

How did the Babylonians do arithmetic?

They used a system of numerals which were made up of rows of wedge-shaped marks in clay tablets. An upright wedge represented the number 1, and a bigger wedge lying on its side was number 10. 100 was a vertical wedge, about twice as big as the wedge for 1, with four small wedges lying on their sides.

Where was the Minoan civilization?

Minoan civilization was centred on the longish, thin island of Crete, in the Mediterranean, about 80 kms (50 miles) south of the Greek mainland. It lasted from about 3000 to about 1400 BC. The Minoans, because they lived on an island, were a great seafaring race and traded between the countries on the mainland of Europe and Asia, and even Egypt. Their principal city was Knossos.

Why does a bull figure so much in Minoan art?

Minoans believed that the island had once been terrorized by a beast that was half-man, half-bull, the top-half being the bull. This beast was called the

Minotaur, and it devoured seven maidens from the ruling class every year.

Who were the Hittites?
They were an Indo-European race from southern Russia who successfully settled in what is now Turkey in about 2000 BC. They built towns in the valleys near the Taurus mountains. Their civilization lasted for about 1000 years.

What was the secret of the Hittites' success?
The Hittites were the first people to use iron to any extent. Iron weapons were harder than bronze weapons and the Hittite armies were better armed than their enemies. They also edged their ploughshares with iron, and this enormously improved their agricultural production.

Who was Suppululiumas?
The man with this splendid name was one of the best Hittite kings. He reigned in the 14th century and improved the Hittite capital city, Hattusas. He made his power felt outside his own land.

Who were the Sea Peoples?
A strange thing happened to Mediterranean and Near Eastern peoples in the 1200s BC. They were, for the most part, quite suddenly overrun by an enormous invasion of peoples from central Russia and south-east Europe. The invaders came to be called the Sea Peoples because they travelled in ships. They destroyed the Hittite and the Mycenaean civilizations and threatened Egypt, too.

What kind of civilization was the Phoenician?
The Phoenicians were maritime people. They built towns and harbours along the coast of the Levant, that is, the East Mediterranean. They traded with each

other and with peoples in other parts. They may have been descendants of the Sea Peoples.

Where did the Indus civilization begin and what were its principal towns?
The Indus civilization grew up on the banks of the Indus river, in what is now Bangladesh. The main towns of the early Indus peoples were Mohenjo-daro and Harappa, both of which were excavated early in this century.

How did the ancient Indians plumb and drain their houses?
The Indians of the old Indus civilization (which lasted from about 3000 BC to about 1500 BC) constructed houses of baked clay bricks. They inserted clay pipes into floors and walls for water circulation from storage tanks at roof level and for drainage into sewers in the streets.

Did the Indus people know of other civilizations?
Yes, it is thought they were in contact with Sumer and Babylon. Artefacts from these civilizations were found in the excavated streets and houses of Mohenjo-daro and Harappa.

What were the main crops of the Chinese in their earliest days?
The Chinese, who first became civilized between 3000 and 2000 BC grew millet, a grassy plant with a head of many seeds. They also grew rice, particularly in the warmer parts of the country.

Where did Chinese civilization begin?
It began on the banks of the Hwang-Ho (Yellow) river in central China, near what is today the Chinese capital, Peking. It has continued uninterrupted, despite many conquests by foreign armies, up to the present.

What is alabaster?
A fine and translucent plaster, white usually, though it can also be found in yellow or red. It is very soft and can easily be mistaken for marble from a distance.

What is porcelain?
It is a fine white pottery made from kaolin, a white clay, and petuntse, a feldspar mineral, which are bound together at a very high temperature and then glazed. It was invented by the Chinese in the 6th century AD.

Why is some porcelain called biscuit ware?
Because it is smooth but unglazed, and looks like biscuits. It was popular in the 18th century.

What do the letters EPNS stand for?
They stand for electro-plated nickel silver. It is a form of silver-plating that produces a good imitation of Sheffield plating. The item is made of nickel-based metal and silver.

What is Parian ware?
Real marble and high-quality porcelain have always been popular for making statues and figures but the price of these had grown so much that by the 19th century various makers devised substitutes. One was Parian ware, a mixture of unglazed porcelain and some glaze material which was easy to model. It was called Parian ware from the marble of the island of Paros in the Aegean Sea, which was famed for its genuine white marble.

What has bone china to do with bones?
Well, believe it or not, it is a typically British porcelain, mixed with bone ash, sometimes as much as half bone-ash to half porcelain. It has been widely used

138

since the 1800s, and resembles the best porcelain.

What has Ironstone China to do with iron or stone?
Ironstone china is a hard earthenware in white, which is said to have some ironstone slag in its make-up. It was popularized by the firm of Mason's in the 1830s, and has been imitated since, though not with the iron content.

How is brass made?
It is an alloy of copper and zinc, and has been used for making a variety of utensils, such as candlesticks, saucepans, coalscuttles, warming pans. It is difficult to say when it was first used, but it must be four centuries or more in Britain since it came into use. Because it corrodes, and is worn away by polishing, few pieces can have survived from that period.

What does 'tin-glaze' mean?
It is a form of decoration on pottery made by putting tin ashes into an ordinary lead glaze. This makes the glaze opaque. It is sometimes called tin-enamel. Famous ware in tin-glaze was English Delftware, Italian maiolica and French Faience.

What has pâpiér-mâché to do with paper?
It is a mixture of waste paper, chalk, glue and sand, which is stirred up to produce a sort of paste or plaster. The resulting plaster can be moulded into all sorts of shapes to trays, chairs, cigarette boxes, flower vases and much more. These could be painted, inlaid with mother of pearl, and polished very highly to make extremely attractive objects.

How do you print a transfer?
If you want to put a transfer decoration

on to a piece of pottery or porcelain, you engrave the design on a copper plate, print it on paper tissue and normally from there on to the glazed pottery, although it can be done under the glaze as well.

What's slip?
Slip is a word for pottery decorated with a mixture of clay and water, and painted before glazing and firing. The mixture itself is called the slip because it is usually runny and 'slips' through your fingers.

What was Britannia metal used for?
Britannia metal is a kind of pewter which has more lead in it than normal pewter. It was widely used in the earlier decades of the last century because it cost much less to produce, but it is readily distinguished from the better material.

Why was 'pinchbeck' metal widely used in the 18th century?
Pinchbeck metal is a mixture of copper and zinc, not unlike brass, but with more copper. It was used as a base for gilding in making things like watch cases, so that when the gilt was worn, the under metal still had the appearance of gold. It was invented by Christopher Pinchbeck, a London watchmaker, who flourished in the reigns of Queen Anne and George I.

What is spelter?
Another cheap metal for decorative objects, popularly in use in the 19th century. It consists of nearly 97 per cent zinc and the rest lead.

What is a lacquered cabinet?
Lacquering is a process which originated in China but which was developed in Japan. The sap of particular trees is tapped to produce a 'lac' or resin which is coated on to a surface for decoration. Each coat is left to dry and then polished. The final coat is then painted with landscapes or figures in one colour or in several colours. A lacquered cabinet is made of panels thus treated. The process is also called 'japanning'.

Why do we talk about jet black?
Because of the hard, black naturally-found form of carbon called jet which was in wide use for jewellery in the later part of the 19th century. Jet polishes up well.

What is jade?
This is a hard stone which has been used for many centuries for making jewellery, ornaments and figures. Popularly thought to be exclusive to China, it has in fact been widely employed in such diverse areas as Mexico, New Zealand and the Indian sub-continent. It is more generally a green stone, but many other colours have been found and used.

Why was feldspar used by the Spode china factory?
In order to make the bone china it manufactured from the 1800s more delicate and better able to stand comparison with foreign ware. Feldspar is a white or pink mineral which is mixed with porcelain to achieve this result.

What animal provides ivory for such things as handles, piano keys, etc?
Ivory comes from the tusk of an elephant or the canine teeth of the hippopotamus.

Which was the earliest metal used by civilized man?
Bronze, a mixture of copper and tin. It is cast easily, can be carved, engraved, polished, shaped with little trouble, and it acquires a soft green patina over the years.

139

What would the doctor use a sphygmomanometer for?
To measure blood pressure.

Why does a car have an ammeter fitted on the dashboard?
To register the number of amperes of electrical current being charged by the dynamo.

Who invented the mirror galvanometer?
William Thomson, Lord Kelvin of Largs (1824–1907), OM GCVO, possibly the greatest scientist produced by Britain since Newton.

What's a taximeter?
It is the apparatus fitted to a taxi-cab which registers the mileage covered and the time spent during a journey in a taxi. It also registers the cost to the passenger.

There is a piece of apparatus that you can carry in your pocket while you are walking along the road, which will measure the distance you have travelled by the number of steps you took. What is it called?
A pedometer, and its information is more of a rough guide to the distance that an accurate measurement.

What's a centimeter?
It is not an instrument, but is merely the American way of spelling a centimetre.

What is a comptometer?
It is a calculating machine.

What is a photometer?
An instrument for measuring illuminating power by the comparison of two sources of light.

What is a colorimeter?
A piece of apparatus for chemically
140

analyzing liquids by comparing their colours with various standard colours.

What is a calorimeter?
An instrument for measuring quantities of heat, or for calculating specific heats.

What is an electroencephalograph?
It is an instrument used in hospitals for measuring and recording brain waves, and it is helpful in determining the the nature of some brain illnesses. It is known, for short, as an EEG.

What is an electrocardiograph?
Known as an ECG, it records and interprets the electrical activity of the heart.

What is an autograph?
It is a specimen of someone's handwriting. It may be a signature but it is not necessarily so, and anything written by someone is their autograph.

What's an odontograph?
It is an instrument that marks out the outlines of the teeth of gear wheels.

What is a micrograph?
It is a drawing of an object as seen through a microscope, or it is also an instrument for recording very small movements by magnifying them.

Would you write a monograph at school?
If you were asked to write an essay on one subject, and you put some work into it to produce interesting reading, you could say you had written a monograph. It is a word meaning a researched piece of writing on one particular subject.

What is palaeography?
It is the science of studying and deciphering ancient manuscripts or inscriptions.

What would you use a hygrograph for?
To measure and record changes in the humidity of the air.

What's glyptography?
It is the process of engraving gem stones.

What does a cosmographer do?
He is someone skilled in cosmography, that is, the all-embracing study of the structure of the universe, which includes geography, geology and astronomy. *Kosmos* is the ancient Greek for world.

What is graphology?
It is the study of handwriting which can lead to suggestions of the characteristics of the person whose handwriting has been studied.

Little Quiz 21
Answer these questions about the Earth

1. What is its circumference at the Equator?
2. What is its approximate surface area?
3. How much of that is land?
4. Can you estimate its weight in tonnes?
5. How old is it?
6. How far is it from the Sun?
7. How far is it from the Moon?
8. How many continents are there?
9. What are they?
10. How many oceans are there?
11. What are they?
12. What is the estimated population?
13. What is the population expected to be in the year 2000?
14. Is it possible to estimate how many other living things share the Earth with human beings?
15. How many people speak Mandarin Chinese?
16. How many people speak English as their first language?
17. How many people speak Russian as their first language?

Who were the following?

18. The Brown Bomber
19. Citizen King
20. Fair Maid of Kent
21. Kingmaker
22. 1st Gentleman of Europe
23. Prime Minister of Mirth
24. Red Dean
25. Mrs Morley
26. Winter Queen
27. Garbo
28. Swedish Nightingale
29. Iron Chancellor
30. Hammer of the Scots
31. Jersey Lily
32. Old Hickory
33. Boney
34. The Virgin Queen
35. Old Rowley
36. Old Noll
37. Mrs Freeman
38. Uncle Sam

Who were the husbands of the following?

39. Calpurnia
40. Eva Braun
41. Livia
42. Anne of Cleves
43. Mary I of England
44. Clara Schumann
45. Mary, Queen of Scots
46. Cleopatra
47. Queen Victoria
48. Sarah Jennings
49. Anne Hathaway
50. Josephine
51. Marie Antoinette
52. Christina of Sweden
53. St Helena
54. Empress Maria Theresa
55. Eleanor of Aquitaine
56. Elizabeth Moulton Barrett
57. Joan of Arc
58. Queen Anne of England, Scotland and Ireland

?ism

What is cubism?
It was an art movement which arose in Europe at the beginning of the present century. It may be defined as the expression of reality by means of abstract forms. These forms do not bear much resemblance, if any at all, to recognizable things, but they give an impression of their solidity and their abstract qualities. Picasso was for part of his long art experience a Cubist.

What is despotism?
It means absolute rule, or dictatorship. It is generally used with régimes that are tyrannical.

What is hedonism?
It is the word used to describe living for pleasure and giving that way of life a philosophical basis.

What is a solecism?
It is a slip in grammatical or syntactical terms; it also refers to a slip in good manners.

What is voodooism?
It is a religion mixed up with black magic, practised among some peoples of African descent, in particular in certain West Indian islands.

What would be the matter with you if you had an astigmatism?
It would mean that the lens of your eye did not focus properly. This can be corrected with spectacles.

What is nepotism?
Favouritism, with special reference to promoting relatives to higher positions that they would not achieve it on the grounds of ability alone.

What is cannibalism?
It is the act of one animal eating the flesh of another animal of the same kind, and the word is used principally in connection with humans that eat other humans. This is very rare in the world today.

What's a mannerism?
With a small 'm' it means affecting a gesture or manner of speaking, and is used generally in a slightly critical sense.

What's Mannerism with a big 'M'?
A 16th century style of architecture and painting, in which the human form is represented in elongated or distorted shapes to sharpen the emotional effect.

What is a spoonerism?
It is a mixing up of the starting letters of words, generally with funny results, such as 'Kinquering kongs their tatles tike' instead of 'Conquering kings their titles take'. It was a habit of the great scholar, Dr William Spooner (1844–1930), who was Warden of New College at Oxford.

What was the Great Schism?
A serious split in the Christian Church in the West in the 14th century when there were two popes, one at Rome and one at Avignon in France. Schism means division, with special reference to divisions within a religion.

What's an aneurism?
It's an expansion, usually sudden, of an artery that results in a haemorrhage.

What is feminism?
It's really another word for believing in Women's Lib; that is, accepting the equality of women with men in all things, especially social, political and economic matters.

What's botulism?
Food poisoning, generally associated

with bad meat, sausages, or some kinds of preserved food. It comes from the bacillus *Clostridium botulinum.*

Would you like to be accused of egotism?
It depends if you do spend much too much time thinking about yourself and refer to yourself all the time in speech and writing, for that is what egotism is.

What is alcoholism?
The inability to stop drinking alcoholic beverages and eventually the inability to control most of the normal functions of the body.

What is evangelism?
Preaching the Christian Gospel with force and missionary zeal in areas where perhaps Christianity has been allowed to lapse.

Is there such a word as antidisestablishmentarianism?
Well, there is, and it means being opposed to the idea of disestablishment of the church from the state. It was first coined when Gladstone, prime minister of Britain in the later years of the 19th century, campaigned to disestablish the Church of Ireland.

Little Quiz 22

Here are the ten biggest cities in the world (in terms of population): what is their correct order?

Chicago (US)
Tokyo (Japan)
Buenos Aires (Argentina)
Los Angeles (US)
Moscow (USSR)
Sao Paulo
Mexico City (Mexico)
London (Britain)
New York (US)
Shanghai (China)

Little Quiz 23

The elements in chemistry are often referred to by their abbreviations, or symbols. Do you recognize these?

1. H		14. Mo
2. Mg		15. Ba
3. Hg		16. Mn
4. Pb		17. Ca
5. O		18. Cr
6. Sn		19. I
7. Ag		20. Cu
8. Au		21. Ra
9. U		22. As
10. C		23. Co
11. Sb		24. Cl
12. K		25. Fe
13. Na		26. Fm

Could you give the atomic number of these?

27. Silver
28. Oxygen
29. Sulphur
30. Fluorine
31. Mercury
32. Aluminium
33. Plutonium
34. Hydrogen
35. Radium
36. Zinc
37. Nitrogen
38. Neptunium
39. Carbon
40. Uranium
41. Lead
42. Iodine
43. Gold

Some general questions

44. Which are the four halogen elements?
45. Which are the five inert gases?
46. How many transuranian elements are there?
47. How many elements are gases?
48. How many elements are liquids?
49. How many elements are lighter than oxygen?
50. How many elements are heavier than lead?

What is an element?

In chemistry an element is a substance that cannot be broken up by chemical means into anything simpler. All matter consists of elements, either individually or in combination.

How many elements are there?

There are 92 naturally occurring elements and several elements that are called transuranic elements which are prepared artificially.

What is the lightest element and what is the heaviest?

The lightest is hydrogen, whose atomic weight is 1.0080 and the heaviest natural element is uranium, whose atomic weight is 238.03.

Which metal is liquid in its normal state?

Mercury, or as it is popularly known, quicksilver. It is one of the liquids used in thermometers, barometers and other instruments.

What are the constituents of water?

Two parts of hydrogen and one part of oxygen. The chemical formula is simply H_2O.

What is heavy water?

It is water which contains a high proportion of deuterium, or heavy hydrogen, so the chemical formula becomes D_2O – deuterium oxide.

Where is heavy water used?

In a nuclear reactor.

What is ozone?

It is a kind of oxygen which has a pungent smell, and is used for purifying air or sterilizing water.

What is an inert gas?

A gaseous element (an element that is a gas in its natural state) which does not react with other elements. There are several, including argon, neon, krypton, xenon and helium.

What is radium?

It is a soft, white metal which tarnishes in the atmosphere and is extremely radioactive. It was discovered by Pierre and Marie Curie.

What is ammonia?

It is a gas formed by the combination of hydrogen and nitrogen. It is pungent, so much so that it makes you screw up your face if you sniff at it. Dissolved in water it forms a solution that can be used for fertilizers, for cleaning purposes and it has its application in refrigeration.

What is an acid?

It is a chemical compound that has a sour taste, contains hydrogen and reacts with an alkali to form a salt.

Why does a balloon filled with hydrogen rise upwards so easily?

Because hydrogen is a much lighter gas than air.

What are the principal kinds of radioactive rays?

Alpha rays, beta rays and gamma rays. Alpha rays are a stream of alpha particles which are the nuclei of helium atoms and which are emitted from radioactive substances like uranium and radium. Beta rays are very fast electrons emitted by some radioactive substances. Gamma rays are of the same nature as X-rays, that is, they are electro-magnetic rays but they have shorter wave-lengths.

What is an atom?

For a long time an atom was said to be the smallest particle of matter. Since Lord Rutherford and his successors have managed to break atoms up into their constituent parts, the definition has changed, and now we speak of an atom as the smallest particle of an element that still has the chemical properties of that element.

What is a molecule?
It is the smallest particle of any substance that can exist yet still demonstrate all the chemical properties of the substance. A molecule is made up of a number of atoms. A helium molecule has one atom and complex organic substances may have thousands.

What is the difference between inorganic and organic chemistry?
Inorganic chemistry is concerned with compounds made from substances other than carbon as well as some of the simpler compounds containing carbon; while organic chemistry deals with the remaining compounds of carbon which originate from living tissues.

What is a compound?
A combination of elements bonded together, for example, common salt, is a compound of the elements sodium and chlorine and is called properly sodium chloride.

How many forms does the element carbon have?
It has four main forms, coke, graphite, diamonds and charcoal.

What are the proper names for common salt, epsom salts, saltpetre and spirits of salt?
They are sodium chloride, magnesium sulphate, potassium nitrate and hydrochloric acid.

What is a simple laboratory way to produce hydrogen gas?
Pour diluted sulphuric acid on to a piece of zinc in a glass beaker or flask and very soon bubbles will be seen forming on the metal surface. This shows that hydrogen gas is being given off.

Why is it dangerous to inhale the exhaust fumes of a motor car?
Because they contain poisonous gases, notably carbon monoxide which can kill. They are the result of the combustion of petrol vapour and air in the engine cylinders.

What are the two main gases in ordinary air?
The two main gases are nitrogen and oxygen. Air in the dry state at sea level contain about 78 per cent nitrogen, 21 per cent oxygen and the rest is a jumble of carbon dioxide, ozone and tiny quantities of the inert gases.

What is a vacuum?
In theory it is a part of space in which there is no matter. In practice this is impossible because the container of the vacuum must give off a vapour which will destroy the vacuum. The word has come to mean a space almost entirely exhausted of air.

Little Quiz 24
Give the dates of the terms of office of these US Presidents
1. George Washington
2. Thomas Jefferson
3. Quincy Adams
4. Abraham Lincoln
5. Ulysses Grant
6. Grover Cleveland
7. William McKinley
8. Theodore Roosevelt
9. Woodrow Wilson
10. Herbert Hoover
11. Franklin Roosevelt
12. Harry Truman
13. John Kennedy

What caused the American War of Independence?

The colonists in America, hard working and wealthy, had to pay heavy taxes to the British government in London. Increasingly they disliked this, but the taxes went on, or if they were lifted, others were raised in their place. By the 1770s, the colonists knew they would never change this position without fighting, and war broke out with the British government forces, in 1774.

What was the Boston Tea Party?

One of the British government's taxes on the colonists was on tea. In 1773, in protest, some colonists in Boston, Massachusetts, dressed up as Indians, boarded some ships carrying tea and tipped the chests into the harbour. This sparked off the war.

What did the Boers and the British fight about in the 19th century?

The Dutch settlers in South Africa, called Boers (from a Dutch word for farmers), clashed with British settlers in the same land. They decided then to move away northwards and found new states (Transvaal and the Orange Free State). Later in the century when the Boers were in trouble with native tribes, they appealed to the British for help. But help was offered only on condition that the Boers placed themselves under British rule. When the fighting was done, the Boers hoped to be released from their subjection, but it did not happen. So they went to war.

What was the Moghul Empire?

An empire in India, at its greatest power dominating what is now India, Pakistan and Bangladesh. It was founded by Babur, a Mongol chief, in about 1525. Babur was great-grandson of Timurlaine. His empire lasted until the 18th century.

146

Who are the Maoris?

They are the people of Polynesian descent who occupied New Zealand for several centuries. When Europeans – chiefly British – came to New Zealand in the 1800s to explore and settle, they clashed with the Maoris, who resented inroads into their way of life.

A Maori chief

What was the Treaty of Waitangi?

It was a treaty between the Maori chiefs and the settlers in New Zealand under the first governor, Hobson, in 1840. This ensured that the Maoris should keep their possessions and their lands in return for accepting British sovereignty. The agreement did not last long. Within three years it had been disregarded by British settlers and the First Maori War broke out.

When did the Japanese civilization begin?

Japan was nominally under the control of China for a long time, and it was greatly influenced by Chinese culture, learning and so forth. Then in the 4th or 5th century AD the first attempts at a centralized form of government were made and efforts began in the direction of curbing the strong powers wielded by local warrior chiefs. By about 1200 AD Japan was beginning to be effectively governed by one ruler, the shogun, who was a military commander-in-chief as well as the political ruler.

What was the Industrial Revolution?

It was the change from making goods by hand in small workshops or in the home to turning them out in their hundreds by machine in the factory. It was helped by the invention of steam power for machines, the building of canals for easier transport of goods, and by improvements in iron-making. The Industrial Revolution spread from Britain in the 18th century.

Who said 'After me, the deluge'?

It was supposed to have been said by Louis XV, king of France (1715–1774). During his reign France plunged further and further into debt because of court extravagance and inefficient government. It was, however, said by one of the king's ministers, and he said 'After us, the deluge', which meant 'When we've gone, all hell will be let loose' – and eventually it was.

When did the French Revolution break out?

In 1789, technically with the storming of the Bastille prison in Paris on 14th July. The grievances had, however, been mounting for more than a generation. The Revolution was far-reaching and France was never the same again.

What happened to the king and queen in France?

Louis XVI, grandson of Louis XV, was a well-meaning ruler who tried to do something to put right the national grievances, but it was too little and too late. Encouragement from him opened the floodgates and he came to be regarded as a puppet by various new assemblies, governments and so forth until he tried to escape. He was captured, tried and executed, in January 1793. His wife, Marie Antoinette, was similarly dealt with later in the year.

Who were the Hapsburgs?

A royal family in Europe, whose members were emperors, kings and princes in many lands. The family began with a Count of Hapsburg, Rudolf I, who was king of Germany, 1273–1291. Among his descendants were Charles V, Emperor of the Holy Roman Empire (1519–1555), and Empress Maria Theresa of Austria–Hungary (1740–1780).

How did the British first become involved in India?

Through trade. They set up trading interests in India at the beginning of the 17th century, when the East India Company was founded. In the 18th century, these traders and others associated with them clashed with similar French traders and adventurers and also with Indian princes.

Where did the Polynesian peoples come from?

It is thought that the Polynesians, who live in many of the islands in the more southerly parts of the Pacific, originally lived in the Indian sub-continent. They made voyages of enormous distance and duration, probably about 2000 years ago, and settled in the Pacific, in places like Hawaii, the Friendly Islands.

147

What is Cubism?

This is a form of Expressionist art, in which the work is produced as an assemblage of solid shapes with no immediately recognizable meaning. The subject becomes fragmented and redefined in terms of the artist's vision. Picasso was a leading cubist for a while, and when, for example, he painted pictures with people in them, he portrayed them much more as collections of geometric shapes than actual humans. Cubists believed they were giving demonstrations of genuine feelings, and although their appeal was never widespread they made a lasting impression on the work of 20th-century painters and sculptors.

Who brought Impressionist painting to Australia?

Tom Roberts (1856–1931) was English born but emigrated to Australia when he was twelve. He studied art and began to establish himself as a sound representative painter. In 1881, he went to Europe and fell under the influence of the Impressionist school. Then he returned to Australia with new ideas about painting which he put into practice and very quickly made popular. He won national renown, and his fame spread far beyond the shores of his adopted home.

Who is Sidney Nolan?

Sidney Nolan, born in 1917, enjoys the reputation of being Australia's foremost living painter, and this fame is well deserved. Although he had little training to start with, he taught himself and developed a technique of recording the landscape of Australia and also something of the society which Australians have built for themselves. His work is sharp and direct and it has attracted attention far beyond his native Australia.

148

Are there any world-famous painters in New Zealand?

New Zealand has not yet produced a painter to compare, say, with Sidney Nolan of Australia, but it cannot be long before some great artists emerge, since there is rapidly growing interest in painting and other arts throughout the country. The famous political cartoonist, Sir David Low (1891–1963), who created such well-known characters as Colonel Blimp and the Trades Union Congress horse, was New Zealand born.

Who was L. S. Lowry?

Laurence Stephen Lowry, who died in 1976, was a British artist who spent nearly all his life in his native Lancashire. He painted industrial and crowd scenes from the heart of the working north-west of England. His own life was extremely simple, and he lived almost as a hermit for years. His pictures were often in bright greys and whites, and the people in them were portrayed like ants rushing about their business. Certainly one gets a feeling of living movement in his work.

What is lithography?

Lithography is a form of printing based on the principle that oil and water do not mix, but reject each other. A drawing is made on an absorbent stone using an oil based ink. The stone is washed with water, then it is inked and the watered parts repel the ink while the drawing part attracts it. It is then printed on paper. The process, invented by an Austrian, Aloys Senefelder, in the 1790s, has been very popular. Leading lithographic artists include Barnett Freedman.

How is so much known about the Renaissance artists?

Very largely because one of them, Giorgio Vasari (1511–1574), a painter who studied under Michelangelo, decided to become an art historian and set down for the record something about the work of the marvellous artists who were flourishing in his time. Vasari wrote *Lives of the Artists* in the middle of the 16th century, and this great work gave details of the painters' lives as well as helpful criticisms of their works.

What is varnish?
Varnish is the word for the resinous gums which are dissolved in linseed oil, turpentine and other fluids to provide transparent covering for pictures, furniture and other forms of decoration. Some varnishes may be coloured and these would be used for furniture or woodwork (though polishes and waxes are much better). Varnish for paintings is clear and it helps preserve them from the effects of dust, dirt and smoke.

How did Stubbs learn to paint horses so well?
George Stubbs (1724–1806) was an anatomist by profession and taught at York Hospital. He was also interested in painting and earned a small living on the side as a portrait painter. In the 1750s he decided to leave the hospital, gave up portraits and took a farm where he set out systematically to dissect a horse, tissue by tissue, and draw each piece as he lifted it out. This took a long time, but at the end he was able to publish a remarkable work, *The Anatomy of a Horse*, which was immediately successful. From then on he painted horses and horse scenes and never lacked work, for rich people loved horses and horse-racing and often wanted faithful representations of their favourites. Stubbs was elected to the Royal Academy in 1781.

What is water colour painting?
Water colour painting is done using pigments or dyes dissolved in water. It was practised in China over 2000 years ago and in ancient Rome. It became popular in Britain in the 18th century. It is said this was because the continual variations in the weather in the UK were more easily captured in water colours than in oils.

What is Titian Red?
Titian red is a particular shade of colour, a bright golden auburn, with which the great Venetian painter Titian sometimes used to colour people's hair in his pictures. Tiziano Vecelli, to give him his right name, lived for over 90 years, from the 1480s to 1576. He was for a long time the leading painter in the Venetian School, and he was also court painter to the Emperor of Austria and the Holy Roman Empire, Charles V. One of Titian's most famous works is the *Entombment of Christ*. Another, the *Death of Actaeon*, sold for over £2m in a London saleroom in 1971.

What was so remarkable about Picasso?
To begin with he was a mature painter by the age of ten and was still painting vigorously when he was over 90. Pablo Picasso, born in Spain in 1881, became a painter of quite exceptional merit. His early work was mainly representational, but in his time he was to embrace all the new forms, however different they were from each other – Expressionism, abstract painting, Cubism, to mention a few, but whatever form he used he dominated it. His work was sometimes very hard to understand. It was often daring, and it was often irritating, but it hardly ever failed to attract attention. Even in the year of his death (1973) he was still painting as commandingly as ever, but he is particularly remembered for the paintings from his 'blue period', that is, from 1901 to 1904.

149

What is music-hall?
Basically it is a theatre which specializes in light entertainment shows – comedy turns, acrobatics, individual singing, group singing, dancing and so forth. Such a show normally lasts two to three hours, probably with an interval or two. It was greatly affected by the cinema and TV, and most music-hall theatres closed down. But there has been a sign or two of revival.

Where is Hollywood?
It is a unique district, a suburb of Los Angeles in California. It has been the principal place of the US film industry since 1911, and with the decline in the number of films made there, it has been used for television feature production.

What's Beverly Hills?
It is a smart district near Hollywood chiefly inhabited by film stars – and ex-film stars, many of whom live in the most luxurious homes.

Who was Cecil B. de Mille?
Cecil Blount de Mille (1881–1959) was a US film director who became a leading Hollywood character, best known for his mammoth productions like *The Ten Commandments*, and *The Sign of the Cross*.

Who was Sam Goldwyn?
Another leading US film producer, born in Poland in 1882. For a while he worked with Cecil B. de Mille, but broke out on his own and founded the Metro-Goldwyn-Mayer Company, one of the most celebrated of all film companies. He specialized in making films of famous books, such as *All Quiet on the Western Front, Wuthering Heights*, and became famous for strange remarks such as 'Include me out' and 'Anyone who visits a psychiatrist needs his head examined'.

150

Who were the principal stars in 'Gone with the Wind'?
Clark Gable as Rhett Butler, Vivien Leigh as Scarlett O'Hara, Olivia de Havilland as Melanie Hamilton and Leslie Howard as Ashley Wilkes. Only Olivia de Havilland is still alive. The film was made in 1939.

What was Walt Disney famous for?
He was an American film-maker who set up his own company and studio in Hollywood in 1923 and from then on produced a wide variety of cartoon films. Some of the characters in these films became extremely popular almost overnight and have passed into history, including Mickey Mouse, Donald Duck, Goofy, Pluto (the dog), and Dumbo. He made full-length cartoon films like *Snow White and the Seven Dwarfs, The Lady and the Tramp*. He also made some fine nature study films, including the very successful *The Living Desert*.

Which film in 1951 predicted man landing on the moon?
Destination Moon. Within eighteen years what had seemed a complete fantasy became a reality when Neil Armstrong stepped out of a lunar module and walked on the moon's surface, 20th July 1969.

Who is Bunuel?
Luis Bunuel, born in 1900, is a Spanish film director who left his country because he did not agree with the Franco regime. He has made a number of brilliant films in Europe, one of which was *The Discreet Charm of the Bourgeoisie*.

What was the basis of Charlie Chaplin's fame?
Charles Chaplin (born 1889) made films in America in which the central character (acted by himself) was a

down-trodden scruffy tramp in bowler hat and badly-fitting black suit, wearing a short black moustache. He started in silent film days, then continued through early 'talkies', and among his successes were *The Gold Rush, City Lights* and *Modern Times*. Then he began to make films in which he played more conventional parts. He was knighted in 1974.

When were moving pictures first made?
In England, by William Friese-Greene, in 1889.

Who was Eisenstein?
Sergei Mikhailovitch Eisenstein was a Soviet Russian film director who lived from 1898 to 1948. He devised many new cinema techniques, including editing film, use of montage (especially in his epic film, *Battleship Potemkin*, in 1925). He always used vast crowds of extras in his films.

Who were the stars of the film 'The Alamo'?
John Wayne, Richard Widmark and Laurence Harvey.

What was 'Citizen Kane'?
This was a remarkable black-and-white film by Orson Welles in 1941. He wrote, produced, directed and acted in this picture which introduced revolutionary camera techniques.

What is a documentary film?
It is a fact film, as opposed to a fiction, or feature, film. Documentaries include newsreels, travelogues and educational films as well as more artistic films.

Who was John Grierson?
He was a British film-maker who created the documentary school of film-making in Britain. His films were Britain's chief

contribution to film art and have also had a great influence on feature films.

What was the first talking picture?
The Jazz Singer, starring Al Jolson and made in 1927, could be called the first talkie although it had only part sound with synchronized songs and a few words of dialogue. The first fully talking picture was *The Lights of New York*, made in 1929.

What was the first British talking picture?
Blackmail made in 1929 and directed by Alfred Hitchcock. Originally intended as a silent film it was discovered, when it was decided to add sound, that the star, the Czech actress Annie Ondra, could not speak English. Her dialogue had to be dubbed by another actress.

. . . and the first French talkie?
Sous les Toits de Paris, made in 1930 by René Clair. Its title tune became extremely popular and is still heard today.

What are the best-known of Danny Kaye's films?
Up in Arms, Secret Life of Walter Mitty, Hans Christian Andersen, Wonder Man, and probably the funniest of them all, *The Inspector General*. Kaye sings, dances, acts and excels in lunatic monologues, and has in recent years directed his talents to raising funds for UNICEF, the United Nations' Children's Fund.

What are Oscars?
They are the annual awards made by the American Academy of Motion Picture Arts and Sciences. They have been made since 1929 but since 1931 have been called Oscars because, the story goes, the Academy Award statuette reminded a secretary of her Uncle Oscar.

151

What is a Tom Collins?
A cocktail of gin, lemon juice, some caster sugar, ice and some soda water, preferably served in a tall, thin glass, with sugar crusted round the rim.

How do you make a Highball?
A popular American drink, it is simply a tumbler of whisky with a lump of ice dropped in, and filled up with soda, ginger ale, or plain water.

If you get cold, you may be given a hot toddy. What is it?
A measure of whisky or brandy into which are put a slice of lemon peel, a pinch of cinnamon, a clove or two if you like, and also a pinch of white sugar. The glass is then filled with very hot water.

What is a Stinger?
A powerful drink consisting of three parts of vodka to one of crême-de-menthe, preferably the white variety.

What is a Bloody Mary?
This is vodka with tomato juice, into which you also put a few drops of lemon juice, a dash of Worcestershire sauce, a pinch of celery salt and perhaps a sprinkle of black pepper. Some people think they're good for hangovers.

What is an Angel's Kiss?
Take some cream, put in it an ounce or two of crême de cacao (liqueur) and pop in a cherry on a stick.

What is a White Lady?
Gin and cointreau, in the ratio three to one, with a dash of lemon juice.

What is a Black Russian Coffee Cocktail?
A small amount of crême de cafe – or any other coffee liqueur – laced with about three times as much vodka. If you were

152

Russian, the proportion of vodka would probably be much greater than that!

Has gin and orange any special name?
With a pinch of white sugar, and rather less orange than gin, it is often known as 'Orange Blossom'.

What is a Horse's Neck?
Take a tall, thin glass, coil a whole lemon-peel round the inside with a bit sticking out of the top. Put in some crushed ice and then pour in a large whisky (or brandy). Fill up with dry ginger ale. Some people put in a dash of Angostura bitters into the whisky version.

Where did the drink called a Manhattan originate?
It is claimed to have been thought of in the district of New York called Manhattan, and consists of a mixture of rye or bourbon whisky (three parts) and one part of Italian Vermouth, with a dash of bitters and a slice or two of orange peel.

What is Black Velvet?
Probably Irish invented, it's a long drink of cold champagne and cold Stout (Guinness is the best) mixed in equal proportions. It is called 'Black Velvet' because it is very dark and very smooth.

How would you make a Sidecar?
Put one measure of cointreau with two of brandy and throw in some lemon juice.

What is grog?
Grog is rum and hot water. It stems from a drink first made up by the British admiral, Edward Vernon (1684–1757), who had the neat rum ration for his sailors diluted with water. Vernon was often called 'grog' from the cloak he

wore, called a grogram, which is a rough material of silk and mohair.

What are the main characteristics of proper vodka?
It does not smell, nor does it have a taste (though it feels tangy and burning as it goes down the throat). It is a clean drink, but it is also strong.

What is vodka made from?
It is made from distilling rye, wheat or potatoes. Vodka is popularly believed to be of Russian origin, but could have been invented by the Poles in the late Middle Ages. There is a thriving vodka distillery in northern England.

What is a whisky mac?
Generally, it is Scotch whisky with an equal measure of green ginger wine. It is very warming in cold weather.

What is the difference between British cider and American cider?
British cider is an alcoholic drink made from fermented apple juice, while American cider is non-alcoholic and comes from pure apple juice.

What is the difference between whisky and whiskey?
Whisky is made in Scotland, either the Highlands or Lowlands, while whiskey is made in Ireland, Canada and the United States. However it is spelled, all good whiskies are distilled from fermented grains, like rye, barley, maize or corn, oats and wheat. Some inferior whiskies are made from potatoes or beets.

What is Bourbon?
It is the name of one of the two main types of American whiskey. It is distilled from corn (maize) and is named after the county of Bourbon in Kentucky. The other American whiskey is rye, made from the cereal of that name.

What is an opera?
It is a theatrical play set to music. The characters sing as well as speak their parts. The costumes, scenery and props are normally representative of the period of the opera.

What kinds of opera are there?
There is comic opera and there is grand opera.

Where did opera first appear?
In Italy, and it is the Italian style that has, more than any other, remained supreme.

Which were Mozart's best-loved operas?
The Magic Flute (1791), *Marriage of Figaro* (1786), *Cosi fan Tutti* (1790) and *Don Giovanni* (1787).

What was Wagner's role as a composer of opera?
Richard Wagner (1813–1883) attempted – and succeeded in his way – to combine the musical, poetic and scenic elements of his operas so that the audience became involved in the story and feel the emotions felt by the characters in the story.

Which of his operas do this most effectively?
Well, it's a matter of personal view, but *The Flying Dutchman* (1843), *Lohengrin* (1848) and *Tannhauser* (1845) – and some would add *Tristan and Isolde* (1865) – all do this very well.

Who were the composer and librettist of the Savoy Operas?
Sir Arthur Seymour Sullivan (1842–1900) and Sir William Schwenck Gilbert (1836–1911). The Savoy operas were so called because they were staged by Richard d'Oyly Carte at his Savoy Theatre in London (they were also staged as repeats by his company in America) in the late 19th century. The operas included *Patience, Iolanthe, The Yeoman of the Guard, HMS Pinafore, Ruddigore, The Pirates of Penzance, Utopia Limited* and, perhaps the best known, *The Mikado.*

What was the story of Benjamin Britten's opera 'Peter Grimes'?
It comes from a story by the poet George Crabbe (1754–1832), about 'a villainous fellow who 'fish'd by water and filch'd by land' and killed his apprentices by ill-treatment'.

What other operas did Britten write?
He wrote nine other full-length operas including *Billy Bud, A Midsummer Night's Dream* and *Death in Venice* as well as several short operas, such as *Noye's Fludde* (Noah's Flood) and *Let's Make an Opera.* He also wrote many choral works and songs.

Who was the greatest of the Italian opera composers?
Probably Giuseppe Verdi (1813–1901), whose best-loved operas were *Il Trovatore, La Traviata, Don Carlos, Aida* and *Otello.* But Giacomo Puccini (1858–1924) is considered by some to have run Verdi a pretty close second. His best-known works were *Madame Butterfly, Tosca,* and *La Boheme.*

Who was Caruso?
He was an Italian tenor singer, specializing in opera, who lived from 1873 to 1921. He is regarded as perhaps the greatest of all male opera singers, and travelled throughout the world to take the lead in numerous performances of operas.

What is ballet?
It is a theatrical combination of dancing, mime and music.

How long has ballet been performed?
There was a sort of ballet performed in ancient Greek times. But as we know it, ballet began in France about 400 years ago.

Who was Diaghilev?
Sergei Pavlovich Diaghilev (1872–1929) was a Russian theatrical impressario who founded the *Ballet Russe*, not in Russia but in France. He ran it for twenty years and among those who starred in ballet productions were some of the greatest artists of all – Nijinsky, Pavlova and Massine. He also commissioned music from leading composers, such as Stravinsky and Falla.

Who lifted American ballet into the front rank in the world's performers?
Georges Balanchine, Russian born, who fled at the time of the Revolution and worked with Diaghilev. In 1948 he became artistic director of the New York City Ballet Company and brought this company's performances up to standards comparable with any.

Who created the foundations of the British Royal Ballet?
Dame Ninette de Valois, in 1928. She, too, worked with Diaghilev, but later went to London to develop the Sadlers-Wells Ballet which became the Royal Ballet. Dame Ninette encouraged many of Britain's leading performers including Dame Margot Fonteyn, Dame Alicia Markova and Anton Dolin.

What was Isadora Duncan famous for?
She was an American dancer and ballet producer whose life was at least as dramatic and unusual as the ballets she staged. She specialized in dancing, favouring interpretations of the classical Greek forms. She made a considerable impact in Europe. She quarrelled violently in hotels and public places, drank to excess, ran a school of dancing in a very eccentric way, and eventually died, tragically, in a motor accident when her scarf, tied round her neck, got caught in the sprocket of a wheel and it strangled her.

Who is Martha Graham?
She is the founder of the Martha Graham Dance Theater in New York. At first her productions were unpopular because they did not fit in with traditional ideas of what ballet should be, but the company is now accepted as one of the most original and exciting in the world.

Who composed the music for 'Swan Lake'?
Tchaikovsky, perhaps the greatest Russian composer of all times. He also wrote the music for *The Nutcracker, Sleeping Beauty*, amongst others.

Which Russian novel was choreographed to music by Chopin?
A Month in the Country. Sir Frederick Ashton selected several pieces of music by Chopin and choreographed the story for the Royal Ballet in 1976.

What is operetta?
It is a type of light opera with a romantic story and spoken dialogue but containing much light pleasant music. The form was developed in the 19th century by the French composer Jacques Offenbach whose most famous piece is *La Vie Parisienne*, although musically the best known are the Viennese operettas, particularly those by Johann Strauss the younger.

Who wrote the opera 'The Barber of Seville'?
Gioacchino Rossini (1792–1868), one of the masters of Italian opera, who, in fifteen years, composed forty operas.

Who invented

The bicycle?

The first bicycle that really looked anything like a modern one was invented in about 1840 by Andrew Macmillan, a Scottish engineer, who fitted pedals to driving rods between the axles of front and rear wheels of a bicycle.

The parachute?

This is one of the many things that were drawn by Leonardo da Vinci but never actually developed in his time. The first parachute that worked was made by a French balloonist called Blanchard, in 1785.

The submarine?

In 1620 a Dutch engineer, Cornelis van Drebbel, built a wooden elliptical boat with leather covering, which he propelled with oars operated from inside. The oars poked out through water-tight holes in the leather. He navigated this 'submarine' in the Thames, some three fathoms below the surface.

The sewing machine?

The earliest attempts to make a sewing machine were carried out in Europe, but the first successful machine was made in the US by Elias Howe, in 1846.

The piano?

The piano as we know it today is a development of a less refined instrument invented by the Italian instrument-maker Bartholomew Cristofori. In 1710 he introduced the hammer action on the strings which was produced by pressing keys for the notes.

Postage stamps?

Postage stamps were the idea of Rowland Hill, an English schoolmaster who produced a paper on how to improve the British postal system. The government

were impressed by the paper and Hill was encouraged to develop his ideas. In 1840 the penny postage was introduced and the first stamp was a black stamp bearing a portrait of Queen Victoria, and costing a penny. It was the Penny Black.

The refrigerator?

The principle of converting ammonia gas to liquid by compressing it and removing the heat, so that when the pressure is lifted, cold is produced, was worked out by Michael Faraday, in the 1820s. It was a Swiss engineer, Carl Linde, however, who in 1877 made a machine using this principle, which actually worked as a refrigerator.

The semaphore code?

This code, which spells out words by making letters using different positions of outstretched arms, was invented by a Frenchman called Jean Chappe, in 1794. It was soon widely in use, for it was then the quickest way to get a message from one place to another. Operators stood on hill tops and signalled each other.

Braille?

Braille is the alphabet of the blind. It is made from tiny raised dots in different groupings meaning different letters, pressed out on paper. It was invented by a blind teacher, Louis Braille, who lived in Paris (1809–1852).

The miner's safety lamp?

In 1815 Sir Humphry Davy, the famous British chemist, invented a special miner's lamp that would not set light to the dangerous gases in the atmosphere under the ground in a coal mine. It saved many lives then, and in some mines versions of this lamp are still in use.

Shorthand?

A Greek scholar named Tiro is said to have introduced a form of shorthand for taking down speeches by orators like Cicero in Rome in the 1st century BC.

The vacuum flask?

The vacuum flask was invented by the Scottish physicist Sir James Dewar (1842–1923) who had also been the first to liquefy the gas hydrogen. His flask was the same as the modern vacuum flasks which we take on picnics.

The autogiro?

The autogiro is slightly different from a helicopter. It was invented by the Spanish engineer, Juan de la Cierva (1896–1936), in 1920 and demonstrated in 1928.

Logarithms?

Logarithms were first thought of by the Scottish mathematician John Napier (1550–1617) in about 1614. They were extremely useful. Complicated multiplications could be worked out very quickly by adding together the logarithms of the numbers to be multiplied. These were set out in tables devised by Napier. Today, many of these calculations would be done by electronic calculators.

The steam hammer?

The steam hammer is a high-powered hammer used in the iron and steel industry. It is a huge hammer head connected to a piston in a cylinder operated by steam. It was invented by the Scottish engineer, James Nasmyth (1808–1890).

The incandescent light bulb?

The light bulb with carbon filaments was invented by Thomas Alva Edison in 1879. This was the beginning of electric lighting for the house and factory. Sir Joseph Swan, the English physicist, was said to have invented a similar lamp nearly twenty years earlier, but Edison has received the credit.

Gas lighting?

The first practical gas lighting for the home was demonstrated by William Murdoch at his house in Redruth in Cornwall, England, in 1792. Six years later, he installed gas lighting in a big factory in Birmingham.

The rheostat?

A rheostat varies the resistance in an electrical circuit. If you fit one in a light switch you can make the lamp go bright or dim. This was invented by Sir Charles Wheatstone (1802–1875), an English physicist.

The military tank?

This self-propelled armoured vehicle which moves on what are called caterpillar tracks was invented during the First World War (1914–1918) by Major General Sir Ernest Swinton. Its value was immediately recognized by Winston Churchill, then 1st Lord of the Admiralty, who pressed for it to be manufactured.

Swing wing aircraft?

The swing wing aeroplane, whose wings can be moved during flight, was devised by Sir Barnes Wallis.

Electric batteries?

The electric battery stores electricity which has been fed into it by an outside source, such as a generator. Some batteries have wet cells and some dry ones. The wet cell variety can be re-charged. The first battery was successfully devised by Count Alexander Volta, the Italian physicist, in 1800.

Steam carriages?

In 1770, Parisians were amazed to see a three-wheeled carriage going down the streets at about 4 kph (2½ mph), driven by steam power. It had been invented by Nicholas Cugnot (1725–1804).

What was the Palaeozoic Era in prehistory?
It was really the first era in which life beyond simple cell organisms appeared, roughly from 750 million to 250 million years ago. Both invertebrates and vertebrates developed, particularly reptiles, and seed-bearing plants.

Which was the next era?
The Mezozoic, characterized by the appearance of the reptiles in some numbers and varieties. This era lasted from about 230 to about 130 million years BC, and is divided by palaentologists into the Triassic Age, the Jurassic Age and the Cretaceous Age.

What was an Iguanadon?
He was a vegetarian dinosaur of the Cretaceous period (about 165 to 130 million years BC) about 9 metres (30 feet) long, lizard-like, with a large mouth and sharp teeth. He has a sort of descendant in the iguana.

What was Archaeopteryx?
The first animal that could fly. It had a lizard-like tail and sharp teeth, as well as a huge wing span. It appeared during the Jurassic Age.

What was a pterodactyl?
Another flying animal – it seems strange to say bird when these prehistoric flying creatures were so enormous. Pterodactyls looked a bit like huge bats with bird-like head and hind quarters like a lizard. The wing span could be anything up to 7 metres (21 feet).

Who were the Dinosaurs?
They were a group of huge vertebrates, of lizard-like appearance, whose principal characteristic was that they had very small brains. Among the family were Megalosaurs, Brachiosaurs and Brontosaurs.

Which of the Dinosaurs had armoured skin?
The Stegosaurus. He had rows of bony plates sticking upwards from his backbone.

What did Stegosaurs eat?
They look fierce in drawings, and you might think they ate each other or some smaller beasts, but they were herbivorous.

What were ichthyosaurs?
They were one group of reptiles who lived in the sea in the Mezozoic Era, and they were anything from 1 to 10 metres (3 to 30 feet) long, with four flippers and a long, powerful swishing tail.

What was Psittacosaurus?
He was a large lizard with parrot-like features, who lived on land.

Which was the largest of the dinosaurs?
Probably Tyrannosaurus, who walked on two feet, ate flesh and may have been 12 metres (40 feet) or more long. He was also one of the last of the dinosaur family.

What was the Cainozoic Era?
The age of mammals, from about 130 million years BC up to the first appearance of man as we know him.

When was a coelacanth, a prehistoric fish, recently found?
This prehistoric fish lived about 300 million years ago, and was believed to have been extinct for about 70 million years, until in 1938 some were found alive off the African coast. More have been found since.

What was Meganeura?
A huge insect not unlike a dragon fly, with a wingspan of up to a metre.

What was a moa?
A bird which lived in New Zealand and which looked something like an ostrich, only several times bigger.

What was a quagga?
It was an animal like a zebra, which came from South Africa. It is now extinct, but the last one died in a zoo about a century ago.

Who was Neolithic Man?
He was Man who lived in Europe and West Asia from about 6000 BC to about 4000 BC (later still in northern Europe) who is characterized by his making and usage of polished stone tools and utensils of ground horn. He learned to domesticate animals and grow some crops.

Who was Neanderthal Man?
A race of men who lived about 50,000 to 60,000 years ago who were not in the main stream of descent of man as we know him today from his ancestors, but who were nonetheless quite developed. They became extinct. A skeleton of one was found in the Neanderthal valley in Germany in 1856.

Neanderthal man

Which were the two principal mammals which early man knew but which have been extinct for thousands of years?
The Mammoth and the Sabre-tooth tiger. The sabre-tooth tiger had huge canine teeth and lived in north and south America. He became extinct not long before man became civilized, 7000 years ago.

Where was the carcass of a Mammoth discovered in recent years?
One was discovered in a riverbed in Russia (Siberia) at the end of the last century. A Mammoth was an elephant-type mammal but very much bigger, with long hair and huge, curved tusks.

Little Quiz 26
Who was the victorious admiral in these battles at sea?
1. Trafalgar
2. Actium
3. The Saints
4. Jutland
5. Tsushima Straits
6. Straits of Dover (1652)
7. Lepanto
8. Beachy Head
9. Manila (1898)
10. St Vincent

Name the country of origin of the admiral in each of the ten.

Who were the assassins of the following?
11. Caligula
12. Abraham Lincoln
13. Archduke Franz Ferdinand
14. William the Silent
15. Henry IV of France
16. Mahatma Gandhi
17. John F. Kennedy
18. George, Duke of Buckingham
19. Spencer Percival
20. Martin Luther King

What do you know about these buildings?

The Taj Mahal, Agra, India
The Moghul emperor, Shah Jehan (1628–1658) grieved so much over the death of his wife, Mumtaz Mahal, that he built her a most amazing mausoleum at Agra. It is called the Taj Mahal, it is of white marble, and it has a central dome that is 61 metres (200 feet) high. The Taj is one of the most beautiful buildings in the world.

Forum Romanum
The Roman Forum began as a small meeting place and market in Rome. Over the centuries it grew until it filled much of the centre of the city and contained triumphal arches, palaces, basilicas and monuments. It lies between the Capitoline and the Palatine Hills.

The Tower of London
Begun by William the Conqueror (1066–1087) on a site which once held a Roman fort, the Tower started with a rectangular great tower of stone (the White Tower). Over the next generations, other buildings were added, and walls as well. Today it is the biggest tourist attraction in Britain.

Chequers, Buckinghamshire
An Elizabethan mansion house, the official country residence of Britain's prime minister. It was given to the nation for this use by its owner, Lord Lee of Fareham, in 1917. The first occupant was Lloyd George.

Sydney Opera House, Australia
One of the most modern opera houses in the world, this extraordinary structure, built chiefly of concrete, stands near Sydney Harbour. The 'wings' over the main parts of the building reflect in the water like yacht sails. At one time the builders said the architect's design was impossible to construct, but the problems were overcome.

Golden Gate Bridge, San Francisco
A suspension bridge, over 1220 metres (3905 feet) long, more than 62 metres (204 feet) above the water, in San Francisco.

Milan Cathedral, Italy
A remarkable cathedral begun in the late 14th century, which can seat over 40,000 congregation. One of its features is a number of graded rows of spires on the roof.

Leaning Tower of Pisa, Italy
The Leaning Tower is 55 metres (179 feet) tall and is made of white marble. It leans $4\frac{1}{2}$ metres (15 feet) off the vertical, owing to subsidence of the soil on which it was put up, between 1170 and 1350.

Caernarvon Castle, Wales
Edward I of England (1272–1307) conquered Wales in 1282. To establish his authority he had several big castles built to overawe the Welsh and to accommodate his administration. One was Caernarvon Castle, which took over thirty years to complete.

Ziggurat at Ur, Mesopotamia
The city of Ur was one of the cities of Sumerian civilization. The Ziggurat was a temple, approximately pyramidical in shape, and much of it has been recovered in excavations at Ur.

London Bridge, now in Arizona
The famous London Bridge was built by Sir John Rennie in the 1830s. In the early 1970s it was taken down, stone by stone, and transported to Lake Havasu City, Arizona, USA, where it has been re-erected. While the bridge was being dismantled, another was constructed alongside it.

UN Building, New York
The United Nations Building is in New York City, USA. It is rectangular in plan and seems to be made almost entirely of glass. Actually, it is glazed between steel and concrete framework.

Toronto City Hall, Canada
A new city hall for the capital of Ontario state in Canada, it is two separate curved buildings, facing each other, tall and glazed. The plan shape of the buildings resembles a boomerang.

The Great Wall of China
This must be the most astonishing work of construction in all history. It is a fortified wall with parapet along its entire length, and with turrets 13 to 16 metres tall at intervals of about 200 metres. The wall is amazingly long – over 2400 kilometres, and it runs from north to south China. It was constructed largely in the reign of emperor Huang-Ti (247–210 BC).

Temple of Ammon at Karnak, Egypt
Egyptian pharaohs built huge temples for worship either of themselves or of other Egyptian gods. Some were built at Karnak, near Luxor on the Nile, the site of an old capital. One was to Ammon, and this was added to over nearly twenty centuries. One feature is a hall with 134 sandstone columns, twelve of them over 24 metres (80 feet) high, put up by Rameses II in the 13th century BC.

L'arc de Triomphe, Paris
The arc de triomphe was begun by Napoleon I to celebrate some of his victories. It was not finished until the 1830s. It resembles some of the triumphal arches in the Forum at Rome.

Palace of Versailles, France
The Palace of Versailles, about sixteen kilometres south of Paris, was built by Louis XIV in the 1660s and was the chief royal residence of the kings until the Revolution in 1789. Its western facades are nearly 612 metres (2010 feet) long.

Salisbury Cathedral, England
The principal feature of this medieval English cathedral is its very tall spire, 123 metres (404 feet) high. This was added some time after the construction of the main part of the cathedral.

Machu Picchu, Peru
Machu Picchu was an Inca fortress and citadel north-west of Cuzco in Peru, at about 2134 metres (7000 feet) above sea-level. It was probably built about 1000 years ago.

Bridge of Sighs, Venice
The Bridge of Sighs (*Ponte di Sospiri*) connects the Doge's Palace to the Piombi prison, in Venice. It was built in about 1600.

Knossos
Knossos was the main city of the ancient Minoans in Crete. It was destroyed by earthquake, sometime in the 15th or 14th century BC. The ruins were excavated at the beginning of this century.

Appian Way, Italy
One of the major Roman trunk roads built in Italy. It ran from Rome to Brindisi (Brundisium) in the south, some 570 kms (350 miles). Much of it is still visible and is well preserved. It was built by Appius Claudius in 312 BC.

Ka'aba at Mecca, Saudi Arabia
The Ka'aba is a shrine in the courtyard of the Great Mosque at Mecca, in Saudi Arabia. It contains the Ka'aba stone, a black meteorite which Moslems believe was given to Abraham by the archangel Gabriel.

Which language has the most words?

The English language, which has nearly half a million words, not including technical terms which amount to another 300,000 or so. The average English speaking person, however, doesn't use more than about 10,000 different English words.

What is the tallest building in Britain?

The National Westminster Bank tower block in London's Bishopsgate. It is 49 storeys high, and reaches about 183 metres (600 feet).

Which is the oldest steamship still in service?

The 48-ton Bristol Dredger *Bertha*, some 15 metres (50 feet) long. It was designed and built by Isambard Kingdom Brunel in 1844 and works out of Exeter in south-west England.

What is the longest railway platform in Britain?

That at Colchester, in Essex. It is 603 metres (1980 feet).

Who was the tallest human being in the world?

An American, Robert Wadlow, an Illinois citizen who reached 2.7 metres (8 ft 11 ins) by the time he died in 1939. He was twenty-one.

Who was the tallest woman in the world?

Jane Bunford (1895–1922), who lived in Northfield, UK, and who reached 2.3 metres (7 ft 7 ins). Her skeleton is now in the Anatomical Museum of Birmingham University's Medical School.

What was the worst earthquake recorded in British history?

That which happened near Colchester in April 1884. The nearby church of

Langenhoe was destroyed, and the shock was felt as far away as Exeter over 320 kms (200 miles) away.

What was the greatest volcanic explosion in ancient times?

This is thought to have been Santorini, a volcanic island in the Aegean Sea. It exploded in about 1470 BC and may quite probably have been the cause of the destruction of the Cretan civilization, about 128 kms (80 miles) away.

What is the greatest volcanic explosion in modern history?

When the volcanic island of Krakatoa exploded in 1883. Krakatoa is in the Sunda Strait, between Sumatra and Java in Indonesia. More than 36,000 people were killed, many by tidal waves which struck both Sumatra and Java. The dust drifted as far as 5250 kms (3300 miles) away, and the bang was heard over a twelfth of the surface of the earth.

Which is the largest pearl so far found?

That found at Palawan, Philippines, in 1934, in the shell of a giant clam. It weighed 6.4 kgs (14 lbs).

What is the oldest museum in the world?

The Ashmolean Museum in Beaumont Street, Oxford, England.

Who was the shortest woman in history?

In records at least, it was Pauline Musters, a Dutch girl who lived from 1876 to 1895. She was 58 cms (23 ins) only at death.

What is the highest mountain in Britain?

Ben Nevis, in Scotland. It is 1343 metres (4406 feet) high, and was first climbed in 1720.

Which was the worst earthquake of history?
In 1556, there was a frightful earthquake in the Shensi Province in China, in which it was reported that over 800,000 people were killed.

Which was the oldest domestic cat in British records?
A tabby cat called 'Ma', owned by a Drewsteighton, Devon, housewife. She was put to sleep in November 1957, aged 34.

What was the biggest animal of all time?
A Blue whale, 35 metres (114 feet) long, was caught in the Antarctic in the early 1900s. It was bigger than anything so far discovered in the way of remains of any prehistoric animal.

What is the largest animal's egg so far found?
A whale shark's egg, found in 1953 in the Gulf of Mexico, which was about 30 cm (12 ins) long and 13 cm (5 ins) in diameter.

Who was the most famous midget in history?
Charles Sherwood Stratton, otherwise known as General Tom Thumb. He lived from 1838 to 1885, was only 1 metre (3 feet) at death, and had for some time been taken along as a circus freak by the famous Barnum circus show in America.

What is the largest painting in the world?
Unless someone comes up with another, the Battle of Gettysburg, painted from 1881 to 1883 by Paul Philippoteaux, of France, with the help of several assistants. It measures 125 metres (410 feet) wide and 22 metres (72 feet) high and now belongs to a private collector in North Carolina.

Which is the shortest book in the Bible?
It is the third Epistle of John in the New Testament, Authorized Version, which contains 14 verses with 294 words. The Second Epistle of John has less verses – 13 – but has more words – 298.

What is the highest mountain in the world?
It is Mount Everest on the border of Nepal and Tibet. Named after a Surveyor-General of India, Sir George Everest, it is 8840 metres (29,002 feet) high. The first successful climb to the summit was made in May 1953 by the New Zealand climber Edmund Hillary and the Nepalese sherpa, Tenzing Norkhay.

Where is the largest single cave in the world?
It is in the Carlsbad Caverns in New Mexico in the US. It is 1300 metres (4270 feet) long, 200 metres (656 feet) high and lies 400 metres (1320 feet) underground. Not surprisingly, the cave is called the Big Room.

What is the deepest lake in Britain?
It is Loch Morar in Scotland. It reaches a depth of 310 metres (1017 feet) and is reputed to have its own monster in competition with Loch Ness.

What is the smallest continent?
Australia, which has a total area of 7,614,500 square kilometres (29,400,000 square miles). Australia is also known as the largest island.

What are the tallest trees?
The American redwood (*Sequoia sempervirens*) found in southern Oregon and in California. These trees can reach heights of over 90 metres (300 feet) and diameters of over 10 metres (36 feet) and live for three or four thousand years.

163

What is a saltire?

It is an X-shaped cross, and is the cross of St Andrew, the patron saint of Scotland. The word comes from the medieval French *saultoir* meaning fence or barricade over which people could jump.

Who was Madame Tussaud?

She was a Swiss-born craftswoman who lived and worked in Paris. During the French Revolution she earned a living making wax models of heads of famous people guillotined. Then she left to go to London, in 1802, to set up a waxworks museum. It is still there and extremely popular.

Where does the word nicotine come from?

Nicotine is a poisonous substance which is a major constituent of tobacco, and is the one which gives the narcotic qualities to smoking. The name comes from the French–Dutch merchant who first imported tobacco into France, Jean Nicot.

What is a narcotic?

It is a drug which affects the alertness of the senses, alleviates pain and makes you sleepy, in varying degrees according to the amount taken and the manner in which taken. Alcoholic drinks are narcotics.

What happened to Trotsky?

Leon Trotsky, the bitterest rival of Russia's great leader Stalin, went into exile in 1929 and settled in Mexico. An agent of Stalin's wormed his way into Trotsky's confidence over the years, and then, one day in 1940, suddenly assassinated Trotsky by splitting his head open with an axe.

What are stalactites and stalagmites?

Stalactites are deposits of minerals which project downwards from the ceiling of a cave, built up by chemicals in seeping water, and stalagmites are similar things which grow upwards, for the same reason. They look like icicles.

What does the Salvation Army do?

It is a Christianity-based social service, founded in Britain but now operating world-wide, which aims to bring relief to the poor and distressed in the slum areas of towns and cities. It also campaigns for improvements in social service generally, and it has been a splendid influence on governments in many countries.

Who founded the Salvation Army?

William Booth (1829–1912), who came to be known by his followers as General Booth. In 1865, after several years as an evangelist preacher he founded the Christian Mission to the poor in London's Whitechapel, a very depressed area. In 1878 this became known as the Salvation Army.

What does an à la carte menu mean?

It means that you have to pay for each course, which will be clearly marked and priced (you hope) on the menu. It is the opposite of table d'hôte which is a price for a set of courses.

What is a gazetteer?

It is effectively a dictionary of place-names, generally printed alongside an atlas or at least a set of maps, so that you can quickly look up where such and-such a town or village is.

What is the Plimsoll line?

It is a line about 46 cm (18 ins) long painted on both sides of a mercantile ship indicating the point beyond which the water level should not rise when cargo is being loaded. It was introduced about a century ago because unscrupulous shipowners deliberately overloaded their ships, endangering the crews and claiming large amounts from insurers if the ships were lost.

Why were the Wars of the Roses called by that name?
Because the two contending sides (the royal house of York and the royal house of Lancaster, in England) were represented by their badges, a white rose for York and a red one for Lancaster. They were fought between 1455 and 1485.

How many times did Robert Clive (Clive of India) attempt suicide?
Twice, at least. The first, as a young man serving in India, in about 1744, because he was depressed. Then he tried again, thirty years later, and this time was successful. It was the end of what had been a splendid career.

What is the Levant?
It is the name given by some to the eastern Mediterranean coastal countries like Turkey, Syria, Israel, Lebanon.

What does it mean if you say that someone is as rich as Croesus?
Croesus was king of the near-eastern kingdom of Lydia in the 6th century BC. In his reign he acquired immense wealth, partly by conquest of rich and independent cities in Asia Minor.

What was Oscar Wilde's definition of a cynic?
He said it was someone who knew the price of everything and the value of nothing. Its more general meaning is one who considers that self-interest is the motive behind all human conduct.

What is the Snowy river project in Australia?
A huge engineering and agricultural scheme to divert the river Snowy into the Murrumbidgee river to supply water for irrigation and power in both New South Wales and Victoria states. It was started in 1955.

What is frankincense?
It is a resinous substance which comes from several trees of the Boswellia genus, found in Africa, Arabia and India. It is the main constituent of incense which is burned in churches.

What happened to St Lawrence?
He was a Christian martyr who suffered death in about AD 258 by a most excruciating form of torture, roasting alive on a grid-iron.

What is a dulcimer?
A musical instrument, not often made or played these days, but which was a box inside which a frame was strung with wires which the player struck with little hammers.

What time is the fall in the US?
It is the American word for autumn.

Who were the Canadian 'Group of Seven' painters?
J. E. H. MacDonald, Franklin Carmichael, A. J. Casson, Lawren Harris, A. Y. Jackson, Arthur Lismer and F. H. Varley. They were well-known as a group in the years between 1919 and 1933.

What are the principal exports of New Zealand?
Dairy produce, meat, particularly lamb, wool and other agricultural products, as well as some minerals.

What is the veldt?
It is the Afrikaans word for the vast areas of open grass land in South Africa, particularly in Transvaal, where for miles and miles you can see few if any trees.

What is sardines?

As a game, it is played indoors. Players choose one person who is to go off into the depths of the house and hide. After an interval the rest go out of the main room and look for him. The point is that each person who finds the first joins him quietly, so as not to give the game away to the next person, and so on, until the last person does find everyone – probably squashed and half suffocating in a cupboard.

What is falconry?

It is a sport, enjoyed for centuries by kings and noblemen, in which falcons are trained to pursue other birds and bring them down. When not out on the chase, the falcons are kept in captivity and often hooded. If there is a shortage of falcons, hawks can be used.

A falcon

What is charades?

A party game. Two or three (more, if you like) people act out the individual syllables of a word they have chosen. The rest have to guess what the word is.

How do you play musical chairs?

Take a group of people, count them and then put a ring of chairs in the room, with the seats turned outwards. There should be one chair less than the number of people. Start playing some music and get the people to walk or dance round the chairs. Then stop and everyone has to sit down where he is. There will be one person left out, and he drops out, taking a chair with him. The round starts again until there are only two playing.

What was the London Ball Game?

A medieval form of hockey, with few rules, in which quite a lot of small boys got hurt knocking each other with sticks when trying to chase a ball across the ground.

When did horse-racing begin in Europe?

Probably about a thousand years ago, soon after the spread of the use of horses for military purposes. It arrived in England in the time of Henry II (1154–1189) but the first races in anything like the form known today did not take place until the 17th century.

What is the Jockey Club?

The body responsible for administering horse-racing in Britain. Founded in 1751, it has its headquarters in Newmarket, Cambridgeshire, the town where organized horse-racing began.

What is the origin of horse-racing in the United States?

Colonel Richard Nicolls, a commander of British forces in New Amsterdam (later New York), laid out a 3-km (1½-mile) track near the present one at Belmont Park, in 1664. Racing has since become an enormous industry in North America. Over 20,000 races are run in the US every year.

What are the principal American horse races?
The Kentucky Derby, The Coaching Club Oaks, and the Withers Stakes at Belmont Park.

What are the five classic flat races in England?
The Derby, the Oaks, the St Leger, the 2000 Guineas, and the 1000 Guineas.

What is the principal steeple-chase race in the United Kingdom?
The Grand National, first raced at Aintree near Liverpool in 1839.

What is the origin of steeplechasing?
Riders in an ordinary race in the 18th century would be started at a point in a field and expected to make for a neighbouring church steeple, which could be seen in the distance. The races involved jumping fences and ditches, and today this is what differentiates a steeplechase from a flat race.

What is a rodeo?
Once the business of rounding up cattle in America and Canada prior to a big sale or transfer. This was often accompanied by revelry and parties. Gradually some sort of show developed which included contests between cowboys trying to ride – or just stay on the backs of – frisky cattle. It then grew into a regular kind of tournament, held in various areas and is still a popular show in North America.

What is a gymkhana?
It is a typically British day event during the summer in the country featuring a kind of horse show, with riding competitions, some having fairly rough contests not unlike rodeos. But a gymkhana is a very much more quiet and delicate matter.

Where is the International Horse Show held?
Wembley in London, England, and has been held in London since 1907.

What is harness-racing?
A sport enjoyed in the United States and Canada in which a horse pulls a two-wheeled carriage with a driver, usually trotting and pacing. Races consist of heats. One of the best known harness-races is the Hambletonian at Goshen in New York. Harness-racing has also caught on in Australia, but has made little impact in Britain.

What is a pentathlon?
It is an athletics contest in which competitors have to take part in five events.

What is the pole vault?
It's a jumping contest in an athletics competition. A contestant vaults over a high bar lifting himself by means of a long bamboo or metal pole which he pushes into the earth at the end of a run.

Where was the crawl swimming stroke developed?
In Australia, by swimmers adapting a stroke used by South Sea islanders, only using it much more vigorously to get up speed. The Australians are still the world masters of the crawl stroke.

Who was the outstanding swimmer at the 1972 Olympic Games?
It was Mark Spitz of the US who won four individual and three team gold medals, setting a record.

Who was
Alaric the Goth?

In the last years of the 4th and first years of the 5th centuries AD the Roman emperors used to employ barbarian leaders to beat off attacks by other barbarian chiefs. Alaric was leader of the Goths, who served for a time as a Roman commander, but it seems he became disappointed with the rewards and felt he could do better himself by attacking Rome and putting it to sack, in 410. The sack lasted for three days.

Vitruvius?

Marcus Vitruvius Pollio (1st century AD) was a Roman engineer and architect. He left behind him several works devoted to principles and practices of building, and these were used as guides not only by builders who followed, but also, many centuries later, by architects and engineers of the Italian Renaissance, when Vitruvius' works, lost for hundreds of years, were found again.

Delius?

Frederick Delius (1861–1934) was a North Country English-born composer of German descent. He studied music in America and began to compose in a style that owed little to the influences of anyone else. Towards the end of his life he went blind and became paralyzed, but he managed to dictate music to a young musician, Eric Fenby, who wrote it down. In spite of the difficulties, Delius had not lost his touch as one of the greatest of this century's composers.

Nostradamus?

Nostradamus was the name Michel de Nôtre-Dame (1503–1566) took when he became famous as a doctor in the 1540s, in France. He was well-known for being able somehow to predict the outcome of some people's illnesses. One patient whose manner of death he forecast

accurately was Henry II of France. When the king died, his successor, Charles IX, made Nostradamus his court physician.

Toussaint L'Ouverture?

This was the other name for Pierre Dominique (1746–1803), a Negro rebel leader in the West Indian island of Haiti. He led a revolt against the British and Spanish and drove them out. Thereafter he ruled as commander-in-chief, under the guidance of the French, but later on, they dismissed him.

Alexander Hamilton?

This remarkable American statesman was born a British subject in the West Indies in 1757. He became aide-de-camp to George Washington in the American War of Independence, and was later appointed Secretary of the Treasury in the new US government. Hamilton was killed in a duel in 1801. Otherwise he would almost certainly have served as President at some time.

John Brown?

John Brown was a great fighter against slavery in the United States. In 1859 he led a raid on a government-controlled armoury, was barricaded and had to surrender. He was tried and executed for treason and rebellion. The song 'John Brown's Body' was written to commemorate him.

Dick Turpin?

One of the most famous of highwaymen in British history, Turpin (1705–1739) operated chiefly in the counties around London. He murdered, probably by mistake, an innkeeper at Epping and had to flee for his life. He went north and was captured and hanged at York.

Wat Tyler?

In the Peasants' Revolt in England, 1381, Wat Tyler was one of the leaders who marched with a rabble of peasants to the Tower of London. At Smithfield market he presented demands to the boy king, Richard II, who promised they would be met. Tyler then became involved in a scuffle and was cut down by the Lord Mayor of London.

Lady Jane Grey?
Lady Jane Grey (1535–1554) was a cousin of Edward VI of England, who died aged fifteen in 1553. The Lord Protector, the Duke of Northumberland, tried to make Lady Jane queen of England in succession, but the country supported Mary Tudor, Edward's older half-sister. Jane was imprisoned and later executed.

BP?
BP stands for Be Prepared, the motto of the Boy Scout movement. It also stands for the name of the founder of the movement, Robert Stephenson Smyth Baden-Powell, Lord Baden-Powell of Gilwell (1857–1941). He had been a successful general in the Boer War before starting the Scouts.

The GOM?
The GOM (Grand Old Man) was William Gladstone (1809–1898), British prime minister in the latter part of Queen Victoria's reign. He was the only person to be prime minister for four terms. Gladstone was a Liberal who fought for Home Rule for Ireland, reforms in Parliament, improvements in education and social services, and he concentrated on domestic matters rather than foreign affairs. He was one of the greatest of all British statesmen.

Dizzy?
Benjamin Disraeli (1804–1881) entered Parliament in 1836. Determined to overcome the prejudice against a Jew making headway in politics, Disraeli (known as 'Dizzy') eventually became prime minister twice. He specialized in foreign affairs. He bought shares in the Suez Canal enabling Britain to be the majority shareholder – and so its controller.

Mark Antony?
A Roman statesman and general who worked with Julius Caesar. Antony was a good-looking, tough and sometimes irresponsible man, with a good nature. When Caesar was murdered, Antony delivered his funeral oration to stir up the people against his friend's killers. Then he and Caesar's great nephew Octavian divided the empire and ruled it. Antony quarrelled with Octavian and was defeated at Actium. He thereupon committed suicide.

Sir John Monash?
An Australian who became a general in the First World War, and eventually commanded the Australian army corps in France in 1918, Monash was regarded by many as one of the outstanding generals on either side in the whole war.

Belisarius?
The Byzantine Emperor Justinian (527–565 AD) was no military leader and he entrusted his armies to the command of Belisarius, a brilliant general who defeated and captured Gelimer, king of the Vandals, in 534. In 542 he defeated Chosroes I of Persia, and in 559 he beat off a serious attack on Rome by the Huns.

Morning Star of the Reformation?
John Wiclyffe (1320–1384) was an English preacher who attacked the Church for high-living and neglect of religious duties. He was extremely outspoken, questioned many of the very teachings of the Roman Church but was protected by John of Gaunt, uncle of Richard II.

169

What is latent heat?
This is the heat required to convert one gramme of solid into liquid (the latent heat of fusion) and it is also the heat required to convert one gramme of liquid into gas (the latent heat of vaporization). The latent heat of ice is 80 calories per gramme.

What is energy?
In physical terms it is the capacity of a body or substance for doing work. It can be heat, or light, or mechanical energy, or sound, or electrical energy.

What is the speed of light?
Light travels at about 299,000 kms (186,000 miles) per second. A light year is the distance travelled by light in one year, which is just under 9,650,000,000,000 kms (6,000,000,000,000 miles).

What is the speed of sound?
This depends on the temperature of the atmosphere, but under normal conditions sound travels at about 330 metres (1120 feet) per second.

What is a decibel?
It is a unit for measuring loudness of sound, and is equal to the smallest difference of loudness detectable by the human ear. There is a range of decibels within which sounds are bearable to human beings, and this is from 1 decibel (practically inaudible) to 130 decibels at which point the ears begin to hurt.

How long is a micron?
It is one ten-thousandth of a centimetre.

What is friction?
It is the force that resists the movement of one surface over another. Friction in moving parts of a machine uses up energy in the form of heat and can damage the surfaces. That is why moving parts in machines have to be

lubricated with some kind of oil. Some kinds of friction, however, are important, such as with brakes, where friction cuts down motion.

What is an Ångström?
Named after the Swedish physicist A. J. Ångström (1814–1874), it is the smallest measurement of length, and is used to measure wavelengths of X-rays, gamma rays and light rays, and also the distances between atoms in molecules. It is 10^{-8} cm.

What is gravity?
It is the force with which one body or object attracts another body or object, and this force is proportional to the result of multiplying the masses of the bodies or objects. Objects near the earth fall towards the ground because the mass of the earth is so much greater than that of the objects.

What is infra-red light?
It is light that you cannot see, which has wavelengths longer than those of light you can see. Infra-red light has a warming effect.

What is ultra-violet light?
It is also light you cannot see, but its wavelengths are shorter than those of light you can see. It is harmful to the eyes and should be looked at only through specially tinted glasses. Its rays, however, are beneficial to the body, given carefully in small doses.

What is a laser?
It's a device which will produce a narrow and intense beam of light or infra-red radiation, and has an increasingly useful range of applications in communications, rocketry and some industrial enterprises.

What are electromagnetic waves?
They are waves with varying magnetic

and electrical quantities, and they can be light waves, radio waves, X-rays, gamma rays, infra-red waves, micro-waves and so on. Their lengths vary, and the number of cycles they complete in a second is called the frequency of the wave, whilst the distance between two successive crests in the wave is called the wavelength.

What is the Periodic Table of Elements?

A table classifying the elements into groups so that certain chemical and physical properties are repeated at regular intervals. Elements in a group have striking similarities, such as the group embracing chlorine, fluorine, iodine and bromine, which are known as the halogen elements, or the group of the inert gases like argon, neon, xenon and krypton.

What are reflection and refraction of light?

Reflection of light is when the light ray bounces back from the object on which it is directed, and refraction is when the light ray passes through the object (which will be transparent) and is 'bent' once it has gone through.

What is AC and DC?

AC means alternating current and DC means direct current. AC is electric current which flows in one direction and then in the opposite direction in a circuit. DC is current going round a circuit in one direction all the time.

What unit is a volt?

A volt is the unit of electromotive force, and is named after the Italian physicist Alessandro Volta (1745–1827) who invented the electric battery.

What is electromotive force?

It is the electrical pressure generated by a battery or a dynamo or other 'producer' of electricity.

What is an accumulator?

Perhaps a 'wet battery' would be a good description. It is a battery which can be recharged when it has spent its electromotive force. It has plates surrounded by sulphuric acid in dilute form, and can be re-charged by pushing fresh current into the plates for re-storage.

Who invented the Wheatstone Bridge?

Well, it wasn't Sir Charles Wheatstone (1802–1875) the British physicist, but S. Hunter Christie, another British physicist. It is a device for comparing and measuring electrical resistances.

What is electrical resistance?

It is the resistance to the passing of electric current set up by conductors of electricity and it varies with the temperature. In ordinary conductors the resistance increases with the temperature and with semi-conductors it decreases, as it does with insulators.

How do you measure resistance in units?

The unit of resistance is the ohm.

What is horse power?

It is a unit of power equal to 76 kg-force metres (550 ft-pounds) per second.

What is an armature?

It is the coil of electric wire which rotates inside an electric motor or dynamo. It rotates through a magnetic field and so produces electricity.

What is an ampère?

It is the unit of electric current, named after the French physicist André Marie Ampère (1775–1836).

Who introduced printing into Europe?

The first printing press that printed books in Europe was one set up by Johann Gutenburg in Mainz, in Germany, in the middle of the 15th century. One of his earliest books was a copy of the Bible.

How was the Inca Empire organized?

The Inca Empire in Peru was divided into districts of about 10,000 people ruled by officials appointed by the Inca himself (the emperor). They kept in touch with each other and with the Inca by using fast relays of running couriers. Unfortunately, the Inca had absolute power and he did not allow his officials much initiative. When he was betrayed by the Spanish and put to death, his organization collapsed because his officials were quite unused to making decisions for themselves and had no one to turn to for advice.

What was the Safavid dynasty in Persia?

Persia, which had survived many difficulties since its greatness of the 5th century BC, was taken over in about 1500 by one Ismail, a Mongol leader from central Asia, who claimed descent from the prophet Mohammed. He belonged to the Safavid tribe – hence the name of the dynasty he created. Ismail took the title Shah and ruled Persia well.

What did Shah mean?

It meant ruler, and came from the Roman name Caesar (after the great Julius Caesar). Caesar's name also came to be adapted as the title for ruler in other lands, including Kaiser in Germany, Czar in Russia (for several hundreds of years) and in some quarters the emperor of the Holy Roman empire was for centuries referred to as the kaiser.

What was the Spanish Armada?

A huge fleet of fighting ships and transports launched against England in 1588 by Philip II, king of Spain, in order to invade the country. He wished to depose Elizabeth, and restore the Roman Catholic Faith. It failed in its attempt, however, largely because Philip appointed as its commander-in-chief a second-rate general who had never been to sea.

Who was the Spanish commander-in-chief of the Armada?

The Duke of Medina Sidonia (1550–1615). Amazingly, Philip never blamed the duke for his catastrophic failure, which resulted in the loss of the great majority of the ships. Indeed, he kept him on as a senior admiral.

Why was Elizabeth I's favourite, the Earl of Essex, executed?

Quite simply because he went too far. Robert Devereux, Earl of Essex (1566–1601) was a courtier with more courage than sense. The queen favoured him, but when he went to Ireland, was humiliated by the Irish rebel leader Tyrone, returned to London, barged into the queen's private apartments to protest that other statesmen were plotting against him, was ordered out by her, then formed a private army which seemed to threaten her, then it's not surprising that Elizabeth felt she'd had enough. He was tried for treason, convicted and executed, in 1601.

Why did Elizabeth I never marry?

No one will, of course, ever know, for she did not tell. But we may guess it was because the man she did want to marry, Robert Dudley, Earl of Leicester, who would have married her, too, was already married. His wife then died under mysterious circumstances, and as a result the queen felt she could not go any further. But it is likely she never cared for anyone else so much again.

What started the First World War?
Principally the reckless ambition of the Kaiser, Wilhelm II of Germany. He ordered the invasion of Belgium, in August 1914, to get at France. His principal allies, the Austrians, had already come to blows with Serbia who were supported by the Russians. But it is possible that the war could have been confined to central Europe if Kaiser Bill, as he was known, had not had grandiose ideas that he could smash France and Great Britain.

Kaiser Wilhelm II

Where did the Pilgrim Fathers settle in America?
The Pilgrim Fathers, a group of English people who wanted to worship God in their own way and not according to the rigid rules of the national Church, left Plymouth in 1620 and sailed to America in the *Mayflower*. They arrived at Cape Cod in Massachusetts and set up a community there.

Which were the original thirteen states of America?
After about a century or so of British settlement in what is now the USA, there were thirteen distinct colonies: Connecticut, Delaware, Georgia, Massachusetts, Maryland, New Hampshire, New Jersey, New York, North Carolina, Pennsylvania, Rhode Island, South Carolina and Virginia.

What was the Korean War of 1950–1953 all about?
North Korea, influenced by Chinese Communists, went to war with South Korea, backed by the US Army, supported by contingents from armies of other UN countries. The result was a stalemate.

Why was Admiral Byng shot on the quarter deck of his own ship?
In 1756 he had failed to hold the island of Minorca during the Seven Years War (1756–1763). The British government, already under fire at home for various mismanagements, looked for a scapegoat and picked on Byng who was arrested, courtmartialled for cowardice and shot.

What was the Edict of Nantes, in 1598?
An agreement signed by Henry IV of France in which religious freedom was granted throughout the country to Protestants, in a country that was predominantly Catholic.

Who was Frederick the Great?
King of Prussia from 1740 to 1786, Frederick was a great military leader, winning several victories in the Seven Years War (1756–1763). As a domestic ruler he worked very hard, encouraging agricultural expansion, industry and building. He was also a patron of the arts, wrote music and corresponded with many leading authors of the day.

173

What is Salic Law?

It is an ancient law, observed in European countries, in which succession to titles, etc., cannot pass to females or through females. It was not always strictly adhered to, but it was sometimes quoted to justify a challenge to a succession in the royal line, such as the argument over whether Edward III of England should or should not have a rightful claim to the throne of France, in the 1330s.

What is International Law?

It is, of course, a vast subject, but basically it is the law or collection of laws accepted by most nations as binding in relations between one another.

Where is the International Court of Justice?

It is at The Hague, in Holland, and it is the principal agency of justice of the United Nations. Cases of individual grievance against nations or disputes between nations can be taken before this court for adjudication.

What is the Geneva Convention?

It is an agreement between nations which regulates the treatment of wounded prisoners in war, the protection of civilians in war-time and the treatment of prisoners-of-war during war. Several countries are party to the convention, but they sometimes break the rules.

What was the 18th Amendment in the US Constitution?

For thirteen years (1920–1933) there was total prohibition on the manufacture and sale of alcoholic liquor in the United States, enacted by what was the 18th Amendment to the Constitution. It was repealed in 1933 simply because it was so difficult to enforce.

174

What is Habeas Corpus?

It was an act passed in England in 1679 to prevent illegal and indefinite imprisonment. In effect it meant that if you were arrested for any alleged offence you had to be charged and the case heard within a specified time, as swiftly as possible. It is still in force in the UK but not every country in the world has such a law.

Why was there such a fuss over the Corn Laws in the early 19th century?

Corn Laws were heavy duties levied on corn which was imported into England. Landowners wanted to keep foreign corn out by imposing heavy taxes on imports so that the home-grown product could be kept at high level. The laws, however, brought great hardship to the poor because of artificially high prices and also damaged trade relations abroad, and a campaign arose to repeal them. They were repealed in 1846.

What was the Code Napoleon?

A Civil Code of law introduced by Napoleon in France in 1804 which reformed the French legal system. It was a kind of balance between the paternal authority of the old law and the more equalizing principles of the Revolution, but it gave emphasis to the protection of property and property rights.

What was the Peace Preservation Act of 1890 in Queensland?

This was a measure passed by the Queensland Parliament in Australia to enable the state government to deal effectively with strikes. There had been a wave of strikes in several states in the 1888–1890 period which threatened to cripple industry.

What is Legal Aid?

It is the provision of legal services free or at greatly reduced cost for persons who need advice or defence or assistance in obtaining justice in a court, but who cannot afford to pay the whole cost, or any costs. There are of course maximum incomes above which a person cannot receive such aid at all, depending on the circumstances.

What was the New Zealand Industrial Conciliation and Arbitration Act of 1894?

It was an attempt to get on to the statute books legislation that made negotiation between management and labour compulsory in cases of dispute. It laid down procedure for pursuing such negotiation from one stage to another if one failed.

When did Upper and Lower Canada become united by act of Parliament?

In 1840, following the Durham Report. One government was set up for the two parts, with one governor, one legislative council and one elected assembly.

What was the Five Mile Act of 1665?

During the Great Plague of London, English Church clergy had neglected their duties and the non-conformists had carried them out instead. The church, still very powerful, objected and got Parliament to prevent any non-conformist priests coming within five miles of any town (which had mayor and corporation) if they had ever preached there, unless they had to pass through to get somewhere else.

What is the Highway Code?

It is a code of behaviour for road users, motorists, cyclists and pedestrians alike. Although it is not a legal code, it nevertheless carries some weight with magistrates and judges if you are convicted of having committed some traffic offence which is a breach of this code as well as being a breach of the law.

What did the 1875 Public Health Act establish in the UK?

It compelled local authorities to collect rubbish on certain days regularly. Previously, rubbish had been left to pile up in the streets for long periods.

What is the Tennessee Valley Authority in the US?

Set up by Congress in 1933, it is an organization to develop the Tennessee River for a variety of activities, navigation, control of flooding, hydro-electric power generation and agricultural experiment.

What does extradition mean?

It means handing over to a state at the state's request a person or persons who have committed a crime, or may be accused of a crime, and who are sheltering in another state.

What was the 40th Clause of Magna Carta?

Translated, it reads 'To no one will we sell, to no one will we refuse or delay right or justice'. It was one of the few clauses which extended any rights to people beyond the rich and powerful.

What is bail?

It is money placed with the court or the police by a person charged with an offence, together with the promise of money by someone else on behalf of the person charged, which they undertake to forfeit if the charged person does not appear for trial at the appointed time. The idea was said to have been introduced in the time of Richard III (1483–1485).

What is the Court of Session?

It is the supreme civil court in Scotland, whose legal system is different from that of England and Wales. It was established in 1532, in the reign of James V.

Who was Lenin?

To many Russians he was the greatest figure in their whole history. Vladimir Ilyitch Ulyanov (1870–1924) devoted his younger life to agitating for major reforms in Russia, was imprisoned, exiled, forced to lie in hiding, and endured many other trials. Finally, in 1917, he returned to Russia through the cooperation of the German authorities who thought to weaken Russian czarist resistance to German arms by helping Lenin to bring about his great dream, a proletarian revolution in Russia. The provisional government which took over from the Czar was in turn overthrown by Lenin and his associates and from 1918 to his death, Lenin ruled that great land with a rod of iron, forcing into being an unparalleled programme of social reform and reorganization. Many millions were hurt or discomfited, many more lost liberty, but in the end he laid the foundations of what the Soviet state is today.

What was unusual about the Roman Emperor Diocletian?

Several things: to begin with he rose to the highest position in the empire although he was the son of a freed slave; he recognized that the empire was too big for one man to manage, and he split it into four parts under a board of four emperors, remaining the senior one himself. Then, after 21 years of sound and firm rule (284–305 AD), during which time he built up the army, he abdicated to grow cabbages for the rest of his days.

Who was Horatio Nelson?

Nelson was the greatest admiral in the history of the world. Born in 1758, he died in action at Trafalgar at the height of his fame, on 21st October 1805, soon after he heard that the combined French and Spanish fleets under Villeneuve had been decisively defeated by his squadrons. Nelson's first major action was as second-in-command at the battle of St Vincent, in 1797, where his exploits enabled Admiral Jervis to carry the day. In 1898, now in command himself, Nelson smashed the French fleet supporting Napoleon in his Egyptian campaign. Three years later he destroyed the Danish fleet off Copenhagen. These victories and that of Trafalgar once and for all proved Britain's absolute mastery of the sea and meant that Napoleon's chances of successfully invading Britain were reduced to nothing.

Who was 'Jacky' Fisher?

Admiral of the Fleet Lord Fisher of Kilverstone (1841–1920), the greatest admiral in Britain's navy since Nelson. After a long, distinguished and dramatic career studded with acts of bravery and cool resolution, Fisher became First Sea Lord in 1904 and held office for six years. In that time he revolutionized the British navy, brought it up to date and made it the finest fighting arm at sea anywhere in the world. He made enemies, he used favouritism if necessary to get the right man in the right job, he disregarded many feelings, but he won the acclaim of the navy – indeed of the nation – for getting the fleet fit to match and – as it turned out – beat the German High Seas Fleet during the First World War.

What did Lord Lister do for surgical patients throughout the world?

Lister enabled them to risk surgical operations for a variety of complaints and injuries with a far higher likelihood of surviving infection from germs in the wounds than before his great work on germ killing. By introducing the system of antisepsis in hospitals and surgeries he made one of the two major contributions to medical science of the 19th century (the other was the discovery of anaesthetics). Lister was

born in 1827, was made a baron in 1892
(the first medical man to be ennobled),
received countless other honours, and
died in 1912.

What were the principal aims of Oliver Cromwell as Lord Protector?

Cromwell, the foremost general of the
Parliamentarian army that defeated the
king, Charles I, in the Civil War (1642–
1647), was gradually raised to the
supreme position of state in England,
Scotland and Ireland when following the
execution of Charles, in 1649, there was
no proper government of the country. He
was appointed Lord Protector in 1653
and ruled like a king for the next five
years. He aimed to reform taxation, have
the laws of the country examined and
tidied up, to grant religious freedom
(except to Catholics) and to make the
country so strong that European
countries would fear it, and seek
alliance with him. To a large extent he
was successful, but in many of his ideas
he was generations ahead of his time.
He died on 3rd September 1658.

Who was Britain's greatest military commander of all?

Without much question among
historians, it was John Churchill, first
Duke of Marlborough (1650–1722). This
splendid soldier and statesman
dominated British politics and military
affairs from the time of William III to
about 1710. In those years he became a
leading counsellor to William, was
tempted to betray him and spent some
time in the Tower, was restored to
position and later created commander of
the allied armies against France in the
War of the Spanish Succession (1701–
1713). In this he fought and won four
glorious victories, Blenheim, Ramillies,
Oudenarde and Malplaquet. He was later
dismissed for helping himself to funds
passing through his hands and for other
questionable acts, but his fame as a
military genius remained undimmed.

Who was the Mahatma Gandhi?

Mohandas Karamchand Gandhi (1869–
1948) was an Indian political and
religious leader who studied law in
London and spent some time in South
Africa. In 1915 he returned to India to
lead the movement for home rule,
insisting upon a policy of non-violence.
His methods were passive resistance
(that is, lying down on railway tracks
and not moving, fasting almost until
death, and generally refusing to
cooperate with the British authorities).
In the negotiations which finally
resulted in partition of India and home
rule, he played a crucial if background
part. His title, the Mahatma, means
Great Soul, and he was revered
throughout India. This, however, did not
stop one extreme Hindu fanatic from
assassinating him, in 1948.

Little Quiz 27

Where are the following:

1. Medicine Hat
2. St Asaph
3. Poitiers
4. Dnepropetrovsk
5. Haarlem
6. Appomattox
7. Calgary
8. San Sebastian
9. Dresden
10. Llangefni
11. Phoenix
12. Calgoorlie
13. Worms
14. Brindisi
15. Limerick
16. Salt Lake City
17. Carlisle
18. Brno
19. Harlem
20. Callao

Why was the Crippen case so sensational?

Several reasons. Hawley Harvey Crippen, an American born doctor who went to England to work, murdered his wife in 1910 and buried those parts of her body he had cut up but failed to burn successfully. He tried to escape justice with his mistress, Ethel le Neve, by taking ship back to America. A wireless message from London to the ship's captain, however, enabled Crippen to be arrested, taken back to England, tried and executed. It was the first time wireless had been used in a criminal arrest.

What were the Nuremberg Trials of 1945–1946?

The surviving leaders of the German government and armed services, which had caused the Second World War – and lost it – were tried for various crimes against humanity and other war crimes. Several were convicted and hanged. It was the first time a defeated nation's leaders had been tried by the victors.

Who were Sacco and Vanzetti?

They were Italian immigrants in the US who were tried and sentenced to death for murder, in the years 1920–1927. There was a great deal of protest about the case because the two men held anarchist opinions and this was said to have prejudiced the courts against them.

What happened to Oscar Slater?

He was a German Jew who lived in Glasgow, Scotland. He was convicted of murdering a woman on the evidence of three witnesses who picked him out in an identity parade. He was sentenced to death in 1909 but the sentence was commuted to life imprisonment. Slater spent nineteen years in jail, but many influential people did not like the whole proceedings, campaigned to get the case

178

looked into again, and in 1928 he was released and awarded compensation of £6000.

Who was Charlie Peace?

A British criminal who murdered a policeman in Manchester in 1876 while committing robbery. Another man was sentenced to death for the crime but reprieved. Peace escaped and lived undetected for two years. Then he killed someone else, carried out more burglaries, was caught, confessed to the earlier murder as well and was tried and hanged, 1879.

Why did Brutus and his colleagues murder Julius Caesar in 44 BC?

Because they wanted the old Roman Republic to continue, whereas Caesar saw that it had to end and a new form of imperial administration be created to deal with the problems of the time. All the murderers, some sixty of them, were motivated by envy, but Brutus may have been without that. Caesar was killed, but his new ideas survived and were the basis of the imperial system of Augustus.

Why was the Dreyfus Case so sensational?

Alfred Dreyfus, a Jewish-French soldier, was accused of stealing secrets and passing them to the Germans, in 1894. He was court-martialled and sentenced to imprisonment on Devil's Island. Two years later the real culprit, Major Esterhazy, confessed to the crime, but the French Army Command suppressed the truth, forging documents to prove their point. They were motivated by anti-Jewish feelings, and this split French opinion in two. Championed by Clemenceau and Zola and other well-known Frenchmen, Dreyfus eventually had a new trial and was pardoned. But this was not enough, he wanted exoneration. In 1906 the Court of Appeal declared him innocent and re-instated him in the army.

What happened to the baby son of Colonel Lindbergh?

Colonel Charles Lindbergh achieved world fame in 1927 when he flew solo across the Atlantic in an aeroplane, the first such flight. In 1932 his first son, still a baby, was kidnapped and then murdered. It took four years to find the murderer, try him and bring about his execution.

Who was John Reginald Halliday Christie?

He was a Yorkshire-born Englishman who murdered his wife and five other women in London. He concealed their bodies, some in his house behind the wall-paper. He confessed to a crime for which his one-time lodger, Timothy Evans, had been hanged. This helped to bring about the abolition of the death penalty in Britain. Christie was hanged in 1953.

What were the acid bath murders?

John George Haigh, an English company director, murdered at least one woman and then tried to get rid of the body by placing it in a bath of acid. He was detected, however, when a set of dentures which resisted the acid were subsequently found and were proved to belong to the dead woman. The trial was sensational in many ways, not least for the manner in which a leading psychiatrist giving evidence for Haigh was severely mauled in the witness box.

Who was Jack the Ripper?

Nobody knows to this day. It is the name given to the unidentified murderer of several women in East London in 1888, all of whom were mutilated in much the same manner, hence the nickname of the murderer. Several books have been written with many intriguing theories.

Why was Archbishop Becket murdered?

Becket had been Henry II's Chancellor and then Archbishop of Canterbury. He clashed with the king over whether the state should punish people in the church if they were found guilty of crimes. The king lost his temper and complained that none of his friends would get rid of Becket who was troubling him. But at the end of December 1170, four knights took him seriously and went to Canterbury where they cut Becket down.

Who was Francois Ravaillac?

He was the son of poor parents near Angoulême in France, who became a monk, and who, in 1610, murdered Henry IV, king of France. This was a senseless crime, for Henry was acknowledged to have been the best king France had had for centuries. There is a suggestion that it was planned by extreme Catholics who objected to the king's tolerance towards Protestants.

What was the Great Train Robbery in Britain of 1963?

This was when a gang of criminals stopped a mail train and stole about £3,000,000 of used banknotes. Up to then it was the biggest raid of its kind in the UK. Many of the gang were rounded up and sentenced to long terms of imprisonment. One or two escaped but were captured later. One is still free.

Who was the executioner of Charles I of England, Scotland and Ireland?

There has long been doubt about the person who actually wielded the axe that removed the king's head in 1649 at Whitehall in London, but it is almost certain it was Richard Brandon, a son of the London hangman Gregory Brandon.

179

How long have people worn jewellery of some kind?

Ever since they were civilized, possibly longer. They wore jewellery long before they wore costume, and necklaces, bracelets, rings and anklets of the greatest antiquity have been found in many parts of the world.

A Greek female bust found in Spain. It dates from the beginning of the 4th century BC and shows Phoenician influence in the jewellery.

Which are the two most precious gem stones, apart from diamond?

Emerald and ruby.

Where do emerald and ruby come from?

Emerald, a bright green translucent – or sometimes transparent – stone comes from South America, and true rubies are mainly found in Burma. Rubies are rich red in colour.

What is the Koh-i-Noor diamond?

Koh-i-Noor means 'Mountain of Light' and it is the name of a big diamond that is one of the British Crown Jewels. It was given to Queen Victoria by the East India Company.

What is the Cullinan diamond?

This, the largest diamond in the world, was discovered in the diamond mine in South Africa that belonged to Sir Thomas Cullinan (1862–1936). When found it was 12 by 6 by 5 cm (5 by 2½ by 2 ins) in size, and it was cut down so that a stone could be inset in the King of Great Britain's sceptre and another in his crown, both part of the British Crown Jewels. Cullinan gave it to Edward VII.

What is Hatton Garden in London famous for?

It is a street near the City of London in which nearly every building is concerned in some way with diamonds and jewellery, selling, exchanging, repairing, even manufacturing.

What is cornelian?

It is a red-brown translucent stone used in making jewellery. It is not particularly valuable now, but the Romans thought quite highly of it. It is also called carnelian.

What is a paste jewel stone?

It is a hard, shining substance made from glass and lead with which you can make jewel stones to look like real ones, to the untrained eye.

Why is diamond so good for cutting glass?
Because it is one of the hardest substances you can get, and this enables glass to be cut or carved without breaking it. Of course occasionally the glass will break but an expert seldom does this.

What is a tiara?
It is a coronet of precious metal and precious stones and is generally worn by women. Cheaper varieties are also made.

When did rings start to be worn as a symbol of fidelity?
Before Roman times, but the Romans were the first to introduce wedding rings. These were taken up by the early Christian Church.

Why does a bishop wear a ring?
It is a symbol of his 'betrothal' to the Church.

When did wedding rings begin to be worn on the left hand?
Sometime in the 18th century.

What is a carat?
It is an international measure of weight relevant to gems. It is also a measure of purity of gold. Pure gold is said to be 24-carat. Gold is so scarce now and so expensive that usually when you buy a new gold ring it may only be made of nine-carat gold, the remainder being some alloy.

What is a signet ring?
A ring of metal with a flat part in which is carved either your initials or your family crest (if you have one). Alternatively, it may be a ring with a stone in which the crest is carved. These rings used to be employed to press into sealing wax to seal an envelope or otherwise indicate that a document has been 'signed', but this practice is dying out although the rings themselves are as popular as ever.

What sort of stones would be used for such rings?
Chiefly bloodstone, sardonyx, and possibly cornelian.

What is a torque?
A necklace of twisted metal, generally of gold or silver, and favoured by the early Celtic peoples in Europe and Britain.

How long have earrings been worn?
Among African, Asian and Polynesian peoples, probably as long as they have been in existence. They have been worn in Europe among some earlier civilizations, and the Romans wore them, too. Then they seem to have gone out of fashion.

When did earrings come back into fashion?
In Europe it is difficult to say. Probably in the late Middle Ages they became popular again – among both men and women.

What is the story about bracelets?
A long one, but briefly, the Romans gave bracelets as presents. Anglo-Saxon warriors wore large ones on their wrists for protection and they were sometimes awarded to heroes in battle by chiefs afterwards.

Little Quiz 28

Which motorcycle manufacturers made these models?

1. Black Shadow
2. KTT
3. Gold Star Twin
4. Square Four
5. Dominator

Which was the first university in the world?

Probably the college founded in Alexandria in the time of Alexander the Great, king of Macedon (336–323 BC), and ruler of much of the then known world.

What is the oldest university in Europe?

Salerno, in Italy, founded in the 9th century AD. The next oldest is Bologna (also in Italy), established in the 11th century.

Which are the four oldest universities in the United States?

Harvard (1636), William & Mary (1693), Yale (1701) and Princeton (1746). Interestingly, Harvard was founded at a place called New Town, in Massachusetts, which was subsequently re-named Cambridge!

What is a Comprehensive School in Britain?

One which is meant to cater for all children below university level, from all families in a given area. The idea was born out of the 1944 Education Act and most state schools in Britain are now comprehensive.

Why were Grammar Schools so called?

As far back as Richard II's reign (1377–1399) the phrase was used to describe a school where boys were taught Latin grammar, among other subjects. It was essential to know Latin extremely well to get into any of the university colleges. Indeed, Latin was obligatory in some right up to the present decade.

Who was Dr Arnold?

Dr Thomas Arnold (1795–1842) was headmaster of Rugby School in Warwickshire, England, from 1828 to his death. He introduced the system of

prefects, organized school games (to keep boys occupied so that they would not divert energies into bullying others or breaking the rules) and moulded the school regimen round the Christian faith.

What were the hedge schools?

Part of the Protestant laws of repression against Catholics in Ireland in the 17th and 18th centuries were directed against education for Catholics in any form whatever. But some brave catholic priests used to teach pupils in small classes hiding in ditches and under hedges in the fields. These were called 'hedge schools'.

What is co-education?

It is the word to describe learning at school in which the classes are mixed, boys and girls. Some schools also have boys and girls living in the buildings, in dormitories for each sex. The idea is very good for it teaches one to understand the opposite sex from an early age.

Who was A. S. Neill?

He was a British educationist who founded a very progressive school at Summerhill, near Leiston in Suffolk in England. He believed in giving children the maximum scope for individual development at an early age and he had few rules for the children.

What's a Polytechnic?

It is an educational institution that gives you degree courses or similar courses either as a full-time or as a part-time student.

What is to matriculate?

It is to get your name entered in the roll of students of a college, and in many instances this can only be done by special examination.

What does Froebel trained mean?

It refers to a teacher who has been trained in methods of teaching devised by Friedrich August Wilhelm Froebel (1782–1852), a German education expert who believed in the advantages of teaching through play as well as through study. Children's creative instincts should be encouraged through games. He opened the first kindergarten in 1837.

What is 'to major' in American education?

It is to study a subject to a certain level and be considered proficient in it. The subject has to be one of a specified list.

Who founded Eton College?

Henry VI (1422–1461) king of England, in about 1440. It is the most famous school in the world.

What does it mean if you are given a Latin 'unseen' to translate?

It generally means, in an examination, that you are given a paragraph or two from a Latin author to translate from scratch. You are not allowed to use a dictionary or grammar and you have to make the best sense of it you can.

What is 'dictée' in French lessons?

The French master first reads a passage of French to you, clearly enunciating the words. Then he reads it again, more slowly, phrase by phrase, and as he does you have to write down what he is reading. Then he reads it through once more at normal speed, for you to check if you've got it all right – or as near right as you can!

Who was Johann Pestalozzi?

He was a Swiss teacher (1746–1827) who changed the emphasis from memorizing and discipline to understanding the child and relating learning to the child's personal experience.

Little Quiz 29

What is the collective noun for a group of:

1. deer
2. wolves
3. whales
4. ants
5. oxen
6. leopards
7. bears
8. moles
9. kangaroos
10. hounds

What is the name for a group of the following birds:

11. hawks
12. ducks
13. peacocks
14. pheasants
15. swallows
16. goldfinches
17. gulls
18. geese
19. herons
20. larks

What day were or are the following:

21. St Cecilia's Day
22. Hallowe'en
23. Commonwealth Day
24. Noel
25. Victory in Europe (1945)
26. Lammas Day
27. Guy Fawkes Day
28. Hogmanay
29. St David's Day
30. Shakespeare's Birthday

What companies were the original makers of the following cars?

31. Javelin
32. Hornet
33. Dauphine
34. 'Beetle'
35. Silver Ghost
36. Super Snipe
37. Kestrel
38. SS 100
39. Aprilia

Did the Vikings get to America before Columbus?

Yes, Leif Ericsson, a Viking captain, set out westwards from Greenland in about 1000 AD and eventually landed at what we now know as Labrador. This was nearly 500 years before Columbus reached the West Indies.

What did the Greek sailor Pytheas discover in the 3rd century BC?

Pytheas arrived in Britain, probably by accident, and he visited many parts of the island.

What was Marco Polo famous for?

Marco Polo was a Venetian merchant who travelled across Asia with his father and eventually reached Peking, in the time of the great ruler, Khubilai Khan (1259–1294). The Polos stayed there for several years.

Why did Marco Polo stay so long in China?

Because soon after he reached the court of Khubilai Khan he was given a job in the Chinese government service and he seemed to have enjoyed it. He returned to Europe in the 1290s and later on wrote an account of his travels. This told Europeans more than they had ever heard about the Chinese.

Who was the first captain to get round the Cape of Good Hope?

Bartholomew Diaz, who rounded it in 1488. He was a Portuguese sea-captain who later accompanied Cabral on the expedition which was to discover Brazil in 1500. On that voyage Diaz perished in a storm.

Who was Henry the Navigator?

He was Prince Henry, son of King John I of Portugal, and he set up a place of study of navigation and allied matters at Sagres. There he encouraged navigators

184

to take ships to sea to discover new places in the Atlantic and to explore down the coast of Africa. Henry died in 1460, by which time Portuguese ships had reached as far as Sierra Leone.

What was Vasco da Gama's great achievement?

Vasco da Gama was the splendid Portuguese captain who discovered the sea route from Europe to India via the Cape of Good Hope, in the years 1497–1499.

What were the Lusiads?

The name of a long and stirring poem by Portugal's most famous poet, Luis de Camoens (1524–1580), in which he described the historic voyage of Vasco da Gama.

Who were John and Sebastian Cabot?

A Genoese father-and-son team of navigators who persuaded Henry VII of England to support a voyage from Bristol westwards towards North America. They set out in 1497 and discovered Cape Breton Island and Newfoundland.

Who was the first to sail round the world?

Actually, it was some of the crew of one of the ships led by Ferdinand Magellan, the Portuguese navigator, working for Spain. Magellan took the ships round Cape Horn (at the bottom of South America) and across the Pacific as far as the Philippine islands. There he was killed in a skirmish but some of his crew managed to return to Spain in one of his ships.

Who was the first captain to take a ship right round the world?

Sir Francis Drake (1540–1596) set out from Plymouth in *The Pelican* and four other ships in 1577. After a stormy rounding of Cape Horn, in which he renamed the *Pelican* and called it *The Golden Hind*, Drake crossed the Pacific, skirmishing with a few Spanish treasure ships on the way, rounded the Cape of Good Hope, came up the Atlantic and reached Plymouth again in 1580.

Where did Columbus think he had landed in October 1492?

Christopher Columbus (1451–1506) thought he had reached Cathay, as China was called in those days, which is what he was looking for. In fact, he discovered the West Indies. He is credited with discovering America for he did come home to Spain to tell everyone what he found.

What islands did Columbus discover on his first two voyages?

San Salvador (now Watling Island), the first place he reached, the Bahamas, Cuba, Haiti, Guadeloupe, Montserrat, Antigua, Puerto Rico and Jamaica. On his third voyage in 1498 Columbus touched South America.

What were the names of Columbus's ships on his first voyage?

They were the *Santa Maria*, the *Pinta* and the *Niña*.

Which country was Columbus working for?

He was working for Spain. He was Italian (Genoese) by birth and had tried unsuccessfully to interest Portugal in sponsoring him. It took some time to get the Spanish king to take him seriously, when he put forward his plan to find the westward sea route to China.

When was Australia discovered?

In 1606, by the Dutch navigator William Janszoon, though it is not likely that he realized that he had found a separate continent. He was followed by other Dutch captains, and in 1642 Abel Tasman found the island south of Australia, named after him (Tasmania), and also New Zealand.

Who discovered Canada?

Jacques Cartier (1491–1557), a French navigator who in 1536 sailed up the great St Lawrence River and gave the name Montreal (Mount Royal) to the small Indian village of Hochelaga.

What happened to Henry Hudson in Canada in 1611?

Hudson, an English explorer, had discovered the Hudson River in 1609. Two years later, on a second voyage to Canada, some of his crew mutinied and cast him adrift in an open boat. He was never seen again.

When were Captain Cook's three famous voyages?

1768–1771, when he sailed round the world, charted New Zealand and surveyed the east coast of Australia, giving names to Botany Bay and New South Wales; 1772, when he set out to find the southern continent and discovered Easter Island, Norfolk Island and others; and 1776, when he discovered Hawaii.

Where was Captain Cook killed?

In 1779, after sailing up the American coast to survey the Bering Strait in unsuccessful search of a passage to the Atlantic, he was killed on his return to the Hawaiian islands by natives who misunderstood his motives.

Why was 1797 an important year in the story of Africa?

It was when Mungo Park, the Scottish navigator, explored the course of the Niger River. In 1799 he wrote a book 'Travels in the Interior of Africa' which created a sensation.

How does a fish breathe?
Well, a fish doesn't breathe like a mammal. But it does breathe through its gills. It takes in water through its mouth, which runs down the throat and over the gills and out again through slits behind the gill covers. This water has the oxygen the fish needs and which it extracts as it goes through.

How does a snake move along?
On the underneath of a snake are rows of broad scales. These are moved forwards so that the lower edge of every scale can push downwards against the ground or rocks or whatever surface the snake is on. As the snake pushes the scales down, he hoists his body along.

What is a sponge?
A natural sponge is the elastic skeleton of a type of animal which lies in the sea. This animal has no legs or fins or even stomach and it doesn't move. It is almost like a plant.

Why doesn't a fly fall when it walks along the ceiling?
Because it has pads on its feet which 'stick' to the surface, loosen and then 'stick' down again as it moves along. Possibly the pads create suction, or they may produce a minute amount of quick-sticking glue.

Why does a snake shed its skin?
Because as it grows up its skin gets too tight. A new skin grows under the old one and when it is ready the snaks pulls the older one away from its head by rubbing it against a stone or other hard surface. Then it glides out of the sheath and leaves it on the ground.

Why can't a penguin fly?
Because over many centuries it has changed from a flying bird into one that swims about using two limbs as paddles.

A penguin stands upright like a human being and is no longer shaped for flight, even if its wings were big enough.

What is a crustacean?
This is the name for a variety of animals without backbones, which have instead an articulated shell covering their body. They live on the whole in or near water, though there are some which inhabit dry land. The best known crustaceans are crabs, lobsters, prawns. One dry land crustacean is a woodlouse.

What is a Galapagos tortoise?
A tortoise that lives on the Galapagos Islands in the Pacific. It moves very slowly indeed, chiefly because its shell weighs more than the rest of its body. A big Galapagos tortoise can weigh two tons or more.

Why is the stick insect so-called?
Because it disguises itself as a twig and cannot easily be seen. It also moves very slowly indeed, rather jerkily. It can on the other hand remain absolutely motionless for hours. An Australian Giant Stick Insect can be as much as 30 cms (12 ins) long.

Can a frog fly?
In Borneo there is a frog that can. It lives in trees, has long toes with wide webs between them and it can leap from one tree to another using its feet as wings of a glider. It can speed up by flapping its feet rapidly.

Whoever heard of a flying snake?
But there is one, in Asia. It glides through the air from tree to ground, or tree to tree. It does this by breathing out all the air and making itself flat.

Is there an animal called a sloth?
Yes, it is a mammal from central and South America that hangs upside down

on trees, asleep most of the day, and moves very slowly when so inclined.

How fast does a snail move?
Well, a snail moves along on average at 8 cms (3 ins) a minute, in other words, it could do a kilometre in 208 hours or 8 days or a mile in 372 hours or 11 days.

Is there a slow lizard in the forest?
The Tuatara lizard, found in the islands around New Zealand, is extremely slow-moving. It can't run or even jump, it crawls. It is very lazy in its habits, too lazy even to build a nest for itself, preferring to occupy one built by some other animal.

Is there a kind of squirrel that can fly?
There are several, which have flaps of skin along the sides of their body. These form 'wings' and enable them to glide.

What is a Flying Fox?
A kind of bat that looks a bit like a winged fox. It lives on fruit, especially bananas, which it carries in its mouth. It lives in the tropics.

What is the principal difference between a spider and an insect?
A spider has eight legs and insects have six legs. And spiders usually eat insects.

What is a 'Softly, Softly'?
A potto, from West Africa, which creeps about at night in search of food. During the day it sleeps curled up in a ball, in trees or shrubs. A potto is about the size of a squirrel.

Why do birds sing?
It is their way of communicating with each other. A bird may 'sing' to tell other birds to keep out of his part of the woods or fields, or to tell them he has found a new source of food and wants them to come along and share it. If it is a male bird, he may just be trying to attract a female bird.

How do worms burrow through the earth?
Worms actually eat their way through earth, which contains many of the things they need. As a worm does so it digs a tunnel for a home. When the worm is full, it comes to the surface and deposits the earth and waste matter.

Which is the fastest running of all animals?
The fastest animal is the cheetah, a type of leopard. It can run at over 110 kms (70 miles) an hour. A cheetah is one of the cat family of animals, stands about 60 cms high and lives in Africa and South West Asia.

The cheetah, the North African leopard

187

What is a balance of power?

In world politics, it means building an alliance of nations to equal as closely as possible the strength of another group of nations who are considered to be following an aggressive foreign policy. It was a prime factor in British foreign policy in the past to throw in her weight on the side of a weaker alliance of European powers if it were in any way threatened by a more powerful one.

Have the British ever had a plebiscite?

Once, in 1975, when the nation went to vote in the referendum as to whether the country should stay in the Common Market or not. A plebiscite is a referendum, and is a direct vote of an electorate on one question, and not, as at a general election, on a range of issues.

What is absolute monarchy?

A form of government of a country where full power is in the hands of one person, usually a hereditary king or emperor. There are numerous examples in history, though only a few in the present century.

What, then, is constitutional monarchy?

This is a system where a country has a monarchy but the monarch's powers are strictly limited by law.

What is an anarchist?

Most people would define an anarchist as a person who is lawless, and believes in no form of government at all. True anarchists, however, believe in the minimum amount of government and that that government should be truly representative of the people.

Why is the Civil Service called Civil?

Simply to differentiate it from military, naval – and in recent years – air services.

Does aristocracy really work out as government by the best people?

It may have done once in classical Greece, but today the term means a class who expect privileges as their birthright but who in fact find that these privileges are on the whole no longer forthcoming.

Why do so many people in the Western world fear communism?

Possibly because they think that they stand to lose a lot if they were to live under it. Communism works towards the creation of a society that has no private ownership of land, industries, banks and commercial enterprises. Everyone receives what he needs and is supposed to put in the best work possible.

Is fascism the opposite of communism?

Well, fascists think it is. But as it worked out under Mussolini in Italy it meant the sacrifice of the individual need to the interests of the state. Its aims were a strict control of all aspects of national life for the good of the state, and in that respect it was not unlike communism.

What is imperialism?

In the 19th century many Western countries grew rich and powerful by exploiting the resources of weaker, less developed nations.

What is the bourgeoisie?

The word is French and means 'citizen'- or 'middle-class'. It is used in a derisive sense by communists to mean people who have their own business.

What is the difference between the democracy of ancient Greece and today?

Among the Greeks, in theory at least, all adult people in the state could meet regularly in a public place and discuss and vote on issues affecting them and the running of the country. Today, the people of a democracy elect representatives to discuss the issues of the day and to vote on their behalf. These representatives normally meet in a central place, sometimes called the parliament building.

What is nationalism?

It is really the determination of a people to assert their national identity. It is often a movement inside a country where there is more than one racial group. In the United Kingdom, for example, both Welsh and Scots, two separate peoples inside the kingdom and distinct from the third, the English, are increasingly asserting their national identities.

Is nationalism anything to do with National Socialism?

No. National Socialism was championed though not invented by Adolf Hitler (1889–1945), the Austrian born leader of the German people from 1933 to 1945. It was a doctrine which stood for the subordination of the individual existence to the will of the state. At first it had socialist associations, but these were submerged when the National Socialists found they had to rely on non-Socialists' capital to keep the movement going.

What is capitalism?

It is an economic system which operates by the private control of production and distribution of goods and services. It has also come to have political associations. Conservatives, for example, generally seem to support the continuation of this system, whilst socialists want to see it ended.

What is a republic?

It is a country which has no king, emperor or any other ruler whose position is hereditary. The head of state is one person elected for a fixed term of office. Generally, though not always, the head is called a president.

Why are Conservatives called Tories in Britain?

Tory comes from the Irish word for robber. The name was first used in the reign of Charles II for the party which opposed the exclusion of James, Duke of York, as his heir on the grounds that he was a Roman Catholic. It then came to mean the party that stood for the squire, the high-church vicar, the reactionary landowner and the nobility.

What is a social democrat?

He is a politician who seeks to bring about a socialist (or communist) society by proper democratic means, and not by violence or intimidation.

What is the Iron Curtain?

A somewhat out-dated phrase now, it means the theoretical boundary between the countries of the West and the East in Europe. The most famous use of the phrase was in a speech made in Fulton, Missouri in 1946 by Winston Churchill.

What is the difference between Entente and Detente?

Entente is the existence of friendly relations between certain countries whilst Detente means active attempts to ease strained relations between countries.

What is a dictatorship?

It is rule by one person who makes all decisions about the running of the state. He may listen to the opinions of such people as he sees fit to have round him as advisers, but he decides for himself and it is presumed will take the responsibility for such decisions.

189

What was a lettre de cachet?
Strictly speaking, it is the French for a sealed or secret letter. It was a private document issued by the king which ordered the arrest and imprisonment of a subject, without trial. It was a weapon used by the kings from the 1560s right up to the Revolution in 1789.

What was l'ancien régime?
It means 'the old order of things' and it is a phrase to describe the social and political organization of France before the 1789 Revolution which uprooted French society and set out to construct a new order.

What is a cause célèbre?
It means a famous lawsuit or trial. Although the phrase is French it is used widely in English parlance to refer to any case in court that attracts a great deal of publicity, preferably one that has a taint of scandal about it.

What do we mean by esprit de corps?
The feeling of purpose that unites a disciplined group of people and flavours it with loyalty and pride. It was much more apposite in the days when conceptions of public school spirit, army regiment honour and those kinds of feelings held sway.

When would you be likely to have a 'tête-à-tête'?
Any time you wanted a private chat with a friend or with someone whom you wished to advise confidentially. It comes from the French meaning 'head-to-head'.

Would you feel insulted if someone said you were 'nouveau riche'?
Well, you might be, because it is a suggestion that your family were upstarts, that is, they came from humble origins and have risen to wealthy heights. There is in fact nothing wrong

190

in this and the term is really out of date.

What does 'vis-à-vis' mean?
It's a French phrase meaning opposite, or with respect to, or compared with.

What do we mean when we say 'noblesse oblige'?
It means that rank or position imposes obligations or duties of behaviour on the part of the holder.

When French troops used to run off the field of battle crying out 'Sauve qui peut', what did they mean?
They meant, Save himself who can, which is another way of crying out 'Every man for himself'. The advice may not always have been very chivalrous, but on the whole it was sensible.

If you write under a nom de plume, what does it mean?
It means you are using a name other than your own. This may be for a variety of reasons.

What's a faux pas?
Technically a false step, but it means to make a tactless remark or a slip in behaviour. It could be a *faux pas* to ask someone how their father is when he's just gone to prison and you ought to have known about it.

How do you commit lèse majeste?
It's the French term for high treason. But it means a little more, namely, offending the dignity of the sovereign or his (or her) representative.

What is a 'coup d'état'?
It is an attempt to overthrow a government suddenly, usually by violent means, but sometimes without bloodshed. Several well-known 20th-century figures came to power as a result of a *coup d'etat*, including General

Neguib in Egypt, Field Marshal Amin in Uganda.

Whose motto is 'Ich Dien'?
The Prince of Wales, eldest son of the reigning monarch of Great Britain. It means 'I serve', in German.

Which order of knighthood carries the motto 'Honi soit qui mal y pense'?
The Order of the Garter, founded by Edward III of England in 1348. It means 'Evil be to him that evil thinks'.

What's a fait accompli?
Something that has already been done, and, generally, you can't undo it. Nor is there much point in arguing about it!

Why do some people say 'Cherchez la femme!' when discussing a mystery?
Generally, because they consider that there is a woman's hand at the bottom of the mystery. They might say this when a man does something inexplicable.

What does 'chacun à son gout' mean?
It means every person to his own taste. The phrase is used by someone who disapproves of the preferences of another, but who perhaps doesn't want to be too outspoken in his disapproval.

Where would you be staying if you were in a 'pied à terre'?
You would be in a house or flat in a town or district in which you did not normally live, but needed to go there only occasionally.

What does 'caput' in German mean?
It's a word meaning absolutely done for. It is very final, and is perhaps more meaningful than the English 'finished'.

What does 'che sara sara' mean?
It's the Italian for 'what will be will be', made popular by a song.

Little Quiz 30
What nationality were or are these authors?
1. Joseph Conrad
2. Mark Twain
3. Thomas Mann
4. Emile Zola
5. James Baldwin
6. Leo Tolstoy
7. Oscar Wilde
8. James Joyce
9. V. S. Naipaul
10. Vincent Cronin
11. John Dos Passos

Who wrote these books?
12. The Three Musketeers
13. Vanity Fair
14. The Caine Mutiny
15. Nineteen Eighty-Four
16. Goodbye, Mr Chips
17. The Lost World
18. Forever Amber
19. The Thirty Nine Steps
20. Gone With The Wind
21. The Tree of Man
22. Moby Dick
23. Dr Zhivago
24. War and Peace
25. Bel-Ami
26. Cry, the Beloved Country
27. The Code of the Woosters
28. Kim
29. Savrola
30. Coningsby
31. Crime and Punishment

What is the country or origin of these stars?
32. Ingrid Bergman
33. Sophia Loren
34. Helmut Berger
35. Conrad Veidt
36. Katina Paxinou
37. Leslie Howard
38. Omar Sharif
39. Richard Burton
40. Richard Harris
41. John Gielgud

Who was T'ang the Successful?
T'ang was ruler of China in the 18th century BC. He founded the Shang dynasty, which lasted for 600 years or so. He was a practical soldier-statesman who gave the Chinese sound government. encouraged trade and took an interest in farming.

Where did Abraham come from?
Abraham, the father of the Hebrew people, was a Semite from Mesopotamia, that is, the land between the Tigris and the Euphrates. He may have come from Ur. He left Mesopotamia with a group of farmer friends and their families and settled in Palestine in about 2000 BC.

Where was Nineveh?
Nineveh was a splendid city built on the Tigris as the new capital of the Assyrian Empire by Sennacherib, in about 750 BC. Its ruins were discovered by Henry Layard in the mid 19th century AD.

Who was Ashurbanipal?
He was king of Assyria from about 670 to about 625 BC. In that time Assyria stretched from Turkey to Persia. Ashurbanipal was not only a military leader. He was also interested in learning, and he built up a library of clay tablets on which were written books and letters.

Who founded the ancient Persian empire?
This was founded by Cyrus the Great, king of Persia from about 550 to about 530 BC. By the time of his death, in a military campaign, he was master of nearly the whole Middle East. His lands almost bordered on India.

What happened to Cambyses, Cyrus' son?
Cambyses succeeded to Cyrus' throne,

but he was a highly-strung man with a quick temper. He wished to consolidate his father's work but was not able to get all his generals and officers to cooperate. In a fit of depression he committed suicide, in about 524 BC.

Who was the King of Kings?
This was the title, self-bestowed, of Darius, king of Persia, who followed Cambyses. Darius was quite determined to make his power felt throughout his great empire. He did this by establishing complicated rituals for those attending him. He was always to be higher than his people, which meant he sat on a throne high above the ground. When he went out into the sun, servants had to shade him with umbrellas.

What was the King's Highway?
Part of Darius' methods of controlling his empire was to build a huge road right across his domains. It ran from Ephesus in western Asia Minor to Susa, east of the Tigris, about 2575 kms (1600 miles) long. Riders could cover the distance in about a week, but they had to change horses.

How did Xerxes' army cross the Hellespont?
The Hellespont is a narrow stretch of water which separates European and Asian Turkey. Xerxes, who was Darius' son, ruled Persia from 486 to 465 BC, and he spent much of his time doing battle with his father's enemies, the Greeks. He invaded Europe by lining up a fleet of ships, side by side across the Hellespont, and marching his army across the resulting bridge.

Who won the battle of Marathon?
The Greeks beat the Persians at Marathon, not far from Athens, in 490 BC. It was a turning point in the war in which Persia tried to add Greece to its

empire. The Greeks had a far smaller army but triumphed through greater courage and superior generalship.

What was the caste system in India?
After the collapse of their fine Indus valley civilization, the Indian peoples split up into four castes, or divisions. These were the Brahmans (priests and educated men), Kshatriyas (military officers), Vaisyas (merchants and craftsmen) and the Sudra (labourers and servants). The process was extremely gradual.

What were the Silk Routes from China?
For centuries the secret of silk manufacture was jealously kept by the Chinese. Other people wanting silk had to buy rolls of it from traders who journeyed from and to China along special routes across Asia, some of them in caravan convoys.

How did the Chinese write down their language?
They developed a pictorial script of characters which represented complete words rather than individual letters. The first characters appeared probably as long ago as 2500 BC and the present Chinese language is based upon this extremely ancient script.

Why did Huang Ti burn 'The Books'?
Huang-Ti, the first Ch'in emperor (c.275–210 BC), objected to the teachings of Confucius and his followers, because he thought they undermined his ideas of government. So he ordered all Confucius' works and those of many other scholars to be burnt. Copies did survive, however, and Huang-Ti was not able to prevent everyone reading them.

Who built the Great Wall of China?
This was erected by Huang-Ti in the later years of his reign. It is over 2400 kms (1490 miles) long and is one of the most astonishing engineering feats of all history.

What does Spartan mean?
If we talk about a Spartan existence we mean one that is tough and enduring. It comes from the custom in ancient Sparta of taking children from their parents at the age of seven, training them in schools and colleges in the military arts, physical exercise and endurance tests. The aim was to produce a strong, ever alert army.

Why was Socrates put to death?
Socrates was a philosopher of ancient Greece, who lived from 469 to 399 BC. He believed that people should speak out against what seemed to be wrong. Men should examine their environment, see what was missing and put it right. If this upset the authorities, that was too bad. For a while he was able to preach his revolutionary thinking, but when the government of Athens changed from an enlightened rule to one of repression, a number of Greek nobles had him tried and put to death. He was compelled to drink a cup of poisonous hemlock.

How big was the empire of Alexander the Great?
By the time of his death, aged only 33, in 323 BC, Alexander's empire stretched from Greece to India, and from the Black Sea to Egypt.

What happened to Alexander's empire after he died?
Alexander had no children. His great empire was split up between three of his generals. Cassander ruled European Greece, Ptolemaius governed Egypt, and Seleucus held the Asian territories. Soon, however, they started quarrelling amongst themselves.

Why is a silver birch so-called?

Because it is a member of the birch tree family and has a whitish, silvery bark.

What is a cypress tree?

A conifer, whose features include short leaves kept close to the stem (trunk) and branches. There are several kinds of cypress tree, and two of the best known in Britain are the Leyland and the Lawson. Leylands are very fast-growing, and can add a metre (three feet) a year to their height.

What is a cos?

It is a type of lettuce which has long, upright leaves, and is very crisp to eat. It is said to have originated from the Greek island of Kos in the Aegean Sea.

Can you eat quince?

Well, raw quince fruit is not very nice, but cooked and made into jam it is a distinctive and interesting thing to spread on bread and butter.

Why do people take cuttings of plants?

A cutting is usually a small shoot of a plant which has leaf buds on it. Two good reasons for wanting cuttings are (a) to graft a cutting on to another one of similar family to get a new variety of plant (commonly done with roses) and (b) to grow a plant of your own from a plant belonging to someone else.

What is a hybrid?

This is the result, in botany, of cross-breeding of two kinds of plant of similar family, in which characteristics of both are perpetuated.

What has cowslip to do with cows?

Nothing really, except the name. Cowslip comes from the Old English cuslyppe, which means cow-dung. This does not in any way describe the

194

pleasant fragrance of the yellow primrose called cowslip that blooms in the spring.

What is unusual about some wild orchids?

Some wild orchids look as if they are being visited by insects when in fact the 'insect' is part of the plant. Some examples are the bee orchid, the wasp orchid, the early and late spider orchids and the fly orchid.

A bee orchid
Ophrys apifera

Can hollow trees grow leaves?

Some can, because the processes which make a tree grow and sprout foliage go on in a series of small tubes just inside the bark layer and not in the centre of the trunk or branch.

How can you tell the age of a tree?

By counting the rings on a tree stump.

(This of course means cutting the tree down first!) There are two rings for each year's growth, if the conditions for growth have been right. For trees that are still uncut, some experts can make guesses at the age according to the diameter of the trunk.

What is a pollen count?

This is the figure for an estimate of the amount of pollen (the male reproductive cells of plants) there may be floating about in the air in a given space. Pollen affects sufferers from hay fever and other allergies and if a high count is announced, the sufferers can take steps to avoid the area.

What is a puff ball?

It is a fungus consisting of a round white sphere with a fragile skin, inside which are thousands of spores (reproductive cells).

What are algae?

Briefly, they are what go to make up the green scum found in a pond or stagnant pool, or even in some running water. They are minute plants, and there is a great variety of them. They are valuable food for some water animals.

Why do some clovers have four leaves and not three?

There is no special reason for this. It just happens now and again in a field of clover, and if you find one, it is supposed to be good luck.

What are the two kinds of artichoke?

The Jerusalem artichoke, whose plant is like a sunflower and whose root is edible. These artichokes look like potatoes underground and they have a distinctive taste. The globe artichoke belongs to another plant family, the thistle family, and produces heads whose leaves can be chewed. You boil the globe artichoke in water and the leaves are loosened. They can be taken out and one end of the leaf dipped in melted butter and eaten.

What is Morning Glory?

A climbing plant of the convolvulus family which has trumpet-shaped blue and white flowers that come out only in the morning. The flowers die in the afternoon, but next morning, more are in bloom.

Why do some plants have to be grown in a greenhouse?

Chiefly because they will not grow properly outdoors in climates less warm than they are used to. Greenhouses are also used to force plants, such as tomatoes and grapes, to grow more quickly than they would outside.

Little Quiz 31

Which authors invented these characters?

1. Sherlock Holmes
2. Wackford Squeers
3. Man Friday
4. Captain Nemo
5. Umslopogaas
6. Bulldog Drummond
7. Sir Percy Blakeney
8. Ashenden
9. Long John Silver
10. Jonathan Wild
11. Dorian Gray
12. Edmond Dantes
13. Captain Shotover
14. Lewis Eliot
15. Tom Sawyer
16. Biggles
17. Gatsby
18. Tarka
19. Horatio Hornblower
20. Tom Brown
21. Mrs Malaprop

Which is the longest-running play in London?
The Mousetrap, a thriller by Dame Agatha Christie. It has been running continuously since 1952.

What shocked audiences so much about Noel Coward's 'The Vortex'?
This play, written and staged in 1924, was a sophisticated story of a family and its circle, and it was very vividly written. What shocked people most was one of the characters admitting to taking drugs.

Who are Rodgers and Hammerstein?
Richard Rodgers and Oscar Hammerstein combined to produce some of the most famous musicals of history. Rodgers was the composer and Hammerstein the playwright, and they produced, among others, *Oklahoma, The King and I* and *The Sound of Music.* All three were later filmed.

Who is Irving Berlin?
Perhaps the doyen of the musical composers who specialized in musical plays, Israel Baline was born in Russia in 1888. He settled in the US and later changed his name to Irving Berlin. He has been composing ever since, and among his numerous successes are *Alexander's Ragtime Band, Annie Get Your Gun, Call Me Madam* and *White Christmas.*

What is Broadway?
It is a main street in New York and a small part of it has many theatres. People who have plays produced, or appear in one as actors or actresses, on Broadway, can count it as a major achievement.

What is the Old Vic?
A theatre in Waterloo Road, London. Founded in 1818, it was taken over in 1880 by Emma Cons who called it the Royal Victoria Hall. It was a centre for opera and drama, and became affectionately known as the Old Vic.

Who was Lilian Baylis?
She was the niece of Emma Cons, and in 1898 she took on the management of the Old Vic. She converted the style of the presentations and concentrated on producing Shakespeare plays, from about 1914 up to the beginning of the Second World War. The theatre was damaged in an air attack in the Second World War but the company continued. It was rebuilt and became the home of the new National Theatre. Most stage performers considered it a great honour and pleasure to do a play at the Old Vic, although the financial rewards were not as high as elsewhere.

Who is considered the leading actor in Britain today?
Laurence Olivier (born in 1907), who was created a life peer in 1970, the first actor to be ennobled. He has had an astonishing career as stage, film, television and radio actor, has produced and directed numerous plays and films, and was the new National Theatre's first Director, getting the project off the ground.

Who was Dame Sybil Thorndike?
Dame Sybil Thorndike was born in 1882 and went on the stage early. Her first great success was in Bernard Shaw's *St Joan* (1924) which made her reputation. She continued to appear in films, TV and on the stage right up to her last years. She died in 1976.

What is the Comedie Francaise?
It is the French national theatre, founded in Paris in 1680, in the time of Louis XIV who patronized it. It is subsidized by the government today and

runs on rules said to have been laid down by Napoleon.

What was so important about the play 'Summer of the Seventeenth Doll'?

It was an Australian play, written by an Australian, in which the characters spoke in the Australian idiom. It was staged in 1956 and was the first time an all-Australian production of such magnitude was put on. Some saw it as the start of the Australian national theatre.

What is Vaudeville?

A word in common usage among theatrical people for music-hall variety shows and entertainment.

When was pantomime invented?

It's almost as old as the hills. In Roman times, a pantomime was a performance by one person, who mimed all the parts in a mythological story. In 18th century England, pantomime was still silent, but with a full cast of actors and dancers, not just one. At that time only certain theatres, known as Theatres Royal, were allowed to present proper plays, with words. So 'music houses', such as Sadler's Wells, staged elaborate musical pantomimes with the lovers Harlequin and Columbine and clowns.

It was in the 1840s that what we now think of as traditional pantomime was established – a lavish Christmas entertainment for children based loosely on a fairy story, with the Principal Boy acted by a woman, the Dame by a man, and, somewhere along the line, a transformation scene – from earth to fairyland, the Prince's palace to Cinderella's hovel, or something like that!

What were the Miracle Plays?

They were plays enacted in Latin during the Middle Ages and based originally on the scriptures but eventually using also material which did not come from the Bible. The plays were given in series, called cycles, and named after the towns in which they were performed. The longest of the English cycles was the York Plays which actually contained 48 separate plays.

What are Passion Plays?

These are similar to Miracle Plays but are concerned solely with the life of Christ. The most famous of these plays is the one given at Oberammergau in the Bavarian Alps once every ten years. It is performed entirely by local people, and with only three interruptions because of war has been held every ten years since 1634.

Who has revived the art of miming?

Marcel Marceau, the French mimic, has successfully revived the art of mime both in France and in other countries. With the minimum of props and without speaking a word he can create perfect illusions.

Marcel Marceau, the famous French mime

How did Peter Pan say fairies are made?

'When the first baby laughed for the first time, the laugh broke into a thousand pieces,' said Peter Pan – who is the boy who wouldn't grow up in Sir James Barrie's famous play for children. Each little piece of laughter became a fairy, and since then every new baby's first laugh has become a fairy, according to Peter Pan.

And when did Peter Pan ask children to clap their hands?

'Every time a child says: "I don't believe in fairies", there is a fairy somewhere drops down dead,' Peter explains when Tinker Bell, his own fairy, is dying. He asks all little children watching to clap their hands if they believe in fairies. Some don't – but many do, and Tinker Bell's life is saved. *Peter Pan* is performed in London after Christmas every year.

Who was the original Robinson Crusoe?

Alexander Selkirk (1676–1721), the son of a Scottish shoemaker. He ran away to sea in 1703 and was made sailing master of the privateer Cinque Ports Galley. He was not shipwrecked, like Crusoe, but quarrelled with the captain and at his own request was put ashore on the uninhabited island of Juan Fernandez, off the coast of Chile. It was four years and four months before he was rescued by Captain Woodes Rogers. Many stories were written about his adventures, as well as Daniel Defoe's famous novel.

Where does Auld Lang Syne come from?

The words of this old song were written by the Scottish poet Robert Burns for the *Scots Musical Museum*, a collection of songs and poems several volumes long which was published between 1787 and

1803. Burns said he took down the words from an old man's singing, and the refrain which we sing as the old year dies and we let in the new, is certainly very ancient:

> 'For auld lang syne, my dear,
>   For auld lang syne,
> We'll tak a cup o' kindness yet,
>   For the sake of auld lang syne.'

Who wrote 'Drink to me only with thine eyes'?

Ben Jonson, the great Jacobean dramatist who was a friend of Shakespeare. The words form the first line of a song *To Celia* which was published in 1616. The verse goes on:

> And I will pledge with mine;
> Or leave a kiss but in the cup
> And I'll not look for wine.

Who told Alice she could have 'jam tomorrow and jam yesterday – but never jam today'?

The White Queen in *Through the Looking Glass*, Lewis Carroll's second book about Alice. The first was *Alice in Wonderland*.

Who first said 'A cat may look at a king'?

Alice – in Lewis Carroll's *Alice in Wonderland*. She may not have been first to say it, though – she'd read it in some book, she said, but didn't remember where.

'When I use a word,' Humpy Dumpty said in a rather scornful tone, 'it means just what I choose it to mean – neither more nor less.' Was he right?

Yes. We all use language that way – even when we are as good at using it as Lewis Carroll, who featured Humpty Dumpty in *Through the Looking Glass* along with many other famous characters.

What is satire?
A poem, story, play, or film, in which current fashions, vices or attitudes are exposed and made fun of.

What is the greatest satire in the English language?
Gulliver's Travels, written in 1726 by Jonathan Swift. Gulliver – like so many people – came back from his travels and told what appeared to be *tall stories*. He had been to the land of the tiny Lilliputians. Then he had visited the giants of Brobdingnag. He had even been to a country governed by horses. The strange fact emerges that everywhere the people (and even the horses) behaved much better than us.

Are there modern satires?
Yes. One is the film made by the great Spanish director Bunuel called *The Discreet Charm of the Bourgeoisie*. It is about the important place given by the rich upper and middle classes to ritual eating – at lunch parties, dinner parties and so on.

What is a satyr?
Nothing to do with satire, or ridicule. In ancient Greece, a satyr was a woodland spirit, part man, part beast. Sometimes a satyr was depicted in sculpture and by actors in plays with the ears and tail of a horse, and sometimes with horns, dancing on the hind legs of a goat.

Who tilted at windmills?
Don Quixote, the crazy Spanish knight whose adventures were told in a very long 16th century masterpiece by Cervantes, the greatest writer Spain has produced. Accompanied by his servant Sancho Panza, and riding his bony nag Rosinante, Don Quixote searched for lost causes he might champion, and 'enemies' he might vanquish – and ended up charging full tilt, his lance at the ready, at windmills! 'Quixotic' has come to mean selfless and idealistic, in a rather foolish way, and 'tilting at windmills' wasting one's energy attacking problems, or 'enemies', that aren't really there.

Who was the Swiss Family Robinson?
A family – parents and children – whose adventures on a desert island were described by the German author J. R. Wyss in the famous book of that name published in 1813. He probably invented the Robinsons, as well as the ingenious ways they had of coping with the problems of feeding, clothing and sheltering themselves.

Who were the Spectrists?
They were two American poets, Witter Bynner and Arthur Ficke, who in 1916 published a book entitled *Spectra: A Book of Poetic Experiments*, intended as a satire of current styles but accepted by critics of the time as a genuine new literary school.

Who is Pooh Bear?
He is the best-loved bear in literature. He was created by the English writer A. A. Milne together with the boy Christopher Robin and two other famous toy animals, Piglet and Eeyore, in the books *Winnie-the-Pooh* and *The House at Pooh Corner*, published in the 1920s. Originally intended for children, these books have become classics and as popular with adults as they are with children.

What contributed to the success of the Pooh books?
The warm and humorous illustrations by Ernest Shepard which, although simple line drawings, manage to capture exactly all the charm of Milne's characters.

Who discovered Chloroform as a gas?

In 1847, a young Scottish physician, James Simpson (1811–1870) experimented with chloroform vapours on himself and a few friends. They fell asleep. Then Simpson tried it out on some mothers about to give birth to children, and he found it eased their labour pains. This was the beginning of anaesthesia in Britain.

Antiseptics?

Before Joseph Lister (1827–1912) started his work, people who had surgical operations often died from infection in the wound if they did not die under the knife. Then Lister, at Glasgow Infirmary, started using carbolic acid to kill germs, and by this means drastically cut down infection. It was a major landmark in surgery and Lister was eventually made a peer – the first British doctor to be so ennobled.

Ether as a gas?

Surgical operations were, up to the middle of the 19th century, excruciatingly painful, as no anaesthetics were used. Some patients were given alcohol to ease the pain. Then, in 1846, the American dentist, William Thomas Green Morton (1819–1868) gave a patient ether gas and put him to sleep. Morton later demonstrated the effect of ether at Boston Hospital, when the surgeon Professor Warren removed a lump from a patient's neck without the patient screaming in pain.

The colours of the spectrum?

There are seven colours of the Spectrum – red, orange, yellow, green, blue, indigo and violet. They show up when a beam of light is passed through a specially shaped glass called a prism. This was discovered by Sir Isaac Newton (1642–1727), the famous British

physicist and mathematician who also discovered gravitational force.

Radio-activity?

Some materials become radioactive when the nuclei of certain atoms suddenly break up and give off a variety of rays. One such atom is uranium, and it is called a radioactive element. The property of radioactivity was discovered by the French physicist Henri Becquerel (1852–1908) in 1890.

X-rays?

X-rays were first identified in 1895 by the German physicist Wilhelm Rontgen (1845–1923).

Radium?

The metal radium gives off rays which are valuable for medical treatment and atomic research. It was discovered in 1898 by the physicists Pierre and Marie Curie, a husband-and-wife research team at the Sorbonne University in Paris. Pierre was French and Marie was Polish.

Laws of heredity?

Gregor Johann Mendel (1822–1884) was an Austrian monk who studied biology in his spare time. He cultivated peas in his garden and noted everything about their growth. From his research he deduced that there was a natural law of inheritance of characteristics in plants, and he believed this also applied to animals – and humans.

Insulin?

About one person in every thousand may have the complaint diabetes to a greater or lesser degree. This is caused by a malfunction in the pancreas gland – the gland that produces the enzyme insulin. Those who are short of naturally produced insulin can take it by pill or by injection. This is the result of the research achievement of Sir Frederick

EUREKA!

Banting (1891–1941), a brilliant Canadian doctor who isolated insulin in experiments with animals and used it to control diabetes in humans.

Diagnosis?
The first person to try to diagnose an illness from its symptoms and effects on patients was Theophrastus Bombastus von Hohenheim, otherwise known as Paracelsus (1493–1541), a Swiss physician. He also introduced the treatment of some illnesses by immersing patients in mineral baths.

The detailed anatomy of the human body?
In the 16th century the human body was considered sacred. But Andreas Vesalius, a Belgian anatomist, risked everything by dissecting dead bodies so that he could draw what he saw and explain how the body worked. His ideas were opposed to many accepted notions of the time and when he published them he got into serious trouble.

Vitamins?
Vitamins are organic substances essential to good health in human beings. Some are present in our bodies, others are found in the food we eat. Deficiencies in vitamins cause diseases and disabilities, even death. They were isolated by various people, but the pioneering work was done by Sir Frederick Gowland Hopkins (1861–1947).

That the Earth moves round the Sun?
Nicolaus Copernicus (Kopernik) (1473–1543) was a Polish astronomer who in the last years of his life stated that the earth and the other planets moved round the sun. He observed this over a series of studies of the solar system. Up to then it was believed that the Sun moved round the earth, and the Church had ruled it heresy to say otherwise.

Sodium and potassium?
These two important elements were discovered in 1807 by Sir Humphry Davy (1778–1829), the Cornish-born chemist and physicist who was Director of the Royal Institution in London. In 1808 he also isolated the elements of calcium, barium, boron, magnesium and strontium, and was the inventor of a safety lamp for miners.

Little Quiz 32
Who painted these pictures?
1. The Fighting Temeraire
2. The Laughing Cavalier
3. Mrs Siddons
4. The Light of the World
5. Derby Day
6. The Boyhood of Raleigh
7. Napoleon's Retreat from Moscow
8. The Hay Wain
9. The Bathers
10. The Last Supper

What nationality were these painters?
11. Cézanne
12. Chagall
13. Baldung
14. Lely
15. Alexander Calder
16. van Gogh
17. Watteau
18. Sir Henry Raeburn
19. Klee
20. Paul Nash

In which country is each of these galleries?
21. Uffizi
22. Rijksmuseum
23. Tate
24. Metropolitan Museum of Art
25. Prado
26. Walker Art Gallery
27. The Hermitage
28. Shoso-in
29. du Pont Winterthur
30. Wallace Collection

Who discovered Penicillin?

Penicillin, the first antibiotic substance for fighting infection, was discovered by the Scottish bacteriologist Sir Alexander Fleming (1881–1955) in the late 1920s. It was some time before he could convert the mould into a form suitable for clinical use but when it was available it saved countless lives.

Vaccination?

Edward Jenner (1749–1823), an English doctor, discovered that if a sample of the mild disease, cowpox, was injected into some-one's arm, this would prevent them catching smallpox. He made his discovery in 1796 when smallpox was a major killer disease. Vaccination comes from the Latin word, vacca, meaning cow.

Red corpuscles in the blood ?

These were first noted by Anton van Leeuwenhoek, the Dutch anatomist who had developed a microscope for studying minute organisms. Leeuwenhoek also discovered bacteria, though neither he nor anyone else appreciated their importance at the time.

The tubercle bacillus?

Tuberculosis was a major cause of death right up to the present century. That it was caused by the tubercle bacillus, an infectious organism, was the discovery by the German bacteriologist Robert Koch (1843–1910) who also discovered an inoculation against anthrax.

Circulation of the blood?

The blood circulates round the body, pumped along by the heart, down the arteries and back through the veins to the heart again. The process cannot be reversed because the valves in the heart will only operate if the blood flows in a constant direction. This was discovered by the English doctor, William Harvey (1578–1657) but he encountered furious opposition to his ideas.

That the atom could be split?

Up to the end of the last century people believed that an atom was the smallest particle of matter. Then physicists discovered that the atom had a structure of its own, and contained a nucleus and electrons. Ernest Rutherford (1871–1937), a New Zealand physicist, investigated the atom in great detail and proved these ideas correct. He suggested other things in its structure, and he capped his work by splitting an atom of nitrogen in 1919. This revolutionized man's conception of matter.

Explosive properties of gunpowder ?

The ancient Chinese used a kind of gunpowder for fireworks nearly 2000 years ago, but they did not develop it as a weapon. The explosive properties of gunpowder were discovered in the Western world by Roger Bacon (1220–1290), an English monk and chemist.

Boyle's Law?

Boyle's Law was stated in the 1660s by the Hon. Robert Boyle (1627–1691), an Anglo-Irish chemist. It says that if you compress a gas in a vessel, at constant temperature, you decrease its volume in inverse proportion to the amount of pressure applied. This led him to observe how water expands when it is frozen.

Electrons?

Electrons are negative charged particles that orbit the nucleus of an atom, just as the planets orbit the Sun in our solar system. They may be just waves, but they can be detached from their orbits, whereupon they travel in straight lines. They were first identified by Sir Joseph John Thomson (1856–1940), one time

EUREKA!

Cavendish Professor of Physics at
Cambridge University in England.

Wireless Waves?
Marconi was the first person to send
wireless waves over long distances, but
the actual waves had been discovered
several years earlier by the German
physicist Heinrich Hertz (1857–1894),
who called them electromagnetic waves.

Cosmic rays ?
These are sub-atomic particles which
bombard the earth from outer space.
They were discovered by the American
physicist Robert Milliken (1868–1953) in
1925.

Little Quiz 33
**In which country were the following
famous and beneficial drugs
introduced?**

1. Streptomycin
2. Cocaine
3. Adrenalin
4. Aspirin
5. DDT
6. Quinine
7. Salk vaccine
8. Sulphonamide drugs
9. Iodine
10. Digitalis

**The following people were Nobel
Prize winners: what country did they
come from (1) and which prize did
they win (2)**

11. Lord Rutherford
12. Fridtjof Nansen
13. W. F. Libby
14. Henri Becquerel
15. Albert Einstein
16. Ernest Hemingway
17. Sir Macfarlane Burnet
18. Albert Luthuli
19. Sir Frederick Hopkins
20. Samuel Beckett
21. Theodore Roosevelt

---

22. Theodor Mommsen
23. Ivan Pavlov
24. Svante Arrhenius
25. Guglielmo Marconi

**What are the English names for
these Latin-name orders of insects?**

26. Odonata
27. Lepidoptera
28. Coleoptera
29. Hemiptera
30. Saltatoria
31. Siphonaptera

Classes of birds?

32. impennes
33. pelecaniformes
34. anseriformes
35. columbiformes
36. strigiformes
37. struthioniformes

Classes of plants?

38. musci
39. filicales
40. cyanophyta

**What is the English name in
common usage for these?
Animals**

41. Gallus gallus
42. Vulpes
43. Bos
44. Felis domestica
45. Equus caballus
46. Ursus
47. Oryctolagus cuniculus
48. Mus musculus
49. Anthropopithecus troglodytes
50. Loxodonta

Plants

51. Citrus limonia
52. Daucus carota
53. Coco nucifera
54. Piper nigrum
55. Zea mays
56. Brassica oleracea
57. Avena sativa
58. Paeonia
59. Helianthus
60. Ranunculus

N

Who discovered the position of the North Magnetic Pole?

This was determined by Sir John Ross (1777–1856), a Scottish admiral, and his nephew, Sir James Ross, the explorer, in 1831. Both men also made voyages of exploration in the Arctic separately, and Sir James explored Antarctica as well.

What was Sir John Franklin famous for?

Franklin (1786–1847) was a British admiral and explorer who fought at Trafalgar, explored the Arctic, made expeditions to Australia, and died while searching for a North West Passage over the top of Canada.

Who discovered the mouth of the huge Congo River?

The Portuguese sea captain Diogo Cao, in 1482. The extent of the great river, however, was not known until the time of Livingstone.

When was the North West Passage finally navigated for the first time?

In 1905 by Roald Amundsen, the remarkable Norwegian explorer, but it had been partially discovered fifty years before by Sir Robert MacClure.

Who discovered the course of the Zambesi River, found the Victoria Falls and discovered Lake Nyasa?

These were the achievements of the Scottish missionary and explorer Dr David Livingstone (1813–1873) who spent the best part of the last thirty years of his life in Africa. He searched for the sources of the Nile but these were found by someone else. He opened up Tanganyika and Nyasaland.

Who, then, did find the source of the Nile?

John Hanning Speke (1827–1864), a British explorer who also found Lake

Tanganyika. He found the source of the White Nile in 1862. Two years later, his claim was disputed, and two days before he was to appear at a public debate to argue his claim, he died from a gunshot accident.

Who discovered the North Pole?

The American explorer Robert Peary, in 1909. He reached the actual spot by sledge. A short while afterwards, Amundsen, unaware of Peary's success, started to look for the Pole. But on the way he discovered that Peary had got there. So he abandoned his search and decided to look for the South Pole instead.

Did Amundsen discover the South Pole?

Yes, late in December 1911. Strangely enough he reached it a few weeks before Britain's Captain Robert Falcon Scott who was racing to get there first.

What happened to Captain Scott?

He reached the South Pole in January 1912 only to find that Amundsen had beaten him to it. On the return journey, Scott and his four colleagues, Wilson, Bowers, Oates and Evans were overcome by the weather and died.

Who was the first person to fly over the South Pole?

Admiral Richard E. Bird, US Navy, on the 28th and 29th November 1929.

After whom is America named?

Amerigo Vespucci (1454–1512), an Italian navigator who took part in several voyages to the New World (as it was then called). He said he was on the Ojeida expedition of 1499 which first found the mainland of North America, and his claim was backed by a German geographer who in 1507 gave the name America to the lands. The name stuck.

Who tracked down the course of the River Congo?

Sir Henry Stanley (1841–1904), the Welsh born explorer who was brought up in America, became a journalist, searched for and found Dr Livingstone (1871) and spent years in Africa exploring.

Who discovered the Great Lakes of Canada?

Samuel de Champlain (c.1567–1635), a French explorer who founded the colony of Quebec and became its governor. He also sailed up the St Lawrence River.

Who discovered the North-East Passage?

The route from the Atlantic over the top of Asia into the Pacific was discovered and navigated for the first time by the Swedish explorer Nils Adolf Nordenskjold (1832–1901).

Who first planned to search for the North-East Passage?

Sebastian Cabot (1476–1557), who, with his father John Cabot, had discovered Cape Breton Island in Canada.

When was Iceland discovered?

The Norwegian Vikings almost certainly touched on Iceland in the early 9th century AD, and the first settlements were founded in about 875.

Which people first visited the Azores islands?

They were visited by the Carthaginians in the 3rd century BC, but not settled. The first settlements were by the Portuguese some time in the 14th century AD.

Why was Tasmania once known as van Diemen's Land?

Because van Diemen was governor general of the Dutch colonies in the East Indies in the 1630s when he sent a captain, Abel Tasman, to explore the east coast of Australia. Tasman found the island and named it after his chief. Tasman won out in the end: the island's name was changed in 1853.

When Lieutenant Bligh (of the 'Bounty') was cast adrift in an open boat after the famous mutiny, in 1789, how far did he navigate before coming to dry land?

Over 5790 kms (3600 miles), all the way from a point not far from Tahiti to Timor Island near Java. It was the most amazing open boat feat of all time, for he had no instruments. Not one of the loyal crew who had left the *Bounty* to accompany him died on the voyage.

Who discovered the South Magnetic Pole?

Sir Douglas Mawson (1882–1958), the Australian explorer who accompanied Ernest Shackleton, the Irish-born explorer, on the latter's famous voyage to the Antarctic, 1907–1909.

Were there any Chinese explorers?

There has been only one of any note, Hsuan-tsang who between 629 and 646 travelled as far west as India and beyond. His discoveries were not exploited, however, as the Chinese rulers at that time were more concerned with administering the huge territory of their own land.

Who was Giovanni Carpani?

This intrepid monk (c.1180–1252), a companion of St Francis, was sent in 1245 by Pope Innocent IV to the court of the Mongols. His journey of some 4800 kms (3000 miles) across Europe and Russia took 106 days on horseback. On his return in 1247 he wrote the first travel book, *Liber Tartarorum*, a detailed record of his journey and of Mongolian life.

When did Canada become a Dominion?

In July 1867. The British North America Act was passed by the UK Parliament, and it united Nova Scotia, New Brunswick, Canada East (Quebec) and Canada West (Ontario) as the Dominion of Canada, a federation of four provinces each of which continued to have self-government but which came under a central government for foreign affairs, defence and so forth.

What happened to the other provinces?

In time they joined the Dominion, Manitoba in 1870, British Columbia in 1871, Prince Edward Island in 1873, Saskatchewan and Alberta became provinces in 1905 and Newfoundland joined in 1949.

Who were the 'reffos' in Australia?

They were refugees from Germany, Austria and Czechoslovakia who in 1938 and 1939 were admitted into Australia to make new lives because they could not survive under the dictatorship of Hitler.

How is the New Zealand Government operated?

New Zealand is governed by an Executive Council which works through the Governor-General and by a General Assembly of one house, the House of Representatives, which has 80 members including four Maoris. These members are elected every three years. Women were allowed to vote, by the way, as far back as 1893, some quarter of a century before they were allowed to vote in the UK.

What is apartheid?

It is the racial policy of the South African government, which means separate development. In South Africa the white population, the Asiatic and the African peoples live separately and are in theory allowed to develop separately. In practice, of course, it means the white people are much better off than the coloured people. As a policy it is disliked by practically every other nation in the world.

When did South Africa cease to be a member of the Commonwealth?

In 1961, Dr Verwoerd, prime minister of the republic of South Africa, took his country out of the Commonwealth because of the apartheid policy which he and his party intended to pursue and which the other Commonwealth members could not accept.

How long has the Isle of Man had self-government?

Legally, since 1866, but before that it had been the property of the Dukes of Atholl, and the Earls of Derby previous to the 1730s. It is an ancient Celtic nation, held for a time by the Vikings and then tossed to and fro between England and Scotland during the Middle Ages. It has its own Parliament, the Tynwald, which consists of the Legislative Council and the representative House of Keys.

At what age can Americans vote in elections?

People of eighteen and over have a vote in the United States. This may be qualified by which state in which they live, or used to live in.

What is the composition of the US Senate?

The US Senate, the American second house of parliament, as it were, has two senators from each of the states who are elected to serve for six years. One-third of the members retire every second year. The Senate is presided over by the Vice-President.

Who cannot vote in British elections?

The only people who cannot vote in the UK, even if they are eighteen or older, are peers, lunatics and criminals. You will also find it impossible to vote if you have not got your name down on the register of electors.

Who is the head of the Russian Government?

The USSR has a president, but he is merely a figurehead. The effective head of government is the first secretary of the Communist Party or the chairman of the Council of Ministers.

Why is Australia known as the Commonwealth of Australia?

Australia used to be divided into separate colonies under the British Crown. In 1901 they agreed that important matters concerning defence, foreign affairs, and the judiciary should be dealt with by a central government, but at the same time the states would retain individual control over domestic matters such as education, building and so forth. The federation was called the Commonwealth of Australia.

For how long can someone be president of the United States?

The president is elected for a term of four years, and can only be re-elected for a further four years, making eight years in all. But if a president dies in office, the vice-president automatically assumes office. If he then stands for the presidency at the next election, is successful and is subsequently re-elected for a second term, his total time in office would be longer than eight years.

What is the US Congress?

It is the national legislature of the USA. It is made up of the Senate and of the House of Representatives which has over 400 members elected for two-year terms.

Does the United Kingdom have a written constitution?

No, not as such. Because the United Kingdom has not experienced a fundamental political upheaval such as a revolution, its constitution has become embodied in its laws and in the traditions of its parliamentary practice.

Little Quiz 34

What numbers do these Roman letters represent?
1. VI
2. M
3. D
4. MCDXXVII
5. IM
6. MCMLXXVII
7. LXXXV
8. CCCXXXIII
9. MCXLVI
10. XIX

Which authors wrote these novels and in what year were they first published?
11. Catch-22
12. The Sun Also Rises
13. Der Tod in Venedig (Death in Venice)
14. Jane Eyre
15. L'Etranger (The Outsider)

Which composers wrote the music for these operas, and in what year were the operas first produced?
16. Cavalleria Rusticana (Rustic Chivalry)
17. Un Ballo in Maschera (A Masked Ball)
18. Ariadne auf Naxos (Ariadne on Naxos)
19. Jenufa
20. Eugene Onegin
21. Owen Wingrave
22. The Trojans
23. L'Enfant et les Sortileges (The Child and the Magic Spells)
24. Die Zauberflote (The Magic Flute)
25. Manon

And who wrote the music for these ballets and when were the ballets first performed?
26. Giselle
27. The Miraculous Mandarin
28. Scheherazade
29. The Rite of Spring
30. Ondine

Who was Dürer?

Albrecht Dürer (1471–1528) was the first important German painter and engraver. He produced many engravings on copper plate and on wood, and some are regarded as among the finest in the world. He went on to study painting at Venice, and in the early 1500s he produced several major pictures, including *The Martyrdom of St Bartholomew*. In 1520 he was appointed court painter to the Austrian emperor, Charles V.

Why was Rembrandt always short of money?

Harmensz van Rijn Rembrandt (1606–1669) studied painting and engraving in Holland. His father was a wealthy miller, and he left Rembrandt a lot of money, but Rembrandt had no idea of how to manage it. He became in time the greatest of all the Dutch painters, received and carried out numerous commissions for work, hardly ever stopping to relax, but still failed to meet his bills. Much of the time he undercharged for his work, and sometimes he never got paid anyway. In 1656 he went bankrupt and a great number of his pictures were sold for ridiculously low sums. His housekeeper and his son Titus formed a partnership to protect him from his creditors, and he was able to spend the last twenty years of his life painting many of his masterpieces.

Which Flemish painter designed his own house?

Sir Peter Paul Rubens (1577–1640), the famous Flemish painter, designed his house at Antwerp at the beginning of the 17th century. It was partly completed by 1610 when he moved in and settled there, regarding it as his home until his death. It is still standing today and it houses some of his greatest work.

208

Which Flemish painter was knighted by a foreign monarch?

After years as a painter at various foreign courts and capitals, Rubens was sent to England on a diplomatic mission by the Spanish court, in 1630. Charles I, always an eager patron of artists, commissioned Rubens to paint him and his wife, Henrietta Maria, and was so pleased with the result that he knighted him. Rubens' pictures are notable for their vigour and colour, and the women in many of them were often painted on the plump side. This has given rise to the adjective 'rubenesque' to mean plump and curvaceous.

What is a palette?

A palette is a small oval board which an artist uses for mixing his colours. It has a shiny surface, and a small hole towards one end. The artist holds the board by gripping it with a thumb through the hole.

Why was the painter David called The Darling of the French Revolution?

Jacques Louis David (1748–1825) studied painting in France during the last years of Louis XV (1715–1774). France was already beginning to be shaken by writings of people like Rousseau and Montesquieu who challenged the whole order of French society. David sympathized, and when the Revolution did break out in 1789 he had already established himself as a leading painter. He produced many important works which reflected the hopes and ideals of the revolutionaries. When Napoleon took power and ruled France, David became his court painter.

What was the Gobelins factory?

Gobelins was the name of a dyeing business founded on the outskirts of Paris in the 15th century. The firm later specialized in making tapestries and in the 1660s, Colbert, chief minister of Louis XIV, took it over and organized the firm to make tapestries and other decorative materials for the Court. Its products became famous throughout the world, and today a Gobelins tapestry will fetch a huge sum when it is sold.

What were the van Meegeren forgeries?
Hans van Meegeren (1889–1947), a Dutch artist, believed he could paint as well as some of the masters of the 17th century Dutch School of Painting. So he set to work to fake pictures by the artist Jan Vermeer (1632–1675) and produced a number which deceived art experts all over the world. One, *Christ at Emmaus*, was sold to a famous Rotterdam museum as genuine Vermeer. van Meegeren was only found out when he was arrested and tried for quite a different offence, that of collaborating with the Nazis during the occupation of Holland in the Second World War.

Where did Holbein come from?
There were in fact two Holbeins, father and son. Both were called Hans and came from Augsburg. Hans the Elder (1465–1524) became well-known as a painter in Germany, but his son, Hans (1497–1543), proved to be greater. He was influenced by the Reformation and he engraved illustrations for Martin Luther's new German translation of the New Testament. In 1527 he went to England and carried out a number of commissions, chiefly portraits, and ended up as court painter to Henry VIII (1509–1547) whom he painted several times.

Who were the Impressionists?
Impressionism was a movement in art that began in France in the mid-19th century. Some painters no longer felt compelled to reproduce faithfully what they saw in accurate detail, but they began to put down what their first impressions had been of a scene. They believed that colours were no more than the effects of light upon objects, and that these changed constantly. In their works they indicated colour mixtures by lumping one colour next to another rather than by mixing them. Among the earliest Impressionists were Monet, Degas, Pissarro, Renoir and Manet. They in turn influenced people like the American James McNeill Whistler and the British Wilson Steer.

What happened to the first Impressionist exhibition?
The Impressionists submitted several pictures for display at the Paris Salon in the 1860s. They were rejected with a storm of abuse. So they held their own exhibition which was attacked in the Press and largely ignored by other artists. They persevered, however, and within a decade, Impressionist painting had become the major form of painting in Europe of the time.

When was the Royal Academy of Arts founded?
The Royal Academy was founded in 1768 by George III (1760–1820) after talks with one of the leading painters of the day, Sir Joshua Reynolds. There were to be a president and forty academicians. The Academy was to hold regular exhibitions of art, which were to include not only members' work but also contributions from outside. Soon after it was set up the Academy instituted its own school which acted as enormous encouragement to young artists, of whatever background. The king selected 36 of the 40 members, which included Thomas Gainsborough, the famous portrait and landscape painter, and the first president was Reynolds who held the position until his death in 1792.

Who was
Titus Oates?

Titus Oates (1649–1705) was an English preacher who was sacked for misconduct. He then spread stories about London of a plot by Catholics to murder the king (Charles II) and overthrow the government. This resulted in many innocent people being jailed.

Tumbledown Dick?

This was the nickname of Richard Cromwell, son of Oliver Cromwell, Lord Protector of England, Scotland and Ireland (1653–1658). When Oliver died, Richard succeeded but he had no real interest in politics nor any special abilities and soon resigned.

Tum-Tum?

Edward VII, King of Great Britain (1901–1910) was known to some friends as Tum-Tum, usually behind his back, because of the portly way he held himself and the fact that this was due largely to very good living. Despite his concentration on the pleasures of the flesh, Edward was a popular and able monarch.

The Sun King?

Louis XIV of France reigned for a very long time, 1643 to 1715. It was his aim to make France the greatest nation in the world and Paris the finest city in Europe. He spent lavishly, employing the most brilliant artists and craftsmen to build and decorate houses, palaces and so forth, and generally brightened the lives of some of his people. He also embarked upon wars against neighbours to add to his territories.

The Lion of the North?

Gustavus Adolphus, king of Sweden from 1611 to 1632, was the champion of the Protestant armies of Europe in the great Thirty Years War (1618–1648). He
210

defeated several catholic armies in great battles. At his last victory, at Lutzen, in 1632, however, he was killed by a stray bullet after the major fighting was over.

Ned Kelly?

Ned Kelly (1854–1880) was an Australian bush ranger who led a gang of roughs that terrorized the states of New South Wales and Victoria, in the 1870s. They robbed banks, rustled cattle and generally destroyed property. Ned used to wear a tin shield round his head, which was in some respects bullet proof. He and the gang were eventually rounded up and tried. Kelly was hanged. Since his death he has become a figure of Australian folklore.

Teddy Roosevelt?

Teddy Roosevelt was the American president (1901–1909) who first made Americans aware that they had a decisive rôle to play in world affairs. He sent the US Fleet on a tour to several countries to impress them. He offered to intervene in disputes between warring countries. His motto was 'Speak softly but carry a big stick'.

Sir Wilfred Laurier?

Wilfred Laurier was the first French Canadian and Roman Catholic to be prime minister of Canada (1896–1911). In his long term of office he worked to make Canada an important nation within the British Empire and he authorized the beginning of the first transcontinental railway in Canada.

'WG'?

Dr William Gilbert Grace (1848–1915) was perhaps the most famous cricketer of all time. Born in Gloucestershire, England, he became a doctor, but he turned to cricket in the 1870s. He captained England many times, and scored over 54,000 runs.

John Henry Brodribb?
John Henry Brodribb wanted to be an actor. Not surprisingly, he changed his name and became Henry Irving, and it is as Irving that he is remembered as perhaps the greatest of the late Victorian actor-managers in London.

Ludwig the Mad?
Ludwig II of Bavaria (1845–1886) was king from 1864 to his death. He was a patron of the arts and music, and championed Richard Wagner. He spent vast sums on new buildings and improving existing ones, and decorated and furnished them sumptuously. But he also broke the Bavarian national exchequer and his government declared him insane, taking power out of his hands. He thereupon committed suicide.

Mistinguett?
This was the stage name of the famous French actress and dancer, Jeanne Bourgeois (1874–1956). She became the most popular music-hall artiste of the early 20th century in France, but she also showed, in several plays, that she could act serious parts well.

The Lionheart?
This was the popular name for Richard I (1189–1199) of England. He led an army to the Holy Land on the Third Crusade, distinguished himself by bravery, defeated the Turks in several battles but failed to take Jerusalem. He was captured on his way home, ransomed and returned to England, only to stay for a few months before setting out for France. He was killed at the siege of Chaluz.

Garibaldi?
Giuseppe Garibaldi (1807–1882) was a great Italian patriot leader who took Sicilian rebels to war against their government. He created an army of 1000 or so men, dressed them in red shirts, and together they cleared the government out of the island. Then he crossed over to Italy, marched on Naples and drove the king off the throne. His successes helped in the unification of the Italian states into one Italian nation, finally achieved in 1871.

Juarez?
In 1861, Benito Pablo Juarez was elected president of the new republic of Mexico. Born in 1806 of Mexican Indian parents, he had helped his people to win their freedom from Spain. In 1866 he was driven out by French forces who put Maximilian, brother of the Austrian emperor, Francis Joseph I, on a new throne as emperor. A year later, however, Juarez returned and had Maximilian put to death. Juarez was made president again, and remained so to his death in 1872.

Agrippina the Younger?
Agrippina was sister of the lunatic emperor of Rome, Caius (Caligula) (37–41 AD). She was married to her uncle Claudius (emperor from 41 to 54 AD) but she murdered him so that her son by her first marriage, Nero, should succeed. Nero tried then to get rid of his mother who was too bossy and sent her to sea in a collapsible boat. The boat did collapse, but Agrippina swam ashore. Nero then had her cut down.

Henry of Navarre?
Henry of Navarre became Henry IV of France in 1589. He was one of the best kings of all French history. Most notable of his achievements was unifying the Catholic and Protestant factions in France by granting toleration to the latter but adopting Catholicism as his own faith, so as to set an example. He was assassinated in 1610.

How does a fly catch its food?
A fly spits out saliva through its nose. This wets the food it has set its eyes upon, and it then sucks up the saliva again.

What does the large White Butterfly eat for nourishment?
It eats nectar from flowers, which it sucks up through a tube. This tube is kept coiled up when it is not being used.

What is nectar?
Nectar is the sweet and sugary fluid given out by plants, from which bees get honey. Nectar is also the name of the drink which the gods of ancient Greece and Rome were said to have drunk to make them immortal.

What happens to wasps in winter?
Most wasps die during the winter. The Queen wasp then starts a new colony of wasp eggs from which wasp grubs hatch for the next spring.

What is the difference between a spider and an ant?
A spider's body has no separate head. An ant's body has a head, a chest and an abdomen, articulating with each other.

Why do dogs pant?
Dogs have few sweat glands, so they can't sweat when they get hot through exercise or just through very warm weather. If they breathe hard their breath creates air currents which do the same thing for them as an electric fan might do for a human being.

What makes a bull see red?
A bull doesn't see red at all. He is in fact colour-blind and sees things in black and white. So, if a bull charges at you when you are wearing a red jersey it is nothing to do with the jersey. It may be because he is angry at being disturbed,
212

or perhaps he is just being curious.

What is the fastest fish that swims in the sea?
The barracuda, which may be between three and five feet long, can swim at about 50 kms an hour, but only for short distances. This doesn't seem very fast, but it is difficult to make progress through water.

Can frogs breathe under water?
No, fully grown frogs can't breathe under water. They need air as they have lungs. They can, however, spend long periods under water without breathing.

Why is a stoat sometimes called an ermine?
A stoat lives in warm and cold countries. In warm lands it is generally a reddish-brown colour on its back, but in colder countries this coat is white, except for the top of the tail. Then it is called an ermine.

Is a whale a fish?
No, it is a mammal. A whale has to breathe air and to come to the top of the sea to do so. And its babies, called calves, are born alive like the calves of a cow.

Is there any difference between frogs eggs and toads eggs?
The spawn of a frog is in biggish lumps or masses, like jelly, whereas a toad's spawn is in ribbons like streamers.

How do toads and frogs begin their lives?
They start as water animals. They hatch as tadpoles from eggs which are small cells with tails that grow longer and then, later on, shorten as arms and legs appear out of the sides of the body. Tadpoles don't breathe air. They breathe in water through their gills like fish.

What is unusual about lizard eggs?
A lizard's young sometimes hatch out of their eggs while they are still inside the mother's womb.

Is a bat a bird?
A bat is a mammal, not a bird. It is like a mouse with wings, roughly, and it can fly. Bats do not generally fly gracefully like birds. Nor do they like flying by day.

How does a woodpecker cling to the bark of a tree?
With its feet which are oddly designed. It has two toes pointing forwards and two backwards, and this gives the woodpecker a good grip.

Can you see a Great Auk these days?
No. This splendid bird, which could not fly, died out about a century or so ago. It had a huge, curved beak and fierce eyes. But some members of its family still exist, such as the puffin and guillemot.

How does a thrush get into a snail's shell?
If a thrush wants to capture and eat a snail and cannot find one outside its shell, it will take a stone and crack the shell open. The stone is often called an anvil when used in this way.

What is the main difference between the plumage of a male and a female bird?
In many birds, the feathers of a male bird are more colourful and bright than those of a female bird. This may be because the male bird's rôle is to attract female birds to him for mating purposes.

Does a kingfisher feed on seeds and land insects like other birds?
No. A kingfisher generally looks for small fish in the sea or in rivers, darts down and snatches them up. It will eat water insects, however.

What does a kingfisher build its nest from?
The kingfisher constructs its nest from bones stripped from a dead fish. These are collected and built into a nest, usually in a hole in the river bank.

How are swimming birds' feet different from tree perching birds' feet?
The 'swimming' bird's feet are webbed between the toes, whereas the 'perching' bird's feet are not. This webbing makes the feet operate like paddles.

What was a moa?
A moa was a large bird in New Zealand, which became extinct about five centuries ago. It stood over two metres high, but it could not fly as it had no wings.

Reconstruction of the moa

213

Why was Servetus put to death?
Miguel Serveto (1511–1553), or Michael
Servetus, as he was also known, was a
Spanish born doctor who became a
strong supporter of the Reformation.
His written views got him into great
trouble so he fled to Geneva where John
Calvin, the great reformer, was ruling
the city. Calvin and he quarrelled over
certain doctrinal matters. Servetus
refused to budge and was burnt at the
stake.

Who were the Methodists?
They were followers of John Wesley
(1703–1791), the English clergyman who
gave up his parish because he
disapproved of the high life of Church
leaders. He founded a new approach to
Protestant Christian belief and
worship. There was to be no hierarchy of
bishops and meetings of believers were
to be held in circumstances of equality.

What was the Inquisition?
It was a permanent organization within
the Roman Catholic Church set up in the
Middle Ages to investigate reports of
people not conforming to the rules of the
Church and its beliefs. It had wide
powers, including trial, imprisonment
and even execution of offenders.

What is Christian heresy?
Heresy is the holding of opinions that
are contrary to the orthodox teachings
of the Christian Church. Usually it
meant disagreements with the principles
or practices of the Roman Church. A
person found guilty of heresy was known
as a heretic.

Who were the Jansenists?
They were followers of the Dutch
theologian Cornelius Jansen (1585–1638),
who was a bishop in France. He attacked
the Jesuits and other Catholic bodies,
and sought to revert to the ancient ideas
214

of St Augustine. The French Church
split into two factions as a result of his
preachings and there was sharp
controversy for several decades.

Who was St Theresa?
St Theresa was a Spanish nun who
entered a Carmelite nunnery when she
was young. She disapproved of the lax
discipline, slapdash work and insincere
worship, so set out to reform the nunnery
with the help of other nuns. Soon her
ideas spread to other Carmelite
nunneries. St Theresa was born in 1515
and died in 1582.

**What have Plymouth Brethren to do
with Plymouth in England?**
The Plymouth Brethren are a Christian
sect founded in 1826 in Dublin, Ireland,
by John Nelson Darby. They follow a
very simple line of belief. The movement,
an off-shoot of the Protestants, gained
strength and in 1831 held its first
meeting in England, at Plymouth in
Devonshire. From then on members
came to be known as Plymouth Brethren.

Why was Sir Thomas More executed?
Thomas More (1478–1535) was Henry
VIII's Lord Chancellor. He refused to
acknowledge Henry's claim to be called
Supreme Head of the Church and he was
tried and executed. More, a brilliant
lawyer and scholar, wrote several books,
including a *Life of Richard III* and
Utopia, the story of an imaginary and
almost perfect state.

**Why did Henry VIII break with the
Church of Rome?**
Henry wanted to divorce his first wife,
Catherine of Aragon, and marry Ann
Boleyn who, he hoped, would give him a
son and heir. The Pope, who was in the
custody of Charles V, Emperor of
Austria, who happened to be Catherine's
nephew, refused the divorce. So Henry

broke from the Church, founded the Church of England as an independent organization and persuaded Archbishop Cranmer to pronounce the divorce.

What is a hymn?
A hymn is any set of words and music which are intended to be sung in honour of a god. Most religions have a collection of hymns for appropriate occasions. Many are verses of great beauty, some written by famous national poets.

What is a monastery?
It is a building, or group of buildings, which houses people who devote themselves to the service of God and their fellow humans. In the centuries after the collapse of the Roman empire in the West monasteries were the only places where learning and art survived. Monasteries are for men. Women wanting to follow the same kind of life have nunneries or convents.

Which was the first monastic order in the West?
It was the order of St Benedict, a scholar who founded many monasteries in Europe, including one at Monte Cassino in Italy. During his work he formulated rules for members to obey. Benedictine monks came to England at the end of the 6th century AD, led by St Augustine. There were nearly 300 Benedictine monasteries in England by 1500.

What were the mendicant orders?
Some monks believed it was more effective to go out and work among people rather than stay inside a monastery and work and pray there. These monks were usually called friars. They did not have money and had to keep going by begging food and shelter among the people for whom they worked. Among the mendicant orders were those of St Francis (Franciscans) and St Dominic (Dominicans).

Is it true that St Francis talked to animals and flowers?
St Francis of Assisi always found time on his travels to wonder at the marvels of nature. He loved birds and flowers and animals. He was said to be able to charm angry wild animals by the soothing nature of his voice.

What is the Missal?
The Missal is the prayer book and order of services of the Roman Catholic Church. Its use goes back many centuries, and it has been revised several times, sometimes drastically. One great revision was following the Council of Trent, 1545–1563.

Little Quiz 35

Which of these countries is still a monarchy today (1977)?

1. Switzerland
2. Albania
3. Great Britain
4. Portugal
5. Zaire
6. Monaco
7. Tonga
8. Spain
9. Sweden
10. Iceland

In which American states were these Civil War battles fought?

11. Bull Run
12. Chancellorsville
13. Shiloh
14. Charlestown
15. Gettysburg
16. Fredericksburg
17. New Orleans
18. Richmond
19. Vicksburg
20. Chattanooga

Where did playing cards originate?
Probably China, though not in the form
you know them now. They were first
seen in Europe in the 14th century,
introduced by the Arabs. The present
pack of 52 cards was formalized in the
15th century.

A French playing card from *c*.1830–40.
among the earliest double-headed cards

What is bezique?
A Spanish card game, popular in other
countries too, in which two players use
two packs, from which all cards below
number seven have been removed.
Winston Churchill particularly enjoyed
playing bezique.

Where does canasta come from?
This is a variation of rummy developed
216

by ladies in Uruguay, and introduced in
the United States at the end of the
Second World War, from where its
popularity spread to other countries.

What is cribbage?
A card game played by two, three or four
people. The score is kept on special
boards with pegs in holes.

How do you play pontoon?
Pontoon, also known as *Vingt-et-un*
(French for 21), is played with a pack of
cards and – for comfort – not more than
four people. The aim is to make a trick
with cards whose numbers add up to 21,
or as near to it as possible. One player is
banker. Pontoon can be played without
money, or it can be a gambling game.

Where did poker begin?
In the US, probably, as is often shown in
films, among the richer people of the
South, who sometimes spent hours or
days of luxurious travelling in great
steamboats up the Mississippi River.

What is the objective of poker?
It is played with a pack of cards and
money – in some cases very great sums
of it. The aim is to win tricks, and there
are a variety of hands in a special order
which can do so. There are also a
considerable number of variations to the
game.

How many cards are dealt?
In straight poker, five cards are dealt.
You can exchange them either by buying
one, two, three or four fresh ones and
handing over the ones you don't like, or
by exchanging the whole hand.

What is the order of poker hands?
In descending order they are: Royal
Flush (Ace, King, Queen, Jack and ten,
all of one suit); Straight Flush (five
cards of one suit in sequence); Four of a

kind (such as four tens); Full House
(three of a kind plus two of another
kind): Flush (five of one suit); Straight
(five cards in sequence, irrespective of
suit); three of a kind; two pairs; a pair.

What is tiddlywinks?
A game played with counters, chiefly
small ones in different colours. Players
press a big counter on the edge of a
small one and 'flick' it upwards and
forwards (hopefully) towards or into a
container. The game is taken very
seriously by a lot of people and matches
are played in many districts, especially
in the UK.

What's ping pong?
It's the colloquial name for table tennis,
but before the formation of the
International Table Tennis Association
in 1926 the game was called ping pong by
everyone. First played, it is thought, in
the late 19th century by British Indian
Army officers, it is now enjoyed all over
the world.

What are quoits?
Quoits is a game in which you throw a
sharp edged iron ring (quoit) over or
near to an iron hob from about fourteen
metres (48 feet) away. The game is played
like bowls.

What's croquet?
A centuries-old game in which you use a
long-handled wooden mallet to try to
steer or hit a largish ball along the
ground to go through a series of hoops
sticking out of the ground.

What is the Davis Cup?
It is a bowl presented as a trophy by
Dwight Davis (1879–1945), an American
tennis player, in 1900, for the winner of
an annual international competition
between lawn-tennis players of world
status.

What is Badminton?
It is a game played by two or four
players using rackets and shuttlecocks.
It is thought to have been introduced in
India by British officers in the Indian
army in the 1850s, but in fact it was
played by Indians many centuries
before. The name Badminton comes
from the home of the Dukes of Beaufort
(in England). One of the dukes, in the
1860s, enjoyed knocking a tennis ball
around his picture gallery, damaging
many of the paintings. The duke was
persuaded to try using a shuttlecock
instead, which is very much lighter,
When the game was formalized in
England in the 1870s, it was given the
name Badminton.

What is bridge?
Basically, it is a card game for four
people, who play as two pairs, sitting
round a four-sided table. One player is
called dummy, that is, his hand is spread
out face upwards on the table after it is
dealt, and the cards will be played by his
partner, opposite. Bridge has developed
extensively into a highly skilled game
over the past several decades.

What is the objective in whist?
Four people, playing as two pairs, on the
four sides of a table, are dealt thirteen
cards each. They try to take tricks, a
trick being obtained when the highest
card of a round is played that takes the
other three. The winning card may be
the highest of a suit, or it may be a
trump. Whist is part of the basis of
bridge.

What are the two main types of bridge played now?
Auction bridge and Contract bridge. In
Auction bridge, the trumps are
determined at the start by auction. In
Contract bridge, trumps are settled by
contract.

What is a fresco?

This is a method of painting a picture in water colour paints on fresh plaster which is still damp. (*Fresco* is the Italian for fresh.) The artist has to work quickly because the picture must be painted on the plaster before it has set hard. Usually, frescoes are painted on walls or ceilings, and should last as long as they do.

Who was Raphael?

Raffaello Sanzio (1483–1520) was a Renaissance painter of the first rank who also became an architect. His pictures included many portraits, cartoons of Biblical scenes, frescoes and a variety of representations of The Madonna and Child (Virgin Mary and her son, Jesus). He was a supreme draughtsman, and the strength and nobility of his painting put him almost on the same level as Michelangelo and Leonardo.

Who was Kandinsky?

Vassili Kandinsky (1866–1944) was a Russian Expressionist painter who settled in Germany. He produced works that did not represent anything he saw but were colours and squares and circles put down to express feelings. A lot of artists claimed to understand him and to be influenced by him.

Why are Hogarth prints so famous?

William Hogarth (1697–1764) was a leading artist in mid-18th century Britain, and he was a celebrated engraver as well. He had a strong social conscience which was sharpened by his mixing with people in high society. He disliked the gap between the rich and the poor, and to make his point he produced engravings of whole sets of prints which he made into books, drawing attention to social evils. One was *The Rake's Progress*, another was

218

Marriage à la Mode. These and other books sold extremely well and were reprinted several times.

Who were the great English miniaturists?

Among the best miniaturists were Nicholas Hilliard (1537–1619), Samuel Cooper (1609–1672) and Isaac Oliver (died 1617). Hilliard did miniatures of many of the leading figures of Elizabeth's reign, including a famous one of the queen herself. His reputation in Europe was extremely high. Cooper is perhaps best known for miniatures of Cromwell and his family, but he was much in demand among people on the Royalist side as well. Oliver was second only to Hilliard in skill.

Which famous soldier studied mezzotinting?

Prince Rupert of the Rhine, nephew of Charles I of Britain, the dashing cavalry leader of the Royalist Cause in the British Civil War (1642–1647) studied the process in Europe and introduced it to Britain in the 1670s.

What, then, is an aquatint?

This is not unlike a mezzotint. You cover the metal plate with resin, polish the resin and cut in the design, and then pour acid over the plate, leaving it to work into the surface. When this is printed, it looks like a water colour.

How did artists colour engravings?

Colouring engravings was done by using different coloured inks in the correct places when inking the plate. Or you could make several plates of one picture and use one plate per colour inked only where that colour was needed. The results were not usually very good, and artists more often than not finished black and white prints by hand-colouring afterwards.

Who was 'The Blue Boy'?

The Blue Boy was the title of a portrait by Thomas Gainsborough (1727–1788) of Master Buttall, dressed in a blue silk costume. It has become one of Gainsborough's most famous pictures, but it is not by any means his best. Gainsborough painted landscapes as well as portraits, but it is of course as a portraitist that he excelled.

What is Constable country?

Constable country describes the gently rolling vales and small hills on the borders of Essex and Suffolk in England. It is named after John Constable (1776–1837), Britain's greatest landscape painter who lived there and painted many rural scenes, like Flatford Mill, the Hay Wain and Dedham Vale. He paid great attention to the beauties of the clouds, the sky, rivers and woodlands.

Which engraver was born in Italy, worked in Britain and died in Portugal?

Francesco Bartolozzi (1727–1815) was a Florentine painter and engraver. He emigrated to England in the 1760s. When the king and Reynolds created the Royal Academy, Bartolozzi had made a good enough reputation as an engraver to be elected as one of the first members. Over 50 years Bartolozzi produced an enormous number of pictures and engravings, specializing in the stipple-engraving technique which was then most in demand. Early in the 19th century he was invited to run a school of art in Lisbon by the Portuguese Regent, and he left England for good.

What is bronze?

Bronze is an alloy (a mixture of metals) produced by melting copper and tin. The proportions are usually a little over three-quarters copper to a little under one-quarter tin. It is a fine material for casting sculpture from a clay or wax original, and it is still used widely today.

What is sculpture?

Sculpture is the art of creating a likeness or an idea in carved or moulded form. It is created by chiselling down from a block of solid material until the desired shape is produced, or by adding piece to piece of a plastic material until a similar result is achieved. The latter sculpture then has to be cast in a tougher material, one which can be hardened so that the shape is permanent. Clay or wax are the most common materials for casting in plaster, bronze or concrete, while the most widely used materials for chiselling are stone, marble, wood and ivory.

Part of a sculpture by Bernini

Who was the Iron Duke?
Arthur Wellesley, first Duke of
Wellington (1769–1852), an Anglo-Irish
soldier-statesman whose career
dominated British – indeed European –
history in the first half of the 19th
century. Wellington was one of the
greatest generals Britain ever had. He
drove the French out of Portugal and
Spain in the Peninsular War and then
defeated Napoleon at Waterloo in 1815,
bringing to a close that remarkable
man's career. Wellington went on to
become prime minister from 1828 to 1830,
but resisted reform which temporarily
clouded his otherwise immense
popularity. In his last years, people
overlooked this and accorded him the
veneration usually given only to kings.

Who was the Little Giant?
Isambard Kingdom Brunel (1806–1859),
the greatest engineering genius of
modern times. He built railway systems,
bridges, tunnels, steamships (one of
them, the *Great Eastern*, was the
biggest vessel afloat for a generation), a
portable hospital for troops in the
Crimea, a model housing estate, docks
and harbours, and much else besides.
Brunel was short, had immense courage
and endurance, made his staff and
employees work very hard but none
worked harder than he. He smoked long
cigars incessantly, travelled all over the
place in a specially built carriage fitted
out as an architect's drawing office, and
riskd his life on many occasions on big
projects to save those of others.

Why was Alfred of England called
The Great?
For a long time the English people
remembered, and their descendants
recalled, the times of Alfred who was
king from 871 to 900 AD. They
remembered his crushing victory over
the Vikings at Slaughterford in 878, his
220

creation of the English navy, his
encouragement of scholars (native and
from abroad), his own translations of
Latin works, his coding of the law, and
his patronage of the Church. He gave
Englishmen a sense of national pride and
left behind him a son and a grandson
who were to prove almost as able and
popular rulers as he was. He was the
only English king to be called 'the
Great'.

What kind of ruler was Canute?
Canute the Great, king of Denmark,
Norway, England, and for a while of
Sweden, was one of the foremost rulers
in 11th-century Europe. He was king of
England from 1016 to 1035 and in that
time endeared himself to his new
subjects, encouraged trade and
agriculture and took a close interest in
schooling. He was no less popular in
Denmark and Norway where he
governed with strength tempered with
justice. He had begun his career as a
leader of Viking raiders under his fierce
father, Sweyn Forkbeard, who died in
1014. On accepting the English throne
after the death of Edmund Ironside,
however, Canute began to change, and
in no time he showed his other and
better side.

What was Abraham Lincoln's
achievement in the United States?
Abraham Lincoln (1809–1865) taught
himself almost from scratch and became
a successful lawyer. Then he went into
politics and within a short time became a
leading politician with Republican
leanings. He became the Republican
candidate for the presidency in 1860 and
won. Once in office, Lincoln was faced
with the split between northern and
southern states over the question of
slavery, and in 1861 the Civil War broke
out. He worked throughout the whole
war for the preservation of the union of

the states, and he also proclaimed slavery abolished in the southern states. After the battle of Gettysburg in 1863, Lincoln made a famous speech in which he declared that the war was being fought to preserve 'a nation conceived in liberty and dedicated to the proposition that all men are created equal' and to ensure that 'government of the people, by the people, for the people shall not perish from the earth'. This is the simplest definition of democracy ever stated. Lincoln was assassinated five days after the end of the war in 1865.

What did William I do for England?
William, Duke of Normandy, king of England from 1066 to 1087, transformed the country. He defeated Harold the king and destroyed the flower of his army at Hastings. He then set out to build a new England, imposing upon its people his own brand of feudalism. He made every landowner, even his relatives and friends, swear fealty to him. He instituted the *Domesday Book*, a comprehensive survey of the contents of nearly every manor in the land, down to the last sheep and cow. He kept order throughout his realm, ruling sternly but on the whole with justice.

Who was Sir Isaac Newton?
Isaac Newton (1642–1727) was the greatest scientist ever to emerge from Britain. He applied his unique scientific gifts to a number of fields of enquiry, and he introduced the differential calculus, stated the famous laws of motion, discovered the law of gravitation, stated the corpuscular theory of light and put forward the binomial theorem. He was a member of Parliament, president of the Royal Society, sometime warden of the royal mint. He was, over and above all this, a very nice and gentle man, who never allowed his superior knowledge to make lesser men feel humble.

What did Cardinal Richelieu do for France?
This remarkable statesman and prelate, born in 1585, re-structured France and brought the country from being a faction-torn second-rate power to the highest strength and influence in Europe. Armand Jean du Plessis de Richelieu, cardinal of France and principal minister of Louis XIII, from 1624 to 1642, made the monarchy almost absolute, for sound purposes, divided the country into districts which were to be governed by superintendents responsible to the king and him, encouraged explorers and merchants to travel abroad in the undiscovered parts of the world and build an empire for France, and broke the supremacy of the Catholic powers of Europe by supporting the Protestant powers in the Thirty Years War.

Little Quiz 36
Some ruling groups
1. Who were the Twelve Caesars?
2. What are the names of the English royal dynasties since 1066?
3. Give the names of the Tudor monarchs.
4. Who was the first king of all Ireland?
5. Who was the first king of Scotland?
6. What were the dates of Louis XIV, Louis XV and Louis XVI of France?
7. What was their relationship to each other?
8. Who was the first prince of all Wales?
   Of which country was this person president?
9. de Gaulle
10. Paderewski
11. Carmona
12. Tubman
13. Mannerheim
14. Nasser
15. Nkrumah
16. Sukarno
17. Vargas

How do acorns turn into oak trees?
An oak tree doesn't begin to produce seeds until it is about twenty years old. Acorns, its seeds, appear during the summer and autumn and fall to the ground. If the soil conditions are right, the acorn will begin to grow into another oak tree.

Why do cacti have thorns?
A cactus plant is usually found in North and Central America (though it will grow elsewhere). It does not have leaves to store water, but water is stored in its spines. Spines also protect the plant from desert or other animals that try to chew the stem to quench their thirst.

What is chlorophyll?
This is the green colouring material in plants, and it is formed in those parts that are exposed to the sun. Chlorophyll enables the plant to take in carbon dioxide and alter it to produce oxygen and other substances for its growth.

Why does a dandelion change its appearance?
When the yellow blossom of a dandelion begins to die, it leaves behind a lot of seeds. These would all fall to the ground and only a few would grow up into new dandelions. So, the blossom changes into white fluff matter which can be blown away by the wind, carrying the seeds with it.

What's blossom?
Blossom is a flower which appears on trees (especially fruit trees) early in the summer to herald the growth of the fruit for the season. Some blossom is extremely pretty and colourful.

How does ivy stick to the wall?
Ivy is a climbing or spreading plant. It grows quickly and sticks to the wall by means of tiny sucker-like discs. It

doesn't matter if the wall is rough or smooth. A well built wall would be protected from ivy, but if the mortar between the bricks is soft and crumbly, then ivy will send its tendrils into the mortar and eventually break up the bricks.

What is the difference between a fruit and a vegetable?
The real difference is that a fruit encloses its seeds inside a skin whilst a vegetable does not. Some things we think of as vegetables, such as tomatoes, runner beans and even cucumbers, are really fruits. Real vegetables are things like lettuce, potatoes and cauliflowers.

What is a fungus?
It is a simple plant that is not green because it has no chlorophyll, and which does not make its own food. It lives by absorbing food from dead plants like tree stumps or from the earth in which there are decaying plants. The best known fungus is a mushroom.

The British Fungus 'Fly Again'

What is osmosis?
In botany, it is the process by which fluids pass from one part of a plant to another through a porous membrane, carrying foods with them. The membrane slows down the process and ensures that all parts of the plant get enough.

How do peanuts grow?
Peanuts grow inside pods like peas or beans. These pods grow on bushes. When the petals of the bushes fade away, the pods lengthen and bury their tips into the earth. There they get larger still. Inside, the nuts are maturing.

What is a pomegranate?
It is a fruit with a tough, yellow-red skin, about the size of an average orange. It is juicy inside with masses of crisp, small seeds which are very sweet. Pomegranates grow on short trees, chiefly in West Asia and North Africa.

Why do plants wilt?
Plants need water constantly. If they are starved they begin to wilt and will eventually die. This is because they cannot manufacture the food for growth and life without water.

How do nettles sting?
Nettles are covered with tiny hairs. The longer hairs are hollow and contain a minute gland which secretes droplets of formic acid. As the tops of the hairs are sharp, they prick the skin and let the formic acid into it, causing a stinging sensation.

What is a conifer?
A conifer is an evergreen tree that produces cones which protect the tree seeds. Best known of the conifers are fir trees, cypresses, pine trees and yew. There are one or two conifers that are not evergreen but deciduous, such as the larch.

What is an evergreen tree?
An evergreen tree is one whose leaves stay on the branches all the year round. They are usually smallish leaves, very tough, so that they can stand all weathers. Holly is an evergreen.

What is a deciduous tree?
Trees whose leaves turn brown and then fall off in the autumn or early winter are called deciduous trees. They grow fresh leaves again in the next spring.

What is peat?
Peat is a kind of compost of dead plants, compressed over the years into a spongy mass. It is used to improve the soil in gardens. When dried, it can also be burned as a fuel.

What gives a flower its smell?
The pleasing smell of a flower comes from chemicals that are in the petals. The various smells you can enjoy in the garden depend upon the mixture of the chemicals.

Are there any plants that eat animals?
Yes, several. One is the Venus flytrap, and another is the pitcher. The Venus flytrap has leaves with spikes along the edge. When a fly settles on the leaf, the leaf closes and entraps it. A pitcher plant has tubes down which an insect can slide but which it cannot get out of again.

How do plants produce starch?
Starch is made by plants by the action of water and chlorophyll on the carbon dioxide in the air. This produces sugar which the plant converts to starch.

Is cotton a plant?
Yes, it is a shrub which holds its seeds in long white strands inside a capsule. The strands, or fibres, are woven to make cotton thread for cloth.

When was the first artificial satellite launched into space?
Sputnik I was sent up by the USSR on 4 October 1957.

Which was the first animal sent into space?
A dog, Laika, which was sent up in the USSR's second satellite, on 3 November 1957.

Who was the first American astronaut to go into orbit round the earth?
Colonel John Glenn, in the Mercury capsule Friendship 7, on 20 February 1962.

What was Telstar?
Telstar was the first active communications satellite sent into space on 10 July 1962 and which began to relay live television programmes from 23 July.

What objective did the spacecraft Mariner 2 achieve on 14 December 1962?
It flew past the planet Venus after a voyage of over three months.

What did Mariner 4 achieve in 1965?
It flew past the planet Mars and photographed Martian craters. The journey took from 28 November 1964 to 14 July 1965.

Who was the first man in space?
Yuri Gagarin, the Soviet cosmonaut, who made a two-hour orbital flight in Vostok I on 12 April 1961.

Who was the first woman in space?
Second Lieutenant Valentina Vladimirovna Tereshkova, aged 26, of the Soviet Air Force. She spent 2 days, 22 hours, 50 minutes orbiting the Earth alone aboard Vostok 6 in June 1963.

Which country achieved the first unmanned spacecraft flight round the moon and brought the craft back to Earth?
The USSR, in September 1968. The vehicle was Zond 5.

Which country achieved the first soft landing on the moon?
The USSR, with Luna 9, a spacecraft which photographed the surface, on 3 February 1966.

What was the Apollo–Soyuz Test Project?
It was a joint American–Russian mission on which the US astronaut Thomas Stafford and the USSR cosmonaut Alexei Leonov met and shook hands in the interconnecting hatch of the Apollo–Soyuz complex, that is, the two spacecraft linked in space, 17 July, 1975.

What other nations apart from the USA and the USSR have launched satellites into space?
France (1965), Britain (1969), China (1970), Japan (1970), India (1980).

When was the first soft landing on Venus?
On 17 August 1970, by the USSR, when a capsule from Venera 7 settled on the surface. The craft was of course unmanned.

What was Lunokhod I?
This was the world's first remote-controlled lunar roving vehicle. It was landed successfully on the moon by the USSR on 17 November 1970.

Who sent up the first orbiting space station?
The USSR sent up Salyut I on 19 August 1971, and it remained in space until early the following October.

Which spacecraft took the first close-

up pictures of Saturn's rings?
Voyager I (USA) in November 1980.

Who was the first man to land on the moon's surface?
Colonel Neil Armstrong of the USA. He was followed closely by Edwin Aldrin, and both stepped out onto the surface on 20 July 1969.

What were Colonel Armstrong's words when he stepped down onto the moon?
'That's one small step for a man, one giant leap for mankind.'

What did Helios I achieve?
This space probe launched jointly by the USA and West Germany, went as close as 45 million km (28 million miles) to the Sun. This was in 1974.

Which spacecraft made the first return trip into space?
The space shuttle orbiter Columbia. It first blasted into orbit on 12 April 1981. It made a return journey on 12 November 1981.

Who was the first spaceman to die of natural causes?
Colonel Pavel Ivanovich Belyayev of the Soviet Air Force, who had commanded the Voskhod 2 flight in March 1965. He died of a stomach complaint in January 1970.

Where is Tyuratam?
Tyuratam, originally referred to as Baikonur, is the USSR equivalent of Cape Canaveral. It lies in Kazakshtan, to the east of the Aral Sea.

What lunar fly-by mission almost ended in disaster?
That of Apollo 13 in April 1970. Following an explosion aboard the service module, the crew of three were able to use the lunar module as a refuge which saved their lives.

Who was the first Western European to travel in space?
French astronaut Jean-Loup Chrétien, who accompanied a Soviet commander aboard Soyuz T-6 in June 1982.

Who has made the most flights into space?
John Watts Young, who made his first flight into space in 1965 and his fifth in 1981.

Who was the first man to die during a space mission?
Colonel Vladimir Mickhailovich Komarov of the Soviet Air Force, who died aboard Soyuz I when it crashed to Earth in April 1967. According to the official Russian account, the accident was due to parachute failure.

Little Quiz 37
   In which countries do these rivers mainly flow?
1. Irrawaddy
2. Ganges
3. Po
4. Tagus
5. Scheldt
6. Rhone
7. Tay
8. Taff
9. Liffey
10. Test
11. Red
12. Flinders
13. Dnieper
14. Maranon
15. Xingu
16. Yukon
17. Yangtze
18. Orange
19. Clutha
20. Menderes

?ism

What is populism?
A doctrine whose advocates believe they represent the common people irrespective of political persuasions.

What is capitalism?
It is the economic system based on private or corporate ownership of the means of production of wealth, the distribution of whose goods depends upon competition in a free market.

What would it mean if you were a communist and were accused by your colleagues of deviationism?
It means that you had a tendency to think, speak or act contrary to the orthodox communist line.

What is Post-Impressionism?
It is the term used to describe French art styles of the very late 19th century and the early 20th century, immediately following those of the impressionists. Notable exponents of post-impressionism were Cézanne, Gauguin and Van Gogh.

What is a mechanism?
It is a system or process made up from components which work together and function like a machine.

What is holism?
It is the belief that some wholes are greater than the sum of their component parts.

What is atavism?
It means reverting to primitive instincts from Latin *atavus* a great-great-great-grandfather.

Is atheism a religion?
No, it is the refusal to accept the existence of God, or of any supernatural being, past or present.

What is an aphorism?
It is a short and pithy saying.

226

What is a euphemism?
The use of a mild word or phrase in place of a harsh or offensive one, for example, 'a stranger to the truth' instead of 'liar'.

What has Castroism to do with Fidel Castro?
It has everything to do with him. When Castro overturned the US-backed government of General Batista in Cuba in 1959, he set up a new communist state in the island, in which the communist ideas were tempered with the traditional Latin-American revolutionary aims of giving the peasants and industrial workers a fair deal.

What is an organism?
It is a living being, plant or animal, with components that work together.

What is metabolism?
A word describing the continuous processes of the building up and breaking down of cells in living organisms, which accounts for the sustaining of life and growth.

What is pantheism?
This has two meanings. It means the worship of, or belief in, many gods, as in ancient civilizations. It also means belief that one god is everything and everything is that god.

What is transvestism?
It means the habit of wearing the clothes of the sex opposite to that of the wearer.

What is Zionism?
It is the movement for establishing and maintaining a national community for the Jews in Palestine. It is also the belief that such a home is the destiny of Jews.

What does syllogism mean?
It is a logical argument constructed from two propositions, one following another, and a conclusion arrived at.

What is Fabianism?

It is an early socialist philosophy developed in Britain in the later 19th century, which stated that the changes required in society would be better and more permanent if they were achieved slowly instead of by violent revolution.

What is prognathism?

It is the state of being prognathous, that is, having a projecting jaw.

What is a micro-organism?

Any organism which is extremely small, such as a bacterium, virus or tiny cellular structure like an amoeba.

In what play is there a character called Miss Prism?

The Importance of Being Earnest, by Oscar Wilde.

What is a malapropism?

A misapplication of a word with humorous, or even ludicrous results. The name derives from a character, Mrs Malaprop, in Sheridan's comedy *The Rivals*, a lady given to such misuse of English.

What is Zoroastrianism?

A religion founded in Persia by the prophet Zoroaster in the 6th century BC. Its holy book is known as the Avesta, its supreme god is referred to as Akura Mazda. Most of its adherents now live in and around Bombay.

What is Lamaism?

The name for the form of the Buddhist faith developed in Tibet. Its spiritual leader, the Dalai Lama, is considered to be divine; however, the present holder of this position was forced by the Chinese occupation of his land to flee to a life of exile in India in 1959.

What is Arianism?

This was a Christian heresy, first expressed by one Arius of Alexandria in the 4th century. This denied the full divinity of Christ. It was condemned by the Council of Nicaea. After remaining dormant for over a millennium, Arianism enjoyed a limited following in 17th and 18th century England and had some influence in the development of Unitarian thought.

What is Wahabism?

This was a movement within Islam that was developed in Arabia in the 18th century by Muhammad ibn Abd-el-Wahhab. Since Saudi Arabia achieved statehood following World War I, Wahabism has been the official creed of that country.

What is deism?

The belief that there is a god, but that he (or she) has not revealed himself (or herself) except in the normal courses of nature and history.

Little Quiz 38

What are the capital cities of:

1. West Germany
2. Burma
3. South Africa
4. Ecuador
5. Bolivia
6. Mexico
7. Cuba
8. Trinidad
9. Northern Ireland
10. Iceland
11. Uruguay
12. Chile
13. Egypt
14. Israel
15. Sudan
16. Bulgaria
17. Malta
18. Albania
19. Malawi
20. Malagasy

What is a *de facto* ruler?
A monarch who rules not because he is
the legitimate successor of the previous
monarch but because he has seized power
by a coup d'état or by war. Henry VII of
England was *de facto* king by virtue of
having won the throne at the battle of
Bosworth in 1485 from the rightful king,
Richard III who was killed.

**What do we mean when we say 'do
something pronto!'?**
Pronto is Spanish for quickly.

**Would you find it advantageous to be
given *carte blanche* in a new job?**
Yes, for it means virtually that you can
do what you like in the position, though
there would obviously be some limits.
Carte blanche means white card or sheet,
and the term comes from the idea of
giving someone a blank sheet of paper
and allowing them to write out their own
terms.

What is *parvenu*?
Parvenu means 'having arrived' in
French, and refers to people who have
come from humble beginnings and made
good, generally through the acquisition
of wealth.

**What has happened to you if you are
described as *hors de combat*?**
It means you are temporarily out of
action. Generally, it is used if you have
been disabled through illness or accident.
It is the French for 'out of the fight'.

What is *sang froid*?
It is the French term for coolness or
composure in moments of crisis (literally,
cold blood).

What are *pince nez*?
They are a special type of spectacles in
which the two lenses and frame are
supported by clips on the nose. (French,
pinch nose.)

What is a *cul-de-sac*?
A blind alley. If you come to a road
marked cul-de-sac, you will not normally
be able to get out of it at the other end.

**Why would someone use the phrase
jacta alea est, or its English equivalent,
the die is cast?**
It was the phrase used by Julius Caesar
when he stood by the Rubicon river in
north Italy, deciding to cross and go
south, thereby starting what he believed
to be a necessary civil war. So, it means 'I
can't turn back now.'

What does *in vino veritas* mean?
It means, the truth comes out in wine,
and that you are more likely to show
your real feelings if you have had a lot to
drink. The idea, however, is certainly
open to question.

**Where would you expect to see a
gendarme?**
Usually in France. *Les gendarmes* are
soldiers used for police duties, but
foreigners often use the word *gendarme*
to mean any kind of policeman.

What is a *snorkel*?
It is a piece of simple apparatus of
mouthpiece and tube, enabling one to
swim for long periods under water. It
probably comes from the German
snarchen to snore.

What is *karate*?
A Japanese form of unarmed combat. It
is taught and used as a form of recreation
so widely now in the West that the term
has come to be regarded as any kind of
unarmed combat.

**Would you feel honoured if you were
presented with a *festschrift*?**
Probably. It is a book of essays or papers
specially written by scholars on the
subject on which you are a leading
authority, and presented to you on

retirement or on reaching a certain age. It comes from the German meaning festival writing.

What is _cologne_?
It is short for _eau de Cologne_, (French, water from Cologne), a scented water, refreshing especially in hot weather when applied to the skin.

What is a _boutique_?
From the French for shop, the word is now used to indicate a particular kind of small store that specializes in ready-made fashion clothes, and perhaps crafts, scents and soaps.

Why do children shout 'Cave!' when a master is approaching the classroom?
Because they want to warn their friends to stop fooling about, etc. _Cave_ is Latin for Beware!

What is _poste restante_?
Part of a post office where letters are kept for collection.

What does _in toto_ mean?
Entirely or completely.

What does _id est_ mean?
Simply 'that is'; however, you are already likely to be familiar with its abbreviated form, ie.

Who or what is an _aegrotat_?
Literally meaning 'he (or she) is ill', an aegrotat is one considered worthy of being awarded a degree or similar honour, despite having been unable through illness to sit the examination or test required for such an award.

Who or what is a _sabra_?
A Jew, born in Israel, considered to have the qualities of the sabra or desert pear which is prickly on the outside and soft on the inside.

When a papal pronouncement is made _urbi et orbi_, to whom is the pope speaking?
To everyone! It means 'to the city (Rome) and to the world'.

What is _l'esprit de l'escalier_?
This is 'staircase wit'. The phrase refers to the witty answer one wishes one had made in the drawing room but only thought of later on, going down the stairs on the way out!

What did the hand write on the wall of Belshazzar's banqueting hall, and what did it mean?
Mene, mene, tekel, upharsin (_Daniel_ v: 25). These words are Aramaic and they can be translated as 'God has numbered your kingdom and brought it to an end; you are weighed in the balance, and are found wanting; your kingdom is divided'.

What is the meaning of _mens sana in corpore sano_?
What we all strive for, doubtless. Expressed by the Roman writer Juvenal, its meaning is 'a sound mind in a sound body'.

What is _chili con carne_?
This is basically meat cooked in a spicy sauce, a dish emanating from Mexico and neighbouring parts of the USA.

What was _suttee_?
This was a custom abolished by the British in India, by which a Hindu widow would throw herself onto the funeral pyre of her husband.

What is _jai alai_?
This is a handball game, native to the Basque country in Spain, which is played in a court by two or four players with long curved wicker baskets strapped to their right wrists.

How was the wireless first used at sea to help in crime detection?
The murderer, Dr Crippen was travelling to the US in a liner in disguise. A radio message was sent by the police to the ship's captain and he was discovered, arrested and brought back to Britain in 1910.

When was the BBC established?
In 1922, as the British Broadcasting Company. This was dissolved in 1927 and the British Broadcasting Corporation founded with a 10-year charter.

Which famous abdication speech was broadcast on radio in December 1936?
The speech by Edward VIII. It was broadcast from Windsor.

Who was the first director-general of the BBC?
John Reith, later Sir John and later still, Lord Reith. He retired in 1938.

When was Radio Times first published?
1923.

Who was the first commentator on the Oxford–Cambridge Boat Race?
John Snagge, who started in 1928.

Which famous West Indian cricketer became a governor of the BBC?
Learie Constantine, later Lord Constantine.

What did the initials ITMA stand for?
It's That Man Again, the name of a highly popular radio comedy show, starring Tommy Handley (who was 'that man').

When were radio waves discovered?
In 1864 by James Clerk-Maxwell, and first successfully transmitted in a laboratory by Heinrich Hertz in 1888.

Who were the most regular and most popular members of the long-running weekly radio programme, the Brains Trust?
Professor C. E. M. Joad, Professor (later Sir) Julian Huxley, and Commander Campbell.

When did a member of the Royal Family first use radio to speak to the nation?
Indirectly, in 1924, when George V gave his speech opening the British Empire Exhibition at Wembley, and was recorded.

Who succeeded in transmitting radio waves across the Atlantic?
Guglielmo Marconi, the Italian born physicist, who directed radio waves from a point at Poldhu in Cornwall to a point in Newfoundland, in 1901.

Which is Britain's longest running radio serial?
The BBC's farming family programme, *The Archers*, begun in 1948.

Which famous London musical concerts were saved by the BBC?
The Promenade Concerts, which had been founded in 1895 by Sir Henry Wood and held at the Queen's Hall (which was destroyed during World War II) and then at the Royal Albert Hall.

Who was the Radio Doctor?
Dr Charles Hill, later Lord Hill of Luton, who eventually became chairman of the BBC.

Who said, 'The Martians have landed' and frightened a whole city?
Orson Wells produced a radio drama in New York in 1938, about invasion from outer space, opening the programme with the announcement 'The Martians have landed'. Many thought the statement to be true, and panicked.

Who was Uncle Mac?
Derek McCulloch, introducer of
Children's Hour.

Three valve battery receiver made by
General Electric Company 1923

**How many recordings on discs and
tapes are there in the BBC's Sound
Archives Library?**
About 101,000.

**How many broadcast receiving
licences were issued in the first full
year of broadcasting, 1927, and in the
last completed year?**
(1927), 2,269,644 and (1983), 18,494,235.
The latter figure, by the way, is not the
highest recorded. The 1981 figure was
18,667,211.

**Who plays the part of June in the
popular BBC TV series** *Terry and
June*?
June Whitfield, who also played the part
of Eth in the regular sketch about Ron
and Eth and Mr Glum in the weekly
radio serial *Take It From Here*, one of the
top BBC radio programmes of the 1950s
and early 1960s.

**What dramatic incident took place
during the famous BBC Radio
programme,** *The Archers*, **on the same
night on which commercial television
opened in 1955?**
During the episode of *The Archers* on
22 September, Grace Archer, wife of Phil
Archer, lost her life through rushing into
a burning stable to rescue a horse. The
incident attracted widespread publicity,
and was described by the *Daily Herald* as
a 'mean, callous stunt'. Phil Archer,
incidentally, was played by Norman
Painting, who is still playing the part, 29
years later (1984).

**How long has the BBC's External
Service by radio been operating?**
Since 19 December 1932, when it started
as the Empire Service, broadcasting
throughout the old British Empire.

**When did both king and prime
minister address the nation over BBC
radio on the same day?**
On the day of the outbreak of World War
II, 3 September 1939. The prime
minister, Neville Chamberlain, spoke at
about 11.00 in the morning, and the
king, George VI, about 6 o'clock in the
evening.

**When did the first Scottish national
radio service, Radio Scotland, begin
broadcasting?**
On 23 November, 1978.

At which battle was a king of Sweden killed in the moment of victory?
Lutzen in 1632. King Gustavus Adolphus of Sweden, commander of the Protestant forces fighting in Germany during the Thirty Years' War, defeated the Catholic Imperial forces under Wallenstein, but was himself wounded. As evening fell after his army had triumphed, he was killed by a fleeing enemy soldier.

At which battle was a king of Ireland killed in the moment of victory?
At Clontarf in 1014. King Brian Boru had just routed the Vikings not far from Dublin, when one of the Viking leaders running from the battlefield came upon him in his tent and slew him.

What was the Battle of the Bulge?
At the end of 1944, when the German armies were being pushed back into their own territory in Europe, the German leader Hitler launched one final attempt to stave off total defeat by an assault upon the US forces in the Ardennes Forest. For a few days, the Germans managed to punch a hole in the US lines and formed a pocket of recaptured territory. This came to be called The Bulge. The attack was not sustained, and with British help, the US forces drove the Germans back into their Rhineland.

What was achieved by the Battle of Omdurman?
Lord Kitchener, in command of the Anglo-Egyptian army, defeated the fierce and bold warriors of the Dervish army in the Sudan on September 1898 and the Sudan was absorbed into the British Empire.

At which battle did Alfred the Great defeat the Vikings in 878?
At the battle of Ethandune in the west country of England. The site was either near Edington in Wiltshire, or near Slaughterford in south Gloucestershire.

At which battle was the son of Napoleon III of France killed?
At the battle of Isandlwana in Zululand in 1879, when the Zulu chief, Cetewayo, defeated a British army in which the prince imperial, eldest son of Napoleon III, was serving.

Where was the siege of Dien Bien Phu?
Dien Bien Phu was a town in French Indo-China (now Vietnam). In 1954 French and allied troops were besieged by communist forces under Ho Chi Minh, and they had to surrender. This led to the withdrawal of France from Indo-China altogether.

At which battle did Julius Caesar defeat Pompey the Great?
At the battle of Pharsalus in Greece, in 48 BC. Caesar defeated an army more than twice the size of his force, and by so doing established himself as supreme in the Roman world.

Which battle stopped the Arabs from conquering all France in the 8th century?
This was the great battle of Tours, near Poitiers, in central France, where in 732 Charles Martel, king of the Franks, crushed a huge Arab army under Abd-Er-Rahman over several days' fighting.

What was the battle of Tsushima in 1905?
It was a great naval victory for the Japanese fleet over the Russian fleet during the Russo-Japanese War of 1905–1906. The battle was fought in the strait of water beside the island of Tsushima off Korea.

At which battle did Nelson put a telescope to his blind eye?
Copenhagen in 1801. Nelson was second in command under Sir Hyde Parker, but ignoring a signal to break off action, he

sailed into the Danish fleet when it was not expecting him and destroyed or disabled the entire fleet.

Which famous siege in France was conducted and won by a cardinal?
The siege of La Rochelle, by Cardinal Richelieu, in 1627. The fortress of La Rochelle was held by Huguenots who held out for over a year, but the cardinal finally compelled them to yield after a relief force promised from England failed to arrive.

At which battle in 1571 was the Turkish fleet defeated?
Lepanto – a tremendous sea battle between the Turkish fleet and a Christian combined fleet of Spaniards, Venetians, Genoese and others under the command of Don John of Austria, illegitimate son of the emperor Charles V of the Holy Roman Empire.

Which was the decisive battle of World War I on the Western Front?
It was the battle of the Marne, fought in early September 1914, where the Allied British and French forces stemmed the advance of the German Army through France on its way towards Paris. The war went on for another four years, but the Germans lost their only chance to take Paris.

What happened at the Battle of the Falkland Islands in 1914?
This was a naval victory by the British fleet under Admiral Sir Doveton Sturdee over the German fleet under Admiral von Spee.

What battle is depicted in the famous Bayeux Tapestry?
The battle of Hastings in 1066 when Harold of England was defeated and slain. This date marked the beginning of the Norman conquest of England by William of Normandy.

At which battle was Sir Philip Sidney killed?
At the battle of Zutphen in the Netherlands, in 1586, where he led an English contingent on the Dutch side against the Spanish.

What English general named his palatial residence after his greatest victory?
John Churchill, Duke of Marlborough, named Blenheim Palace after the battle of Blenheim in the war of the Spanish Succession.

What was the result of the Battle of Cannae in 216 BC?
The Carthaginian army under Hannibal utterly defeated the Roman army in a desperate battle by the river near Cannae, in South Italy. About 50,000 Romans were killed or wounded. The victory left the way open for Hannibal to march on Rome, but he failed to do so.

How did the rain help Clive to win the Battle of Plassey, in 1757?
During the battle, the Indian forces under Suraja Dowlah, the Nawab of Bengal, neglected to cover their barrels of gunpowder. It rained, and the powder was soaked. The British supplies, on the other hand, had been well-protected. As a result, Clive completely routed the Nawab's army.

Who destroyed one part of an enemy's fleet before breakfast, breakfasted, then destroyed the remaining part?
Admiral Dewey, the US commander fighting the Spanish at the Battle of Manila Bay in 1898.

Who defeated whom at the battle of Tannenburg in 1914?
The Germans defeated the Russians, thus reversing the latters' advance into what was then Prussia.

What is the highest British decoration for bravery?
The Victoria Cross, instituted by Queen Victoria in 1856 to decorate heroes of the Crimean War.

Why have there been no new Knights of the Order of St Patrick since 1922?
Because of the creation of the Irish Free State in 1922, a first step towards the complete separation of Ireland politically from Britain.

What is the emblem indicating 'mentioned in despatches'?
An oak leaf or leaves, worn usually on the ribbon of the Victory Medal for World War I, the Victory Medal for World War II, or on other ribbons by order.

When did the orders of the Star of India and the Indian Empire stop being awarded?
In 1947, when British India was given self-government and partitioned into India and Pakistan.

When was the Order of Merit founded?
In 1902, by Edward VII. It carries no title, but it is one of the highest awards that the sovereign can bestow.

How many OMs can there be at one time?
Twenty-four. At one time it was divided into twelve military members and twelve civilian members.

When is a 'bar' awarded to the holder of a decoration?
When the person is awarded the same decoration a second time, for a similar service, such as a second act of great bravery. Bars are awarded to DSOs, MCs, DFCs, DSCs and some others. Only three bars have ever been awarded to holders of the Victoria Cross. One was a New Zealander, Second Lieutenant Charles Upham, who was first awarded the medal during the German attack on Crete in 1941, then won a bar in the Western Desert in 1942.

Why is the Order of the Bath so named?
In medieval times, the bestowal of knighthood was generally accompanied by a ritual taking of a bath. The order is generally accepted as having been established by Henry IV (1399–1413) as a mark of distinction he conferred on several knights and lords at the time of his coronation.

What is the order Pour le Mérite?
Though French in title, it was in fact a high Prussian decoration, introduced by Frederick the Great (1740–1786) as an adaptation of the earlier Order of Generosity. In the early 19th century the Pour le Mérite was limited to military services.

Who founded the Legion d'Honneur?
It was founded by Napoleon Bonaparte in 1802. He introduced it to encourage civilian and military achievement; as he said, it is easier to manage men by giving them toys.

What is the highest award of the United States?
The Medal of Honor, for military or naval services. It was instituted in 1861 and is generally known as the Congressional Medal.

What is the Purple Heart?
It is an old US decoration (which began in the 1780s) that in recent years has been awarded to any US member of the armed forces who is wounded in action, and it is also awarded posthumously.

Who was the only person to receive the Grand Cross of the Iron Cross of Nazi Germany?
Reichsmarschall Hermann Goering.

Who founded the French Order of Liberation?
This was instituted by General de Gaulle in 1940, when he came over to England after the French government surrendered to Hitler. It was to be given to military and civilian people who gave distinguished service towards the cause of liberating France. Holders of the award are *Compagnons*.

Which is the highest order awarded in Denmark?
The Order of the White Elephant, which goes back to the 15th century.

What was the origin of the English Order of the Garter?
It was founded by Edward III (1327–1377) in 1348. He intended the members to be a brotherhood of knights and lords who had distinguished themselves in battle, especially those who had helped to win the great victory over France at Crécy (1346). There were to be 25 members. It is England's highest award, after the Victoria Cross, and is no longer restricted to military personnel.

Can a medal cease to be awarded, its previous recipients then being given another decoration?
Yes. Of the total of 113 Empire Gallantry Medals awarded, all but one were later exchanged for the George Cross which was instituted in 1940.

What is the most recent British campaign medal?
The South Atlantic Medal, which was instituted after the Falklands campaign of 1982. This award is suspended from a ribbon consisting of five vertical stripes, shaded and watered in empire blue, white, sea green, white and empire blue.

What is the highest decoration awarded in the Soviet Union?
The Order of Lenin.

What was the Order of Polonia Restituta?
It was created in 1921 by the newly restored Polish state that rose out of the ashes of World War I. It was a civilian, not a military decoration, and it is still in existence.

When were Companions of Honour instituted, and are their numbers restricted?
In 1917, by King George V. The number of ordinary members is restricted to 65, while foreigners are only admitted as honorary members.

In which country was the Order of Leopold instituted in 1832?
In Belgium. Reflecting the bilingual nature of this country, the legend on the Order's medallion appears in both French and Flemish; on the other hand the title of this Order is only listed in French.

At what age do British field marshals retire?
Officially, field marshals never retire. They remain on what is called the active list for the rest of their lives.

What was Nelson's rank when he was killed at Trafalgar in 1805?
In spite of his unparalleled achievements as a naval commander, Nelson was still only a vice-admiral at the time of his greatest – and last sea battle.

Which is the highest rank in the United States Army?
General of the Army.

What is a non-commissioner Officer?
An officer of lower rank, such as sergeant or corporal, in the armed forces, who has not been awarded a commission.

Why did some officers in the British Army have the word Brevet before their rank?
This usually meant that the rank was honorary, and carried no extra pay. Often it was a sign that in due course the actual rank would be granted and the pay increased.

Which are the equivalent Army and Royal Navy ranks for the Royal Air Force Wing Commander?
Commander, Lieutenant-Colonel.

Who are the first five people in the Order of Precedence, after the Royal Family, in England?
The Archbishop of Canterbury, the Lord High Chancellor, the Archbishop of York, the Prime Minister, the Lord President of the Council.

Is a bishop senior to a dean in the Church of England?
Yes, but a dean is the head of the chapter of a cathedral or collegiate church.

What was the title of the commander of a Roman legion?
He was a *legatus*.

Which British field marshal was drowned at sea?
Field Marshal Earl Kitchener of Khartoum, KG. After a very distinguished military career, he became secretary of state for war in World War I, and prepared the British Army for eventual victory. On 5 June 1916, he set out in HMS *Hampshire* for a visit to Russia, but the ship struck a mine, or was torpedoed, and it sank with all but a handful of passengers.

Who was the 'Father of the RAF'?
Sir Hugh Trenchard, the first marshal of the Royal Air Force.

What was Captain Bligh's rank at the time of the famous mutiny on the *Bounty*?
Bligh was a lieutenant in the Royal Navy. He survived the mutiny to distinguish himself in many later naval actions, and ended as a vice-admiral.

How many US generals later became presidents of the USA?
Four – Ulysses S. Grant (1869–1877), Andrew Jackson (1829–1837), George Washington (1789–1797) and Dwight Eisenhower (1953–1961).

What does a quarter-master sergeant do?
He is a non-commissioned officer who provides the clothing, food, weapons, and accommodation for a body of troops.

How was it that Winston Churchill, a statesman, was allowed to wear the uniform of a British air commodore?
He was made honorary air commodore of the No 615 Fighter Squadron of the Royal Auxiliary Air Force in 1939.

Who was known as the Little Corporal?
Napoleon Bonaparte, who became emperor of the French, 1804–1815.

Who was in command of the English fleet which defeated the Spanish Armada in 1588?
It was Lord Howard of Effingham, a relative of the then Duke of Norfolk. Drake was effectively second-in-command.

Which Nigerian general and statesman afterwards became a post-graduate student at a British university?
General Yakubu Danjuma Gowon, at one time head of the Federal Military Government and commander-in-chief of the forces of the Federal Republic of Nigeria (1966–1975). He later came to Britain to study at Warwick University.

What is a sergeant-at-arms?
In Britain, he is an official who attends the speaker of the House of Commons or the lord chancellor.

Where did the rank of colonel-general appear in the Nazi German Army list?
Below field marshal and above general.

What are the functions of Black Rod?
Black Rod is an official of the House of Lords, his full title being 'Gentleman Usher of the Black Rod'. The name of the post derives from the nature of the staff the bearer carries, an ebony rod topped with a golden lion. He is the principal usher of a number of court and political ceremonials, including those concerning the Order of the Garter. He has responsibilities for maintaining order in the House of Lords and has the power to arrest offending peers. He is best known for summoning the attendance of the Commons to the House of Lords to hear the sovereign's speech from the throne.

What were the ranks of the men who were posthumously awarded the Victoria Cross for gallantry during the Falklands campaign of 1982?
Lieutenant Colonel H. Jones and Sergeant Ian McKay.

Does a rector enjoy a higher rank than a vicar in parishes of the Church of England?
Not really. The essential difference was that a rector enjoyed the greater and lesser tithes of the parish of which he had the care, while a vicar only received the lesser tithes. Such a distinction vanished with the abolition of tithes in 1936; for parishes which are still served by a single clergyman, the historical title of either rector or vicar has been retained.

What were the German army equivalents of these British army ranks in World War II: company sergeant-major; captain; major-general?
Oberfeldwebel or Hauptfeldorwebel; Hauptmann or Rittmeister; Generalleutnant.

Little Quiz 40
What were the earlier names of these countries, once part of European empires?
1. Ghana
2. Zambia
3. Malawi
4. Tuvalu
5. Tanzania
6. Zaire
7. Guyana
8. Campuchea
9. Sri Lanka
10. Malagasy

237

What was a *civitas* capital?
The administrative town of a *civitas*, or tribal state, in Roman Britain. *Civitas* capitals were self-governing and their magistrates were elected by local electors.

What was Crambeck ware?
A type of pottery made in kilns in North Yorkshire, principally near Malton, in the 4th century.

How long was Hadrian's Wall?
It was 80 Roman miles, which is about 73 English miles or 117.53 km from Wallsend on the east to Bowness-on-Solway in the west.

Where was the Antonine Wall?
It ran between the Forth at Carriden to the Clyde at Old Kilpatrick, in Scotland. The Wall was built of turf, though some of the fort buildings along it were of stone.

What was the *Classis Britannica*?
It was the Roman fleet operating in British waters.

Which were the Roman forts of the Saxon Shore?
There were nine, from north-east to south, namely: Brancaster (Norfolk), Burgh Castle (Norfolk), Walton (Suffolk), Bradwell on Sea (Essex), Reculver (Kent), Richborough (Kent), Lympne (Kent), Pevensey (Sussex) and Portchester (Hampshire). The fort at Dover is sometimes included as a tenth.

Briefly, how did the Romans build their roads?
They built them straight where possible, changed direction on hill-tops, and skirted round major obstructions if the need for the road was urgent. The foundations were slabs of stone or small stone blocks. On top of these were spread layers of rammed down gravel or cinders.

Occasionally roads were paved with blocks. Most roads were built on raised banks to allow drainage.

What was the *annona militaris*?
It was a tax raised from the provinces of the Roman Empire which was directed towards paying for the upkeep of the military forces in the provinces. It was paid in cash or in kind (notably farm produce, grain, etc.).

What was a winged corridor villa?
It was a villa building with a central range of rooms having a wing of rooms at one end, or both ends, and with a corridor or verandah at front or back, or both, along the central range. The style began to appear in Britain in the 2nd century.

What was a *mansio*?
It was a large inn or hotel, built round a courtyard, often with an associated bath-house. *Mansiones* were official resting-places, and were erected in *civitas* capitals, towns or occasionally beside main roads in the countryside.

Who was Cartimandua?
She was queen of the Brigantes tribes from about the 50s to the 70s. While she reigned, her tribes maintained relatively peaceful relations with the occupying Roman forces. Towards the end of her reign, her husband Venutius left her and formed an opposition movement, and even rebelled against the Romans, and the queen had to ask them for help.

Did the Romans actually win the battle of Mons Graupius in AD 86?
The historian Tacitus says that they did, but he was prejudiced because the Roman army commander, Agricola, who was governor of Britain at the time, was his father-in-law. The Romans are said to have killed and wounded about 10,000 Caledonians at the battle in North East Scotland, but another 20,000 got away.

And after the battle, the Romans pulled back many miles to the south.

Where were the principal gold mines in Roman Britain?
At Dolaucothi, near Pumpsaint, in Carmarthenshire, Wales.

Why are inscriptions so important to archaeologists?
Because they can often establish the date or the period of the sites at which they are found, or by relating them to other inscriptions with some of the same information on them, they can enlarge knowledge about a particular person, or event, or building.

Wine amphora

What was an amphora?
It was a large, two-handled container for transporting wine, oil or other liquid.

What was an aisled building?
It was a long timber building with one or two rows of posts down the length, to support the roof, like a church nave. It was used for residential quarters for workers on a villa, or for storage or as workshops.

Which Roman emperors died in Britain?
Severus in 211 and Constantius I in 306.

What was the top rank in the magistracy in the Roman Republic?
Normally, it was that of consul, of which two were elected to serve for one year. In certain instances, notably of supreme danger to the state, a dictator might be appointed to govern as long as the emergency lasted. That office was normally held for a very short time, until the time of Julius Caesar who was appointed dictator for life.

What is the Pharos at Dover?
The Pharos, or lighthouse, is one of the most remarkable survivals from Romano-British times. It is in the grounds of the great medieval castle there. It is a stonework tower of octagonal plan, of the 2nd century, which today reaches to about 19m (61ft). The top 5¾m (19ft) of stonework are a medieval rebuilding, but the lower 13m (43ft) are of Roman flint-rubble construction which was faced with smooth stone blocks (which have now mostly disappeared). It is thought the tower originally rose to about 24m (80ft), and would have supported a contrivance for a beacon of fire that could be seen by ships in the Straits of Dover.

When was the first sustained flight by man and vehicle through the air?
On 21 November 1783, when Jean Pilatre de Rozier and the Marquise d'Arlandes piloted a balloon over Paris.

Who first took a balloon across the English Channel?
John Jeffries and Jean-Pierre Blanchard, who crossed from Dover to Calais on 7 January 1785.

When was the first man-carrying airship tested?
In France by Henri Giffard in 1852. His vehicle was powered by a 3 hp engine and managed about 9 kmh (6 mph).

When was the first flight by man in a powered heavier-than-air craft?
This was the famous flight by Orville Wright on 17 December 1903 at the sands at Kitty Hawk, North Carolina. The craft was built by him and his brother Wilbur. Orville sustained the flight for a distance of over 259.25 m (850 ft).

Which is the first recorded air raid during wartime?
In the Italo-Turkish war of 1910–11 in North Africa, a Lieutenant Cavotti flew over the Turkish lines in Libya, on 1 November 1911 and dropped four bombs weighing about 2.042 kg (4½ lb) each.

Who said 'Aviation is good sport, but for the army it is useless.'?
This was said by General (later Marshal) Ferdinand Foch of France. He was to become commander-in-chief of the Allied Armies on the Western Front in the last months of World War I, in which aeroplanes did in fact play a small but useful role.

Who first flew an aeroplane across the English Channel?
Louis Blériot, of France, on 25 July 1909.
240

Photographs were taken of M. Blériot in flight.

When was the first Zeppelin airship flight?
On 2 July 1900. Zeppelin airships were invented by Count von Zeppelin.

How many Zeppelin airships were built between 1900 and the outbreak of World War I?
At least 25. The most celebrated was the Viktoria Luise, built in 1912, which made more than 400 flights, carried over 8500 passengers and flew for more than 47.334 km (29,400 miles).

How many passengers were killed in Zeppelins during the years 1900–14?
Miraculously, none. Although several accidents happened to Zeppelins, there were no fatalities.

When was the first Zeppelin air raid on Britain in World War I?
A Zeppelin dropped several bombs on East Anglia on 19 January 1915, and 4 people were killed, 17 injured.

Who produced the first British official paper on ways of dealing with enemy airships in time of war?
Winston Churchill, when he was first lord of the Admiralty. He wrote a paper about it in 1913.

When was the Royal Flying Corps founded?
In April 1912, with two wings, one for the navy and one for the army.

What armament did the Sopwith Camel fighter plane carry?
This was built in 1917, and it carried two Vickers synchronized machine guns and also four 11.3 kg (25 lb) bombs. It flew at about 193.2 kmh (120 mph) maximum speed.

Which nation first produced anti-aircraft guns?

The Germans. The Krupps armament factories introduced at least three types of A.A.gun in the last years before the outbreak of World War I, a 65 mm, a 75 mm and a larger 105 mm gun which fired a shell weighing 18.16 kg (40 lb). It is believed that about 35 of these guns were ready by the outbreak of the war. The United Kingdom had none.

Who were the first commanders of the R.F.C.?

Captain, later Admiral Sir Godfrey Paine, and Major, later Marshal of the Royal Air Force Viscount Trenchard.

What was Baron von Richthofen's favourite aircraft for aerial combat?

In the last year or two of his life the German airman favoured the Fokker Dr.I (dreidecker), a triplane. Richthofen was killed in combat 21 April 1918.

Which German air ace of World War I was an air force general in World War II?

Ernst Udet. In the middle of the war, however, Udet grew increasingly unhappy about the way Hitler and the Nazis managed the war and treated the people they had conquered, and he committed suicide.

Which was the first aircraft carrier in the Royal Navy?

HMS *Furious*, a battle-cruiser which was converted in 1918 and provided with a long, flat upper deck for take-off and landing. The *Furious* also served in World War II.

Who was the first British pilot killed in an aeroplane crash?

Charles S. Rolls, of the Rolls-Royce partnership. His plane crashed at Bournemouth during Aviation Week, 12 July 1910.

When was the first commercial airline between England and France opened?

In August 1919, when Air Travel and Transport Company Ltd organized flights from London to Paris, using converted de Havilland DH9 bombers. These craft were open to the elements and passengers had to wear flying helmets.

How many Supermarine Spitfire fighters were produced in World War II?

22,759.

Which was the last biplane heavy bomber to serve with the Royal Air Force?

The Handley Page Heyford, which was withdrawn in 1939. It had two engines, carried a ton of bombs and could fly at about 225.4 kmh (140 mph).

When was the retractable undercarriage first used on a monoplane in the RAF?

In March 1935, with the Avro Anson general reconnaissance plane.

Who was Lord Brabazon of Tara?

J. T. C. Moore-Brabazon (1884–1964), a pioneer of British aviation, who made the first three flights by any British aviator (1909) and won a £1000 prize for flying over one mile in a Short–Wright biplane. He received the first flying certificate, No. 1 in 1910. Later, he became a politician and was minister of transport, 1940–41.

PATRICIA

The Liberator
Daniel O'Connell (1775–1847), the Irish national leader who championed the cause of Catholic Emancipation in the 1820s in England.

Lord Haw-Haw
William Joyce (1906–1946), the American-born (of Irish parents) political agitator who became a fascist and went to Germany at the beginning of World War II, where he broadcast anti-British speeches over German radio. He was tried and executed after the war. The name came from the pretentious voice he used.

The Ladies of Llangollen
Lady Eleanor Butler and Miss Sarah Ponsonby, two Irish women who were close friends and lived together at Plas Newydd in Llangollen, Wales, from 1774 to the 1820s. They were visited by many famous people.

The Wolf of Badenoch
Alexander Stewart, Earl of Buchan (c.1343–1405), a son of Robert II of Scotland, who was lord of Badenoch and spent much of his life in violent quarrels with neighbours, particularly the bishop of Moray. He burned Elgin Cathedral and did much other damage.

The Sage of Chelsea
Thomas Carlyle (1795–1881), Scottish-born writer and historian who settled in Chelsea and through his writings and speeches exerted a major influence upon British literature and historical writing. His works included histories of the time of Frederick the Great and of the French Revolution.

Bell-the-Cat
Archibald Douglas, 5th earl of Angus (c.1449–1514), who seized and put to death Robert Cochrane, the unpopular adviser of James III of Scotland.

Satchmo
Louis Armstrong (1900–1971), the American Negro trumpeter and jazz composer.

Vinegar Joe
General Joseph Stilwell (1883–1946), commander-in-chief of the US forces in China, Burma and India in World War I.

Philippe Égalité
Louis Philippe Joseph, duke of Orléans (1747–93), cousin of Louis XVI of France (1774–1793) who supported the French Revolution and hoped he would succeed as king when Louis XVI was deposed.

Bloody Mary
Mary I of England (1553–1558), who as a devout Catholic attempted to reverse the Protestant settlement in England arranged during the reign of her half-brother Edward VI (1547–1553) by persecuting and sending to the stake hundreds of Protestants.

The Young Pretender
Prince Charles Edward Stuart, Bonnie Prince Charlie, 1720–1788, son of Prince James Edward Stuart who was the heir of James II of England and Scotland. Prince Charles came to Scotland to try to win the throne for his father in 1745, but his cause collapsed after defeat at Culloden in 1746.

Toom Tabard
John Baliol (1249–1315), chosen king of Scotland in 1292 but forced to abdicate in 1296. Toom Tabard means Empty Jacket.

General Tom Thumb
Thomas Sherwood Stratton (1838–1883), an American dwarf who was never taller than 1.01 m (3 ft 4 in).

Ike
General of the US Army Dwight David Eisenhower (1890–1969), who was also 34th president of the USA.

Q
Sir Arthur Quiller-Couch (1863–1944), Cornish-born author and poet.

Steenie
George Villiers, 1st duke of Buckingham (1592–1628), favourite of James I (1603–1625) who heaped honours and estates upon him.

Che
Ernesto 'Che' Guevara (1928–1967), the Argentine-born revolutionary leader who became a hero among the young all over the world. (See also p 144.)

K of K
The affectionate abbreviation of Field Marshal Earl Kitchener of Khartoum (1850–1916), a great military figure who as secretary for war became the organizer of the army in World War I.

Prinny
George, prince of Wales, eldest son of George III who became prince regent and ruled in place of his incapacitated father, 1811–1820.

Capability Brown
Lancelot Brown (1715–1783), famous landscape gardener who was employed by many rich and famous people to lay out their gardens and estates, notably Blenheim and Kew.

Bird
Charlie Parker (1920–1955), the American jazz composer and virtuoso of the alto saxophone.

The Pelvis
Elvis Presley (1935–1978), the American rock singer, was given this nickname which conveniently rhymed with his first name in the early part of his career. It is supposed to have derived from his gyrating hips.

Rakehell
John Wilmot, 2nd Earl of Rochester (1647–1680) was a member of the licentious set of courtiers who attended Charles II. Despite his profligacy, which earned him his nickname, he was a poet of some note and a patron of the arts.

Caligula
This is an example of a nickname that has been passed down as if it were the real name of its bearer, the Roman emperor Gaius Caesar who ruled from 37–41. Caligula derives from the Latin word for soldiers' boots. He had worn a diminutive pair as a child in the company of the legions on the Rhine, who accorded him that nickname.

Scarface
The derivation of the nickname of Al Capone (1899–1947) hardly need be stated here. Head of a bootleg and vice syndicate in Chicago in the 1920s and early 1930s, he was also known as Public Enemy Number One.

The Red Dean
The Very Reverend Hewlett Johnson, (1874–1966), dean of Canterbury from 1931 to 1963, who was famous for his support of the Communist cause.

Little Quiz 41
Re-arrange the following into the correct pairs:
1. Clive   Gaul
2. Wolfe   Mexico
3. William of Normandy   Peru
4. Cortes   Alamein
5. Pizarro   India
6. Caesar   Hastings
7. Montgomery   Quebec
8. Marlborough   Crécy
9. Edward III   Bannockburn
10. Robert Bruce   Blenheim

What were the real names of these people?

Anthony Hope, novelist
Sir Anthony Hope Hawkins (1863–1933), author of *The Prisoner of Zenda* and *Rupert of Hentzau*.

Ouida, novelist
Marie Louise de la Ramée (1839–1908). English-born woman novelist who died in poverty in Italy is best known for *Under Two Flags*.

AE
The pseudonym under which George William Russell (1867–1935), the Irish writer, nationalist and poet wrote his verse. He was also editor of *The Irish Statesman* newspaper, 1923–30.

Sapper, novelist
Lt Colonel Cyril McNeile (1888–1937); after a career as regular soldier in the Royal Engineers, he wrote the 'Bulldog Drummond' stories.

Tito, Yugoslav general and statesman
Josip Broz (1892–1981) organized guerrilla opposition to the Nazi occupation of Yugoslavia in World War II and afterwards became premier of post-war Yugoslavia. He called himself Tito, and was created a marshal.

Voltaire
François-Marie Arouet (1694–1778), one of the most celebrated of all French philosophers and writers, whose ideas helped significantly to shape the course of the French Revolution.

Marilyn Monroe, American film star
Norma Jean Baker (1928–1962).

Stalin
Joseph Vissarionovich Dzhgashvili (1879–1953), Russian revolutionary leader and dictator of the USSR from the early 1930s to his death.

Currer Bell
Charlotte Brontë (1816–1855), who is best known as the author of *Jane Eyre*.

Ian Hay, Scottish novelist
Major General John Hay Beith (1876–1952), who was both professional soldier and novelist/playwright.

Lenin
Vladimir Ilyich Ulyanov (1870–1924), leader of the communist revolution in Russia, 1917–18 and founder of the Soviet Union.

Trotsky
Lev Davidovich Bronstein (1879–1940), Russian revolutionary leader, second to Lenin, but driven out of Russia after Lenin's death by Stalin, and eventually assassinated in Mexico.

O. Henry, American writer
William Sidney Porter (1862–1910), American short-story writer, who spent some of his early years in prison on fraud charges.

Molière
Jean Baptiste Poquelin (1622–1673), French playwright and satirist, author of *Tartuffe, Le Misanthrope, Le Bourgeois Gentilhomme* and many others. He revolutionized the theatre in France.

Hugh MacDiarmid
Christopher M. Grieve (1892–1978), Scottish poet and nationalist.

Kemal Ataturk
Mustafa Kemal (1881–1938), Turkish general and statesman who founded modern Turkey after the fall of the Ottoman Empire.

Alcuin
Ealhwine (735–804) English-born scholar and abbot, who became adviser and tutor to Charlemagne.

Tintoretto
Jacopo Robusti (1518–1594), Venetian painter. Among many works he completed the largest canvas by any great master, *The Paradise*.

Donatello
Donato di Betto Bardi (1386–1466), Florentine sculptor, generally regarded as the founder of modern sculpture.

Baron Corvo
Frederick Rolfe (1860–1913), British writer. His best work was *Hadrian VII*.

Malcolm X
Malcolm Little (1925–1965), the American radical black politician and activist, adopted the name Malcolm X. He took the view that X reflected his true yet unknown African family name, whereas 'Little' had come from the slave-owner who had been master of his forebears. For similar reasons, the British black power activist Michael Abdul Malik (1933–1975) renamed himself Michael X.

Twiggy
Lesley Hornby, born 1950, the English fashion model, actress and singer, adopted this pseudonym in the late 1960s at the beginning of her career. Derived from her slim build, it might in other circumstances have been used as a nickname.

John Paul II
Born Karol Wojtyla in Poland in 1920, the then cardinal adopted the above name upon becoming pope in 1978. Throughout the history of the papacy, popes have always relinquished their lay names.

J J Marric
Or 23 others! For John Creasey (1908–1973), the English crime novelist and thriller writer, used his own name and 24 pseudonyms throughout his career as an author.

Spy?
This was the pseudonym of Sir Leslie Ward (1851–1922), the English caricaturist, who became famous for his caricatures of prominent people in the journal, *Vanity Fair*, between 1873 and 1909. Ward was the son of a well-known Victorian painter, Edward Matthew Ward.

Harry Houdini
This Jewish-American magician and escapologist was born Erich Weiss in Appleton, Wisconsin in 1874. He adopted his stage name in 1891.

Rock Hudson
Born 1925 as Roy Scherer, at the age of eight he adopted his stepfather's surname of Fitzgerald. The talent scout who discovered him in 1946 named him Rock after the Rock of Gibraltar and Hudson after the Hudson River. Hudson is on record as disliking his stage name, although it has certainly not inhibited his career. In any case the forename Rock was perhaps preferable to Crash or Brick, alternatives considered by his 'discoverer'.

Little Quiz 42
   Where are these British monuments?
1. The Wallace monument
2. Cabot's Tower
3. King Alfred's statue
4. Martyrs' Memorial
5. Mayflower Stone
6. King Richard's Well
7. Marquess' Column
8. Locomotion I
9. Prince Charles Edward Monument
10. HMS Victory

What is a cruciform plan church?

A plan in the shape of a cross, with – generally but not always – a tower over the centre where the arms of the cross meet.

Where are the transepts of a church?

They are the north and south arms of the cross plan, and where they meet is called the crossing.

What is a chapter house?

This is the room, square or polygonal, where the dean and canons of a cathedral meet to conduct their business. The room is usually a separate part of the cathedral.

Where in the church is the baptistery, or baptistry?

Usually, the baptistery is at the west end and it contains the font. In some cathedrals, notably some of the magnificent Italian ones, the baptistery is a building separate from the main cathedral.

What is a baldachino?

It is a canopied structure, of marble or stone but sometimes of wood, placed over an altar. It may be suspended, or supported on columns.

Where is the clerestory?

It is in the nave, transept and choir walls, or in one or two of these parts. It is at the upper level below the roof and is pierced by windows to let in more light. Not all churches and cathedrals have clerestories.

Is the pulpitum the same as the pulpit?

No, the pulpitum is a solid screen, generally of stone but occasionally of wood, which shuts off the choir from the nave. In many instances it has a gallery above.

Why is a flying buttress so called?

It is a stone buttress in the form of an arch that acts as a prop against an outer wall of a church (or cathedral). The upper part rests against the wall (of the nave, transept or choir) and the lower part rests against a pier, to absorb the outward thrust of the wall.

Where would you expect to find misericords?

They are part of the choir stalls. A misericord is a carved wooden bracket or ledge underneath a hinged seat in the stalls, which when the seat is tipped up provides support if you have to stand for long periods. Many misericords were most beautifully carved.

Lancet windows

246

Has the tympanum anything to do with a drum?

No, it is the space above the lintel and beneath the arch of a doorway, and this space is usually decorated.

What is an apse?

A round, polygonal or rectangular recess or projection, usually though not only, at the east end of a church. An apse usually has a vaulted roof. In some Gothic cathedrals, the east end was a cluster of rounded apses set symmetrically, with a chapel in each of the apses.

Where is the reredos?

It is the screen at the back of an altar, and is generally elaborately decorated.

What is a triforium?

It is an arcaded wall passage below the clerestory and above the nave arcades (and continuing round the transepts and choir in some cathedrals).

What is the difference between the undercroft and the crypt of a church?

None, really, for they mean the same thing, that is, a vaulted chamber under a church.

What is a retable?

The retable is a shelf behind and above an altar. It carried the cross and other ornaments.

Where is the presbytery?

This is part of the eastern end of the church between the choir and the high altar. In some cases, the word is used to describe the whole of the east end, but chancel is a better word for this.

Why are the entrances to some churchyards covered with a roof?

When they are, they are known as lych-gates, and this is where coffins rested before being admitted into the church by the priest.

What is the name of the building that contains the church or cathedral's principal bell?

This is the campanile, and it is usually a bell tower that is separate from the church building. There are several famous campaniles in Italy, most famous of all being the Leaning Tower of Pisa.

What is a lancet?

It is a tall, narrow window with a pointed top.

What are voussoirs?

Wedge-shaped stones which form an arch.

Little Quiz 43

To which countries do these civil aircraft markings refer?

1. CCCP
2. OY
3. YR
4. YU
5. TF
6. GB
7. HB
8. N
9. OO
10. PP

And these international car registration letters?

11. CH
12. RA
13. V
14. SF
15. T
16. FL
17. SK
18. GBG
19. PL
20. U

Who was the first Russian aviator to fly successfully?
Van den Schrouff, in a Voisin biplane at Odessa, 25 July 1909.

When did women begin to fly aeroplanes?
Probably the first woman pilot was Miss Spencer Kavanagh, whose real name was Edith Maud Cook, who made several flights in the Pyrenees in 1910.

Which nation built and flew the first four-engine aeroplane?
Russia. The Bolshoi biplane with four engines flew at St Petersburg on 13 May 1913. The pilot was Igor Sikorsky, the inventor of the single-rotor helicopter. Sikorsky also designed the first 4-engine air bomber.

Which was the first aircraft carrier specially built for the purpose?
The Japanese carrier, Hosho, launched in 1922.

Which was the largest flying-boat built for military uses in Britain?
The Short Shetland, but only two were constructed. It was tested in December 1944. Its wing span was 47.75 m (150 ft) and it could fly at up to 421.82 kmh (262 mph).

What was a *kamikaze* attack?
This is the name of a special air attack by Japanese pilots who volunteered to crash their planes on their targets in 1944–5.

What was the Hughes H2 Hercules aeroplane?
It was an enormous 180 ton flying boat with eight engines, a wing span of 97.6 m (320 ft), which could carry up to 700 passengers. Only one was built, by the eccentric billionaire, Howard Hughes of the USA, and it flew only once, for about 1.61 km (one mile) in 1947.

Who was Amy Johnson?
A woman pilot who flew a De Havilland DH 60 Gipsy Moth monoplane from England to Australia, 5 to 14 May 1930. It was the first such flight.

What was the 'Comet'?
This was the famous De Havilland DH 106 Comet I jet-propelled airliner, which had four engines. It was the first jet airliner to fly regular commercial air services anywhere.

What was the R 101 disaster?
The R 101 was a commercial airship which crashed at Beauvais in France on its flight from Cardington in Bedfordshire en route for Egypt and India in 1930. On board were 54 people, 48 of whom were killed, including Lord Thomson, secretary of state for air.

What is the Harrier jump jet?
It is a jet-propelled military aircraft which can take off vertically, without the need of a runway, and land again, also without runway. It is ideal for aircraft carriers, difficult terrain and for use on airfields perhaps rendered useless to other aircraft in an enemy raid in war time.

What was the Schneider Trophy?
It was a seaplane contest with a trophy for the winner. It was first competed for in 1913, and it was won three times in succession by Britain, 1927, 1929 and 1931. The last competition produced a world speed record of 544 kmh (340 mph).

Which British bomber pilot accompanied the US air crew which dropped the second atomic bomb on Japan?
Group Captain Leonard Cheshire, VC, OM, DSO, DFC, who was so appalled by the destruction the bomb caused that he decided to devote his life thereafter to helping disabled people, founding since

1945 numerous Cheshire Homes all over the world.

What machine first flew on 28 March 1910?
This was the date of the first flight of a seaplane which was made at La Mède near Marseilles. The machine, constructed and flown by the French pioneer, Henri Fabre, bore some resemblance to a flying fence!

Which leading fighter ace of World War II had no legs?
Group Captain Douglas Bader of the RAF had lost both his legs in a flying accident in 1931. Undeterred, he not only learned to walk again using artificial legs, but also resumed his flying career. He was shot down over France in 1941 and spent the remainder of the war as a prisoner of the Germans. He was awarded the DSO with bar, the DFC with bar, the Croix de Guerre and the Legion of Honour and later was knighted.

Who were the Blue Eagles?
This was a helicopter display team, part of the British School of Army Aviation, which was formed in 1968 and which flew until 1977.

What is the significance of Leonardo da Vinci in aviation history?
In about 1500, Leonardo drew design sketches for a helicopter with a rotating helical wing which demonstrated the possibility of vertical lift-off.

Who is regarded as one of the most successful German fighter pilots of World War II?
Major Erich Hartmann of the Luftwaffe, who achieved a total of 352 confirmed aerial victories during service on the Russian Front in World War II. His decorations included the Knight's Cross with Oak Leaves, Swords and Diamonds.

What was the most disastrous day in terms of losses ever experienced by a single air force?
Contrary to what might have been expected, the losses suffered by the Luftwaffe when Germany was on the crest of a wave on 10 May 1940 make that the most disastrous day. The Luftwaffe then lost 304 aircraft with another 51 damaged; casualties amongst their aircrew and other personnel (killed, wounded and missing) amounted to 1066. Those figures, for the day in which Germany invaded the Netherlands and Belgium, exceeded their cumulative losses from the start of World War II.

What was the first jet aeroplane to make a successful flight?
This was the German Heinkel He 178, which flew for the first time on 27 August 1939. The Luftwaffe were not, however, able to use a jet-propelled aircraft in operational service until 1944.

What was the great achievement of the American woman aviator, Amelia Earhart?
She was the first woman to fly across the Atlantic. This feat was undertaken on 17 June 1928 in a Lockheed Vega aircraft, between Newfoundland and Burry Point in Wales. She was lost on a flight over the Pacific in 1937.

For what unusual purpose did Canadair develop the CL-215 twin-engined amphibious flying boat?
This aircraft was specifically developed to fight forest fires, a major threat to the economy of the country. The first flight was made on 23 October 1967. The aircraft picks up water by means of two probes and has been able to drop 545,520 litres (120,000 gallons) in one day.

Which is the largest planet in our Solar System?
Jupiter. It is about ten times the diameter of the earth, and rotates on its axis in about ten hours, which is faster than Earth.

What are the rings round the planet Saturn made of?
Probably lumps of rock and ice. The three rings visible from Earth have been shown by space probes to be made up of hundreds of separate ringlets. The rings appear to be less than 1 km thick.

Why is Mars called the Red Planet?
Because it appears orange-red to the naked eye and through a telescope. When the United States Vikings probes of 1976 landed on Mars, they sent back photographs that confirmed the reddish colour of the surface.

What is a light year?
It is the distance that light travels in a year, which is about 10 million million kilometres (6 million million miles).

Which is the nearest star to Earth?
Proxima Centauri, which is 4.3 light years away.

How many stars are there in our Galaxy?
Probably about 100,000,000,000 (one hundred thousand million).

Where did the Moon come from?
Although it is not known for certain, the Moon probably was formed at the same time as the Earth. It was once thought that it might have come from the Earth.

What is a comet?
It is a member of the Solar System made up of dust, gas and ice. It becomes visible when it approaches the sun, developing a shining 'head' and a 'tail' that streams away from the Sun.

What is the average temperature on the surface of the planet Venus?
Over 450°C. which is four and a half times the temperature of boiling water.

Who discovered the planet Uranus?
Sir William Herschel (1738–1822) on 13 March 1781.

How long did it take to discover the last planet of our Solar System, Pluto?
The search began in 1906 at an Arizona observatory, later called Lowell Observatory, named after Percival Lowell who started the search. Pluto was found in 1930 by Clyde Tombaugh, at the same observatory.

Is the Sun a planet?
No. It is a star.

What is a sunspot?
It is an area on the Sun's surface where the temperature is somewhat colder than its surroundings, producing a dark effect in contrast.

What are the equinoxes?
There are two, the vernal (spring) and autumnal equinox, and they are the dates (about 21 March and 23 September) when the position of the Sun in relation to Earth is such that day and night are of almost equal length everywhere.

How hot is the Sun's surface?
It is estimated to be about 5,800°C.

What is the Milky Way?
It is the name given to our Galaxy, which is shaped like a disc with a central bump. It is also the name for the dense band of stars that spans the sky.

How far is the Sun from Earth?
About 150,000,000 km (93,000,000 miles).

What is the Sun's corona?
It is the 'halo' of gas that surrounds the Sun. The corona can only be seen from Earth during a total eclipse of the Sun, or by means of a special apparatus called a colonograph in an observatory.

What is a lunar eclipse?
This is when the Moon passes into the shadow of Earth, which cuts out the sunlight. The Moon appears dim rather than bright and remains so until it comes out of the shadow. The eclipse may be partial or total, and one occurs fairly frequently, occasionally at the rate of two or three a year, or only once in two years.

What is the Big Bang theory?
It is the theory that the Universe began in a cataclysmic explosion. A tiny, very dense and very hot mass blasted apart about 15–20,000 million years ago to create the universe, which has been expanding ever since.

Has it been established that the changes in the dark areas on Mars are not due to growing vegetation?
The American astronomer Carl Sagan suggested that the seasonal changes in the dark areas on Mars were caused by wind-blown dust; this suggestion was subsequently confirmed by photographs from the Mariner 9 probe.

In simple terms, what is a black hole?
A black hole cannot be observed directly, although this theoretical object may be implied through the effects that it has on other matter. It is assumed that beyond a certain point, a star that has been shrinking is impelled by its massive surface gravity to disappear within a single mathematical point within which is trapped both space and time themselves. Beyond this 'black hole', the density of the star would then rise to infinity – but outside the space-time continuum that is our Universe.

Saturn's rings

Which are the two main species of oak tree native to Britain?
The common oak and the durmast oak.

What is the main difference between the two?
The common oak has its leaves on short stalks or no stalks at all, and its acorns singly or in bunches of several on stalks generally no more than 127 mm (5 in) long. The durmast oak has its leaves on stalks at least 25.4 mm (1 in) long, but the acorns have no stalks or are clustered close to the twigs.

Why is the locust tree so called?
The locust tree, otherwise the false acacia tree, came from North America. It was brought to Europe, especially to France, by missionaries in North America who thought it was the acacia tree from which John the Baptist obtained locusts in the wilderness.

Why is the hickory tree good for making axe and other tool handles?
Because it is very tough, light in weight and springy. Hickory trees are common in the United States.

What is an arboretum?
It is a collection of trees of different kinds, generally of the rare kinds, that are grown for display. Many stately homes have an arboretum in their grounds, in some cases planted more than a century ago.

Many trees are called hybrids: what does this mean?
A hybrid is an 'offspring' produced by cross-breeding of two different kinds of trees.

What is a monkey puzzle tree?
It is a pine tree native to Chile, which is also grown in the US and Britain, and is notable for its whorled branches and stiff leaves arranged in spirals.

What is a Leyland cypress?
This is a well known example of a hybrid that is very popular in Britain. It is a conifer bred from a Nootka cypress from North America and a Monterey cypress. The Leyland grows very fast, up to over a metre (4 ft) a year if the conditions are good, and should reach about 12 m (40 ft).

Which tree grows and flourishes in salt water?
The mangrove tree throws its roots out above water level and the root tips droop into the water and mud. Mangroves grow in swamps as a rule, in central America, along the Florida and Atlantic coasts, and also in Africa and the Philippines.

What is a deciduous tree?
It is a tree which sheds all its leaves once a year.

What is a Judas tree?
This is a most attractive broadleaf tree that has small, pretty pink flowers that flow out of the trunks of the branches as well as from the branch ends. It is called the Judas tree because it is thought to be the tree from which Judas hanged himself.

What is the General Sherman Tree in Sequoia National Park?
This is an example of the sequoias dendrosa giganteum species of tree which is said to be nearly 4000 years old. It is over 82 m (270 ft) tall.

Why are mulberry trees associated with silk manufacture?
The leaves of some species of mulberry provide food for silkworms.

Why do you so often find a yew tree in an English churchyard?
The yew tree has a very long life, sometimes of several hundreds of years. It was a symbol of eternal life in pagan times, and this was adopted by the

Christians. But it is also probable that the tree proved useful as a shelter for congregations on sites of churches before the buildings were completed.

What is Dutch elm disease?
A particularly virulent disease attacking elm trees by means of a fungus Ceratostomella Ulmi, which is carried by bark beetles. The leaves turn yellow and drop off, and the tree dies. Elm trees in Britain were hit by the disease in the late 1970s and over 10,000,000 were affected.

What are other names for the linden tree, the mountain ash and the great maple?
The lime, the rowan, the plane.

What is Robin Hood's larder?
It is a hollow oak tree in Sherwood Forest in which Robin Hood is said to have hidden deer he had killed.

When were the first fig trees grown in Britain?
It is possible that fig trees were introduced by the Romans during their occupation (1st to 5th centuries), but the first known fig trees were planted in Lambeth in the reign of Henry VIII.

What were the original cedars of Lebanon?
They were tall conifers which reached as high as 30.5 m (100 ft) and which grew in the Lebanon and the Taurus Mountains in Turkey, which Solomon used for the construction of his famous temple in Jerusalem. The trees in this instance were given to him by Hiram, king of Tyre.

What is the cricket bat willow tree?
A species of willow (salix coerulea), also called the blue willow, which can be as tall as 30.5 m (100 ft). In England, the wood is used for cricket bats, and the trees grown for this purpose are cut down usually when the trunks have reached a width of 457–482 mm (18 to 19 in).

What is the rarest native British tree?
The whitty pear *Sorbus domestica*, of which only one example is known. It grew in the middle of the Wyre Forest in Worcestershire, but after being damaged in 1862 was only kept alive in cultivation. Happily, this tree, which was first recorded in 1678, was successfully replaced on its old site. Elsewhere, the nearest whitty pears are found in Brittany.

Why is it considered unlucky to bring hawthorn into a house?
Because of the tradition that its thorns were fashioned into a crown for Christ at his Passion.

Mangrove tree

How old is Skara Brae village, in Orkney?

This prehistoric village of stone-built houses is at least 5000 years old. The settlement appears to have flourished for several generations, and depended upon sea food and cattle. It was overwhelmed by some natural disaster but when it was excavated it was found to be in a remarkable state of preservation.

What is a passage grave?

An artificial burial mound of stone construction. At the centre of the inside there is a vaulted chamber that is connected to the outside by a straight passage.

What was so remarkable about Maes Howe passage grave, in Orkney?

Its state of preservation after 5500 years of existence. The stone blocks appear to have been cut and shaped with astonishing skill, so accurately that it is almost impossible to slide a knife into the joins.

What was a causewayed camp?

An enclosure of two or more concentric rings of ditches and banks, the banks being levelled at one or two points and the earth tipped into the adjacent ditching, to provide causeways in and out of the camp.

How many periods of building were there at Stonehenge?

At least three, the first being about 2600 BC. The huge, tall sarsens (sandstone blocks) are probably from the third phase, which was at least 4000 years ago.

What is a henge monument?

It is a round or oval enclosure of raised bank outside an inner ditch, used for religious or ceremonial purposes. There were entrances in the bank. Most henges were built during the 2nd millennium BC, a few earlier.

What is the age of the famous passage grave at Newgrange in Ireland?

At least 5000 years old. At the entrance is a fine stone slab which is decorated with carved whorls and lozenges.

What is a dun?

It is an Iron Age fortlet built from stone blocks resting on each other, without mortar, which is called dry stone construction.

When were hill forts first built in Britain?

It used to be said they were a Celtic invention of about the 9th century onwards up to Roman times, but it is now clear that they were built by pre-Celtic Iron Age people, probably as far back as about 1000 BC.

What does megalithic mean?

It refers to structures built from huge stone blocks weighing several tons each.

What was an *oppidum*?

It is the Latin for town (often in a loose sense), and was used by the Romans in their first contacts with the Gauls and Britons, to indicate their settlement areas, often on hill tops.

What is a vitrified fort?

More generally found in Scotland than anywhere else in Britain, a vitrified fort was an enclosure of dry stone wall construction interlaced with timber posts. When the timber was set alight and burned, the heat melted the surface of the stonework, creating a glassy, slippery surface on the wall. It is not known if the burning was deliberate as a defensive technique or if it was the result of fire-raising by enemy assault.

What was a barrow?

A mound of earth covering a grave. Barrows were round or rectangular, the latter usually called long barrows.

What is a wheelhouse?
An Iron Age round house of dry stone and wattle walling in which the rooms were arranged by partitions set in radiating lines, like the spokes of a wheel.

What was a cist?
This was a grave or burial pit, sometimes lined with stone, with a cap stone as a lid. There were many shapes and sizes of cist.

What do we mean by crouched burial?
A custom of burying the dead by folding the body with the knees drawn up to the jaw, and lying on its side.

What is a trilith or trilithon?
It is a construction using three very large stones, two upright with a third across the top. Stonehenge has a ring of trilithons.

What marked the end of the Stone Age?
It did not end at the same time everywhere, but it was when Stone Age people gave up using stone tools and started to work in copper and bronze.

Where and what are Grime's Graves?
They are near Brandon on the Norfolk–Suffolk border and are an interesting series of over 360 flint mining shafts which began to be worked as far back as about 3000 BC. They appear to have been worked for hundreds of years. When one shaft was worked out, the craftsmen dug another shaft and began to work that.

Who was the first British tribal chief to be mentioned by Caesar in connection with his invasion of Britain?
Cassivelaunus, chief of the Catuvellauni tribe who occupied Hertfordshire, parts of Buckinghamshire, Bedfordshire, Cambridgeshire and Essex. He was defeated in battle by Caesar at Ravensburgh in south Bedfordshire.

Where is the Icknield Way?
This prehistoric trackway runs from the North Norfolk coast near Wells-next-the-Sea to Goring in Oxfordshire. It passes through Swaffham, Newmarket, Royston and Luton – towns which did not, of course, exist when this route came to be formed. For much of its length the Icknield Way has become incorporated into the modern road network; beyond Goring it continues as The Ridgeway along the Berkshire Downs, eventually reaching Salisbury Plain.

How long have Celtic languages been spoken in Britain?
A wave of newcomers, perhaps already in the Bronze Age, brought the first Celtic tongues to Britain about 1000 BC; they were reinforced in the Iron Age about 500 years later by a second wave. The former, or Goidelic, groups gave us the languages which developed into Scottish and Irish Gaelic, and Manx; the latter, or Brythonic, groups likewise Welsh and Cornish (and the Breton tongue of Brittany).

Little Quiz 44
  What is the French for:
  1. eight
  2. thirty
  3. ninety
  The German for
  4. three
  5. twenty
  6. thousand
  Italian for
  7. forty
  8. five hundred
  9. eight
  and the Spanish for
  10. five

What is the origin of the game of tennis?
The game seems to have been played in some form in the 15th century in England and France, and it was played in a covered court. Real tennis (or Royal, or Court Tennis) is still played indoors. Henry VIII of England was one of the best players of his time.

When did tennis begin to be played outside and on grass?
In the 1870s, in England. It came to be called Lawn Tennis, but the game can be played on surfaces other than grass.

How did Wimbledon become the centre for the world's greatest Lawn Tennis Championships?
Because the meeting which founded the Championships took place at the offices of the All England Croquet and Lawn Tennis Club in Worple Road, Wimbledon, at the beginning of June 1877. The first tournament was held on 9 July.

What does 'seeding' mean?
This is the process of putting selected players in a tournament in certain places in the draw so as to prevent them meeting until the later stages of the tournament. It was first used at Wimbledon in 1924.

What is the origin of the scoring method in tennis?
The beginnings of scoring 15, 30, 40 and Game are not known, but it is generally agreed that they go back to the earliest years of the game in the late Middle Ages, and they may relate to the four quarters of the clock. A game was finished at the end of an hour. The intervals may have been marked by rest periods at the quarters.

What is the Grand Slam in tennis?
The achievement by an individual of winning the Singles Championship of

Britain, the US, France and Australia all in one year. Several people have won it. The first was Donald Budge for the US in 1938.

Who was Little Mo?
Maureen Connolly, who won the Women's Singles Championships at Wimbledon in 1952, when she was only 17, and at her first attempt. She won again in 1953 and 1954, and in 1953 was also the first woman to win the Grand Slam.

What rules govern the size of a tennis racket for championships?
It has to be not more than 812.8 mm (32 in) long including the handle, and not more than 317.5 mm (12½ in) wide. The string surface must not exceed 393.7 × 292.1 mm (15½ in × 11½ in).

Who was Suzanne Lenglen?
One of the greatest of all tennis stars. Born in 1899, she was a French player of exceptional skill, who won six Wimbledon Singles' Championships (1919, 1920, 1921, 1922, 1923 and 1925). She died in 1938.

Which international tennis star was Czechoslovakian born, played for his country, for Egypt and for Britain?
Jaroslav Drobny (born 1921) left Czechoslovakia when the country was absorbed into the Eastern bloc and was offered refuge in Egypt. In 1954 he became Men's Singles Champion in 1954 representing Egypt. Later on, he became a naturalized Briton and played for the UK.

What is the make-up of the tennis ball?
Basically, it is a rubber sphere covered with a 'furry' cloth or 'nylon' substitute. Its diameter should be 63.5 mm to 66.7 mm (2½ in to 2⅝ in) and it should weigh between 275 g and 284 g (2 oz and 2$\frac{1}{16}$ oz).

Who was Gorgeous Gussie Moran?
She was an American women's singles
player in the 1950s who startled
Wimbledon spectators with the frilly lace
edges of her tennis skirt and underskirt.

**What is the height from the ground to
the top of the centre of the tennis net?**
It should be 0.914 m (3 ft), a regulation
introduced in 1882.

**Has a left-handed player ever won a
Wimbledon Championship?**
Yes, several times. The first was Norman
Brookes, in 1907. Other famous left-
handers are Drobny, Rod Laver, Jimmy
Connors and John McEnroe.

**What is the greatest number of Men's
Singles Championships at Wimbledon
won by the same player since 1922.**
Five, by the Swedish player Bjorn Borg,
who won five years running, 1976 to
1980. Rod Laver has won four, but not all
in a row.

**How many times has Billie Jean King
won a Wimbledon Championship?**
Twenty, including six Women's Singles.

What was Sphairistiké?
This name was given by Major Walter
Clopton Wingfield to the form of lawn
tennis which he developed and marketed
over the years from 1869 to 1875. The
name was derived from an ancient Greek
ball game known as *Sphairisis*.
Wingfield's game was played on an
hourglass-shaped court, with service
being delivered from one side only; it
rapidly lost popularity once an official
code for lawn tennis was drafted in 1875,
to which Wingfield graciously agreed.

**What traditional English summer
sport did lawn tennis begin to replace
in the late 19th century?**
Croquet. It must, however, be recorded

that this ancient game did not vanish
completely from the lawns of England. It
is still played widely, and its rules are
governed by the Croquet Association of
the Hurlingham Club, London.

**Which member of the royal family
played in the Wimbledon
Championships?**
The Duke of York, later George VI,
played in the men's doubles of the
Fiftieth Anniversary Jubilee
Championship of 1926. He and his
partner, Wing Commander Louis Greig,
were defeated in the first round.

**Which former men's doubles
champion wore a leg iron?**
Sydney Howard Smith (1872–1947), was
a doubles champion in 1902 and 1906. He
was particularly noted for his fierce
forehand drive. Apart from his successes
at lawn tennis, he also played badminton
and was the All England singles
champion in that sport in 1900.

**What are the most northerly and most
southerly lawn tennis clubs in the
world?**
The most northerly is at Hammerfest in
Norway, where the sun in fact never sets
from 19 May to 29 July each year; the
most southerly is at Punta Arenas, Chile.

When was a tennis court first floodlit?
At Cheltenham in 1881.

**Has lawn tennis been played as part
of the modern Olympic Games?**
Yes, in all the Olympics from 1896 to
1924 inclusive – except in 1916 during
World War I when the Games did not
take place. Bad weather and controversy
surrounding control of the sport at Paris
in 1924 led to its being withdrawn. The
game was once again included as a
'demonstration' sport in Mexico City in
1968.

What is a dinghy?
It is a small, open boat for sailing, which can also be rowed. The word comes from the Hindi for little boat, *dingi*.

What does clinker built mean?
It means that the hull of the boat is built with the outer planks overlapping, downwards and fastened with clinched nails.

Where is the bilge of a boat?
The part of the hull where the sides meet the bottom, usually from the keel to the point where the sides start to rise.

What is the difference between a round bilge vessel and a hard chine vessel?
A round bilge vessel has a curved bilge where the bottom meets the sides, whereas a hard chine vessel has the sides meeting the bottom at an angle.

What is a sailing boat's rig?
It is the term that covers the boat's masts, yards and sails.

Is rig the same as rigging?
Rigging describes the lines (of rope) and chains aboard a boat used for controlling the sails and for supporting masts and spars.

What is a Bermudan sail?
A triangular sail, the shortest of the three sides being the lower edge (or foot).

What are sails made of?
They are made from sail cloths sewn together. These cloths are manufactured in different weights, measured as a rule in ounces per square yard of cloth (or grams per square metre). Heavier cloths are for larger boats and stronger winds.

What is a taffrail?
It is the rail across or around the stern of a boat.

How are glass-fibre boat hulls manufactured?
Layers of glass-fibre matting are laid in a hull mould, each being soaked in resin. When the resin cures, the hull is taken out of the mould and is ready.

What is a sloop?
It is a fore-and-aft rigged vessel, generally having two sails (mainsail and headsail).

What is a ketch?
A two-masted sailing boat, rigged fore and aft, with the smaller mizzen mast stepped forward of the rudder post.

What does it mean to 'heave to'?
It means to stop. This is generally done by backing the headsail and lashing the helm to leeward.

Trimaran

What is a spinnaker?
A large, light, generally triangular sail carried on a long, light pole, on the side opposite the mainsail.

What is close-hauled?
This means having the sails trimmed for sailing as close to the wind as possible.

What do windward and leeward mean?
Windward means towards the wind, leeward means downwind or away from the wind.

What are the scuppers on a boat?
They are small holes that let water taken on board run off the deck.

How long is a nautical mile?
About 1,854 m (6,080 ft) that is, the distance equal to one minute of longitude at the Equator.

What is the Beaufort Scale?
A scale for measuring the force of the wind according to a set of numbers devised by Admiral Sir Francis Beaufort in 1806.

What is the world's largest yacht?
HMS *Britannia*, the British royal yacht launched in 1953. Her displacement is 4715 tons.

What is a trimaran?
This is an unballasted single-hull boat constructed with twin floats port and starboard which provide excellent stability.

What was the first fully crewed Round the World race?
This was organized by the Royal Naval Sailing Association and started on 8 September 1973. The winner was the 19.5m (64ft) ketch *Sayula II* owned and sailed by the Mexican, Ramon Carlin.

What is a sheerstrake?
The topmost plank of the topsides of a vessel.

Who made the first single-handed ocean crossing?
The Danish-American, Alfred Johnson, who sailed his 6m (20ft) dory *Centennial* across the Atlantic from Nova Scotia to Wales in 46 days in 1876. As the name of the craft might suggest, this was a celebration of the centenary of the American Declaration of Independence.

What is the national authority for yacht racing in the United Kingdom?
The Royal Yachting Association, which was originally founded in London in 1875.

When did yachting become popular in England?
Yachts were widely used in Holland in the early 17th century. Charles II of England spent part of his exile in Holland and it was there that he became familiar with these craft. Upon his Restoration in 1660, the Dutch presented the monarch with a 15m (52ft) armed yacht called *Mary*. English boatbuilders then tried to improve on the Dutch design, and yachts and yachting thus gradually grew in popularity.

Little Quiz 45
  In which countries are these mountains?
  1. Snowdon
  2. K2 (Godwin-Austen)
  3. Nanda Devi
  4. Elborus
  5. Great Ararat
  6. Mount Logan
  7. Watkins
  8. Mount Massive
  9. Cotopaxi
  10. Fujiyama

What is a Hiram Codd's bottle?
A fizzy mineral water or fruit juice bottle that is sealed by means of a glass ball held against a rubber ring by the pressure from the gas. They are now collectors' items.

What is treen?
It is an old word meaning wooden, and is used as a collective term for small antique articles of wood, such as pepper mills, napkin rings, platters, salad servers, spice boxes, back-scratchers and so on.

What is a Staffordshire flatback?
An item from a considerable range of coloured glazed earthenware figures produced in the later 19th century by the Staffordshire pottery firms. They are known as flatbacks because only the front view is properly shaped and coloured, the remainder being glazed white. Models included Queen Victoria, Prince Albert and other famous people.

What is pressed glass?
A process invented in the United States in the 1820s whereby molten glass is forced into patterned moulds by mechanical means to produce objects in glass that look as if they were of better quality mould-blown glass.

Is amber a rare stone?
No, it is a fossilized resin which occurs in some quantity in Scandinavia and on the east Baltic coast, and has also been found in Britain.

Why is an Apostle jug so called?
It is a straight-sided jug with relief modelled figures of the apostles on its sides, surmounted by Gothic arcading, looking like a heavily decorated pulpit. The style was introduced in the 1840s by Charles Meigh of the Staffordshire potteries during the great Gothic revival of the early Victorian period.

What is the difference between pewter and Britannia metal?
Pewter is an alloy of tin, lead, copper and antimony (or bismuth) which has been used for plates, cups, tankards and vessels for at least 2000 years. Britannia metal is a cheap copy of the same, first produced in the 18th century but more popular in the 19th century. Britannia metal is an alloy of tin, copper and antimony, produced by a spinning process, and is generally much shinier than pewter.

What is a what-not?
A light, portable stand of three or four wooden shelves graded downwards small to large, supported on uprights at the corners, used for ornaments or books.

What is a pouncepot?
A vase-shaped bottle for sprinkling powdered pumice (or pounce) upon writing paper, used before the days of blotting paper.

What is soapstone?
A brown-green mottled stone which can be carved and shaped for a variety of decorative objects or utensils. Among the best known figures popular since the 19th century are the famous Three Monkeys – see no evil, hear no evil, speak no evil.

What was a Meerschaum pipe?
A smoker's pipe whose bowl and part of the stem were carved, often intricately and with skill. Meerschaum pipes were usually made of a soft white claylike mineral from the Near East, called meerschaum, which became stained through usage and often in the end looked like amber.

What is a bygone?
An increasingly popular term for any object no longer in use, such as an old farm implement, a pair of bellows etc.

What is a trivet?
A three-legged stand on which utensils rested in front of a fire, though there were many varieties, some of which had no legs but instead had hooks which gripped the bars of the fire.

What is a chain mail purse?
A purse with a clip at the top two edges, the sides made of thin steel links, like medieval chain mail armour only much thinner. This type of purse was popular in the late Victorian age.

What was a moustache cup?
A special cup with an arrangement across an arc at the top which allowed a moustache wearer to drink a cup of tea or coffee down to the dregs without wetting his moustache.

What is a fairing?
It is the word applied to a great variety of objects made of glass or china in the later 19th century, and sold at stalls at travelling fairs as souvenirs. They were made in Germany and France and imported into Britain in great quantities. Later it meant any present bought at a fair.

What were lazy tongs?
These were a contrivance enabling women, when dressed in fashionable billowing crinolines, to pick up objects off the floor. They were a strip of trellis (wood, metal or ivory) with finger holes at one end and 'grippers' at the other. When you squeezed the finger holes together (like scissors) the trellis extended and reached beyond the dress to clasp the object.

What is bentwood?
Introduced in central Europe in the mid-19th century, it was a type of furniture made of beechwood stick, steamed and bent into shapes. The curving lines, uninterrupted by joints, allowed for an interesting range of flowing furniture styles, especially rocking chairs.

What is a stereoscope card?
This is a long, rectangular card consisting of two identical photographs of the same size placed side by side and set at a very slight angle to each other. The card was placed in a stereoscope, a 19th century invention which was a gadget consisting of a strip of wood with an eye-piece at one end and at the other end a slot for the card. The eye-piece could be adjusted forwards or backwards for the right distance from the card, so that when you looked through the lenses you obtained a three-dimensional view of the picture.

How did the 19th century polyphon work?
The polyphon was our Victorian ancestors' juke-box. The mechanism was in a glass-fronted cabinet, often fixed to the wall in a place of public entertainment, such as a public house or café, and it was coin-operated. For one penny, a steel disc dotted with perforations would rotate, causing small pieces of metal to drop down and strike a series of metal keys in an order that produced a popular tune, say, a favourite music hall song or an air from a Gilbert and Sullivan comic opera.

Little Quiz 46

Who were the husbands of?
1. Messalina
2. Roxana
3. Boudicca
4. Cartimandua
5. Empress Matilda
6. Madame de Maintenon
7. Hatshepsut
8. Mary II of England, Scotland and Ireland
9. Philippa of Hainault
10. Berengaria of Navarre

What is hepatitis?
It is a serious disorder of the liver, generally caused by a virus infection. It can be cured, but this takes time and much care has to be taken with diet.

What is lumbago?
It is a term for backache in the lumbar region of the backbone.

How does a disc slip?
Each of the vertebral bones in the spine is separated from the next by a thick pad of fibrous tissue. The pad is roughly disc-shaped and has a soft centre. If the tissue is damaged, the soft centre can bulge out to squeeze a nerve and so cause pain.

What does hardening of the arteries mean?
The arteries are normally quite elastic, and they allow the passage of blood at speed as it moves round the body. But some people's arteries become less elastic when the artery walls get too thick, which may be caused by a variety of problems such as high blood pressure or too much smoking or by too much eating of rich food. The condition is technically called arteriosclerosis.

What is a coronary?
This is short for coronary thrombosis, which is the medical term for heart attack, and it occurs when a branch of a coronary artery gets blocked, which stops oxygenated blood reaching the heart muscles, so affecting the operation of the heart.

What is laryngitis?
The larynx is the proper name for the vocal chords. If this organ becomes inflamed, the condition is called laryngitis.

What is catarrh?
This is an inflammation of the membranes of the nose and throat with a thick mucous discharge. Catarrh

sometimes accompanies a heavy cold, or may occur without a cold, and sometimes may be of nervous origin.

What is heartburn?
This is an uncomfortable, sometimes painful, condition in which a burning sensation occurs behind the ribs and in the pit of the stomach. It has nothing to do with the heart, normally, but is a digestive complaint caused by a spasm at the bottom end of the oesophagus (windpipe) aggravated by acid bubbling back from the stomach.

What are chilblains?
These affect the fingers and toes (and occasionally the ears) when they get very cold in winter. An inflammation sets in and produces red swellings that can hurt and/or itch once the coldness wears off.

What is diphtheria?
It is an acute and dangerous bacterial infection affecting the mucous membrane in the throat. It is highly contagious and can, if not treated swiftly, be fatal. Children can now avoid diphtheria altogether by having an injection when only a few months old, and a 'booster' injection when they are about five.

How do you get malaria?
Usually, if you are in the tropics, or hot countries, and are bitten by the *anopheles* mosquito.

What is tetanus?
It is the medical name for lockjaw, and is caused by the tetanus bacillus that can get into a simple wound, such as a cut, and which produces a poison that makes the muscles move in spasms. Tetanus can be treated, and it is usually dealt with by having an anti-tetanus injection.

What is gingivitis?
A disease of the gums which starts round

the arcs where the gums meet the teeth. The gums swell and become tender. It can be treated.

Is gingivitis the same as a gumboil?
It may feel like it, but it isn't. A gumboil is an abscess on the gum caused by a decaying tooth.

What is Parkinson's disease?
It is a term to describe a range of nervous diseases in which the main symptoms are trembling and weakness of the muscles. It develops very slowly as a rule, often starting with a slight tremor in the hands, and progresses to a more widespread muscular debility.

What are kidney stones?
These are stones, usually very small, that can be formed from excessive salts and uric acid. They can obstruct the proper functions of the kidney and cause much pain. The condition can be treated.

What makes you faint?
Fainting occurs when there is a sudden drop in blood pressure which reduces the blood supply to the brain, and so produces temporary loss of consciousness.

What is arterial grafting?
This is a technique whereby a diseased or damaged section of artery is replaced with tubing prepared either from synthetic materials, or with a section of healthy artery from the patient or from another person.

What is a boil?
This is a subcutaneous infection which derives from bacteria invading a hair follicle or sweat gland. The body responds to such an attack by sending millions of white cells to the area, and many boils are thus resolved without need of medical assistance.

What is pleurisy?

This is inflammation of the pleura, the membrane enveloping the lungs and which lines the inner wall of the chest cavity. It can be caused by a number of factors, especially by bacterial, viral or fungoid infections of the lungs, by tumours, or by such general disorders as rheumatic fever or rheumatoid arthritis. Treatment includes pain-relieving drugs and the draining of excessive fluid accumulations, as well as measures directed at the underlying condition which has triggered off this illness.

What is scarlet fever?
This is an infectious disease most prevalent among children but which is relatively uncommon nowadays. There is a rash on the face and body, accompanied by fever. The rash flakes off after a few days. The principal treatment is penicillin. As with many infectious diseases, once a patient has recovered from scarlet fever he or she is normally immune from a further attack.

What is stuttering or stammering?
This is a disorder of speech in which some sounds are difficult to produce. It may bear some relationship to tensions experienced by a growing child. Treatment is usually through psychotherapy or speech therapy to which it responds well, and the earlier the better.

Little Quiz 47
  Where are?
  1. Dallas
  2. Meerut
  3. Bretton Woods
  4. Biarritz
  5. Quimper
  6. Grenada
  7. Geneva
  8. Kiel
  9. Beirut
  10. Quatre Bras

Who said?

The Holy Roman Empire was neither holy, nor Roman nor an Empire.
Voltaire.

The English country gentleman galloping after a fox – the unspeakable in full pursuit of the uneatable.
Oscar Wilde.

Do not do unto others as you would they should do unto you. Their tastes may not be the same.
George Bernard Shaw.

He has occasional flashes of silence that make his conversation perfectly delightful.
Sydney Smith.

War is much too important a matter to be left to the generals.
Georges Clemenceau.

Mad dogs and Englishmen go out in the midday sun.
Noel Coward.

Russia is a riddle wrapped in a mystery inside an enigma.
Winston Churchill.

There are three kinds of lies: lies, damned lies, and statistics.
Benjamin Disraeli.

Genius is one percent inspiration and ninety-nine percent perspiration.
Thomas Alva Edison.

They say kings are made in the image of God. I feel sorry for God if that is what He looks like.
Frederick the Great.

All Gaul is divided into three parts.
Julius Caesar.

No man but a blockhead ever wrote except for money.
Samuel Johnson.

I don't know who my grandfather was: I am much more concerned to know what his grandson will be.
Abraham Lincoln.

Soldiers win battles and generals get the credit.
Napoleon Bonaparte.

Well, if I called the wrong number, why did you answer the phone?
James Thurber.

A radical is a man with both feet firmly planted in the air.
Franklin Delano Roosevelt.

History is the essence of innumerable biographies.
Thomas Carlyle.

A man's a man for a' that.
Robert Burns.

A week in politics is a long time.
Harold Wilson.

Cauliflower is nothing but cabbage with a College education.
Mark Twain.

I would never read a book if it were possible to talk half an hour with the man who wrote it.
Woodrow Wilson, later US president.

Those in the cheaper seats clap. The rest of you rattle your jewellery.
John Lennon.

The physician can bury his mistakes, but the architect can only advise his client to grow vines.
Frank Lloyd Wright.

What is a centrifuge?
A machine that rotates at high speed a container holding mixtures in order to separate them, such as mixtures of solids and liquids or liquids of different densities.

What is a cyclotron?
A particle accelerator, which accelerates atomic particles to a very high speed. The particles move in spiral paths in a magnetic field.

What is a dynamo?
A kind of electricity generator which produces direct current. A simple dynamo has a powerful magnet between the poles of which an armature is rotated to produce the electrical energy.

What is an electron microscope?
A kind of microscope that uses beams of electrons to form an enlarged image of a very small object on a fluorescent screen or photographic plate.

What is a geiger counter?
A special instrument for detecting and counting nuclear radiations and particles. It is named after Hans Geiger (1882–1945), a German professor of physics who along with others developed it.

What is a solenoid?
A cylindrical coil of wire that creates a magnetic field within itself when fed with electric current, thus drawing a core of iron or steel into its body.

What is a rheostat?
A piece of apparatus that varies the resistance to electric current.

What is a thermostat?
A piece of apparatus that is sensitive to temperature changes, which keeps the temperature of something, such as a water boiler, within a narrow range.

What is a cloud chamber?
A device for observing the movement of fundamental particles by means of the tracks they leave. The best known kind is the Wilson Cloud Chamber invented by Sir C. T. R. Wilson (1869–1959).

What is a radio telescope?
A special instrument that collects radio waves from space.

What is a Pitot tube?
This instrument is used for the measurement of speed or velocity of a fluid, either in gas or liquid form. It works on the principle that an open-ended tube facing the flow of a liquid will experience a pressure build-up which will increase according to the velocity of flow; a pressure gauge placed at the outlet of the tube can be contrived to indicate this velocity.

What is a Bunsen burner?
A laboratory tool giving a hot, non-luminous flame, which does not leave sooty deposits on the articles it heats. Gas is injected under pressure through a narrow jet into a vertical tube. As it enters this tube, it causes air to be drawn in through holes level with the jet, the amount of air which can be drawn in being regulated by a rotating collar.

Little Quiz 48
  What were the dates of the reigns of?
1. Alfred the Great
2. Joanna the Mad (Spain)
3. Frederick the Great
4. St Louis IX of France
5. Edmund Ironside
6. Casimir III of Poland
7. Suleiman the Magnificent
8. Catherine the Great
9. Macbeth
10. Llewelyn Fawr (the Great)

What is ballet?
In simple terms, it is a form of theatrical art using specially devised dancing, music and scenery to tell a story or convey an atmosphere. The performers always act in mime.

How long has ballet been performed?
Certainly since ancient Greek times, but modern ballet began in France in the later 17th century.

What is a prima ballerina?
She is a female ballet dancer who has performed a range of leading rôles in classical ballets. One of the first ballerinas was the French dancer Marie-Anne Camargo, who in the 1720s introduced the shorter skirt, allowing freer movement.

When did ballet first come to Britain?
Apparently, foreign dancers performed ballet as early as the mid-18th century, but most audiences in Britain regarded these as music-hall turns. Towards the end of the 19th century, Adeline Genée, a Danish-born ballerina (1878–1970) came to London and made regular appearances as a prima ballerina in ballets at London's Empire Theatre.

What is a *pirouette*?
It is a ballet movement in which the dancer makes a rapid spin or whirl of the body on one toe, with the other foot touching the knee-cap. There are several varieties of *pirouette*.

What is choreography?
It is the art of arranging a ballet performance and the notation representing the steps of the dances.

What is a *divertissement*?
It is a collection of unrelated dances performed in interludes during classical ballets.

266

Who is the *maître* or *maîtresse de ballet*?
The ballet master or mistress. The job is to supervise the classes and rehearsals of a ballet company. At one time ballet masters were also expected to compose ballet.

What is so special about the Romantic Ballet?
It was an age of ballet, lasting roughly from the late 1820s to the early 1850s, when ballets consisted chiefly of fairy tale, make-believe themes, in which the characters were as a rule immortal or fantastic, like wood-nymphs, swan-maidens, goblins, beautiful young demi-gods and so on.

Which are the seven principal dancing movements in ballet?
tourner (to turn), *glisser* (to glide), *sauter* (to jump), *élancer* (to dart), *plier* (to bend), *étendre* (to stretch), *rélever* (to rise).

Prima Ballerina

When were ballet 'tights' introduced?
By a Paris costumier, Maillot, in the
1820s. Another tight-fitting costume, the
leotard, was introduced in the mid-19th
century by Jules Leotard, a trapeze
artist.

**What was the achievement of Dame
Marie Rambert?**
Dame Marie Rambert was born in 1888
in Poland, danced with the Diaghilev
ballet, and in 1926 founded the Ballet
Rambert which she directed for over 50
years.

Who was Nijinsky?
Vaslav Nijinsky (1890–1950), a Russian
born ballet dancer, made his debut in
1908, then joined Diaghilev in Paris, and
for about ten years was one of the
greatest of the Diaghilev dancers.
Nijinsky also choreographed many
ballets.

**How did the Moscow audience react
to the first performance of** *Swan Lake*
in 1877?
The performance was a disaster and the
audience booed and stamped their feet.
This was for a variety of reasons – the
interference of the choreographer with
Tchaikovsky's lovely music, the
drabness of the costumes and sets and
the poor performances of individuals.

**What were Dame Ninette de Valois'
origins?**
She was born Edris Stannus in Wicklow,
Eire, in 1898, of French Huguenot
descent. She became a dancer with
Diaghilev, then prima ballerina at
Covent Garden in 1919. Dame Ninette
has dominated British ballet since the
1920s. She was made DBE in 1951.

Whose music is the basis of the ballet
*Les Sylphides***?**
Frederic Chopin, and it was orchestrated
in the early part of the 20th century by
Glazunov. It was first performed at St
Petersburg (now Leningrad) in 1908.

Who was Diaghilev?
Sergei Pavlovich Diaghilev (1872–1929)
was a Russian ballet producer who
introduced a whole scheme of new ideas
into ballet centred on the coordination of
dancing, mime, music, costume, stage set
and lighting. He adapted ballet to famous
orchestral compositions, such as Rimsky-
Korsakov's *Scheherazade* and Debussy's
L'après-midi d'un faune. He founded Le
Ballet Russe in France in 1909 which he
ran for twenty years, employing the
greatest names of the day, such as
Pavlova, Nijinsky, composers like
Stravinsky and Prokofiev, and artists
such as Picasso and Braque.

What is a tutu?
This is the ballet skirt which became
standard for female dancers in 1832. It
has three forms, which, from longest to
shortest, are the romantic, the classic,
and the horizontal.

What is the *corps de ballet***?**
It is the term to describe all those
members of a ballet who are not principal
or solo performers.

Who was Pavlova?
Anna Pavlovna Pavlova was born in
St Petersburg in 1881 and entered the
Imperial Ballet Academy there when she
was ten. Upon graduating in 1899 she
joined the Maryinsky Theatre where she
became prima ballerina in 1906. In 1907
she created the *Dying Swan* which
became her most famous solo dance.
Subsequently, she embarked upon
numerous foreign tours. She was
motivated by conservative aesthetic
principles, and had little sympathy with
the new ideas promoted by Diaghilev
with whom she worked for a few years
before World War I. She died at The
Hague in 1931.

When and where was the Chavin de Huantar civilization?
In Peru, South America, and it lasted from about 1300 BC to about 400 BC. It was one of the first civilizations in South America, and remains of several important buildings of the period have been found.

Who defeated the armies of the cities of ancient Sumer in the 24th century BC?
Sargon I, king of the Akkadians, who captured the cities of Ur, Lagash and others, and built a new city called Agade.

Who was Murshili the Hittite?
He was king of the Hittite people who occupied what is now Turkey, during the 2nd millennium BC. In the 1590s he captured the city of Babylon, far away in the land between the Euphrates and the Tigris rivers.

Where was the city of An-Yang?
It was in China, north of the Huang-ho or Yellow river. Here, the Shang dynasty which ruled in China from about 1600 to about 1025 BC, built its last capital city. It has been excavated and many remains of large buildings found.

What was the result of the great volcano eruption on the Aegean island of Thera?
The shock waves destroyed several of the towns of the Minoans on Crete and led to the decline of Minoan civilization in the 15th century BC.

Who were the Mycenaeans?
They were wandering peoples who settled in southern Greece in the middle of the 2nd millennium BC, about 1600–1500. They built several fine cities, notably a capital at Mycenae. They took advantage of the decline of the Minoan civilization in Crete, and overran the island in the 15th century BC.

Who were the Chou rulers?
They were Chinese kings who followed the Shang dynasty. They ruled China for nearly eight centuries, in two distinct periods and from two different capitals, one following the other. The first was near Sian, in what is now Shensi province and this has been excavated. The Chou were warlike rulers and appear to have spent much of their time fighting.

Who were the Dorians?
They were a warlike race from Eastern Europe who descended upon Greece in the early 1st millennium BC, overturned the ruling Achaeans and founded new cities such as Corinth, Megara and Sparta.

How did the ancient Indus civilization come to an end?
The Indus civilization began to decline in the period 1700 to 1600 BC, and by the middle of the millennium it had given way to hordes of invaders from Asia Minor, notably the Kassites who had been ravaging Babylonia.

Why was the old Hebrew State of Saul, David and Solomon divided?
Largely because, although these great rulers had managed to unite the Hebrew peoples under one government, it was not really the wish of the Hebrews to be one people. When Solomon died in about 930 BC, his kingdom was broken up into two, Israel and Judah.

What is the origin of the Celts?
They were a group of peoples speaking two basic languages, who came to central Europe, probably from the Near East (and also perhaps from central Russia) in the last years of the 2nd millennium BC. They were skilled metal workers, they bred horses, and they held deep religious beliefs.

What happened at the battle of Karkar?

The Israelite king, Ahab, led a combined army of Hebrews, Phoenicians and other Levantine peoples against the all-powerful Assyrians and crushed the Assyrian army in a splendid victory, in about 853 BC.

What was the Hallstatt period of Celtic civilization?

Hallstatt was a site of big salt deposits in Austria which Celtic people worked and used for trading with Mediterranean people, chiefly in the period 750 to 500 BC. These people were iron users, skilled artists and craftsmen, and also warriors.

Who were the Olmecs?

One of the earliest civilized peoples in Mexico and central America, who built cities at La Venta, Santorenzo, and Tres Zapotes, and other sites, in the 1st millennium BC.

What happened to the kingdom of Judah in 586 BC?

Nebuchadnezzar II, king of Babylonia, invaded Judah and captured Jerusalem, destroying the principal buildings. The people of Judah were taken into captivity, many of them being transported to Babylon.

What were the Vedas?

They were hymns written in ancient Sanskrit in India during the 2nd millennium BC.

What were the Upanishads?

They were sacred teachings of the Hindu faith, going back to the 1st millennium BC, and were compiled in more than 100 volumes.

What is an Ashoka pillar?

A column of sandstone, finely polished and bearing a symbol on the top, and sometimes with an inscription carved into the main trunk. Many of these pillars were set up in ancient India by the Mauryan king, Ashoka (3rd c BC), generally at holy Buddhist sites.

What was a *quipu*?

A string and knot device for calculations, employed by the Incas, probably as far back as about AD 1100. The *quipu* consisted of strings of different colours which, with the knottings, could be permutated to represent a range of calculations, statistics and other information.

Where did the La Tène Celtic culture begin?

At and around the village of La Tène near Lake Neuchatel in Switzerland, in the 6th century BC.

Where is Leptis Magna?

It is a now ruined city in Libya, about 120km (75 miles) east of Tripoli. It was originally founded by the Phoenicians, later occupied by the Carthaginians, and became a Roman colony in the 1st century BC, possibly in Caesar's time. It was the birthplace of the Roman emperor, Septimius Severus (AD 193–211). The ruins have been excavated, and among them are fine remains of a theatre, a forum, a senate house, and some baths built in the time of Emperor Hadrian (117–138). Severus also erected major buildings there.

Who were the Kassites?

They were a people from Persia who moved from Mesopotamia in the 1800s BC. They may have come from the Caucasus, originally. In the 1500s they established a ruling dynasty in Babylon and gradually absorbed Mesopotamian culture. The Kassites survived until the 12th century BC when they were overthrown by Elamites from what is now south-west Iran and the border district with Iraq, near the Persian Gulf.

What is the Commonwealth?
It is a free association of sovereign states which at one time had been part of the old British Empire. The term Commonwealth of nations was suggested as long ago as 1917 by Field Marshal J. C. Smuts of South Africa.

Why are the British known as 'Pommies' in Australia?
It is the slang word for British emigrants to Australia. Their fresh complexions remind Australians of the colour of the flesh of a pomegranate.

What happened at the Treaty of Waitangi?
The Maori inhabitants of New Zealand accepted British sovereignty by this treaty in 1840.

Who was the Father of Modern Kenya?
Jomo Kenyatta (1893–1978), who led the nationalist opposition to British rule in the 1950s and, after several years' imprisonment, became the first president of the new independent state of Kenya in 1964, three years after the formal granting of independence.

Where is Belize?
This used to be known as British Honduras, a small British colonial territory in central America adjacent to the republic of Guatemala.

What was the condominium of the New Hebrides?
An archipelago of islands in the western Pacific until 1978 administered jointly by Britain and France as an Anglo-French condominium.

Where is Tristan da Cunha?
It is a group of islands in the South Atlantic, between South America and South Africa, which is a British dependency.

Where is the 'outback'?
It is a word to describe areas in Australia that are far away from principal urban and populated rural areas.

Why was South Africa 'dropped' from the Commonwealth in 1961?
Technically, the Union of South Africa withdrew from the Commonwealth following a referendum in 1960, but the other Commonwealth members did not want South Africa to remain within, because of its national policy of *apartheid*, which discriminates against coloured people.

What was the Partition of India?
When, after World War II, the British government withdrew from India to give the sub-continent independence, it was decided that, because India was partly Hindu dominated and partly Moslem dominated, the country should be divided into two parts, India (Hindu) and a new state of Pakistan (Moslem). This arrangement was put into effect in 1947.

Why is Singapore a separate state from Malaysia?
In 1963, a federation was formed of the old British colonies of Sarawak, North Borneo, the Federation of Malaya and Singapore. The Federation of Malaya became known as Malaysia, and Sarawak, Sabah (formerly North Borneo) and Singapore joined. But in 1966, Singapore decided to drop out and remain an entirely independent state.

What is Malaysia's principal export?
Rubber.

Who brought Jamaica into the British Empire?
A Spanish possession from 1509 to 1655, it was taken from Spain by Admiral Penn during the Protectorate of Oliver Cromwell. Jamaica became an independent state in 1962.

Where do the Gurkhas come from?
They are, in military terms, soldiers
recruited in the kingdom of Nepal in the
Himalayas, who serve with the British
Army. They have a very well deserved
reputation for bravery, and many
individual Gurkha soldiers have won the
Victoria Cross.

**Who was the first prime minister of
the old Union of South Africa?**
Louis Botha (1862–1919), one of the
leaders of the Boer army in the Second
South African War (1899–1902), who
after the surrender to Lord Kitchener in
1902, became a firm friend of Britain. He
was appointed first prime minister of
South Africa in 1910, and brought his
country into World War I in 1914, on the
British side.

**When was the Sudan brought into the
British Empire?**
In 1898, after Lord Kitchener defeated
the army of the Khalifa at the battle of
Omdurman. The Sudan became an
Anglo-Egyptian condominium in 1899
and this arrangement lasted until 1956
when it was given full independence.

**What Commonwealth country in
Africa was once known as
Bechuanaland?**
Upon achieving full independence in
1966, the former British protectorate
of Bechuanaland in Southern Africa
adopted the name of Botswana. The
capital of the republic is Gaborone
(Gaberones).

**Where is Heard Island, and what
physical feature is it noted for?**
Heard Island is situated in the sub-
Antarctic zone of the Indian Ocean and
belongs to Australia. It has an active
volcano called Big Ben, 2745m (90,000ft)
covered with a mantle of snow.

Where is Pitcairn Island?

Pitcairn Island is a remote island in the
South Pacific Ocean. It is a British
dependent territory, subject to the
authority of the governor who is the
British high commissioner in New
Zealand. It does, however, have an Island
Council, made up of representatives of its
inhabitants – only 61 in number in 1980.

**What Commonwealth country in East
Africa was once a German colony?**
Tanzania, or rather the mainland part of
this country, once known as Tanganyika,
which was mandated to Britain at the
end of World War I. Offshore, Zanzibar,
too, once belonged to Germany; it passed
into British control in 1895.

**What parts of the former Indian
Empire have not remained within the
Commonwealth?**
Burma became an independent republic
outwith the Commonwealth on
4 January 1948; Pakistan left the
Commonwealth in January 1972
following the recognition of its former
Eastern Province as the independent
republic of Bangladesh by British and
other member states.

**When was the Isle of Man granted
self-government?**
In 1866.

Little Quiz 49
  Who was the winning commander at?
  1. Naval battle of the Falklands (1914)
  2. Austerlitz
  3. Omdurman
  4. Teutoburg Forest (AD 9)
  5. Oudenarde
  6. Tel-el-Kebir
  7. Qarqar
  8. Pharsalus
  9. Brunanburh
  10. Naval battle of Camperdown

What is magma?
It is very hot molten matter underneath solid rock.

What is lava?
It is magma that is shot out onto the surface when the Earth's crust is ruptured by volcanic action.

What is the Earth's crust?
It is the outer 'skin' of the Earth, and is anything from about 6 km to 70 km (3 to 43 miles) deep.

What are metamorphic rocks?
They are hard, solid rocks whose composition or texture have been altered by heat or pressure in the Earth.

What are sedimentary rocks?
They are rocks formed out of layers of sediment bonded together.

What is loess?
It is a fine yellowish dust or silt spread and deposited by the winds in the interior of central Asia, in parts of Europe and in North America (especially the United States). This material is very fertile.

What is alluvium?
It is a mixture of silt, sand and gravel deposited by flowing water, such as rivers and streams.

Where is the Continental Shelf?
It is a shelf or ledge round the Earth's continents, that continues descending very gradually under the water edging the continents. When it reaches 182.8 m (100 fathoms) or so, the ledge drops sharply to deep ocean.

What were Continental drifts?
It is believed that the Earth's present continents were formed when two huge continents broke up into smaller parts by a very slow drifting process.

Where is the Great Rift Valley?
It is a long valley in the Near East and East Africa, created by the landmass having sunk between two geological faults, or breaks in the Earth's crust. The Rift runs from Syria down to Zimbabwe.

What is an estuary?
It is the part of a river near the coast into which the sea flows.

Where are the pampas?
They are huge areas of grassland totally without trees in South America, especially around the estuary of the River Plate.

Where is the Great Barrier Reef?
It is a huge coral reef off the north-east coast of Australia.

What are Zones of Latitude?
The Frigid Zones, within the Arctic and the Antarctic circles, the Torrid Zone in the region north and south of the Equator and including the Equator, and the Temperate Zones, those areas between.

What is savanna?
It is tropical grassland which has tree clumps scattered about it.

What is a flood plain?
It is the floor of a valley that is regularly flooded by a river and which receives a layer of alluvium each time.

Where are the Roaring Forties?
They are areas of ocean, south of about latitude 40° South, in which the prevailing winds come from the north-west to west, and blow fiercely more or less all the time.

What is tundra?
Tundra is the name given to areas of land in the higher latitudes where short, cool summers do not permit trees to grow.

The frost which grips the tundra for much of the year does melt sufficiently to allow carpets of bright flowers, mosses and lichens to grow, and the whole area attracts a wealth of insect, bird and animal life. Much of Siberia and Canada are covered by tundra, as is the coast of Greenland and parts of Iceland; in the southern hemisphere tundra is restricted to the extreme south of South America and a few isolated islands.

What are moraines?

Moraines consist of material borne along by, beneath or within glaciers. This debris has been worn away from the Earth's surface by the action of the ice, or has merely fallen onto it. If the glacier becomes stationary, this material is left as a 'terminal' moraine. When a particular glacier has terminated at a number of positions throughout its long history, such spots are marked by 'recessional' moraines – each one having once been a 'terminal' moraine.

Volcano erupting

What is seismology?

The study of earthquakes and the waves of energy generated by them. It is an aim of seismologists to work towards accurate predictions of earthquakes, thus avoiding loss of life and material damage.

What is a mesa?

This is a flat-topped hill or mountain left isolated by the erosion of softer rocks all round it. Mesas are common in the south-western United States and can often be seen in 'Western' films. Masada in Israel is a mesa made famous by its defence by Jews against the Romans in the 70s.

What is a nunatak?

A hill or peak sticking through an ice cap, mostly found in Greenland or Antarctica. It is an Eskimo word.

What is a fumarole?

A vent in the Earth's surface which emits steam and gases, essentially associated with volcanic regions. The best known fumaroles are situated in California, Alaska and Iceland.

What is an oxbow lake?

Currents of a slow moving river meandering across a flood plain dictate that eventually the channel will cut through the neck of each meander. When this occurs, the ends of the abandoned loop silt up to leave a crescent-shaped, oxbow lake. In time, it too silts up and becomes a marsh.

2, 5, 7...

Who were the Twelve Apostles?
They were the twelve disciples of Jesus,
namely, Simon Peter, Andrew, James,
John, Philip, Bartholomew, Matthew,
Thomas, James son of Alphaeus, Simon
Zelotes, Judas (brother of James) and
Judas Iscariot (who later betrayed Jesus).

**Who were the Gang of Four in
politics?**
They were former Cabinet ministers in
the Labour Party who in 1981 founded
the Social Democratic Party, and were
Roy Jenkins, Shirley Williams, David
Owen and William Rodgers.

**How long did the Hundred Years'
War really last?**
Of course the fighting did not last all the
time, but the war began in 1337 and only
ended in 1453. It was the struggle
between England and France for the
throne of France.

When was the Six Day War?
It was a lightning strike by Israeli forces
against Egypt early in June 1967, in an
attempt to prevent Egypt and other Arab
countries attacking them. The Israelis
caught the Egyptian army and air force
unprepared and within six days had
reached and taken the east bank of the
Suez Canal.

**What happened at 11.00 am on the
11th day of the 11th month of 1918?**
World War I officially came to an end by
an armistice which was ordered to start
from that moment.

**Who was the Third Man in British
fiction?**
It was Harry Lime, an unscrupulous
racketeer who made money out of the
distress of the defeated German and
Austrian people after World War II. He
was the 'hero' of a story by Graham
Greene, which was made into a most
successful film in 1949.

274

**In what sports does the cry 'Seconds
Out' occur?**
In boxing or wrestling. Contestants are
attended by seconds, or helpers, who
assist them in the intervals between
fighting bouts. Seconds are told to get out
of the ring before a fresh round starts.

When was the Six Weeks' War?
1866, a short war between Prussia and
the Austria-Hungarian Empire, which
Prussia won as a result of the victory at
the battle of Sadowa.

**Why did people in England in 1752
say 'Give us back our eleven days'?**
In September 1752, it was decided to
correct the calendar in Britain which had
already been corrected everywhere else
in Europe in 1582, and which had slipped
by about eleven days. September 3rd was
changed to September 14th, the next day
September 15th and so on. But many
people felt they had been cheated.

Who were The Few?
They were the pilots of RAF fighter
planes, who in the days of the Battle of
Britain, 1940, shot down hundreds of
German fighters and bombers, thus
denying the German air force the air
supremacy it needed to ensure that
Hitler's projected invasion of Britain
could be successful. The term comes from
Winston Churchill's tribute to the pilots
– 'Never in the field of human conflict
was so much owed by so many to so few.'

What is a baker's dozen?
13.

**What does being at sixes and sevens
mean?**
It means being in a state of considerable
confusion.

What was a four-in-hand?
A carriage drawn by four horses and
driven by one person.

What is the 64,000 Dollar Question?
Originally, it was the top prize on an American TV quiz game in which a contestant could win up to that sum of money in stages, by answering correctly questions put to him. The phrase has come to mean 'the important question'.

What is a nine-days' wonder?
Something that creates sensational interest for a short time and then is forgotten.

What is talking nineteen to the dozen?
A phrase meaning to talk incessantly.

How many eyes did the Cyclops have?
One, in the middle of his forehead.

Who were the Three Musketeers?
Athos, Porthos and Aramis in the novel by Alexandre Dumas.

What was 'the Fifteen'?
An unsuccessful attempt by James Edward Stuart, the Old Pretender, to gain with the help of the Jacobites, the throne of England in 1715.

Who were the Five Members?
They were five members of Parliament whom, in 1642, the king, Charles I, attempted to arrest in the House of Commons for opposing him. They were John Pym, John Hampden, Arthur Haselrig, Denzil Holles and William Strode.

What was the Five Mile Act of 1665?
Because the established church priests abandoned their churches during the Great Plague, non-conformist ministers took them over. This angered the established churchmen so much they persuaded Parliament to pass this act ordering these ministers not to go within five miles of their churches or of any town where they might have preached.

What was the Seven Years' War about?
Fought between 1756 and 1763, with Britain and Prussia on one side against France, Austria and Russia on the other, it was a conflict over Prussian aggression in Europe and rivalry between Britain and France in India and North America.

What were the Six Acts?
These were tough, repressive laws introduced in 1819 to prevent rioting among the working classes. There was much distress among the workers in the newly industrialized parts of the country, about which the government did nothing. The acts enabled the authorities to search houses for arms, to ban printed propaganda and protests etc.

Where is the 38th Parallel?
It is the border between North and South Korea as determined at the Potsdam Conference between the victorious allies at the end of World War II in 1945.

When is Twelfth Night?
It is the evening of the twelfth day after Christmas Day, and in the Christian calendar is the Feast of the Epiphany. On that day it is usual to take down Christmas decorations and cards.

What was the Third Estate in France?
A term describing the various classes in pre-Revolutionary France below the nobility and the clergy. The third estate paid almost all taxes.

What were Luther's 95 Theses?
These were the complaints Luther had against the practices of the orthodox church in Europe, and in 1517, he listed them in some detail and nailed the sheets of paper to the doors of Wittenburg Cathedral. This is often taken to be the starting point of the Reformation.

What is the origin of boxing?
The ancient Greeks used to box with bare hands, though it is not known for certain if they staged special bouts in their Olympic or other games.

When did boxing become organized in Britain?
In 1719 James Figg opened a stadium in Oxford Street in London where among other things boxing bouts were put on. Incidentally, Figg also gave coaching in the sport.

When were gloves first used for boxing?
In the mid-18th century, John Broughton, once champion prize fighter of England, began to use bandaging to protect his hands for practice purposes. Gloves began to be worn in contests on a wide scale after the introduction of the Queensberry Rules in 1867, which included regulations on gloves.

What were the Queensberry Rules?
In the 19th century boxing had become a most brutal sport, with fighters hammering each other for hours on end, often encouraged by heavy betting on the outcome. In 1866 the 8th Marquis of Queensberry and some associates drew up a set of rules. These eliminated fouls, introduced points scoring and limited rounds to three minutes and made glove-wearing obligatory. These rules, with few amendments, have governed the sport ever since.

What was the particular winning punch of Britain's Henry Cooper?
His left hook, known as 'Enery's 'ammer', with which he floored many opponents. He once put the world's greatest boxer of the day, Muhammad Ali, on the floor with such a punch. Cooper was British heavyweight champion for ten years (1959–69) and again 1970–71.

Who was Jack Dempsey?
One of the most popular world heavyweight champions, he was born in Colorado, USA in 1895. He won the world heavyweight championship in 1919 and held it until 1926 when he was knocked out by the challenger Gene Tunney.

What is the maximum weight allowed for a boxer to be admitted to the featherweight class?
Nine stone.

Who was the only British-born boxer to win the world heavyweight title?
Bob Fitzsimmons.

What are the correct dimensions of a boxing ring?
Boxing rings are not exactly the same size everywhere, but the rules state they should be between 1.3 and 1.86 m square (14 and 20 ft square), must have three horizontal ropes on the four sides and properly padded corner posts.

Which body governs the sport of professional boxing throughout the world?
The World Boxing Council, founded in 1963.

How many rounds should be boxed for a world title fight?
Unless one contestant is knocked out or the referee stops the contest, the fight should go for 15 rounds of 3 minutes each.

Who was Freddie Mills?
He was a British light heavyweight champion who won the World Championship in 1948. He was challenged in 1950 and beaten by Joey Maxim, and then retired to run a restaurant in London. Freddie Mills was murdered in a gangland quarrel in London in 1965.

How many challenges to his world heavyweight title did Joe Louis defeat?
Joe Louis became world heavyweight champion in 1937 when he was twenty-three, and he held it for twelve years against twenty-five challengers. In the end he retired undefeated, but made a come-back a few years later, himself to challenge another world champion, Rocky Marciano, but he was knocked out.

What happened to Rocky Marciano?
He was a most remarkable heavyweight boxer who became world champion in 1952, held it against six challengers and then retired. He was killed in an aeroplane crash in 1969.

Who taught the poet Byron to box?
John Jackson (1769–1845), who had been British Boxing Champion from 1795 to 1803.

Why was Muhammad Ali stripped of his World Heavyweight title?
Because he was called up and refused to serve in the US Army in Vietnam. He had been boxing as Cassius Clay, but he adopted the Muslim faith and changed his name to Muhammad Ali. This did not absolve him from military service.

Who defeated the American world champion Sugar Ray Robinson?
Randolph Turpin, British middleweight, in London in 1951, by beating Robinson on points. Just two months later, Turpin had to meet a return challenge by Robinson and lost when the referee stopped the fight towards the end.

Who was the oldest man to win a world championship?
Bob Fitzsimmons, the English-born New Zealander, won the light-heavyweight title in 1903 aged 40 years and six months. He outpointed George Gardner over 20 rounds.

Who was the heaviest heavyweight world champion?
Italy's Primo Carnera, who weighed just over 19 stone.

When was the last prize ring world title bout fought?
On 8 July 1889 at Richberg, Mississippi, when John L. Sullivan beat Jake Kilrain over 75 rounds.

Which British monarch first showed an interest in boxing?
George I, who set up a 'Ring' for the populace in Hyde Park in 1723.

When was Muhammed Ali's first professional defeat?
On 8 March 1971, when Joe Frazier beat him on points at Madison Square Gardens, New York. Ali did, however, win two subsequent fights with Frazier.

What championships has John Conteh held and when did he retire from the ring?
From 1973 to 1978, Conteh gained the British, Commonwealth, European and World light-heavyweight titles (World Boxing Council). After losing the latter body's recognition as champion, he tried to regain a title but won no more fights. He retired from boxing in 1980.

Little Quiz 50
  What are the manufacturing nations of these motor cars?
1. Citroën
2. Lada
3. Buick
4. Ferrari
5. Datsun
6. Skoda
7. DAF
8. BMW
9. AC
10. Saab

When was the first photograph printed?

In 1826, by Nicéphore Niepce (1765–1833), a French amateur scientist. He began to make copies of drawings by contact printing in about 1822, and four years later produced the first photograph from nature on a bitumen covered plate.

What was the Daguerreotype process?

It was the earliest practical method of photography whereby a positive image could be produced upon a silvered plate. It needed between 15 and 30 minutes' exposure for brightly lit views. The process was introduced by Louis Daguerre (1787–1851), also French, who had been in partnership with Niepce to develop the latter's process.

What is a fish-eye lens?

It is a very wide-angle lens capable of covering at least 100° of viewing, but it produces pictures which are distorted at the edges.

What is hypo?

It is sodium thiosulphate (once called sodium hyposulphite), a chemical in solution which is used for fixing photographs after developing. The chemical was introduced in 1839.

What is the origin of the word Kodak?

It was a word invented as a trade mark by George Eastman (1854–1932), the American amateur photographer who introduced the first simple camera for the amateur in 1888. The name was thought to be easily remembered or pronounced in any language.

What other process did Eastman introduce with his Kodak popular camera?

Developing & Printing (D & P) service, which was offered to customers buying his films.

What is the aperture of a camera lens?

It is the hole that regulates the amount of light coming in through a lens, affecting the brightness of the image and it can be varied in size.

What does it mean to retouch a negative or print?

It means to improve it by removing blemishes, creases and scratches by using a fine brush or pencil.

What is photogravure?

A process for printing in ink by mechanical means from an etched plate.

What is the origin of the word photography?

From the two Greek words, *photos* (light) and *grapho* (I write), which when combined were to mean 'writing by means of light'. The term was coined by Sir John Herschel in discussions with William Fox Talbot, the British photography pioneer, probably in 1839.

What was Fox Talbot's contribution to photography?

He made many, but perhaps the most significant was producing the first permanent photographic negative on photographic paper, which he patented in 1841 as the Calotype process.

Who was Julia Margaret Cameron?

She was an eccentric, wealthy amateur photographer of the mid-Victorian period who lived for a time in the Isle of Wight, near the poet Tennyson. She took numerous photographs of celebrities which were striking in the way they caught the sitter's personality.

What is a telephoto lens?

It is a long-focus lens which provides a large image of a distant object or individual, rather like the image produced in a telescope.

Why do you have to wash photographs during the printing process?
To remove all unwanted chemicals and reduce the risk of unexpected chemical reactions taking place.

When did the twin-lens reflex Rolleiflex camera first appear?
In 1928, as a German invention.

Early Rolleiflex camera

How does an exposure meter work?
It converts light into electric current, by means of an electric cell. The apparatus measures the intensity of light in the area in which the picture is to be taken, to allow the photographer to adjust the aperture.

What is panchromatic film?
It is black-and-white film whose photographic emulsions (that is, light-sensitive salts in gelatin) are equally sensitive to every colour, thus producing the differences in correct tones of darkness and light.

When was the first flash-bulb produced?
In 1929, and it was devised for newspaper photographers.

Why do people still talk about black and white prints as bromides?
Because the process of using photographic paper covered with silver bromide in a gelatinous base for printing black and white pictures is still being used, nearly 120 years after its invention.

What was Peter Henry Emerson's major contribution to photography?
Emerson (1856–1936) led a revival of nature photography. He is particularly noted for his studies of the life and landscape of the Norfolk Broads, where he worked over a ten-year period in the late 19th century.

Little Quiz 51
  What do the following abbreviations stand for?

1. DNA	21. pp
2. HMSO	22. lbw
3. CIA	23. oz
4. SS	24. cc
5. UCH	25. ie
6. Bart or (Bt)	26. inst.
7. OUDS	27. etc.
8. CUP	28. mph
9. NUS	29. rpm
10. Litt. D	30. bhp
11. LJ	31. ca.
12. ICBM	32. cwt
13. JFK	33. aux
14. SJ	34. non seq
15. RAM	35. pub
16. NSPCC	36. pa
17. MFH	37. del
18. IOW	38. v
19. TT	39. CID
20. op. cit	40. Ky

Where can Rodin's *Le Baiser* (The Kiss) be seen?
In the Tate Gallery, London.

Donatello was a sculptor of the 15th century to whom Michelangelo was indebted. They both did sculptures of a famous Biblical character. Who was it?
David, king of Israel.

Statue of David by Michelangelo

Why did Degas turn to wax and bronze figure sculpture?
The great Impressionist painter began to lose his eyesight in his later years.

Early sculpture was done from wood and stone. What other materials are commonly used today?
Bronze and lead.

What famous Florentine goldsmith and sculptor wrote an autobiography which is still read today?
Benvenuto Cellini (1500–1571).

What is the word for the structure on which a sculptor puts his clay?
An armature.

Picasso's early painting was influenced by examples of primitive sculpture. From which country in particular?
Negro sculpture from the Ivory Coast.

What is the difference between relief sculpture and intaglio?
In the first the image is raised from the material used, and in the second it is carved out of it.

Who made the bronze doors to the baptistery at Florence Cathedral?
Lorenzo Ghiberti (1378–1455). The doors took nearly half a century to complete and Michelangelo described them as 'the gates of Paradise'.

When does a sculptor make a plaster cast?
When a piece of sculpture has not been directly carved and is to be cast in metal.

Where are these three famous sculptures executed by the artist Jacob Epstein (1880–1959); *The Rima; Christ in Majesty; St Michael and the Devil*?
Hyde Park, London; Llandaff Cathedral, Wales; Coventry Cathedral.

What other art form most resembles sculpture?
Collage, because it is done by the application of many varied materials to make a picture.

What is the 'Laocoon'?
A Hellenistic statue of the agonies of

Laocoon and his sons being crushed to death by serpents. It was discovered in 1506.

What happened to the *Unknown Political Prisoner*?
This was an almost abstract sculpture executed by Reg Butler representing an unknown political prisoner. It was exhibited in 1953 and won a major competition prize. But it gave offence to many former victims of persecution in Europe under the communist group of powers, and one refugee smashed the sculpture in a moment of anger.

Who is regarded as the greatest modern British sculptor?
Henry Moore (b 1898) OM, CH.

Who executed the recumbent statue of Lord Kitchener in St Paul's Cathedral in London?
Sir William Reid Dick.

What is a mobile?
It is a form of sculpture whose component parts are suspended from a ceiling or pole and which move more or less continuously in the varying air currents around it.

What was Eric Gill's major contribution to sculpture?
Gill (1882–1940) was most famous for his bas-reliefs, often in the form of friezes. Such work can be seen on many buildings throughout the world.

What woman has made the greatest contribution to sculpture in the 20th century?
Without doubt, Barbara Hepworth (1903–1975), D.B.E. A near contemporary of Henry Moore, Barbara Hepworth has concentrated far less on purely figurative themes. In 1939 she moved to St Ives, Cornwall, a much

favoured resort of artists working in a wide range of media, spending the rest of her life there. Equally skilled with stone and with wood, her forms in the latter medium were often threaded with string or painted.

Who was Moholy-Nagy?
Laszlo Moholy-Nagy (1895–1946) had been a Hungarian law student who took up painting and drawing while convalescing from wounds received in World War I. Later moving to Berlin, he turned his attention to solids, and after an exhibition of his work there in 1922 he was invited to teach at the famous Bauhaus Academy. He became particularly concerned with the relationship between the artist and the space surrounding his work, which ideas he expressed in his book, *From Materials to Architecture*. After moving to the United States in 1937 to found a New Bauhaus in Chicago, he became fascinated with the properties of a type of plastic called *Plexiglass*.

What is a maquette?
It is a preliminary wax or clay sketch for a sculpture.

Little Quiz 52
  What are the homes of these animals?
1. hares
2. foxes
3. wasps
4. bees
5. badgers
6. squirrels
7. wolves
8. eagles
9. spiders
10. rabbits

What are the main recognition features of mayflies?
They have two or three long tails, one or two pairs of wings, the hind wings if present being much smaller than the front ones. They also have short antennae.

What is a stick insect?
A long thin insect with long legs, looking like a tiny stick (or in some non-European species, like a leaf). Stick insects are green or brown in varying shades. Stick insects are not common in Europe, and the European kinds usually have no wings.

Why are earwigs so called?
They are longish brown insects with short wings, as a rule easily identified. It used to be thought they crawled into the ears of sleeping human beings and chewed their way through the ear-drums.

Why are cockroaches unpopular?
Cockroaches tend to seek out warm areas, usually travelling at night time, and rest during the day, hidden under floorboards or behind dados or in air ducts. They tend to stay there and multiply, coming out from time to time to look for scraps. They create an unpleasant smell which is associated with rotting food, and so they can probably spread germs.

What sort of material do termites eat?
Termites have biting mouths, and are very destructive. They go for the wood of trees, shrubs, and houses where there are old timbers.

Why are book lice so called?
They are wingless insects which like to live among materials like old paper, where they feed upon moulds that grow there.

What are the antennae of an insect used for?
They are two sensory organs projecting from the head, which act as feelers.

How many species of insect are there in the United Kingdom?
Over 20,000.

What is a larva?
It is a baby insect, distinguishable from its parents because it is different in shape. A good example is the caterpillar, which is the larva of a moth or butterfly.

Which is the biggest flea you are likely to meet in Britain?
The mole flea, which is more than $\frac{1}{2}$ cm ($\frac{1}{4}$ in) long.

What is the human flea?
This is a species of flea called *Pulex irritans*. It is well known for being able to hop as far as 0.305 m (1 ft).

What is the largest order of insects?
The beetle order, of which there are said to be more than $\frac{1}{4}$ million species, 4000 of which are distinguishable in the UK.

What are the distinguishing features of a dragonfly?
It is a long-bodied insect, with two pairs of wings whose network of veins is readily visible, and which has two very big compound eyes (that have thousands of facets). The colouring of a dragonfly is most striking and often extremely beautiful.

What is the chief characteristic of bumble bees?
They make a loud humming noise when in flight.

What do the springtail, bristletail and silverfish have in common?
They are all primitive insects without wings.

What are the whirligig beetles?

They are beetles of the Gyrinidae family which spend their lives skimming around on the surface of still or gently moving water. They are small, shiny, black, and they dive into the water when disturbed or when in search of food.

What sort of food do grasshoppers eat?

They depend chiefly on grass, and on some other plant life.

Grasshopper

How does a mole cricket sing?

By rubbing its legs against its wings. Not all species of mole cricket have wings.

What do ants, bees and termites have in common?

They are in the main social insects, that is, they live in colonies, each with their own job to do to help the colony survive.

Why do some insects shine?

Some insects, such as the fire-fly and the glow-worm, produce a chemical light to attract a mate. Other types use the light to frighten creatures which would otherwise try to eat them. The headlamp click beetle, which dwells in the South American jungles, has two spots of light behind its head. To any creature coming upon it at night, the spots look like huge shining eyes.

How do you tell moths from butterflies?

Moths and butterflies make up the order of insects called *Lepidoptera*. There are many differences. Butterflies come out during the day, rest with their wings pointing upwards and have a blob on each antenna. Moths are nocturnal insects, are not as brightly coloured, and when they rest they fold their wings across their bodies. They have no blobs on their antennae.

What do butterflies live on?

They feed on nectar, the sugary substance found at the bottom of a flower. They suck up the nectar with a long, thin tube which, when it is not in use, they keep rolled up under the head.

What is a bed-bug?

It is a brown, flattened insect without wings, which gives out an unpleasant smell. Bed bugs are found as a rule in old, deteriorating houses and they come out at night time to suck the blood of people when they are sleeping.

Who was the first statesman to try to create a united west Europe?
Julius Caesar, who by his conquest of Gaul (France and part of Belgium) between 59 and 50 BC transformed the Roman Empire from a Mediterranean to a European empire.

What other rulers attempted to create a united Europe?
Charlemagne, king of the Franks and first emperor of the Holy Roman Empire, and Napoleon Bonaparte, emperor of the French.

What was the origin of the European Economic Community?
World War II (1939–45) had devastated Europe and over 50 million people had been killed. Winston Churchill saw that the future peace of Europe could best be guaranteed by the formation of a United States of Europe.

What was the first step taken towards creating this union?
The Organization for European Economic Cooperation was created in 1947, and in 1949 the Council of Europe was formed, holding its first meeting as the Consultative Assembly, at Strasbourg, in August 1949.

Who were the member states of the new Council?
Britain, France, Belgium, the Netherlands, Italy, Sweden, Denmark, Norway, Ireland, Luxembourg, Greece, Turkey. Other states including West Germany joined later.

What was the ECSC?
The European Coal and Steel Community, which was founded in 1952, basically to pool the coal and steel resources of western Europe under one authority, and to create a single market. It was the first practical step towards a United States of Europe.

What is the Common Market?
It is the popular term for the European Economic Community (EEC), founded in 1957 as a development of the Coal and Steel Community. There were six member states, France, West Germany, Italy, the Netherlands, Belgium and Luxembourg. They reached agreement at the Treaty of Rome to form an economic union. A Council of Ministers was set up.

What is the make-up of the Council of Ministers?
It is a council with one member from each member state, according to the subject to be discussed, such as agriculture, finance, foreign affairs, etc. The headquarters are in Brussels.

What is the European Commission?
It is a body which initiates policy in the EEC and advises the Council of Ministers. It has at least one member from each member state and two from each of the larger nations. Its president is chosen from its members, and he or she is in office for two years.

Who was the first British president of the European Commission?
Roy Jenkins, PC, who had been both chancellor of the exchequer and home secretary in the government of Harold Wilson (1964–70). He entered his presidency in 1977.

What is the European Parliament?
This is a representative assembly having members directly elected from each member country. It sits at Strasbourg and has to be consulted on all major issues affecting the EEC. It has the power of veto over the European Commission, and also has control over the EEC's budget.

What is the role of the European Court of Justice?

It exists to safeguard the interpretation of the various treaties making up the EEC and its constituent bodies, and to decide if necessary on the legality of decisions of the Council of Ministers or the Commission. Member states can bring cases to the Court, as indeed individual people in the member countries may also do.

When did the United Kingdom join the EEC?
The UK applied to join in 1961, and was refused. It applied again in 1967 and was refused again. But in 1970, negotiations began once more, and on 1 January 1973 the UK became a full member, along with both Denmark and Ireland.

What was the difficulty regarding United Kingdom memberhip?
Largely, it was because of the opposition of General de Gaulle, president of France and a leading influence in the EEC. He objected to the special relationship between the UK and the United States of America, notably over defence policies. De Gaulle ceased to be president in France in 1968 and died in 1970. His departure from the sphere of power removed most of the obstacles to British entry.

Which country refused to join the EEC in 1973?
Norway, which had originally applied to join, along with the UK, Denmark and Ireland. A national referendum produced a majority against membership and the application was dropped.

What is the Common Agricultural Policy?
It is the issue that has caused the greatest difficulties among the member states. Basically, it is a system that guarantees the incomes of the farmers in the member states by fixing prices that are charged to consumers for agricultural products, including cereals, milk, beef, pigs, eggs and poultry, fruit and vegetables, wine, and sugar.

Who was the European statesman generally regarded as the architect of the Coal and Steel Community?
The French statesman Jean Monnet (1888–1981). He was its first president (1952–55).

Which other European states are considering application to join the EEC?
Spain, Portugal and Turkey.

Has any other state joined since 1973?
Yes, Greece.

What was the result of the referendum held in the United Kingdom in 1975 to confirm or change the decision to join the EEC?
Two thirds of the electorate approved the decision to join. It is said today that if the same question were asked now, the proportions would be very different.

Which is the only EEC country with which the United Kingdom shares a land frontier?
The Irish Republic.

With which potential EEC member has the United Kingdom been involved in a territorial dispute?
Spain, in respect of Gibraltar.

What overseas territory of a member state voted to leave the EEC on 1 January 1984?
Greenland, which has home rule but remains a Danish possession.

In what EEC country might you hear a language called Frisian?
In the Netherlands. Frisian is spoken in the islands which bear that name, and very locally on the northern mainland.

285

What were the names of the ships that Columbus took on his first voyage across the Atlantic in 1492?
The *Santa Maria* (his flagship), the *Niña* and the *Pinta*. The *Santa Maria* was wrecked off Haiti after his first discoveries, and the remains of it were discovered in 1968.

What was the name of Drake's flagship on his voyage round the world?
He set out in the *Pelican* in 1577 with four other ships. The four became detached in the Cape Horn area, and he went on alone, changing the name of the *Pelican* to *Golden Hind*.

Who were the travellers in the *Mayflower* in 1620?
They were the Pilgrim Fathers, political and religious victims of persecution who set out for the Americas. They left Plymouth and set up the first colony in New England.

Which ship was the flagship of the British Grand Fleet at the battle of Jutland?
HMS *Iron Duke*, a battleship, flying the flag of Admiral Sir John Jellicoe (later, Admiral of the Fleet Earl Jellicoe), commander-in-chief of the British Grand Fleet. The battle was fought at the end of May, 1916.

Which famous warship was sunk by the German battleship *Bismarck* in the Atlantic in 1941?
HMS *Hood*, a 42,000 ton battle-cruiser. The magazine is thought to have been hit by shells from the *Bismarck*, for the ship blew up and all but a handful of the crew were drowned.

What happened to the *Lusitania*?
This Cunard trans-Atlantic liner was

Columbus' flagship, the *Santa Maria*

sunk off the Irish coast by a German submarine on 7 May 1915, and over 1200 people were drowned, some of them women and children.

How old was HMS *Victory*, Nelson's flagship at Trafalgar in 1805?
It had been launched in 1765 and it weighed over 2160 tons. The *Victory* survived the battle, though Nelson lost his life, and the ship is still in dry dock at Portsmouth Harbour.

What happened to the *Marie Celeste*?
This small ship left the United States in 1872 with a captain and crew, and was later found abandoned in the Atlantic, with no sign of anyone aboard or any evidence as to where the ship's complement had gone.

What happened to the liner *Titanic* on its maiden voyage in April 1912?
It struck an ice-berg in the north Atlantic and sank within about two hours, with the loss of over 1500 lives, largely because there were too few lifeboats on board.

What was a monitor in the Royal Navy?
An unusual warship of shallow draught and of cruiser size, but which mounted very heavy guns. Two of the best known British monitors of this century were HMS *Erebus* and HMS *Terror*, both of which mounted 15 in guns.

What was a dreadnought?
It was a type of battleship built in the early years of the present century for the Royal Navy, named after the first of the series, HMS *Dreadnought*. The *Dreadnought* displaced about 18,000 tons, carried ten 12 in guns and was protected by 11 in armour. It could travel at 21 knots. Dreadnoughts were the idea of Admiral of the Fleet Sir John (later Lord) Fisher, first sea lord.

Who was aboard the cruiser HMS *Hampshire* when she was sunk off Orkney on 5 June 1916?
Field Marshal Earl Kitchener of Khartoum, secretary of state for war, who was travelling to Russia to help bolster up the Russian war effort against the Germans in World War I. Kitchener was drowned.

What was the *Great Michael*?
It was a splendid battleship built for James IV of Scotland at the beginning of the 16th century. At 72 m (236.16 ft) long and 11 m (36.08 ft) wide, and carrying a crew of 300, it was the largest battleship anywhere in Europe at the time. It took most of the oak trees of the kingdom of Fife to build it.

What was the *Charlotte Dundas*?
It was the first steamship to operate successfully. It plied the Forth-Clyde Canal in Scotland, starting in 1802.

What principal armament did the battleships HMS *Nelson* and HMS *Rodney* carry?
They carried three turrets of three 16 in guns, mounted in line, one higher than the next, in the fore part of the ship.

What are the characteristics of battle cruisers?
Basically, they were warships that displaced a similar tonnage to that of the battleship and carried similar armament, but at the same time had less protective armour and could travel considerably faster.

Which is the largest aircraft carrier in the world today?
There are two: the USS *Nimitz* and the USS *Dwight D Eisenhower*, both of them displacing 91,400 tons, over 332 m (1090 ft) long, nuclear-powered, and capable of carrying over 90 planes.

Where are?

The Champs-Elysées
A long, wide boulevard in Paris, stretching from the Place de la Concorde up to L'Arc de Triomphe.

The Kremlin
A huge, walled citadel, with eighteen towers, in the middle of Moscow, begun in the 12th century and containing, among other buildings, three cathedrals, the Ivan Veluki tower over 90 m (300 ft) tall, several palaces and museums.

The Grande Place
The main central square in Brussels, Belgium, containing many fine buildings including La Maison du Roi.

Princes Street
The main street of Edinburgh, and one of the finest streets in Europe.

The Four Courts
A splendid composite building of the late 1790s in Dublin, Eire, rebuilt after damage in the civil war, 1922. It used to house four separate courts, the Court of Exchequer, the Court of Common Pleas, the Court of King's Bench, and the Court of Chancery.

Cathays Park
A park in the centre of Cardiff, Wales, containing several public buildings including the law courts and the City Hall.

Table Mountain
A remarkable rocky prominence, some 1067.5 m (3500 ft) high, which lies on the edge of, and dominates the city of Cape Town in South Africa.

The Hradcany
A fortified palace and castle in Prague, Czechoslovakia, now containing the president's palace and various government headquarters.

The Prado Museum
One of the best museums and art galleries of Europe, it is in Madrid, Spain. It houses a fine collection of one of Spain's most celebrated painters, Velasquez.

Kenwood House
In Hampstead, London, this 18th century mansion standing in beautiful grounds, houses a fine collection of paintings, notably the famous self portrait by Rembrandt and Romney's portrait of Lady Hamilton.

The Wedding Cake
It is the *Vittoriano*, or Monument to Victor Emanuel II in Rome.

Fifth Avenue
The smartest and perhaps most famous street in New York, USA.

The Deichstrasse
A street in Hamburg, West Germany, which has several late medieval houses that, miraculously, survived the devastation of the city during World War II.

The Horse Guards
A splendid building by William Kent, in Whitehall, London, which backs onto a huge parade ground used for Trooping the Colour and other ceremonies.

The Doge's Palace
An amazing structure beside St Mark's Cathedral in Venice, Italy, it was begun in the 9th century. Its principal external feature is the superb Gothic front of the 14th century.

Trogir Cathedral
A splendid Romanesque cathedral of the 13th century, with some fine Gothic additions, situated on an island along the Dalmatian coast in Yugoslavia, connected to the mainland by causeway.

The Red Fort
Once the imperial palace of the great
Mogul emperors of India, this is in Delhi.

Berchtesgaten
The village in south-east Bavaria,
Germany, near which Adolf Hitler lived
in a fortified country house called the
Berghof on the top of the Obersalzburg.

Grace Cathedral
An imitation Gothic cathedral, built of
structural steel and concrete, in San
Francisco. It is a very fine building, and
has some stained glass in the rose
window at the east end specially made
for it at Chartres in France.

The oldest surviving timber building in England?
The church of St Andrew at Greensted,
about 12 miles west of Chelmsford, in
Essex. The nave is constructed of tree
trunks split in half and stood on end, and
the timberwork is mid-9th century.

The Balearic Islands?
In the Mediterranean, they include some
of the world's most popular holiday
destinations: Majorca, Minorca and Ibiza.

Bouvet Island?
This has the distinction of being the most
isolated place on earth, situated in the
South Atlantic Ocean 1600km (1000
miles) from any other land. This bleak,
icy island bears the name of the French
explorer who discovered it in 1739, but it
actually belongs to Norway.

Botany Bay?
Now a suburb of Sydney, it marks the
spot from which Captain Cook
proclaimed British sovereignty over the
eastern coast of Australia on 29 April
1770. Later it achieved notoriety as the
name of a penal colony, although this
was actually situated a short distance
away from the locality where Cook
landed.

Electric Brae?
A section of the coast road near Ayr in
Scotland where an optical illusion is
created giving the impression that the
road is descending, whereas the opposite
is the case. The effect is brought about by
the nature of the configuration of the
land on either side of the road in this
locality.

Smoo Cave?
One of the more famous caves on the
mainland of Scotland, it is situated on
the north coast of Sutherland near
Durness. The outermost of its three
chambers can be readily entered; Sir
Walter Scott visited it in 1814. Like
many names in this part of Scotland, it
probably derives from an old Norse word
for rock.

The Blarney Stone?
This feature forms the sill of a
machicolation (projecting battlement) of
Blarney Castle in county Cork, Ireland.

Little Quiz 54

When were these major Civil Wars or Revolutions?
1. French Revolution
2. Indian Mutiny
3. Irish Civil War
4. Boudicca's Rebellion
5. Spanish Civil War
6. Russian Revolution
7. American War of Independence
8. English Civil War
9. Civil War between Caesar and Pompey
10. Chinese

In which countries were playing cards first used for games?
China and Japan, probably over 1000 years ago.

What were the earliest symbols used on these cards?
The Chinese reproduced designs from their paper money notes.

What was the Japanese Flower Game?
This was a card game in which the cards used had four flower pictures to represent each month of the year, making 48 in all. This was because the months were known by names of flowers. Each card was assigned a value of a certain number of points. The cards were generally very small, less than 5 cms (2 in) square.

How did playing cards reach Europe?
No one knows exactly, but it is thought they came from India, brought by wandering fortune-telling gypsies.

What is a court card?
Originally called a coat card, it is the clothed or 'coated' figures of the king, queen or jack of any of the four suits in a pack.

Can the game of whist ever be played without a partner?
Whist is a game for four players in which two partners play against another two. In solo or solo whist, however, there is a different set of rules and a player may play without a partner.

What does 'misère' mean?
This is a term used in solo whist, when the bidder contracts to win no tricks, playing a no-trump contract against the other players.

What is a flush?
A run of cards of the same suit. In poker,

a hand containing cards from the ace (high) to the ten in one suit is called a royal flush.

What is to revoke?
To fail to follow suit, even if able and required to do so, for which a penalty may be exacted.

Where did playing cards first come to be used in Europe?
In France. There is a record of three sets of playing cards being made up for King Charles IV in the 1390s. Some of the cards have survived and are in the Bibliothèque Nationale in Paris.

What was the origin of the suits in packs of cards as we know them today?
The origin is in the game of piquet, a game of knights and chivalry that was introduced in France in the early 15th century by a French knight, Étienne Vignoles. He devised the suits, namely spades, hearts, clubs and diamonds.

What did the four suits represent?
Spades represented the lance points of the knights, or the knights themselves, hearts represented the Church, clubs were clover leaves representing husbandmen, and diamonds were arrowheads, representing vassals from whom the archers were drawn.

When and where were playing cards first printed in Europe?
In Germany in the late 15th century. The designs were cut into wooden blocks and inked for printing, using a technique said to have been learned from merchants who had visited China where woodblock printing had been in use for centuries.

How did playing cards come to England?
Probably through the lords and knights

who fought in France in the later period of the Hundred Years' War (1337–1453).

Where did the term 'jack' come from?
The third court card used to be called the knave, which meant son or male child, but in time knave came to mean 'rogue', and so 'jack' from 'jack-a-napes' was substituted.

Which king of England actually recorded his losses at cards?
Henry VII, who entered in the royal accounts sums for card debts. The costumes worn by the kings, queens and jacks on cards in Britain today are typical costumes worn in the time of Henry VII.

What is a wild card?
A card that represents any card the holder wants it to, particularly in wild card poker, and wild card rummy.

What is the strongest trick in the game of vingt-et-un (or pontoon)?
A five card trick, which cannot be beaten unless the banker himself has another five card trick, which is extremely rare.

What is a rubber?
It is a match or tournament in cards, the winner being the first to win a fixed number of games. The word generally applies to bridge.

What is the origin of the joker?
The joker, usually two jokers, found in present-day packs of cards is often superfluous. Its ostensible place as a 'wild' card originates in the unnumbered trump of the tarot of the Middle Ages, the fool (le fou) or otherwise jester.

What European country's traditional playing cards were introduced to Japan in the 16th century?
Portugal, with its forty-eight card pack.

What does grand slam mean in the game of bridge?
It is the winning of every trick.

What is 'to throw in the cards'?
It means to give up or admit defeat and the expression comes from some card games, such as poker. If a player is dealt a very poor hand he may throw in the cards and wait for a new deal.

What does 'to meld' mean?
This is to declare a card or a combination of cards that one is holding for a score, usually by placing it or them face up on the table.

English court card c. 1750

Little Quiz 55
   What are the correct names for the following heraldic colours?
   1. gold
   2. silver
   3. red
   4. blue
   5. black
   6. green
   7. purple
   8. orange or brown
   9. blood red
   10. purple red

When was the Armourers' Company founded in London?

During the 14th century, but English armourers were not producing armour comparable with European makers in quality or workmanship until the Tudor period.

What was the principal body armour of the Roman legionary during the first two centuries of the Roman Empire?

Known as *lorica segmentata*, it consisted of a flexible system of overlapping strips of metal and two pairs of plates over chest and back. The body portion of strips was held together by leather thongs at the back and fastened in front with hooks and ties, or straps and buckles, loosely enough to allow the wearer to move and bend easily.

What is chain mail?

It is small interlocking iron rings put together to form a garment such as a shirt (hauberk) or a longer tunic, with or without sleeves, enabling the wearer to move freely. The links or rings were made of wire and the ends were generally riveted, though some rings were solid.

How effective was chain mail?

Not as effective as its long period of use (at least three centuries) might suggest. It could be pierced by an arrow and certainly by a lance. It was heavy and uncomfortable. Many wearers first put on one or other of a variety of undergarments as a kind of extra protection, such as thick hardened leather tunic or whalebone vest.

What was a great helm?

A cylindrical shaped helmet with a flat top, having horizontal slits in front of the eyes. It emerged in the late 12th century.

What was a basinet?

An improvement on the great helm, it was close fitting, with a short length of mail hanging from its lower edges to cover the neck and shoulders (the aventail), and it had a hinged vizor to protect the face.

What was the main weapon of the medieval knight?

The sword. It was a weapon made with great skill and craftsmanship. It was treasured by its owner, and if it was not captured in battle or broken, it was often handed down to an owner's son. Many swords were inscribed with the owner's name.

When did plate armour begin to flourish in Europe?

In the 13th century, probably as a result of the ineffectiveness of chain mail, and also because of improvements in swords, particularly the development of sharper sword points which led to swords being used as thrusting weapons as well as cutting ones. The plate armour developed as a series of plates shaped to fit various parts of the body, not all developed at once, and to begin with armour appeared as a mixture of plates joined together with large areas of chain mail. Eventually, plate armour covered the whole body, and there was even armour for parts of the horse on which the armed knight rode.

What is a gauntlet?

A steel glove of mail or plate, which was worn with armour, probably from the 12th century.

What were staff weapons?

They were the weapons used by the infantry in later medieval warfare, such as the halberd, the bill and the glaive. They are also known as pole-arms.

What was a quillon?

A special dagger that resembled a sword, but which was much smaller.

What does 'throw down the gauntlet' mean?

In medieval terms, it was a challenge to a duel. A challenger took off his gauntlet and threw it down on the ground in front of the man he wanted to challenge. If the rival picked up the gauntlet, it meant he accepted the challenge, and a duel followed.

What was a crossbow?

It was a bow placed across a stock that contained a winding mechanism, or a powerful drawing back lever, for pulling back the string and releasing it. The bow fired an arrow known as a quarrel. Crossbows took longer to load and fire than ordinary hand bows, but they were extremely accurate and had a high range.

When was the crossbow introduced and how long was it used?

It emerged in the 11th century in Europe, probably the second half, and it was still being used in the 18th century.

What was the longbow?

It was a development of the simple bow which had been used in war for many hundreds of years (even as far back as ancient Egypt). The longbow was made of yew wood and consisted of a stave over 1.83 m (6 ft) long. This differentiated it from ordinary bows which were only 0.915 to 1.22 m (3 to 4 ft). With a long bow an archer could shoot six arrows a minute with high accuracy and up to 228.75 m (250 yds) or so, nearly twice the range of the shorter bow.

Where did the longbow come from?

It is generally agreed that it was invented by the Welsh in the 13th century, and taken up by both English and Scots early in the 14th century.

What was a halberd?

It had a straight shaft of wood, about 1.83 m (6 ft) long, and at one end was an axe-like blade with a hook on the side opposite the blade.

What is a Scottish claymore?

A big two-handed sword used by the Scottish Highlanders. The word comes from Gaelic *claidheamh mor*, great sword.

Plate armour c. 1500

What was a Todenkopf helmet?

It was a 16th century middle European helmet. The vizor bore a marked resemblance to the front of a human skull.

Which was the first book printed in English?
The *Recuyell of the Historyes of Troye*, printed by William Caxton in English in 1474 at his press at Bruges in Flanders.

Who was the first doctor to be made a peer in Britain?
Joseph Lister (1827–1912), the discoverer of the antiseptic system. He was made Baron Lister of Lyme Regis in 1897. He was also to become one of the original twelve members of the Order of Merit (OM) in 1902.

Who was the first king of Rome?
Romulus, whose dates are generally given as 753–716 BC. He is credited with having founded the city of Rome in 753.

Who was the first Roman governor of Britain?
Aulus Plautius, who was in office between AD 43 and 47. He had led the legions across the English Channel in 43 and defeated the Britons in the south-eastern part of the island.

Who was the first English scientist to write about electricity?
Sir William Gilbert (1540–1603), who in 1600 published a work *De Magnete* which discussed many aspects of magnetism and electric force.

Who was the first general to take an army across the Alps?
The Carthaginian general, Hannibal (247–182 BC). He waged war against Rome and took a huge force over the Alps from Spain in 218, descending into Italy and defeating all armies that the Romans sent against him.

Who was the first archbishop of Canterbury?
St Augustine, who had been sent by Pope Gregory I to spread Christianity in England in 597.

Who was the first reigning queen in Britain?
Cartimandua, queen of the Brigantes tribe, who reigned between the 50s and 70s.

Who was awarded the first Nobel Prize for literature?
René François Armand Sully-Prudhomme (1839–1907), the French poet and philosopher, in 1901.

Who made the first solo voyage round the world in a yacht?
Sir Francis Chichester, 1966–7.

Who was the first president of the Royal Academy of Art?
Sir Joshua Reynolds, the portrait painter, in 1768.

Where was the first castle built in England by William, Duke of Normandy?
On the shore at Hastings, in October 1066. It was an earth and timber structure that was erected in a matter of days. You can see a picture of the construction on the famous Bayeux Tapestry.

Who was the first TT motorcycle rider to achieve a 144.9 kmh (90 mph) average speed for a lap round the Isle of Man TT circuit?
Freddie Frith, OBE, during the Senior TT race of 1937.

Who was the first woman to take a seat as a member of parliament in Britain?
Nancy, Viscountess Astor, in 1919. Her husband William Waldorf Astor, who was MP for Plymouth, succeeded to the title Viscount Astor when his father died in 1919, and so had to give up his House of Commons seat. His wife decided to stand in the by-election that followed, and she won.

Who was the first woman mayor in Britain?
Dr Elizabeth Garrett Anderson, who became mayor of Aldeburgh in Suffolk in 1908. She had also been a pioneer of the movement to allow women to qualify as doctors.

Who was the first footballer to be knighted?
Sir Stanley Matthews (b 1915), one of the greatest footballers of British soccer history.

Who was the first Canadian to be appointed governor-general of Canada?
Vincent Massey (1887–1967), who was in office 1952–9.

What is a first foot?
Especially in Scotland and the north of England, it is the person who first visits a house after midnight on New Year's Eve.

When was the first celebration of the Gunpowder Plot?
Two years after the plot, in fact, when the corporation of Bristol directed the lighting of bonfires on 5 November 1607. Fireworks on these occasions were not recorded until 1660, according to Samuel Pepys's famous diary.

When were old age pensions first introduced?
In Germany, on 1 January 1891. The first Commonwealth country to introduce them was New Zealand, in March (but retrospective to 1 January) 1899. They were not introduced in Britain until 1 January 1909 when, it is recorded, a recipient in Bishops Stortford died as he was signing his first receipt.

Where were the first traffic-lights erected?
At the corner of Bridge Street and New Palace Yard near the Houses of Parliament in London, on 10 December 1868.

Who was the first living person to have his photograph taken?
The unnamed gardener of the Rev Joseph Bancroft Reade of Stone, Buckinghamshire, by his master in 1838.

What is an antonym?
A word meaning the opposite of another word, such as light/dark, or felicitous/unfortunate.

What is etymology?
The study of the origins of words.

What is a palindrome?
It is a word or phrase that reads the same backwards as it does forwards such as level or Madam I'm Adam.

What do we mean by tautology?
Repetition, in different words, of the same thing, such as 'I have been all alone by myself for hours'.

What is syntax?
It is the part of grammar that deals with the way words are ordered in sentences.

What is accidence?
The study of various forms of words, such as inflexions for gender, number or case.

What is a split infinitive?
It is the error of putting another word or two between an infinitive verb and the word 'to' that should immediately precede it. 'I hope to eventually finish the work', instead of, 'I hope eventually to finish the work'.

What is *oratio obliqua*?
The Latin phrase meaning 'reported speech'. A person may say 'I have paid my bill'. This could be reported by someone else as 'he said he had paid his bill'.

What is bathos?
The same as anti-climax, that is, a figure of speech describing a descent from a higher level of thought to the ridiculous.

What is meiosis?
It is understatement: 'I didn't half enjoy it'.
296

What is a paradox?
A statement which is true but seems false or self-contradictory, such as, James I was the wisest fool in Christendom.

What is hypallage?
The same as transferred epithet, it means emphasizing an adjective or adverb by using it to describe by its position a word to which it does not belong: such as 'the condemned cell', or 'Melissa shook her doubtful curls'.

What is an innuendo?
It is hinting at a thing without actually saying it. Lord Palmerston once said, 'There is never a good champagne year, unless there is a good apple crop in Normandy'.

What is pathetic fallacy?
This is an extreme form of personification, in which objects are made to sympathize with the emotions of the agent. A good example is a famous description of Cromwell's death: A storm was raging outside as if in sympathy with the mighty soul that was passing from the earth.

What is a rhetorical question?
A question put for rhetorical effect, and not meant to be answered: 'How do I love thee? Let me count the ways.'

What is circumlocation?
A roundabout way of saying things. Winston Churchill once described a lie as a terminological inexactitude.

What is antonomasia?
It is a figure of speech in which an individual person is made to represent a class or attribute. He is a Herod, for a tyrant.

What is inversion?
It is the adoption of a rhetorical instead of a grammatical order of words, to

emphasize a statement, or part of a statement, eg 'Not hard for heroes is this death' instead of 'This death is not hard for heroes.'

What is barbarism?
Using a word that is not in current English usage, such as connexity, teached, connote.

What is a synonym?
A synonym is a word which means the same or almost the same as another, for example, song and air; endure and tolerate, plan and scheme, mistake and blunder.

What is bombast?
Strictly, it is pretentious language. 'I perused the daily chronicle of contemporary events', when you mean 'I read the newspaper'.

Is pleonasm a disease?
No, it is using more words than necessary to express what is meant, eg I saw it with my own eyes. You and I both agree.

What is ambiguity?
It is an idea, or statement, or expression, capable of being understood in more than one sense. He hit a man with a stone on his back.

What is anacoluthon?
This is starting a sentence in one way and finishing it in another way, or giving up one grammatical construction in favour of another in the middle of a sentence.

What is paraphrasing?
It is a restating of an idea, or statement, in different words, or a free rendering of a text or passage.

What is the usual order of words in a sentence called?
It is called the grammatical order. A

sentence basically consists of a subject and a predicate.

How many parts of speech are there?
Eight.

What are they?
Noun, pronoun, adjective, verb, adverb, preposition, conjunction and interjection.

What is an elliptical sentence?
It is a sentence in which some words that ought grammatically to be left in are in fact left out, because they do not add to the overall meaning of the sentence. For example; The doctor has done all (that) he can (do).

What is the subjunctive mood?
This states a condition, or purpose, or hypothesis, or wish; such as, *If he should come*, please give him this letter. We eat *in order that we may live*.

What is a diphthong?
A speech sound consisting of two vowels together pronounced as one syllable, as *ae* in Caesar.

What is a diaeresis?
It is the word describing the two dots placed over the second of two vowels together, to show that the vowels are to be sounded separately (eg coöperation). As a matter of fact, diaereses are not so often used nowadays, and when you see COOPERATIVE over a general store, you are supposed to know that the two os should be pronounced separately!

What is a sibilant consonant?
It is one that expresses a hissing sound when pronounced, such as *s, z, sh*.

What is a labial consonant?
It is one that is made with the lips entirely or partially closed, such as *p, b, m, w*.

Who are or who were?

Amazons
They were a mythical race whose leaders and warriors were women, and who occupied land to the south and east of the Black Sea. The women had their right breasts removed so that they could more easily use bow and arrow. Amazon warriors fought on the Trojan side in the great battle for Troy.

Thugs
A murderous sect of Hindus in India who flourished in the 18th century and 19th century, and who specialized in violence against travellers whom they ambushed and strangled.

Black Fellows
Another term for the aboriginal peoples discovered in Australia by the early white European settlers of the late 18th century.

Walloons
Modern Belgium is composed of two races, the more northerly Flemings, of Germanic origin, speaking a Germanic tongue, and the Walloons in the south, a people of Celtic origin who speak a French dialect. There are about 3 to $3\frac{1}{2}$ million of them.

Lapps
Lapland is the landmass spreading across the north of the three Scandinavian countries, Norway, Sweden and Finland, and of north-west Russia. In it are several settlements of Lapps, a people of Mongol origin, numbering perhaps 25,000. They live by hunting and reindeer herding.

Druzes
A people of Syria, they were originally a sect who in the 1000s broke away from orthodox Islam and followed a curiously mixed religion containing elements of Christianity and Islam.

Letts
These are the people of the ancient state of Latvia which enjoyed an independent existence for centuries during the Middle Ages. Latvia was absorbed by Russia in the 1720s, but was freed after World War I, only to be absorbed again by Russia in 1939.

Albigenses
This was a heretical sect of Christians who occupied the lands around Toulouse and Albi in southern France, during the 11th to 13th centuries. Their opposition to the orthodox beliefs of the Church was tolerated at first, but in the 13th century the papacy organized a ruthless campaign of extermination, and their district was invaded and ravaged several times with appallingly cruel treatment of the inhabitants.

Buryats
The vast space of Siberia is peopled by many races and tribes. One of the largest is the Buryat people, of Mongol descent, who lived around Lake Baikal. Most of the Buryats are Buddhists. They have been largely absorbed into the Soviet framework of collective farming and state industry, but some of them still retain their ancient custom of wandering off on lengthy trips during hot months to lead a nomadic life in tents.

Micronesians
Micronesia is part of the South Pacific region of the world (also known as Oceania), and it includes in the large sea area the islands of the Marshalls, Marianas and Carolines.

Negrillos
This is the word for the African pygmies, the race of small-sized people who occupy chiefly the areas of the Congo river basin in central Africa. Negrillos are less than 1.525 m (5 ft) tall, indeed 1.346 m (4 ft 5 in) is an average height.

Waldensians
They were a Christian sect founded by Peter Waldo in the 1170s and now known as the Vaudois, living in the Piedmont hills in the Alps. They followed a simple life, rejecting the worldliness of medieval orthodox Christians, and were persecuted for it.

Saracens
Another name for Moslems or Arabs in the Middle Ages. The word was the Greek for an Arab people of the Sinai desert, but was later adopted to cover Moslems of all kinds, particularly those who clashed with the Christians in the Holy Land in Asia Minor.

Moravians
A Protestant sect in Bohemia who were often persecuted for their beliefs over a long period from the 15th to the 18th centuries. Finally, they left Bohemia and many settled in Britain, and some in North America where they worked as missionaries among the Indian races.

Veneti
Nothing to do with Venice, these were a tough, sea-faring Celtic people occupying Brittany in the last centuries before Christ. They were defeated at sea and on land by Caesar during his conquest of Gaul.

Bhils
A group of hill tribes in the central Indian hills.

Young Turks
A militant group of Turkish nationalists who in 1908 rebelled against the ruling sultan and demanded a new constitution.

Jains
A small religious community in India who are notable for their total belief in pacificism and non-violence and whose way of life is one of compassion and understanding for others, men and women alike. Jains follow the teachings of Vardhamana (6th century BC) and they are distinguished for the high degree of literacy and intellectual attainment of their people.

The Alans?
An ancient people, expert horse-breeders, from the area north of the Caucasus, who in the 4th century were overrun by the Huns and driven westwards into central-western Europe. There, they joined up with the Vandals, and eventually crossed into North Africa, in the 5th century.

The Croquants?
These were peasants who rose in well-organized rebellions, three times between about 1593 and 1645, in the Perigord and Saintonge districts of France. Croquant was a colloquial term for nonentity.

Kipchaks?
Turkish tribes who dominated the Eurasian steppes in the 11th century. They controlled the vast district between the Aral Sea and the Black Sea, and fought continuously with Russians, Byzantines and Hungarians. But in the 1230s they were overwhelmed and absorbed by the Mongols.

Little Quiz 57

In which countries are these cathedrals?

1. Ulm
2. Trondheim
3. Aarhus
4. Lund
5. St Isaacs
6. Hagia Sophia
7. Cefalu
8. Coimbra
9. Albi
10. Esztergom

What is the ILEA?

It is the Inner London Education Authority, the largest education authority in Great Britain, and one of the biggest in Europe. The ILEA is run by a committee of 48 members (with additional co-opted members) and it governs the teaching arrangements and associated responsibilities for about a million children and young students.

What is a mature student?

It is an adult, normally over 25 (and who has held a paid job for at least three years) who goes to a university to study for a degree or diploma. Mature students can claim higher grants than ordinary students.

What is a Public School?

In the UK a public school is a private independent school for which the pupils' parents pay fees. Most public schools are boarding schools, a few are day schools and some are mixed. There are over 1200 such schools in the UK. They got the name public schools because the first ones began as local schools and later opened their doors to people from other districts.

What was School Certificate?

It was an examination taken in England by pupils before leaving school. It prevailed in the education system from the end of World War I up to 1951. A number of subjects were compulsory and pupils could also take extra subjects from choice. It was obligatory to take and pass in English language, and in mathematics, and in three other subjects, in order to obtain the certificate. Good marks earned what were called credits.

What is fagging?

A term to describe the custom in public schools whereby junior boys had to perform jobs, usually of a menial nature for senior boys. The system is dying out.

What did the Robbins Report of 1963 recommend?

Lord Robbins and his committee believed that there should be a significant increase in the amount and choice of higher education. They recommended expansion of university and polytechnic education and the creation of several new universities and colleges.

What is the origin of grammar schools?

The grammar schools probably go back to the days soon after the conversion of England to Christianity by St Augustine, in the last years of the 6th century. The creation of dioceses and the spread of monasteries meant that more people were needed to become priests and monks, and so schools were founded to take young boys in and teach them. The first mention of these schools, which were flourishing in many places in the Middle Ages, is in a document of the 1380s, where the phrase 'gramer schole' appears.

What is a crammer?

It is the word for an individual teacher, or for a small establishment of teachers, who provide special individual teaching privately for young people to help them get through important examinations, where they cannot get such individual help in a school. Crammers began to appear in the UK in the later 19th century, and some of them specialized in helping young men to pass the examinations necessary to get into the army or the navy.

What is a kindergarten?

A school for very young children, between 3 and 6, which helps them to get ready for ordinary school. The name is the German for children's garden and the idea was devised by Friedrich Froebel (1782–1852), a German educational philosopher.

What did the 1870 Elementary Education Act achieve?

It made education compulsory for all young children, and to achieve this it set up special school boards all over the country and allowed funds for building new schools to be raised from the rates. It was a revolutionary improvement in education, and was the work of William Forster.

What was the main achievement of R. A. Butler's 1944 Education Act?

It aimed to achieve 'equality of educational opportunity'. It raised the school leaving age to 15, provided free education for all children at local authority schools, and it established three types of secondary school for children to go to after the age of 11, namely, the grammar schools, (in existence for centuries), technical schools and secondary modern schools (a new creation). Pupils had to take an examination at the age of 11 to determine which type of school they went to. This exam was known as the 11-plus.

What is a prep school?

A preparatory school. This type of school was first introduced in the 19th century specifically to prepare young boys to take the examination necessary to get into public schools.

Which universities offer students the opportunity of taking an external degree?

London University, and the Open University.

What is the Girls Public Day School Trust?

It is a body started in 1872, which founded high schools for girls of the middle classes, where they could be educated to standards enabling them to enter universities. It has a membership of 23 schools.

What is a sandwich course?

It is a scheme whereby a person studies for a degree or diploma or higher certificate and works in a job related to the subject at the same time. That is to say, he or she has the basic job but is given time off to study at a college or other institution.

What does the abbreviation STOPP stand for?

Society of Teachers Opposed to Physical Punishment. Corporal punishment is still allowed in some UK schools. Efforts to get it outlawed are championed by this organization, which consists of teachers and also of parents.

What is the Common Entrance Examination?

At one time, public schools set their own entrance examinations for pupils, in addition to special scholarship examinations for very bright children. In 1903 a common entrance examination system was devised by a group of schools whereby any pupil aiming to get into any of the schools in the group sat a series of papers common to all the schools.

What is the Open University?

An institution created during Harold Wilson's term of office as prime minister (1964–1970), whereby people could obtain degrees by studying at home using correspondence courses organized by the Open University, whose headquarters is at Milton Keynes. Students have to attend one summer course, usually of two weeks, at a recognized centre which is often one of the ordinary universities.

What is the Baccalaureat?

It is an examination, covering a wide field of subjects, taken at the end of one's education at a French secondary school (lycée), which entitles one to apply for a place at a university in France.

Who was Count Basie?
Count Basie (1904–1984) was one of the greatest American jazz musicians and band leaders. He was a favourite before and during World War II.

What is swing?
A popular dance music of the 1930s and 1940s. It came in after the prohibition of liquor was lifted in the USA, when a craze for dancing swept the country. Among the leading swing band leaders were Benny Goodman, Tommy Dorsey and Artie Shaw.

Who was 'The Duke'?
This was Edward Kennedy Ellington (1899–1974), an American jazz pianist and composer who was among the greatest of all jazz musicians.

What is a musical?
It is a development of light opera, emerging in the last year of the 19th century. It is a theatrical performance of popular music, songs and dancing, loosely connected by a story line. It became fashionable in London and New York at about the same time in the 1890s. Later, musicals were specially written for films. Among the composers of musicals were George Gershwin, Cole Porter, Jerome Kern, Rodgers and Hart, Lerner and Lowe, Stephen Sondheim and in the UK, Noel Coward, Ivor Novello, and more recently Tim Rice and Andrew Lloyd Webber.

What is a glockenspiel?
An instrument consisting of a frame of tuned steel bars which is played with two hammers, or by a keyboard.

What is *crescendo*?
It means increasing in loudness.

What is the word for dying down of sound?
Diminuendo.

Who wrote the musical *Annie get your Gun*?
Irving Berlin, the composer who was born in 1888 in Russia and taken to the USA when a baby. He began his musical career as a singing waiter soon after the turn of the century. Since then, he composed over 800 popular songs, one of the earliest of which was 'Alexander's Rag Time Band'. Among the other musicals he composed are *White Christmas* and *Call Me Madam*.

Who was Scott Joplin?
Scott Joplin (1868–1917) was an American pianist and composer, who specialized in ragtime. Among his compositions were 'The Entertainer' and 'Maple Leaf Rag'. Joplin's ragtime has enjoyed a revival in recent years.

What is ragtime?
It is syncopated music for the piano, a forerunner of jazz, and was popular in the 1890s and 1900s.

Who was born Robert Allen Zimmerman?
Bob Dylan, the great folk and rock singer and composer.

Who was Carl Nielsen?
Carl Nielsen (1865–1931) was in his own lifetime recognized as the greatest composer produced by Denmark. His reputation internationally rests largely upon his six symphonies, the last of which he completed in 1925.

What is the nature of the work *Pictures from an Exhibition*?
This is a suite for solo piano by the Russian composer Mussorgsky (1839–1881). It was composed as a tribute to his friend Victor Hartmann, the artist, who died in 1873, and represents ten of his paintings with a 'promenade' as a linking passage. It has adapted well to orchestration by a number of composers, most notably Ravel.

2,5,7...

What is the game of fives?
A hard ball game played by two or four players in a court with three or four walls. The ball is hit by the hand, bare or gloved. The game probably began in the 15th century, and may be named from the five fingers.

What was a hundred?
It was a division of a shire of England. Each hundred had its own court which met every month.

What are hundreds and thousands?
They are tiny sugar sweets in different colours, used to decorate cakes and trifles.

How many pounds are there in a hundredweight?
112, though in American measurement, there are 100.

How much is a milliard?
1,000,000,000 (thousand million).

What is one-track?
It is a derogatory term to describe an attitude of someone who is obsessed by one particular idea.

What does 'two-bit' mean?
It is a word meaning worthless.

Who were the two main stars in the film, *The 49th Parallel*?
Leslie Howard and Eric Portman.

What were the Five Articles of Perth (1618)?
These were ordinances by which James I (1603–1625) compelled the General Assembly of the Church of Scotland to restore bishops in their church, to agree to kneel for the Communion, private communion if necessary, private baptism, observing of feast days, confirmation in church, all of which deeply offended the Scots.

Which army commander was affectionately known as One-Leg?
Field Marshal Henry William Paget, 1st Marquis of Anglesey (1768–1854). Paget had been second in command at the battle of Waterloo, where he lost a leg.

What is the Fourth Estate?
The Press.

What is a .22 rifle?
A rifle which fires a bullet whose diameter is 0.22 of an inch.

What railway services serve Seven Sisters station in London?
The Victoria Line of the Underground and the Eastern Region of British Rail.

What was the *Inn of the Sixth Happiness*?
A 1958 film, starring Ingrid Bergman as Gladys Aylward, a missionary in war-torn China.

Little Quiz 58

In which countries are these cities or towns?

1. Salamanca
2. Kirkcaldy
3. Topeka
4. Edirne
5. Nablus
6. Montreux
7. Odense
8. Oaxaca
9. Rennes
10. Armagh
11. Ghent
12. Omdurman
13. Wiesbaden
14. Srinagar
15. Tbilisi
16. Tatung
17. La Plata
18. Nagasaki
19. Bury St Edmunds
20. Ravenna

Which was the earliest commercially successful motorcycle?
The model produced in 1894 by the German inventors Heinrich Hildebrand and Alois Wolfmuller, known as the H & W. It had pneumatic tyres and would achieve a speed of 45.08 kmh (28 mph). There is a surviving example of the machine in the National Motor Museum at Beaulieu.

What is the origin of the TT Races in the Isle of Man?
TT stands for Tourist Trophy, and the first TT race was run in 1907. The circuit was known as the St John's circuit, the village where it started and ended. The Isle of Man was chosen because there was no speed limit on the roads, and because the island's government was willing to close the roads for the race.

What were the two main features of the motorcycles built by the Scott motorcycle firm?
They were powered by two stroke engines of considerable power and the engines were water-cooled. The first model was built in the late 1890s.

Who was the first British motorcyclist to figure in the Honours List?
Freddie Frith, who received the OBE in 1949.

Which world champion motorcyclist once crashed at over 298.8 kmh (180 mph)?
Barry Sheene, at Daytona, USA, in 1975.

What are the four stages of operation of a 4-stroke engine?
i. induction of air and fuel mixture; ii. compression of the mixture into a small space at the top of the cylinder; iii. combustion of the mixture by means of an electric spark across the sparking plug in the cylinder head; iv. exhaust of the gases that have been burnt.

304

What is a moped?
A motorcycle of 50cc or less, designed to cruise at about 48.3 kmh (30 mph).

Why is the cylinder head of most motorcycle engines provided with fins?
To provide cooling. Air is drawn down between the fins while the motorcycle is in motion, creating cold currents that help to keep the cylinder head cool.

What is the mixture of petrol and air fed into a motorcycle engine by the carburettor?
Usually, 15 parts of air to one of petrol, and this provides the best mix for combustion at an economical level. The engine can work on higher and on lower ratios, but in the case of more air and less fuel, the engine will overheat, and in the case of less air and more fuel, petrol will be wasted.

What does it mean to 'decoke' an engine?
'Decoke' is slang for decarbonize, and all motorcycle engines accumulate layers of burnt carbon on the cylinder head surfaces and on the piston top. After a time, the layers are thick enough to interfere with the engine's performance, and they need to be removed. This is done by taking off the cylinder head and scraping away the carbon.

What does the dynamo do?
It is an electrical motor driven by a gear or a belt from the engine that produces direct current into the motorcycle's battery, keeping the battery charged to perform its functions.

What are the jets in a carburettor?
They are very small components pierced with a tiny hole, which are screwed into appropriate parts of the carburettor and regulate the amount of fuel passing into and out of it.

What was the Black Lightning?

In its time (early 1950s) it was the fastest standard motorcycle in the world, and it was made by the Vincent–H.R.D. stable. The machine could achieve over 241.5 kmh (150 mph).

Which is the longest surviving manufacturer of motorcycles?

The Harley Davidson organization which began to make motorcycles in 1903 and which exhibited models in the 1983 Motorcycle Exhibition.

What is trials riding?

This is an arduous sport involving the riding of a specially adapted motorcycle, non-stop and with the feet clear of the ground at all times over very difficult countryside.

Which motorcycle was T. E. Lawrence (Lawrence of Arabia) riding when he was killed in 1936?

A Brough Superior, given him by a number of friends, including Bernard Shaw.

What does it mean when a motorcycle engine is 'pinking'?

It is an unpleasant metallic noise that sounds like 'pink, pink'. This is caused when the wrong fuel is being used, or if the ignition timing is incorrect, or if the cylinder combustion chamber needs decarbonizing. 'Pinking' is usually accompanied by marked loss of power.

Why do some cylinders require reboring?

When the cylinder lining has become very worn, oil escapes and there is loss of power because the compression is affected. This can be put right by boring out the cylinder to a slightly bigger diameter and relining it with a sleeve of steel, and at the same time fitting new piston rings. Instead of a sleeve, you can fit a slightly larger diameter piston.

What was the most powerful motorcycle built as a normal production machine?

The Kawasaki K2 1300-A1, which had a six-cylinder engine, water-cooled.

Black Lightning Motorcycle

Little Quiz 59

In which English counties are these new district councils?

1. Adur
2. Uttlesford
3. Babergh
4. Breckland
5. Dacorum
6. Langbaurgh
7. Holderness
8. Test Valley
9. Waverley
10. Erewash
11. Fylde

and in which Welsh counties are these?

12. Afan
13. Ynys Mon (Isle of Anglesey)
14. Ogwr
15. Glyndwr
16. Torfaen
17. Ceredigion
18. Brecknock
19. Preseli

What is the generally accepted date of the first Olympic Games held in ancient Greece?
776 BC. Even in those days it was ordained that the Olympiad, as it was called, should be held every four years.

What was the pancratium?
This was a combined wrestling and boxing event introduced to the Olympiad in the middle of the 7th century BC.

Which Roman emperor was the first to compete in the Olympic Games?
Emperor Nero, in the games of AD 65. He entered as a charioteer.

What brought the Olympic Games idea to an end in the ancient world?
Christian leaders decided that the games were undesirable, since they were relics of pagan rituals, and the Emperor Theodosius I banned the games in 393.

When were the Olympic Games re-established?
In 1894, at the instigation of Baron Pierre de Coubertin, the International Olympic Committee was founded. The first games were held in 1896, appropriately in Athens.

What is the ceremony of the Olympic torch?
Before each Games, a torch is set alight and it burns throughout. The torch is ignited by directing on it the sun's rays through a glass at the ancient Greek temple of Altis in the plains of Olympia, and it is carried by a relay of runners all the way to the country in which the Games are being held.

Who was the youngest performer in the Games ever to become an individual champion?
Marjorie Gestring, a US champion diver who won a medal at Berlin in 1936 when she was only 13.

Which member of the British peerage won the 400 m hurdles championship at the Games of 1928?
Lord Burghley, who later succeeded to the title Marquis of Exeter.

What was the amazing achievement of the US athlete Ray Ewry at the Paris Games of 1900?
Ewry had been paralysed as a boy, even confined to a wheelchair. But he was determined to become an athlete, and with tremendous will and application he toughened his leg muscles over many years so that he could compete in standing jump events. In 1900 he won three Gold Medals for the three standing jump events at the Paris Games, did it again at the Games of St Louis in 1904 and won two more at the London Games, 1908.

Which famous US general of World War II competed at the Stockholm Games of 1912?
General George S. Patton, a top American commander in Europe in the closing stages of the war.

Who was the 'Phantom Finn'?
Paavo Nurmi, an extraordinary athlete who, in several Olympic Games, won medals for long distance running, notably Gold Medals in the 1924 Paris Games for 5,000 m and 1,500 m races in the same afternoon.

Which Olympic swimming champion later became a famous film star?
Johnny Weissmuller, best known in the role of Tarzan, won 5 Gold Medals (3 in 1924, 2 in 1928).

Who was the first British woman Olympic Gold Medallist for figure skating?
Jeannette Altwegg won the Olympic title in 1952. She was also World Figure Skating Champion.

What happened to the Olympic champion swimmer Nancy Riach?
Nancy Riach, a Scot, was representing Great Britain in a number of freestyle events at the Olympic Games of 1948 in London. During the Games, Britain was suffering an epidemic of poliomyelitis (infantile paralysis), and between races Nancy Riach contracted the disease. Despite this she continued to compete though in great pain, and won an event. Within two days she died of the disease.

Who was the Flying Dutchwoman?
Fanny Blankers-Koen, who at the London 1948 Games won four Gold Medals, for 80 m hurdles, 200 m, 100 m and her part of a relay race.

Who carried the Olympic torch for the last lap and into the arena at Helsinki at the Games of 1952?
The Phantom Finn, Paavo Nurmi, at the age of 56.

What appalling tragedy occurred at the Munich Games of 1972?
Arab terrorists broke into the Olympic Village on 5 September, and murdered two Israeli competitors. They also kidnapped several others, held them hostage and then killed them that night. Eleven athletes were murdered.

Which four countries have been represented at every summer Olympic Games since they started in 1896?
Great Britain, Greece, Australia and Switzerland.

What are the Winter Olympics?
These were first staged as a separate grouping of events, at Chamonix in 1924. They included figure skating, ski-jumping, bob-sledding, speed skating and ice hockey. Later on, other events were added, such as tobogganing, ski-racing, ice yachting and barrel jumping.

Why did the United States refuse to send their Olympic Team to compete in the 1980 Games at Moscow?
Because the Soviet Union had, in 1979, sent an army into the neighbouring state of Afghanistan and overturned the existing government to install an administration more sympathetic to the Soviet Union.

Why were no equestrian events held at Melbourne, the venue for the 1956 Games?
In these, the first Olympic Games to be held outside Europe or North America, strict quarantine laws did not allow horses to be admitted for equestrian events. To get round the problem, these events were held in Stockholm.

Where would the 1940 and 1944 Games have been held, had they not been cancelled because of World War II?
In Helsinki and London, respectively; locations in reverse order for the first post-war Games of 1948 and 1952. For the record, the 1916 Games cancelled because of World War I would have been held in Berlin.

Little Quiz 60
Some British titled families have surnames different from the titles: Which are the titles using these surnames?
1. Villiers
2. Cholmondeley
3. Wallop
4. Marquis
5. Paget
6. Wellesley
7. Curzon
8. Anson
9. Bigham
10. Dundas

Six times a number increased by 11 is equal to 65. What is the number?
9.

What number multiplied by 11 and reduced by 18 equals 15?
3.

One number is greater than another number by 3, and their sum is 27. What are the numbers?
12, 15.

What are the two numbers whose sum is 30 and one is greater than the other by 8?
11, 19.

If one number is 3 times another and their difference is 10, what are the two numbers?
15, 5.

Which are the two numbers whose sum is 26 and their difference 8?
9, 17.

A, B and C have £72 among them. C has twice B's share and B has £4 more than A. What share has each?
A £21, B £17, C £34.

Divide 75 into two parts, so that three times one part is twice the other.
30, 45.

In 8 hours, C walks 3 more miles than D walks in 6 hours, and in 7 hours D walks 9 miles more than C does in 6 hours. How many miles does each walk in each hour.
C $3\frac{3}{4}$ miles, D $4\frac{1}{2}$ miles.

What number of two digits is 7 times the sum of the digits and if 36 is subtracted from the number the digits are reversed?
84.

Divide £511 among A, B and C, so that B's share equals $\frac{1}{3}$ of A's share and C's share is $\frac{3}{4}$ of A's share and B's share together.
A £219, B £73, C £219.

A is 8 years younger than B and 24 years older than C. $\frac{1}{6}$ of A's age, $\frac{1}{2}$ of B's age and $\frac{1}{3}$ of C's age together amount to 38 years. What are their ages?
A = 42, B = 50, C = 18.

The difference between the squares of two consecutive numbers is 31. What are the numbers?
15, 16.

A has £12 and B has £8: after B has lost a certain sum to A, his money is only $\frac{2}{3}$ of A's. How much did A win?
£2.

How old is a man whose age 10 years ago was $\frac{3}{8}$ of what it will be in 15 years time?
25 years.

Two numbers add up to 54, and there is 12 between them. What are they?
33, 21.

One fifth of the difference of two numbers is 3, and $\frac{1}{3}$ of their sum is 17. What are the numbers?
33, 18.

The digits of a number between 10 and 100 equal each other, and the number exceeds 5 times the sum of the digits by 8. What is the number?
88.

A certain number between 10 and 100 is six times the sum of the digits, and the number exceeds the number formed by reversing the digits by 9. Find the number.
54.

Which number's double exceeds its half by 9?
6.

Two numbers add up to 19. One is twice the other plus 1. What are the two numbers?
6, 13.

Divide £66 between A, B and C, so that B may have £8 more than A, and C £14 more than B.
A £12, B £20, C £34.

What would A and B have if they shared £100 so that B had £30 more than A?
A £35, B £65.

What is the number whose double exceeds its half by 9?
6.

How do you divide 48 into two parts, so that one part is three-fifths of the other part?
18, 30.

Jack is 16 years younger than Fred, and one half of Jack's age is the same as one third of Fred's age: how old are Jack and Fred?
Fred is 48, Jack is 32.

Frances is twice as old as Joan, ten years ago she was four times as old: what are their present ages?
Frances is 30, Joan is 15.

A father is four times as old as his son: in 16 years he will be only twice as old: what are their ages?
Father is 32, son is 8.

George is 20 years older than Mary; five years ago, George was twice as old as Mary. How old are they?
George is 45, Mary is 25.

A father is 24 years older than his son: in seven years the son's age will be two-fifths of his father's age: what are their present ages?
33 and 9.

Two boys have 240 marbles between them; one arranges his in piles of six each, the other in piles of nine. There are 36 piles altogether. How many marbles has each boy?
168, 72.

The sum of two numbers is 97 and their difference is 51. What are the two numbers?
74, 23.

Half Edward's age exceeds a quarter of Cyril's by twelve months, and three quarters of Cyril's age exceeds Edward's age by 11 years. What are Edward's and Cyril's ages?
Edward, 28; Cyril, 52.

In eight hours, Fiona walks three miles more than Jean does in six hours, and in seven hours Jean walks nine miles more than Fiona does in six hours. How many miles does each walk per hour?
Fiona, $3\frac{3}{4}$ and Jean, $4\frac{1}{2}$.

A certain number of two digits is seven times the sum of the digits, and if 36 is subtracted from the number, the digits will be reversed. What is the number?
84.

Find a number which is less than its square by 72.
9.

Divide the number 16 into two, so that the sum of the squares of the two parts is 130.
7, 9.

What was a sabretache handbag?
A large handbag deriving in design from a military bag carried by a cavalry officer on his left side. It was fashionable in the early 19th century, and was generally heavily embroidered.

When would you wear a mantilla?
Only if you were female, and as a rule over your head and shoulders when you went into a church. A mantilla is a veil or scarf, often with lace trimming, or even entirely of lace, and it is carried over the arm when not worn.

What is a chemise?
It is an undergarment, of cotton or linen as a rule, worn by women under a dress or coat and skirt.

What are cami-knickers?
Popularly worn before World War II and for some years after it, they are a combined garment of petticoat top and a pair of knickers.

What was the bustle?
It was a small stuffed cushion arrangement set underneath a woman's skirt at the back, to create a puffed out shape. The fashion began to emerge in the mid-19th century and lasted, with one or two short periods of being out of fashion, to the end of the century.

What is a cummerbund?
It is a sash worn round the waist, by both sexes but more generally by men today with evening dress.

What is a deerstalker?
A special cap of tweed for men, with a peak at both front and back, and with ear flaps which, when not tied under the chin, are folded and tied on top of the cap.

What was a pelerine?
A shoulder cape with pronounced elongated ends at the front.

What was a dormeuse?
A French nightcap worn in the later 18th century, with a loose-fitting, ribbon-trimmed crown over the head and lace flaps, rounded over the ears and curved back to expose the forehead.

Who used to wear a redingote?
Most men, usually of the upper classes, in the 18th and here and there in the early 19th century. It was a long, double breasted overcoat, narrowed at the waist, with large collar, and long cut-away tails.

What was a toque?
A close-fitting cap without brim, usually worn by women.

Day dress with bustle c 1884

310

What was a banyan?
This was a loose coat of the 18th century worn by men indoors. It reached to the knees, had a shortish vent at the back and was fastened by buttons or a sash. The banyan was generally made of simple washable material.

When did women's bathing suits begin to appear in western Europe?
In the later 19th century, probably about 1870. The early style was made of flannel, serge, or alpaca, usually blue or black. The garment stretched from neck to mid-thigh and was tied round the waist, the short leggings also were tied with ribbon.

What was the 'princess line'?
This is a phrase to describe a manner of dress-making in which the back of the garment is close-fitting and has no seam.

Why was the Ulster overcoat so called?
Because the design came from Northern Ireland. It was a double-breasted overcoat, sometimes belted in the middle, with a cape or two capes over the shoulders.

Would you wear galluses today?
You might wear the modern equivalent, which is braces. Galluses first appeared in the 1780s and were of soft, silky material, finely decorated but without elastic which was not then known. They held up the breeches.

What were the characteristics of the dress of the Incroyables?
The Incroyables were a group of dandies of the 1790s who wore their smart clothes in a deliberately messy and unkempt manner, grew their hair exceptionally long and straggly, and sported ear-rings. They wore enormous scarves round their necks, the front bows of which covered much of their faces.

What was a buffon?
It was a square of lace or linen worn like a scarf round the neck and tied into a huge bow at the front, known also as a neckerchief.

What was the trollopee?
A mid-18th century sack-type dress worn indoors by women, generally in the morning only. It hung down below the waist in pleats.

What is a caftan?
A caftan, or kaftan, is a long-sleeved coat, often worn loose. It originated in the Middle East, becoming popular in Britain in the late 1960s.

What is a kimono?
A wrap style of robe with full-cut sleeves and a sash, originating in Japan. The best kimonos are made of silk and often have exquisite designs.

What is a pea jacket?
This is a heavy, double breasted navy blue woollen jacket worn by sailors. The term originates from the Dutch word *pij*, a coarse woollen material.

What is a Basque beret?
A peakless round-crown cap, often made of felt, and originating in the Basque country of France and Spain. It is a garment that will always be associated with the artist, Pablo Picasso.

What is a stock?
A stock is a made-up neckcloth, taking the form of a piece of lawn, silk or muslin pleated into a stiffened band which fastens at the back of the neck. It enjoyed its heyday throughout the 18th century, then fell into a decline for general wear. However, it has remained as part of the huntsman's traditional attire.

Who was the first of the Habsburg royal line in Europe?
Rudolph I (1218–1291), Count of Habsburg, who became emperor of the Holy Roman Empire in 1273 and made his son duke of Austria in 1282. From 1438 to 1806, with one exception, the title Emperor of the Holy Roman Empire was held by a Habsburg.

How did Harold II become king of England in 1066?
He was chosen by the Witenagemot (the English Council), although he was not a member of the royal family. Harold was the son of Godwin, Earl of the West Saxons, and was the most suitable person to rule on the death of Edward the Confessor.

Why was William I succeeded by his *second* son as king of England?
Because the Conqueror left his empire divided between Robert, the eldest who was to have Normandy, and William, the next son, who was to have England.

Who was Pedro the Cruel?
Pedro the Cruel (1334–1369) was king of Castile and León (part of Spain). During the first part of his reign he ruled well, tending to side with the people against the nobility, but he was faced with many baronial revolts, some led by his half-brother Henry of Trastamara. This led him to commit many unjust and severe acts, some against his own family, and in the end he lost his popularity. Pedro died in a duel with his half-brother.

When did the king of Prussia become the emperor of Germany?
Wilhelm I, king of Prussia from 1861, was chosen as first emperor of Germany in 1871 and died in 1888.

When was Queen Victoria proclaimed empress of India?
In 1876.

Why did George I, a cousin of Queen Anne, succeed her in 1714 when there were closer relatives?
Because George, elector of Hanover, was a Protestant. The closer relatives were Catholics and so barred from the succession.

Why was Charles II succeeded by his brother James when he had several sons?
Because all of Charles's children were illegitimate.

Which Scottish king was killed by an exploding cannon?
James II (1437–1460), at the siege of Roxburgh Castle.

What was the relationship between Elizabeth I, and James VI of Scotland who succeeded her?
Elizabeth's father Henry VIII was brother of James's great-grandmother Margaret Tudor (wife of James IV).

Where did John II of France die, and why?
John II (1319–1364) became king of France in 1350. In 1356 he was captured at the battle of Poitiers by the victorious English under the Black Prince and taken to London. Four years later, he was allowed to go back to France, leaving one of his sons as a hostage. But the son escaped in 1363. John thereupon chivalrously volunteered to go back to London in his place, and died in London soon afterwards.

Who was Shakespeare's 'time-honour'd Lancaster'?
John of Gaunt (1340–1399), Duke of Lancaster, fourth son of Edward III and virtual ruler of England during part of the minority of Richard II (1377–1399). The phrase comes from Shakespeare's play, Richard II.

Which English king defeated his brother in battle and then kept him in prison for nearly 30 years?
Henry I (1100–1135) defeated his elder brother Robert, Duke of Normandy, at the battle of Tinchebrai in 1106 and put him in prison in Cardiff Castle where Robert stayed until his death in 1134.

Was George V the eldest son of Edward VII?
No, Edward VII's eldest son was Albert, Duke of Clarence, who died in 1892, without heir.

What happened to Louis XVII of France?
He was the second son of Louis XVI and became heir to the French throne in 1789 when his elder brother died. Louis XVI was deposed in 1792 and executed by guillotine in 1793. The young Louis XVII, who had been born in 1785, was kept in prison where he died in 1795. Many legends arose as to his fate, and some said that he was spirited out of prison to safety. There were even claimants in later years.

Who was the first king of the Belgians?
Leopold I (1831–1865), who was elected in 1831. He was an uncle of Queen Victoria.

Who was the first Stewart king of Scotland?
Robert II, son of Marjorie Bruce (Robert Bruce's daughter) and her husband, Walter the Steward. Robert II reigned from 1371 to 1390.

Has there ever been a king of Finland?
No, though there have been one or two regents, and a number of viceroys and governor-generals – and even some grand dukes. Finland now has a president.

Who was the youngest son of George V?
It is usually said to have been the Duke of Kent, who was killed in an air crash during World War II (1942). But George V and Queen Mary had a younger son, Prince John, born in 1905 who died in 1919.

Has there ever been a king of Brazil?
Yes. Brazil was a monarchy from 1815 to 1889. The first monarch was Queen Maria (1815–1816), who was also Maria I, Queen of Portugal. She was succeeded by her son, John, who was also John VI of Portugal. John handed Brazil to his son Pedro in 1822. Pedro elevated himself to Emperor Pedro I in that year, but abdicated in 1831 and was succeeded by his son Pedro II who was to rule until he was deposed in 1889. Brazil then became a republic which it still is.

Who was the last Emperor of the Holy Roman Empire?
Francis II (1792–1806), who was also Archduke of Austria. The Holy Roman Empire was abolished by him at the insistence of Napoleon, in 1806, and Francis became Francis I, Emperor of Austria, a new title. He reigned until 1835. The last Austrian emperor abdicated in 1919.

Little Quiz 61
  What do these phrases mean?
  1. Blowing your own trumpet
  2. Crying for the moon
  3. Building castles in the air
  4. Looking a gift horse in the mouth
  5. Playing to the gallery
  6. Turning over a new leaf
  7. Tilting at windmills
  8. Flogging a dead horse
  9. Keeping one's feet on the ground
  10. Drawing the longbow

Who was the first woman to be elected a head of state?
Mrs Vigdis Finnbogadottir, who was elected president of Iceland on 30 June 1980.

Who was the first woman to address the House of Commons?
It was not Viscountess Astor, the first woman MP, but Mrs Elizabeth Robinson (1695–1779) who came from Gibraltar to give evidence about the slave trade.

Which was the first university in England?
Oxford, which is generally said to have been founded in about 1167, and whose first college was University College, opened in 1249.

Which was the first university in Scotland?
St Andrews, founded by Bishop Wardlaw in 1412. Its first curriculum was based on that of the university of Paris.

Who was awarded the first Nobel Prize for physics?
Wilhelm Röntgen (1845–1923), the discoverer of X-rays, in 1901.

Who was the first pope?
Traditionally, St Peter, one of the twelve disciples, was the first pope, and his term of office is usually given as 42 to 67. He was martyred in 67.

Who was the first president of the USSR?
Mikhail Kalinin, who held office from 1923 to 1946.

When was the first non-stop transatlantic air flight?
In 1919, when Sir John Alcock and Sir Arthur Whitten Brown took a Vickers Vimy bomber from Newfoundland to Ireland, nearly 3200 km (2000 miles) in just over 16 hours.

Who was the first Ottoman Sultan?
Othman (or Osman), who ruled from about 1299 to 1326. The word Ottoman is taken from him.

Who was the first president of the Royal Society?
An Anglo-Irish mathematician, William, Viscount Brouncker, from 1662 to 1677.

When was the first English Prayer Book issued?
In 1549, in the reign of Edward VI. Much of its matchless prose was written by Archbishop Cranmer.

When was the first public demonstration of television?
On 27 January 1926, when John Logie Baird, its pioneer, revealed it at a gathering in London.

Who was the first Prince of Wales?
Rhodri Mawr (Rhoderic the Great), who was prince of Gwynedd, that is, north Wales, and who was recognized as overlord of Wales between 844 and 878.

Who was the first illegitimate son of Charles II (1660–1685)?
The first known illegitimate son was James Scott, later created Duke of Monmouth. He was the son of Charles and a Welsh girl, Lucy Walter, and was born in 1649, the year of Charles's father's execution. For a time in the early part of Charles II's reign, the king seemed likely to recognize the duke as his heir.

Which Irish king first successfully united the various kingdoms of Ireland?
Traditionally, it was Brian Boru, king of Munster, who was recognized as Ard Ri, or high king, from about 1001 to 1014, when he was killed in battle with the Vikings at Clontarf. He was killed at the moment of victory for the Irish forces.

314

Who was the first surgeon to stitch arteries while operating?
Probably Ambrose Paré (1517–1590), a French surgeon who became a royal physician and served four French kings.

Who was the first president of Czechoslovakia?
Thomas Garrigue Masaryk, from 1918 to 1935. Czechoslovakia was a new state created out of parts of the old Austro-Hungarian empire after World War I. The principal component was the ancient state of Bohemia.

Who was the first and only Englishman to be elected pope?
Nicholas Breakspear (c. 1100 to 1159). He was elected pope as Adrian IV in 1154.

Who is the first lady?
The wife of the president of the USA, or of the governor of a US state. If the president (or the governor) is a bachelor or widower, the first lady is the person he chooses to act as hostess for him at functions.

When were the first rubber bands made?
Elastic bands made from vulcanized rubber were patented by Steven Perry, a member of the firm of Messrs Perry and Co of London, on 17 March 1845.

When was the passenger lift or elevator first recorded?
This was one which was installed in the private apartments of Louis XV at the Palais de Versailles, France, in 1743. The king used it to communicate with his mistress, whose rooms were on the floor above his. It worked through a carefully balanced set of weights, and could be easily raised or lowered by hand.

When were greeting cards first used?
These were designed for use on birthdays and other anniversaries by William Harvey and engraved by John Thompson of London in 1829.

What was the world's first hotel?
This was Low's Grand Hotel, situated in Covent Garden, London, and opened in January 1774 by David Low. Previously, travellers and others requiring hotel facilities had had to rely exclusively upon inns.

Who was the first person to be killed by a motor vehicle?
Mrs Bridget Driscoll of Croydon was knocked down and killed by a car driven by Arthur Edsell at the Crystal Palace, on 17 August 1896. At the inquest it was said that the car was only travelling at 4 mph when the accident occurred. The verdict was 'accidental death'.

Who was the first ombudsman?
Lars August Mannerheim, who held this office in Sweden from 1810 to 1823.

When was the first restaurant opened?
The first establishment to be called a restaurant was the Champ d'Oiseau (bird's field), established by M Boulanger in Paris in 1765.

Little Quiz 62

What time is it in the following capitals of the world, when it is 12.00 noon (Greenwich Mean Time)?

1. Paris
2. Cairo
3. Singapore
4. Madrid
5. Tokyo
6. Peking
7. Melbourne
8. New York
9. Buenos Aires
10. Auckland, New Zealand

Who discovered the laws of planetary motion?

Johann Kepler (1571–1630), the German astronomer, who between 1609 and 1619 showed that the planets move round the sun in ellipses, that the square of a planet's period of revolution is proportional to the cube of its mean distance from the sun, and other fundamental laws, which were later elaborated by Isaac Newton.

Who discovered the periodic arrangement of the elements?

Dmitri Ivanovich Mendeleyev (1834–1907), one of Russia's most distinguished chemists, who in 1869 produced his table of all the elements, in which he predicted the existence of many not then discovered, but which were later found. No. 101 is named *mendelevium* after him.

Who discovered the electron?

Sir Joseph John Thomson (1856–1940), Cavendish professor of experimental physics at Cambridge from 1884 to 1919.

Who discovered the neutrino?

Wolfgang Pauli (1900–1958), an Austrian physicist, who showed that there must be an electrically neutral particle in the nucleus of an atom, which was later proved by Enrico Fermi.

Who identified quasars?

Quasars, the more popular name for quasi-stellar radio-sources, were first identified in 1963 by the scientists Thomas Matthews and Allen Sandage of the United States.

Who discovered the anthrax bacillus?

Robert Koch (1843–1910), the German bacteriologist, in 1876. This remarkable scientist made many other important discoveries, including the tubercle bacillus (tuberculosis) in 1882 and the cholera bacillus. He was awarded a Nobel Prize in 1905.

Who discovered creosote?

Creosote is a mixture of chemicals resulting from distillation of wood tar. It was discovered by Baron Karl von Reichenbach (1788–1869), a German scientist and industrialist, who also discovered paraffin.

Who discovered the leprosy bacillus?

Armauer Hansen (1841–1912), the Norwegian bacteriologist, in 1879.

Who discovered alpha and beta rays in radioactive atoms?

Lord Rutherford (1871–1937), Cavendish professor of experimental physics at Cambridge, who was also the first physicist to split the atom (1919).

Who discovered ozone?

Christian Friedrich Schönbein (1799–1868), the German chemist, in 1839. Schönbein also invented gun cotton.

Who discovered saccharin?

This sharply sweet white powder, used as a substitute for sugar, was discovered by the German chemist Constantin Fahlberg in 1879.

Who first discovered aspirin?

A French chemist, Charles Frederic Gerhardt (1816–1856), who was professor of chemistry at Strasbourg.

Who discovered the element *neptunium*?

Edwin McMillan and Philip Abelson, both in the United States, in 1940. McMillan shared the Nobel Prize for chemistry in 1951, with G. T. Seaborg who had helped to discover plutonium.

Who discovered that sun spots give out radio waves?

Sir Edward Appleton (1892–1965), in 1946. Appleton discovered the region of the upper atmosphere known as the Appleton layer.

EUREKA!

Who discovered streptomycin?
This powerful and effective antibiotic drug was discovered in 1943 by Selman Abraham Waksman (1888–1973), a Russian-born bacteriologist living and working in the United States. He was awarded the Nobel Prize for medicine in 1952.

Who discovered carbonic acid gas?
Dr Joseph Black (1728–1799), the Scottish chemist, who also discovered latent heat. Carbonic acid gas is carbon dioxide.

Who discovered the element chromium?
Louis Nicolas Vauquelin (1763–1829), a French chemist who was professor of chemistry at Paris from 1809.

Who discovered the element selenium, the major component in the photoelectric cell?
The Swedish chemist, John Jakob Berzelius (1779–1848), who discovered other elements, and was also responsible for formulating the present system of symbols for the elements, and laid the basis of chemical formulae.

Who discovered the elements strontium, calcium, magnesium and barium?
Sir Humphry Davy (1778–1829), who also invented the miner's safety lamp.

Who discovered the phenomenon of the super-cooling of water?
Gabriel Daniel Fahrenheit (1686–1736), of temperature-scale fame, discovered that in certain circumstances water can remain as a 'super-cooled' liquid when its temperature is dropped to below freezing-point.

Who discovered the cause of gangrene?
The bacillus causing gangrene was discovered in 1892 by William Henry Welch (1850–1934), the American pioneer of scientifically organized pathology.

Who discovered latent heat?
It was discovered by Joseph Black (1728–1799), the Scottish physicist and chemist, in 1760.

Who discovered the cause of malaria?
The discovery that malaria was transmitted by mosquitoes was due to the collaboration of two British physicians, Sir Patrick Manson (1844–1922) and Sir Ronald Ross (1857–1932). Manson, known as the 'father of tropical medicine', advanced the hypothesis in 1894 that the malaria parasite used the mosquito as its transmitting agent. He then inspired Ross to make the actual discovery that this was indeed true in 1897–98. In addition to Ross's talents as a physician for which he was awarded the Nobel Prize for medicine in 1902, he was also a distinguished poet.

Who discovered Prussian blue?
This was an accidental discovery, made by a German dyer named Diesbach in 1704.

Little Quiz 63

How do the following archbishops and bishops sign their names? They write their Christian names and then add:

1. Canterbury
2. York
3. Oxford
4. Chester
5. Peterborough
6. Rochester
7. Carlisle
8. Salisbury
9. Ely
10. Exeter
11. Durham

When was the first internal combustion-engined car, fuelled by petroleum, driven successfully along a road?
In 1859 by Étienne Lenoir, in Paris.

Which was the first four-wheeled petrol driven car of wholly British design?
It was a car made by Frederick George Lanchester at his Birmingham factory in 1895.

What was the Red Flag Law?
The Road Locomotives Act of 1865 which said that each locomotive powered by steam on the road was to have three persons in attendance, one to stoke, one to steer and one to walk in front with a red flag to warn oncoming horse traffic. The maximum speed was 3.22 kmh (2 mph) in towns and 6.44 kmh (4 mph) in the country.

In which country are car number plates permanent from the day of initial registration to the day of scrapping?
Great Britain. In other countries, plates may be changed on crossing from one state or province to another.

Who designed the best-selling Mini-Minor first produced in 1959?
Sir Alec Issigonis (b 1906), of British Leyland. He also designed the famous and highly successful post-war Morris Minor, which first appeared in 1949.

What was the Silver Ghost?
It was the first car produced by the Rolls Royce partnership, and was so called because it was so well silenced that it was difficult to hear it moving along the road. This high degree of engine silencing has always been one of the characteristics of Rolls Royce motor cars.

How did the great firm of Rolls Royce originate?
C. S. Rolls (son of Lord Llangattock), one of Britain's earliest aviators, met Henry (later, Sir Henry) Royce, an engineer who had a factory in Manchester where he made electrical equipment, cranes, etc., and who had built himself a car. Rolls was so impressed with Royce's car that he offered to market it, and the famous partnership was formed in 1906.

Who is often ranked as second only to Fangio, and cherished as Britain's greatest driver?
Stirling Moss (b 1929). Though he has never won a world championship, he has won numerous international and national races, often with tremendous élan and at colossal speed. Though appallingly badly injured at Goodwood races in 1962 and had to retire when he recovered, he has nonetheless remained by far the most popular motor ace in Britain.

When was the Automobile Association founded?
1905.

206 GT Ferrari

Only three men have held both world land speed and water speed records. Who were they?
Sir Malcolm Campbell (1885–1948), his son Donald Campbell (1921–1967), and Sir Henry Segrave (1896–1930). Both Donald Campbell and Henry Segrave were killed attempting to increase the water speed record.

What is a V-8 engine?
It is an engine which has eight cylinders in two opposing banks of four, set in a 'V'. A few cars were made and fitted with these engines, which were very powerful, but which were heavy on petrol consumption.

Which was the first three-letter car registration?
ARF for Staffordshire, in July 1932.

Which pope was the first to use a motor car regularly?
Pope Pius XII. Pope Pius X had been presented with a motor car in 1909 but he refused to ride in it.

Which was the first mass produced British car?
The small Austin Seven, first produced in 1922. It cost less than £100, could reach about 80 kph (50 mph), was supplied with either a hard top or a canvas folding-down top, and more than a quarter of a million of the cars were made. You can still see the occasional Austin Seven of the 1920s on the roads today, but they are rarity items.

Who is regarded by many as the greatest racing driver of all time?
Juan Manuel Fangio (b 1911), the Argentine driver who was world champion driver five times. He is remarkable for not having started serious car racing until he was nearly forty, an age at which many others retire.

What were the record speeds achieved by the three?
Malcolm Campbell (land: 481.8 kph (301.13 mph), water: 228.2 kph (141.74 mph); Donald Campbell (land: 652.77 kph (405.45 mph), water: 444.89 kph (276.33 mph); Segrave (land: 362.62 kph (231.44 mph).

What German company had made bicycles and typewriters before marketing their first car in 1900?
Adler, which had also made components for Benz before that date. They made private cars until 1939, but only resumed production of motor cycles after the war.

What is peculiar about the French Arola cars?
This firm has made three-and-four-wheeled minicars since 1976; the former having a 47 cc engine, the latter a 50 cc engine. Both have automatic transmission.

What Yorkshire firm with a Lancashire name once made cars?
The Blackburn Aeroplane and Motor Co Ltd of Leeds had made aircraft, but produced the Blackburn 20 hp tourer from 1919 to 1925. They also made bodies for other car makers.

What top class British driver was killed while flying his own aircraft?
Graham Hill, who crashed while returning to Elstree airfield from a test session at the Paul Ricard circuit on 29 November 1975. Among his many successes, he won the Monaco Grand Prix five times.

What hat-tricks were scored at the 1974 Le Mans 24 hour race?
The Matra-Simca team won for the third successive year; Henri Pescarolo achieved his personal hat-trick of wins.

When was the first game of rugger played?
Traditionally, two teams were playing football at Rugby public school one day in 1823, when a player, William Webb Ellis, decided to pick up the ball and run towards the opposing goal and put it down in the goalmouth. The idea of picking up the ball spread to other schools and clubs, but it was nearly half a century before the game of rugby football was formalized.

When was the Rugby Union formed?
In January 1871, and in the same year England and Scotland played their first international match.

What is the Five Nations Championship?
It is an annual series of rugby matches played by teams from England, Scotland, Ireland, Wales and France, and it grew out of the first matches between England and Scotland.

What is the origin of roller skating?
The pastime seems to have begun seriously in the USA in the mid-19th century, when the manufacturer James Plympton introduced a four-wheeled skate and also opened what is believed to be the first public roller skating rink, at Newport, Rhode Island. Roller skates were greatly improved when the wheels were fitted with ball bearings in the 1880s.

What are the three main weapons used in fencing?
The foil, a light, thrusting weapon with tapering, quadrangular section blade and a small bell-like hand guard; the sabre, a flat V-section bladed cut-and-thrust weapon with a half-round guard; and the épée (the duelling sword), a heavier bladed weapon with triangular fluted section, much stiffer than the foil, and which has a large bell-type guard.

What are the familiar names of the rugby teams of New Zealand, South Africa, Australia, and of the combined travelling team of the countries of Britain?
All Blacks, Springboks, Wallabies, British Lions.

Who was the 1983 world champion snooker player?
Steve Davis (b 1957).

Who was probably the greatest snooker player of the 20th century?
Joe Davis (1901–1978) who won 15 world championships between 1927 and 1946, and who in his time also held the world's highest break. Joe Davis was also world champion billiards player four times.

What is the origin of billiards?
There is a record of Louis XI of France (1461–1483) owning a billiard table. The game was certainly enjoyed by Louis XIV of France (1643–1715).

Who is Reg Harris?
Probably the finest and most successful cyclist ever to emerge from Great Britain. He won several championships before World War II and was Britain's fastest amateur cyclist. During the war he served in the army and was badly wounded, but still returned to cycling afterwards and for several years dominated the cycling scene, turning professional and winning the world sprint championships in 1949, 1950, 1951 and 1954. He also set several world records which stood for a generation or so.

What is coursing?
One of the oldest of field sports, and a forerunner of greyhound racing, it is the chasing of hares by greyhounds using sight rather than scent. It is organized today in enclosures and parks.

Who is Mark Spitz?
Born in 1950 in the USA, Mark Spitz won 9 Olympic Gold Medals for swimming events in the Games of 1968 and 1972. Six of the medals were for events in which he also established world records.

What is octopush?
A relatively new sport consisting of a kind of hockey played in swimming pools by swimmers under the water, using snorkel tubes.

Who was the first British woman to succeed in swimming across the English Channel?
Mercedes Gleitz in 1927. It was her eighth attempt.

When did croquet become fashionable in Britain?
In England in the mid-19th century, after some years of popularity in Ireland where it was known as 'crokey'. The game derives from a similar sport in France, probably from late medieval times.

Is karate an ancient Japanese martial art?
No, it was introduced into Japan by Funakoski Gichin after World War I from the island of Okinawa where it had been practised for centuries by the islanders against their Japanese oppressors. They had developed its form from an ancient Chinese style of boxing.

Who invented the game of cribbage?
Sir John Suckling (1609–1642), the English poet and supporter of Charles I.

What is a trampoline?
Invented at the beginning of the 20th century, it is a sprung, webbed bed slung between a frame, from which an athlete – or anyone else – can jump, twist, bounce, somersault.

What is the Royal and Ancient?
The game of golf. It is also the name adopted by the St Andrews Golf Club, founded in 1754 and is the world (excluding USA) authority on the game.

How long has fencing been an international sport?
Since just before World War I when the Fédération Internationale d'Escrimé (FIE) was founded, in 1913. But fencing has been practised by individuals as a recreation, for duelling and for individual combat in warfare, almost since the invention of bronze weapons 5000 or so years ago.

When did the *News of the World* darts championships begin?
In 1927–28 for the London area. The tournament was gradually extended to other areas, a process interrupted by World War I. It resumed in 1947–48 as a national competition.

What is the origin of bullfighting in Spain?
A mural dating back to 3830 BC found at Catal Huyak in Turkey, provides the first evidence for the sport of bullfighting. It had some following in Roman times, but it was the Moors who brought it to Spain from Africa in the 8th century. An enclosure for bullfighting was made in Seville in 1743, although the first rings bearing a resemblance to those in use today were not constructed in Spain for a further eleven years.

In what European country is association football only played in the summer?
Iceland, where for climatic reasons the season lasts from May to October.

What is marine ball?
This is a variation of water polo, played in a shallow pool.

When was Goodwood Racecourse laid out and opened?

In 1801. Racing at Goodwood was introduced by the then Duke of Richmond and Gordon on his Goodwood estate, near Chichester in Sussex, and it is still held there at the end of July every year.

Where is the St Leger run?

At Doncaster Races in September. The St Leger is the oldest of the flat race classics, and was first run in 1776. It was named after Colonel Barry St Leger. The distance of the race is 2.938 km (1¾ miles 132 yd).

What is the leading racecourse in France?

Longchamp, in the Bois de Boulogne north-west of Paris, on the site of a medieval nunnery. Here, the greatest international event of the world, the Prix de l'Arc de Triomphe, is held. The course was opened in 1856.

Where are the One Thousand Guineas and the Two Thousand Guineas run?

The 1000 Guineas and the 2000 Guineas are run at Newmarket.

Which horse has won the Grand National three times?

Only one, and that was *Red Rum*, in 1973, 1974 and 1977. *Red Rum* also came second in 1975 and 1976.

What is a thoroughbred horse?

It is an English breed of horse used for racing or hunting, and is bred from English mares crossed with Arab stallions. All English thoroughbreds are descended from one or other of three famous Arab horses brought to England in the 18th century.

What were the three Arab horses?

The Byerly Turk, the Darley Arabian and the Godolphin Arabian.

Where are the Oaks and the Derby run?

Epsom.

Which king was the first to sponsor racing at Newmarket?

James I (1603–1625), but it was his grandson Charles II (1660–85) with whom one associates royal interest in racing here. He had one horse called Rowley, which he raced at Newmarket. He himself came to be known by many as Old Rowley.

Who was the first jockey to be knighted?

Sir Gordon Richards (b 1905). He began riding in 1920, and by the time he retired in 1954 he had ridden 4870 winners and had been champion jockey in 26 seasons.

Which was the race that always eluded Gordon Richards, until his last full year as a jockey?

The Derby. But in 1953, Coronation Year, he won on Pinza, at his 28th attempt. He had been knighted only a few days earlier. When he retired he became a trainer.

What is the Grand National?

A national steeplechase which is run at Aintree near Liverpool in late March or early April every year. The course is 7.245 km (4½ miles) long and has 30 jumps. It was first run in 1839, though it was not called the Grand National until 1843.

What is point-to-point racing?

Small-scale cross-country steeplechasing for amateur riders.

Who was Fred Archer?

He was the most famous and the most successful champion jockey in the 19th century. Champion for thirteen seasons in a row he rode 2748 winners, including five in the Derby.

What is the totalizator?

It is a system on horse-racing courses (and also on greyhound racing tracks) which records bets and pays out winnings without the intervention of bookmakers. It is known for short as the tote.

What is the Horse-race Totalizator Board?

Founded in 1963 to take over the responsibilities of the previous Racehorse Betting Control Board, it operates totalizators at approved courses in Britain, and it also provides cash and credit offices in places away from courses.

Where is the Horse-racing Museum?

In Newmarket, on the premises of the Jockey Club.

Which was the best known racehorse owned by Winston Churchill?

Colonist II, which won more than a dozen races. In one race, he apparently turned his head to one side to try to bite a rival coming up beside him.

What was so special about the Irish horse Arkle?

Generally regarded as the greatest steeplechaser in the history of racing, Arkle was also the most popular. He won numerous races, often against top competing steeplechasers with such seemingly effortless grace and speed that every time he raced he was greeted with roars of applause. When he broke a foot in 1966 during a race – but still went on to win – he had to retire. He received sackfuls of Get Well Cards, most of them addressed simply to – Arkle, Ireland.

What is the origin of the National Hunt Chase at Cheltenham?

This was instituted in 1859 by 'Fogo' Rowlands with a view to providing a race for steeplechasing hunters over a challenging course which local hunts would both subscribe to and support. The race then became peripatetic, although returning to Cheltenham on occasions until it finally settled there in 1911.

Who said of racing: 'I consider this to be a national sport – the manly and noble sport of a free people, and I deeply feel the pride of being able to encourage these pastimes, so intimately connected with the habits and feelings of this free country . . .'?

William IV. Despite the fact that he felt no personal enthusiasm for the turf, the king acknowledged its worth as a social institution which united all classes.

What religious leader built up one of the world's greatest racing empires?

Aga Khan III (1877–1957), who became the spiritual leader of the Ismaili sect of Shiah Muslims upon the death of his father in 1885. He was raised in India where he acquired his love of racing mainly through his close social contacts with the British raj. He first visited Britain in 1898, and France shortly afterwards; then in 1904 he started to build up his racing interests in those countries. Subsequently, he had 17 successes in classic races, including the Derby on five occasions.

Little Quiz 64

What colour are these gemstones or minerals?

1. amethyst
2. ruby
3. malachite
4. citrine
5. serpentine
6. lapis lazuli
7. emerald
8. moonstone
9. bloodstone
10. zircon

When was St Isaac's Cathedral in Leningrad built?

It was started in the mid-18th century by the Italian architect Rinaldi, in what was St Petersburg. But the huge gilded domed building you can see today was not finished until the later 19th century, to designs by Richard de Montferrand, a French architect who won a competition for the cathedral's completion. It is 111 m (364.08 ft) long, 98 m (321.44 ft) wide and the central dome is 100 m (328 ft) tall. There are 562 steps to the top.

Who designed the splendid cathedral at Brasilia?

Brasilia, the new capital of Brazil, was begun as a new city soon after World War II. It is about 1207 km (750 miles) from Rio de Janeiro. The cathedral was designed by the Brazilian architect, Otto Niemeyer, and it was started in 1959. It is circular in plan and the main floor is sunk about 3.05 m (10 ft) below ground level. The building is shaped like a sheaf of corn, with 16 equidistantly spaced ribs rising from a wide base, narrowing in the centre and splaying out again like a corona at the top, the ribs interspersed with glazed grids.

What are the principal features of Aachen Cathedral in West Germany?

It is really a cluster of chapels set round a central chapel which is known as the Palatine Chapel. It was built in the time of Charlemagne (768–814), and the additions were spread over the next six centuries. It is also where Charlemagne is buried.

What is Fontainebleau?

A palace built for the royal family of France by Francis I (1515–1547) over the remains of an old castle. It was decorated and furnished in Renaissance style (much of which survives) and was refurbished in the time of Napoleon and of Louis Philippe (1830–48).

What is a duomo?

It is the Italian word for a cathedral in an Italian city. It means House of God.

What is the Bull Ring in Birmingham?

It is the new city centre, opened in 1964. The principal feature is a huge drum-shaped building rising out of a vast complex of concrete and glass which is offices and shopping centre.

What is the longest single span suspension bridge in the world?

The Humber bridge which crosses the Humber between Humberside (East Yorkshire) on the north side and South Humberside (N. Lincolnshire). It is 1410 m (4624.8 ft) long and it was opened in 1981. It can cut almost an hour off the car journey from London to Hull and the east of Yorkshire.

Where is the palace of Split?

Split, on the Adriatic coast of Yugoslavia, known also by its Italian name of Spalato, is a port founded by the Roman emperor Diocletian in about AD 300. In the modern town is a huge square-plan palace built by Diocletian, to which he retired in 305 in order, as he said, to grow cabbages.

Where is Coca Castle?

This vast 15th century castle-palace for the archbishops of Seville was built by Moslem workers for Christian masters. Though enormously strong and heavily fortified, it has never been involved in warfare.

Where is the Palace of the Nations?

In Geneva, Switzerland. It is a complex of large buildings which once housed the League of Nations, founded in 1920 after World War I but superseded in 1945 by the United Nations Organization. The Palace of Nations today houses several organizations including the World Health Organization (WHO).

What is Trajan's Column?

It is a monument erected by the Roman emperor Trajan (AD 98–117), to celebrate his various military victories, especially those against the Dacians in south-east Europe. The base is a cube of stone, of 5½ m (18 ft) with a bronze gate in one side. The column is of marble, 3.70 m (12.136 ft) in diameter and reaching a height of 29.77 m (97.64 ft). Inside is a spiral staircase of white marble, with 185 steps. On the top it once had an eagle, then after his death a statue of Trajan replaced it, and this in turn was replaced by a statue of St Peter in 1588. The outside of the column is decorated with a continuous spiralling relief sculpture, depicting various events in Trajan's career, and is a valuable source of evidence for several aspects of Roman military activity.

Which is the tallest building in Britain?

Currently (1984) it is the new National Westminster Bank headquarters building in Bishopsgate, in the City of London. It is 183 m (600 ft) tall and is served by 21 lifts. It is roughly triangular in plan, like the logo on the bank's cheques and cheque book covers, that is, a triangle with flattened corners. It was completed in 1979.

Who built Hampton Court Palace?

Originally, it was built for Cardinal Wolsey in the earliest years of the reign of Henry VIII (1509–1547). In 1526, Wolsey gave the palace to the king who added the Great Hall and other features. The palace remained a royal residence for several generations, and it was restored and enlarged by Christopher Wren for William III.

Where is the Eiffel Tower?

It is on the south bank of the Seine in Paris, near the Champ de Mars. The tower is an astonishing structure, almost 300 m (985 ft) tall, and built of iron in a grid form between 1887 and 1889 – itself a marvel of technology. Much of the ironwork was prefabricated and bolted together on the site. The tower weighs over 9,700 tons, 7,000 tons of which are the ironwork. It was designed and supervised by Gustave Alexandre Eiffel (1832–1923).

Eiffel Tower

Little Quiz 65

These were the Nine Muses in Greek Mythology. What were their arts?

1. Calliope
2. Clio
3. Urania
4. Terpsichore
5. Thalia
6. Euterpe
7. Erato
8. Melpomene
9. Polyhymnia

What is a tabloid newspaper?
A small size newspaper, about half the size of *The Times*, and which is profusely illustrated with photographs and cartoons, many of the photographs taking anything up to a whole page each.

What does a sub-editor of a newspaper do?
He or she gets the copy (text) ready for printing, which means marking the typed sheets of text with directions as to how it is to be set in print. He or she also decides how long the article or news item is to be and cuts the text to fit the amount of space. In this the sub-editor is guided to some extent by the importance of the story in relation to other stories and articles on the same page.

What is newspaper layout?
This is a sketch of a particular page, or set of pages, done in pencil by the sub-editors' department, so that the printer is given a good idea of what the finished page ought to look like when printed.

What does the term freelance journalist mean?
He or she is a journalist who writes for a newspaper or magazine, but is not on the paper's staff. They get paid fees for particular contributions. Many freelance journalists write for a number of papers and magazines.

Which trade unions protect the interests of journalists and other contributors to newspapers and magazines?
The Institute of Journalists, founded in 1884, and the National Union of Journalists, founded in 1907.

What does a press agency do?
It gathers news stories and circulates them to newspapers all round the country, generally by means of a teleprinter.

What is a giveaway newspaper?
Something relatively new in newspapers in Britain, it is a paper whose production costs are entirely paid for by the advertisers who buy space in the pages, and which also makes a small profit for the owners. The paper is given away to readers.

What does the Press Council do?
Briefly, it exists to ensure the continuation of the freedom of the Press in Britain, and to ensure that the Press maintains its standards. It also investigates complaints made against individual papers and journalists. The Press Council is also supposed to draw attention to possible dangers from mergers or take-overs among newspaper proprietors.

Why would a newspaper use a picture agency?
Picture agencies take photographs of events, personalities, disasters and other newsworthy items, and circulate them to newspapers and magazines which may be glad not to have to send their own staff photographers out to the scene. Such agencies usually keep a library of pictures on which newspapers and magazines and other people can draw at short notice.

How old is *The Times*?
Almost two hundred years. It was founded by John Walter in 1785.

Who is reported as having said, 'Publish and be damned'?
The first duke of Wellington.

What does a copy taker do?
Sometimes known as a telephone reporter, he or she is a journalist who sits at a typewriter in a newspaper office, usually wearing headphones, and types out the stories dictated over the phone by reporters from outside.

Who was Cassandra?
Sir William Connor, the famous
columnist wrote under the name
Cassandra a daily column for the *Daily
Mirror* from 1935 to 1967. He was one of
the best known journalists of the present
century, and often produced the perfect
single-line sentence to sum up a
personality or an event. On the death of
Pope John XXIII in 1963, he wrote, 'He
put his arm round the heart of the world'.

What is a newspaper's masthead?
It is the title of the newspaper printed in
large letters at the top of the front page.
The word also means the title where it
appears on the page that carries leading
articles.

**Where is *The Scotsman* newspaper
printed?**
Edinburgh.

What is offset lithography?
It is a method of printing used for books,
some magazines and newspapers from a
flat surface using the principle that
grease (in this case ink) and water will
not mix.

What does a leader writer do?
He or she writes a column expressing the
views of the newspaper on one of the
day's main items or some other topic of
major interest. The views are those of the
editor of the paper or the proprietor but
not necessarily of the leader writer.

**What daily newspaper reflects the
views of the Communist Party in
Britain?**
The Morning Star.

**When did the English provincial
press start?**
With the *Norwich Post*, founded by
Francis Burgess in 1701, probably on
8 November, although there is no copy of
the first issue in existence.

**What is the only daily morning
newspaper to be published in Wales?**
The *Western Mail*, published in Cardiff.

**What is the name of the editors'
professional association?**
The Guild of British Newspaper Editors,
which has about 500 members.

**When did photographs first appear in
newspapers?**
The first ever appeared on the back page
of the *New York Daily Graphic* for
2 December 1873; it was a halftone
illustration of Steinway Hall in New
York.

Little Quiz 66
To what parts of the body or aspect of
medicine do these prefixes refer – eg
gastro = stomach?
1. derm-
2. cerebro-
3. haema-
4. sclero-
5. ophthalmo-
6. myo-
7. psycho-
8. thorac-
9. entero-
10. arthr-
and what do these word endings
suggest?
11. -itis
12. -tomy
13. -rrhea
14. -lapse
Which organs do these complaints
relate to?
15. astigmatism
16. cholecystitis
17. hepatitis
18. nephritis
19. mastoiditis
20. sinusitis
21. cystitis
22. pneumonia

When and where was the first World Cup?
In Uruguay, South America, in 1930. The winners were Uruguay.

When did England win the World Cup?
In a sensational match against West Germany played at Wembley in 1966. The England side was captained by Bobby Moore.

Where was football first played?
In China, in the 3rd century BC. The Chinese played a game called Tsu chu (which means: kick (tsu) ball (chu).

What is the origin of Association Football as we know it?
It began in England in 1863 when a number of London football clubs formed the Football Association and drew up a set of rules. The earliest years saw a number of changes in the rules, partly because clubs outside London did not agree with all the London rules. The game has evolved over the years since then, and there are still occasions when rules are amended.

When was the Football Association (FA) Cup competition inaugurated?
In 1872.

How many people turned out to watch the match between Brazil and Uruguay for the World Cup Final in 1950 at Rio de Janeiro in Brazil?
199,850 the highest number ever to attend a major football match.

Who is Sir Alf Ramsay?
Alf Ramsay was manager of the FA World Cup Team from 1963 to 1974, and this included the great year 1966, when England won the World Cup. Ramsay himself had played for England more than thirty times. He was knighted in 1967.

What was the appalling disaster that struck Manchester United Football Club in 1958?
The first team, with its manager Matt (now Sir Matt) Busby, was returning from a successful game in the European Cup competition, in Yugoslavia, when the aircraft carrying the team crashed on taking off from Munich airport. Eight of the team were killed, Busby and others (including Bobby Charlton) were seriously injured.

Which world famous goalkeeper was compelled to give up playing after a road crash?
Gordon Banks, 73 times player for England and regarded as one of the world's greatest goalkeepers. He was badly injured in a road crash in 1972, which left his eyes permanently affected.

Who holds the record number of goals scored while playing for England?
Bobby Charlton, who in thirteen seasons (1958–1970) scored 49 goals. He was awarded an OBE.

What is the Cup Winners' Cup?
This slightly confusing phrase relates to an international football competition held every year for national cup winners, or runners-up if the winner already qualifies as holder or is in the European Cup.

What is the world governing body of association football?
FIFA (the Fédération Internationale de Football Associations). This was founded in 1904 with six nation members, and now has over 150 members.

What are the recognized dimensions of a football pitch?
The dimensions are variable, between 100.65 and 109.8 m (110 and 120 yd) × 64.05 and 24.4 m (70 and 80 yd) for international matches.

Who is Pelé?
The world famous nickname of one of the greatest footballers, Edson Arantes do Nascimento, a Brazilian who was born in 1940. Pelé was already playing international football by the time he was seventeen, and when he retired from international playing in 1971, he had played 110 matches for Brazil, scored 97 goals in international football, as well as 1216 goals in 1254 matches of all kinds.

What is a *catenaccio* line-up on the football field?
It is a system of tactics of a defensive kind, by which one player (known as the sweeper) operates behind a row of four backs, three midfield players and two strikers (goal scorers).

What does it mean if a player is 'capped'?
It means he is included as a representative of an important team.

What does CONCACAT stand for?
Confederacion Nortecentroamerica y del Caribe de Futbol, which governs football in North and Central America and the Caribbean.

Which famous player was told when young that he would never make a footballer?
Billy Wright (b 1924) by Wolverhampton Wanderers' club management. He went on to captain Wolves (as the team is known) and also England. He played 105 matches for England, 90 of them as team captain, and he did not retire from football until 1959.

Which football team is often described as White Hart Lane?
Tottenham Hotspur (affectionately known as 'Spurs'), whose home ground is in White Hart Lane, Tottenham, in North London.

Which national team has won the World Cup three times?
Brazil, in 1958, 1962 and 1970.

What is the derivation of the name 'Spion Kop', given to parts of certain British football grounds?
This was the name of a hill in South Africa where, in January 1900, the British suffered a bloody defeat at the hands of the Boers. Troops from Lancashire suffered the highest number of casualties, and later the mounds where the spectators stood at football grounds in that country became known as Spion Kops as a tribute. The name is first recorded as having been used in Britain at Anfield, the ground of Liverpool FC, in 1906, then its usage spread rapidly.

What was the worst disaster ever to have occurred at an English football match?
This occurred at Bolton Wanderers' ground, Burnden Park, on 9 March 1946. Because of the sheer size of the crowd already in the ground, or their actions in trying to get in, 33 people died through being crushed or asphyxiated and 500 more required first aid.

What ground was built before the team whose home it became was created?
Stamford Bridge, the home of Chelsea FC. This site which had been a market garden until 1876 then became the headquarters of the London Athletic Club. Twenty years later, the two Mears brothers started negotiations to take over the ground and turn it into a prestige football stadium, but did not succeed until 1904. Having tried with no success to attract another team to play there, one of the brothers, Gus, eventually set up his own team, Chelsea, in 1905.

What is PAYE?

The letters stand for Pay As You Earn, a scheme whereby numerous employees in Britain pay their income tax. Their salaries or wages are assessed for a year's tax, and each pay cheque, or envelope with cash, contains the pay less the amount of tax worked out as a proportion of the year's tax. The amount deducted is determined from a set of tax tables provided to all employers by the Inland Revenue.

What is a franking machine?

A machine that prints the postage rate on a sticky slip of paper or directly on the envelope. This is called 'franking'.

What is collating?

If you have a report, or a catalogue of products, or any multi-page document, and if it is to be duplicated or photocopied for circulation to a number of people inside and/or outside the firm, the sets of papers have to be sorted and then stapled. This is called collating. It can be done by hand, which takes time. It can also be done by collating machines which do the job very quickly.

What is a typing pool?

In larger firms, government departments and other big organizations, there is generally enough typing work every day for a number of typists. It is often convenient for the typists to work together in one room, under a supervisor, and this is generally called the typing pool.

What is an 'Action' slip?

These are internal communications that take various forms, but generally have some kind of arresting feature calculated to encourage the receiver to take some action quickly upon the matter discussed in the communication such as a bright colour for the lettering, or a large printing of the word ACTION.

What is a golf ball typewriter?

A typewriter that does not have the usual type bars (levels with individual letters at one end) but has all the characters mounted on a small typing head which is ball-shaped and approximately the size of a golf ball. This moves across the machine when the keys are pressed.

What international paper sizes are likely to be used in the average office?

A 4, which is 297 mm × 210 mm ($11\frac{7}{8}$ in × $8\frac{3}{8}$ in) and A5 which is half that size. The A 4 size replaces the old foolscap size.

What is filing?

It is the storage of letters, records, documents, carbon copies of letters, etc., kept in folders, binders, wallets, in drawers or cabinets specially designed for the purpose.

What is an 'In' tray?

A rectangular wire-net tray, or a tray made of plywood or plastic, which rests on an office desk. All correspondence, files etc., that are to be dealt with by the person who occupies the desk are put into this tray.

What does a document shredder do?

Papers and documents that are no longer needed but which you don't want other people to read are put into a shredder which reduces them to very thin, unreadable shreds.

What is flexitime?

Staff can choose their own working hours within a basic framework. They have to do a 'core' of work, which is a period of about 4 hours, when everybody works, say from 10.00 am to 12.00 noon and 2.00 pm to 4.00 pm. The other hours may be done more or less when the worker likes.

What is the most valuable contribution of flexitime to people outside the firm where it is operated?
Flexitime means that a workforce does not go into work at one fixed time, thus adding to the crowding on commuter trains, Underground trains etc. It helps to spread the travelling over a much wider range of time. The same applies to finishing work on flexitime principles.

What is a consignment note?
When goods are sent by outside transport firms, they should be accompanied by a consignment note. This is provided by the firm and it gives details of the goods being sent (consigned), the name and address of the sender (consigner), the date of despatch and any other instructions, and the name and address of the firm or person to whom the goods are being sent (consignee).

What is O and M?
It stands for Organization and Methods department of a firm, which is devoted to examining and maintaining checks on the efficiency (or otherwise) of the firm. The O and M department recommends ways to speed up production, cut down waste and improve working conditions.

What does an audio typist do?
Types letters, reports and documents from a tape, or tapes, on which they have been previously recorded by dictation. The tape is played back on the dictating machine through ear phones.

What is Red Star delivery?
It is a fast delivery service for letters and parcels, which is operated by British Rail and which guarantees delivery the next day at any station in the UK.

What is an open plan office?
It is an office arrangement whereby a huge space is not broken up into a lot of partitioned offices but is left open, and laid out with desks and furniture. The furniture and equipment are arranged in groups for each worker, and each working area may be separated by soundproof screens.

What does the abbreviation Ltd mean?
Limited Liability Company, which is a form of business in which a number of people known as shareholders have invested money and have elected directors to run it for them.

What is a status inquiry?
This is one which is, for instance, addressed to a bank by a person or business wishing to discover the credit-worthiness of a prospective customer.

What is a bad debt?
A bad debt is a term used in accounting for one which is known to be irrecoverable, and is therefore treated as a loss.

Little Quiz 67

In the Bible, who was?
1. Abel
2. Abednego
3. Benjamin
4. Melchizedek
5. Belshazzar
6. Elizabeth
7. Jonathan
8. Uzziah
9. Zadok
10. Lot
11. What happened to Lot's wife?

Who were?
12. The Pharisees
13. The Amalekites
14. The Jebusites
15. The Scribes
16. The Rechabites

Who?
17. 'cared for none of these things'
18. had the fatted calf killed for him
19. was cured of 'seven demons' by Jesus
20. wore a coat of many colours

Who introduced the first adhesive postage stamp?

Sir Rowland Hill (1795–1879). He had written a pamphlet entitled 'Post Office Reform' in 1837, in which he had suggested the idea of a prepaid post, with postage stamps to indicate the payment. Up to then, letters were conveyed to the recipient who paid on receipt the cost which was calculated on the distance covered. The first stamps were introduced in 1840.

What was the very first mark of stamp?

A penny stamp, which was the new standard price for up to one ounce weight of postage anywhere in the country. The first stamp was black and carried a picture of Queen Victoria. Actually, these stamps were not issued until four months after the introduction of the Penny Post, because there were delays in getting the printing ready in time.

Who suggested the stamp design?

The design was put out to public competition, and over 2000 people submitted ideas, some of them fantastic. But in the end the postmaster general adopted the simple rectangular shape with the portrait of the queen – which had been suggested by Rowland Hill in the first place.

What happened if you did not prepay postage on your letters?

Your letter was delivered but the recipient had to pay double the postage rate – which still obtains today.

What are the Cinderellas in stamp collecting terms?

They are the once ignored philatelic items that are now collected with great enthusiasm by thousands of collectors. They consist of fakes, forgeries, duty stamps, propaganda labels, registration stamps.

What is a watermark?

In stamps it is a device used on the printing paper to prevent stamp forgery. There are several types of watermark and they can generally be seen if the stamp is held up to a bright light. British watermarks have included the royal crown and the royal monogram.

Have stamps always been perforated along the edges?

Not to begin with. The earliest stamps had to be cut from sheets. Perforation began in about 1852, following experiments by Henry Archer.

Which country produced a stamp which carried as its illustration a few bars of its national anthem?

Venezuela.

What were the Charles Connell Canadian stamps?

Charles Connell was postmaster general for the state of New Brunswick in Canada in 1860, and he had a 5c stamp printed bearing his own portrait. This caused a stir because it was customary to print only the portrait of Queen Victoria in Britain and in the countries of the Empire. Connell portrait stamps are valuable for there were not many run off.

What is a first day cover?

It is an envelope with a new issue of stamp, or stamps, postmarked on the day of issue. Covers are collectors' items. They can be obtained by buying the stamps and sticking them on an envelope addressed to oneself and posting it on the same day.

Where is Britain's National Postal Museum?

It is in St Martin's le Grand, in London's City. It contains vast quantities of material from the archives of the Post Office.

Stamps have generally been printed on paper. What other materials have been used?
Hungary printed commemorative stamps on wax cloth in 1958, metal foil has been used by Tonga, Sierra Leone and the USSR (which has also used silver paper). Bhutan printed stamps on silk. And the state of Latvia, restored to independence after World War I, printed some of its first new stamps on the backs of old German war maps.

Which were the first of the other countries in the world to introduce prepaid postages?
The USA in 1842, Brazil in 1843 and Switzerland, also in 1843.

What was the official cancellation mark for the earliest Penny Post?
A Maltese cross, the design of which varied in some small detail in many of the towns of issue.

Which is the only stamp of the USA to have been printed outside the USA?
During the Civil War (1861–1865), the Confederate states of the South, which had withdrawn from the Union and were at war with the other states, printed their own stamps. One was a 5c of 1862, bearing the portrait of the Confederate president, Jefferson Davis. The stamp was printed by the English firm, De La Rue.

What is Stampex?
It is an annual postage stamp exhibition held in London, at the Royal Horticultural Hall in Westminster, or the Central Hall, also in Westminster.

When did people start to collect postage stamps seriously?
It is not possible to say precisely, but certainly within twenty years of the introduction of stamps there were catalogues of new and used stamps, and there were several philatelic societies and clubs. In 1856 Edward Stanley Gibbons, who was working as an assistant in his father's pharmacy in Plymouth, started to deal in used stamps as a sideline, and thus founded the now world famous firm of stamp dealers.

Which is considered the most distinguished philatelic society in the world?
The Royal Philatelic Society in London, which was founded in 1869 and has about 1000 members who include the majority of the world's best known stamp collectors.

Who has been commemorated with the largest number of mourning stamps?
If we understand by a mourning stamp one issued within one year of a person's death, those issued after the death of Sir Winston Churchill in January 1965 totalled 287 plus 14 miniature sheets.

What are the oldest stamps still valid for postage?
The United States definitive series issued on 17 August 1861.

Have stamps ever been issued for an uninhabited island?
Uninhabited Redonda in the West Indies, has had stamps issued for it since 1979. They were issued in anticipation of the island's commercial and tourist development; this has not, however, so far materialized.

What area of the globe has been simultaneously depicted on the stamps of three nations as belonging to each country exclusively?
A slice of Antarctica shown on stamps of the (British) Falkland Islands Dependencies, Argentina and Chile.

What is a tithe barn?
A long rectangular building of late medieval date (or occasionally a little later) in which the parish priest stored his tithes (that is one-tenth of the produce of the land which were paid to the church). Several very fine tithe barns have survived, including the well-known one at Great Coxwell, Oxfordshire, built in the 14th century.

What is rotation of crops?
The order of growing different crops so that each one contributes to the soil constituents needed by the next, corn one year followed by root crops the next year is an example.

What is strip cropping?
This is the planting of crops in strips in such a way as to prevent erosion.

How did fairs begin in Britain?
A fair is a gathering for the sale of products, and fairs are held from time to time and generally include amusements and sports. The earliest fairs appear to have been held in Roman times.

What was a mop fair?
An autumn fair at which farm-hands and house servants paraded themselves in the hope of being engaged for a year's service with a local farmer.

What is the Forestry Commission?
It is a government-sponsored organization founded in 1919 to encourage growth and protection of forestation in Britain. It now owns about 3 million acres of land, over 2 million of which are planted with trees.

What was a pinfold?
An enclosure inside a village in medieval times in which stray animals were rounded up and held until their owners came to retrieve them on payment of a fee.

What is the Countryside Commission?
It was set up in 1968 to promote conservation and enhancement of the landscape of the countryside in England and Wales.

What is the official definition of a footpath?
A highway over which the public has a right of way on foot only, other than such a highway at the side of a public road.

What is ecology?
It is the study of living organisms within their environment, and this includes human beings and their habitats.

What were turnpikes?
They were gates that had spikes, and they were erected on certain roads for the authorities to use to collect tolls from travellers. These were erected after 1663 and the money was meant to be used to help maintain the condition of the roads.

Why was charcoal-burning an important activity?
Charcoal-burning took place for centuries in areas such as Sussex and Kent, and in Gloucestershire, where the charcoal was used by ironsmiths for their forges. The charcoal-burning industry declined with the gradual move over to the use of coke.

Who was William Cobbett?
William Cobbett (1763–1835) was a Surrey-born journalist and political reformer who championed the distressed labouring classes, particularly those in rural industries and on farms. He owned a newspaper and got into considerable trouble with the authorities for his attacks on abuses. He published his famous *Rural Rides* in 1830, a book of collected articles written over the previous years, in which he illustrated the best and the worst aspects of rural life.

What are the Fens?

They are flat, low-lying tracts of land in East Anglia and south Lincolnshire, particularly round the area of the river Wash. These tracts have been drained by means of a network of canals, started in the 17th century, and this has resulted in the production of a substantial area of extremely fertile land. The Romans made efforts to drain the Fens during their occupation of Britain, but the work was not continued by the Anglo-Saxons.

What is a deserted village?

This is a village abandoned by its inhabitants over the course of a period of years for one reason or another, often because of a plague visitation and resulting depopulation. Interest in these villages, of which there are several hundred, has been growing in recent years as aerial photography has revealed more and more evidence. Villages were also destroyed or allowed to decay by landlords of farms and great estates who wanted extra land for pasturing sheep.

Who are the crofters?

They are Scottish small-holders who rent and cultivate holdings known as crofts in the Highlands and Islands of Scotland. They are protected by acts of Parliament.

What was a hollow way?

An ancient form of boundary marking created by digging a deep ditch between two properties and heaping the earth along each side to form a double line of banking. It was also known as a two-fold ditch.

When was the first Ordnance Survey prepared?

Begun in 1791, under the title of the Trigonometrical Survey, its main concern was to map Great Britain on a scale of one inch to one mile (1/63360), a task completed in 1873.

What is a bridle path?

This is a path over which the public has the right of way on foot and on horseback, and from which vehicles are legally barred.

Little Quiz 68

Who are the patron saints of these?

1. actors
2. archers
3. art
4. beggars
5. blacksmiths
6. bricklayers
7. candlemakers
8. carpenters
9. children
10. cripples
11. domestic animals
12. expectant mothers
13. fishermen
14. glassworkers
15. greetings
16. learning
17. librarians
18. lost articles
19. messengers
20. motorists
21. pilgrims
22. porters
23. scholars
24. shepherds
25. tax collectors
26. teachers
27. watchmen
28. widows
29. writers
30. cabinet-makers

and of these towns or countries?

31. Paris
32. Wales
33. Madrid
34. West Indies
35. Norway
36. Austria
37. Belgium
38. Cyprus
39. Romania
40. Genoa

What is the origin of the marathon?
The ancient Athenians defeated the Persians at a great battle at Marathon in 490 BC. A messenger ran all the way from the battlefield to Athens, about 40 km (26 miles) to bring the news to the city. A similar long distance run was included as an event at the first modern Olympic Games held in Athens in 1896, and there has been a marathon event ever since.

Which England cricketer also held the world record for the long jump?
C. B. Fry, who played for the England cricket team many times between 1895 and 1912, including several matches as captain, and played for the England soccer team as well. He set a world record for the long jump in 1893 at 7.180 m (23 ft 6½ in) which remained unbroken for years.

What is the present world record for the long jump?
8.908 m (29 ft 2½ in) by Bob Beamon of the USA, in 1968.

What is putting the shot?
It is throwing a metal ball weighing about 7¼ kg (15.95 lb) as far as you can, holding it in a prescribed manner and having a limited distance in which to swing yourself into the throwing position.

Who was the first runner to break the 4-minute mile barrier?
For a long time, runners had been trying to run a mile in under 4 minutes. Many had got very close to it, including Britain's Sidney Wooderson, but not until 6 May 1954 was it achieved – by Roger Bannister, at Oxford, who ran a measured mile in 3 mins 59.4 seconds.

What is the best time for the mile run now (1984)?
3 mins 48.8 seconds, by Steve Ovett, in 1980.

336

What is the discus event in an athletics competition?
Competitors throw a heavy disc of wood edged with metal, about 18 cm (7½ in) across and weighing about 2 kg (4¼ lb). They are confined to a circle of about 2.5 m (8.2 ft) in diameter in which to take their stance and twist themselves into the best posture for swinging to throw the discus.

Which South African president at one time claimed to hold the world record for the long jump?
Paul Kruger, who was president of the Transvaal Republic, 1883–1902, and who jumped 7.015 m (23 ft) in 1845.

What great athletic events were the subject of the British film *Chariots of Fire*, made in 1981?
The winning of gold medals at the 1924 Olympics by Harold Abrahams (100 m) and Eric Liddell (400 m).

What is White City's connection with athletics?
The stadium was built for the 1908 Olympic Games held in London, and it accommodated over 90,000 spectators. In 1934 it was refurbished and used for the staging of the British Empire Games. White City continued to be used for athletics (as well as other events) up to 1970.

Where are the Scottish Amateur Athletics Association Championships held?
At Meadowbank, Edinburgh, which was opened in 1970.

Which woman long jump champion won two Olympic medals?
Elzbieta Krzesinska of Poland, who in 1956 jumped a world record of 6.354 m (20 ft 10 in) for women's long jumping, and in 1964 came second with 6.277 m (20 ft 7 in).

What is the world record for the discus throw?
71.192 m (233 ft 5 in) in 1978, by Wolfgang Schmidt of East Germany.

What is the world record for the javelin throw?
96.786 m (317 ft 4 in) by Ferenc Paragi of Hungary, in 1980. Imagine what it might have been like when a whole regiment hurled their javelins in battle, as they did in Greek and Roman times.

Which is the best time recorded for the marathon by a woman runner?
2 hours, 25 mins 29 secs, by New Zealand's Alison Roe, at New York in 1981.

When were the Commonwealth Games started?
They grew out of the old British Empire Games which were first held in Canada in 1930.

When and in what sports were women first allowed to compete in Olympic Games?
In tennis and golf at the Paris Games of 1900; in swimming at the Stockholm Games of 1912; in track and field events at the Amsterdam Games of 1928.

Who was the first black athlete to win an Olympic title?
William De Hart Hubbard of the USA, who won the long jump at the Paris Games of 1924. Hubbard also took the world record for this event from his fellow countryman, Robert LeGendre, in the following year.

When was the first time that two runners in the mile event both broke the 4-minute barrier?
In the Commonwealth Games of 1954, when Roger Bannister and John Landy came first and second respectively, at 3.58.8 and 3.59.6.

What was the most outrageous act of cheating in an Olympic marathon?
At the St Louis Games of 1904, the early leader, Fred Lorz of New York, was taken some of the distance by car. Not surprisingly he finished first, but was subsequently banned for life by the Amateur Athletic Union (USA).

Discus thrower

What is a bonsai tree?
It is a potted tree or shrub which has been rendered almost a miniature version of the original by severe pruning of the roots and stem. The technique is a Japanese one, and bonsai is the Japanese word for it.

What are hardy plants and half-hardy plants?
Hardy plants can survive frost in the open everywhere and every year. Half-hardy plants are those which can survive a normal winter outside but in a sheltered place or in milder areas, such as parts of the UK affected by the Gulf Stream.

Why do you put mulch round the bottom of a flower stem?
Mulch is organic matter such as rotted manure, compost, decayed grass cuttings, and if you put it round a flower stem or rose bush stem it keeps the moisture in and provides food for the plant. It also keeps the weeds down.

What is so remarkable about the rose called 'Peace'?
It is a hybrid rose created in the 1930s in France, which has a huge pale yellow flower with a pink tint on the petal edges. It was given the name 'Peace' in 1945 to celebrate the end of World War II.

Why are tea roses so called?
They were originally grown in China and they have a scent of tea.

What are bedding plants?
These are planted in beds for short term display in the garden.

What are alpine plants?
Strictly, they are plants native to the alpine zone, but the term is nowadays used to cover all small plants that are suitable for a rock garden.

What is so special about orchids?
There are many thousands of species of orchid, and also many thousands of artificial hybrids, but to the expert eye each of the differences is detectable. Orchids are almost always very beautiful flowers. They have been cultivated seriously in the western world for the last two and a half centuries, but the Chinese were growing orchids about 500 BC.

How long ago is it thought that the first flowering plants appeared on Earth?
About 200,000,000 years ago.

What is humus?
A black substance in the earth that is formed out of decaying vegetable and animal matter, and which is the most natural form of fertilizer.

What does cultivar mean?
It is a word meaning a new plant variety cultivated from a natural plant.

What do you plant in a kitchen garden?
Vegetables and herbs and also fruit bushes.

What is a tap root?
The long, central root which goes down vertically into the ground, and which is the principal root of the plant.

What is pollarding?
It is the procedure by which you cut back a tree to the top of its main trunk so that a new and thick head of branches is formed by fresh growth.

Who introduced the first systematic classification of the plant kingdom?
Carl Linnaeus, or Linné, who lived from 1707 to 1778, and who was a Swedish botanist. He visited many countries and studied gardens and botanical collections in great detail.

Are algae plants?
Yes, they are water plants which contain chlorophyll, and range from tiny forms too small to be seen by the naked eye to seaweeds.

What is the death cap?
Said to be the most poisonous of all fungi of the toadstool variety, it looks very like a mushroom.

What is coral spot?
It is a dangerous fungus that affects trees, and if it gets into the living shoots it can kill branches, eventually killing the whole tree. It is detectable by its tiny coral-red coloured spots accumulating in clusters often, though not only, at or near where branches fork, or on branches that have been damaged or broken.

When did the first greenhouses come into use in Britain?
In the mid-17th century, special houses in the garden were erected for plants and vegetables. They are mentioned by the great diarist and gardening enthusiast, John Evelyn (1620–1706).

What is a perennial plant?
A plant that flowers every season, as opposed to an annual plant that begins from a seed, reaches maturity and then dies, all in one year.

What is a cloche?
A cloche is a portable cover used to protect delicate plants and encourage their growth. The Romans are recorded as having dug pits for plants which were protected by sheets of mica, talc or glass; cloches, especially bell-shaped covers from which the name is derived, may have evolved from these Roman covers. They became common in the 17th century and were made of glass. In fact it is only quite recently that plastic and polyethylene have been substituted.

How did grafting originate?
Nobody knows for sure, but a probable explanation is that ancient peoples acquired the technique from observing examples of natural grafting which may happen when neighbouring trees rub together. In Classical times both Geeks and Romans were familiar with several grafting procedures; there is also a reference to grafting in St Paul's *Epistle to the Romans*.

What is topiary?
This name is derived from the Latin word for general gardener. By the first century Roman gardeners were trimming cypress and box trees and shrubs into fanciful shapes, and it was this specific activity which eventually acquired the name of topiary. Following the Dark Ages, topiary again became popular in 15th century Italy and, along with many other Renaissance fashions, spread to England by the time of Henry VIII. The best examples of English topiary are seen in box and yew hedges.

What is a cold frame?
It is a frame made of wood and covered with glass used for protecting young plants from the cold.

Little Quiz 69
What are the trade unions represented by these abbreviations?
1. TGWU
2. NUJ
3. NUT
4. CPSA
5. USDAW
6. NUPE
7. COHSE
8. ASLEF
9. ASTMS
10. NGA

What is equity?

It means fairness and justice, and refers to that common fairness which follows the spirit rather than the letter of justice. It is a legal system in England which supplements statute or common law and corrects, if necessary, its failure to accord with what is morally just and fair.

What is an injunction?

It is an order of a court which restrains someone from doing something injurious to or likely to injure another's interests, or which orders something to be done for the protection of another's interests.

What is an affidavit?

A statement in writing verified by oath or solemn affirmation of the person making the statement, made for the purpose of production in evidence in legal proceedings.

What is affirmation?

Some people refuse to swear an oath when called upon to do so in a court. They are entitled to refuse but have instead to make a solemn declaration, as allowed by Act of Parliament.

What was benefit of clergy?

An ancient privilege, long since abolished, which was granted to ecclesiastics, and later on, to clerks (that is, all persons who could read and write), exempting them from trial in the secular courts in criminal cases.

What does *caveat emptor* mean?

Latin for 'let the buyer beware', it is a maxim that is applied in cases of sale or bargain, where the buyer takes no guarantee from the seller as to the seller's right to sell, or as to the quality or suitability of the thing bought.

What is a peppercorn rent?

A yearly or other kind of rent of purely nominal amount.

What does it mean when it is said that, for example, a local authority has acted *ultra vires*?

It means that the local authority has acted beyond the powers given it by law. This applies also to companies or other incorporated bodies.

What is a deposition?

It is a statement made by a witness on oath in court. It is also a sworn statement made by a witness and used in court in his absence.

What is a curtilage?

An old word for a piece of land that adjoins a dwelling house. It is still used in legal documents concerned with the transfer of property.

What is an Act of God?

For the purposes of a legal document, it is an inevitable event without the intervention of man, such as a flood or tempest. The phrase is used as a get out clause in some contracts, particularly those with insurers and carriers.

What is a codicil to a will?

A document that makes additions to, or alterations to, the provisions in a will. It has to be executed with the same formalities as the will itself.

What is battery?

It is unlawful beating of another person. It is worse than an assault which can be no more than an attempt at battery.

What are letters of administration?

If a person dies intestate, the court may authorize someone to administer the estate of the person who has died intestate.

What are ancient lights?

They are windows or openings which have uninterrupted access to light for not less than twenty years, and which are therefore to be respected when adjoining buildings are put up.

What is intestacy?
The state of being intestate, which means dying without having made a will.

What is alimony?
It is an allowance made by order of the court out of a husband's estate for the support of his wife when a judicial separation or a divorce is decreed.

What are the two main offences of contempt of court?
1 Failure to comply with an order of a superior court, or resistance or insult to the court or the judges. 2 Conduct likely to prejudice the fair trial of an accused person. Offences are punishable by fines and/or imprisonment.

What is a wayleave?
It is a right of way over or through land for the carriage of minerals from a mine or quarry.

What is a test case?
It is an action in the courts, the result of which is applicable to other similar cases that are not taken to the courts.

What is circumstantial evidence?
A series of circumstances which lead to the inference or conclusion that a person is guilty when there is no direct evidence available.

What is to turn queen's (king's) evidence?
An accused person who, instead of being put on trial, is allowed by the Crown to give evidence against persons associated with him in an alleged crime on the understanding that he is not put on trial himself, is said to turn queen's evidence.

What does the queen's proctor do?
He is the Treasury solicitor who represents the Crown in probate, matrimonial and Admiralty cases. In matrimonial cases he can intervene at any stage if he thinks that there has been collusion between the parties or that material facts have not been disclosed, and he can ask for the decree *nisi* of the divorce not to be made absolute.

What was manbote?
It was compensation paid for the unlawful killing of a man or woman particularly if the person was the villein (serf) of a lord.

What is messuage?
Messuage is a term meaning a house, including gardens, courtyard, orchard and outbuildings.

What is a conveyance?
It is a deed or other document by which property is conveyed from one person to another.

When would you be said to be insolvent?
When you have not enough money or other assets to pay your debts.

What are rights of estovers?
They are rights of taking from woods or waste lands a reasonable portion of timber or underwood for use in the home.

Little Quiz 70
  Of which country were these president?
1. Jomo Kenyatta
2. Archbishop Makarios
3. Juan Peron
4. Field Marshal von Hindenburg
5. Marshal Pilsudski
6. J. K. Polk
7. Adolphe Thiers
8. Sun Yat-Sen
9. Douglas Hyde
10. Chaim Weizmann

What is Viewdata?

This is an information system, available like CEEFAXand ORACLE, on the home TV screen by means of a control box, but it is linked also with the telephone, enabling it to retrieve all kinds of information from a network of computers all over the country. The scheme is under development, but before the end of this century it may be possible to use the system as an instant telephone directory, a 'what's on' list, for full sets of prices in local shops, for menus in restaurants, and a hundred and one other things.

What is autocue?

It is a device that allows a TV performer, whether actor, interviewer or speaker, to give the viewers the information or speaking lines he or she would have memorized if on a stage or read out if in a studio in earlier TV history. It enables him or her to speak as if the words have been memorized but they in fact are being read from a screen just below the TV camera.

What does a stunt artist do?

Actors and actresses often have to appear to be involved in a variety of scenes of violence, as part of the story they are acting, such as fights, duels, struggles with wild animals, shoot-outs, bad car crashes and so on. The average actors are not trained to do these things and a special kind of artist known as a stunt man or stunt woman stands in for them. With careful editing afterwards, it is possible to make the shots look as if they really did involve the actor or actress.

What is Channel 4?

It is the second independent television channel to be launched in the UK and began transmission of programmes in November 1982. Channel 4 does not make programmes, but commissions or buys them ready-made from independent television producers.

What is a roller caption?

When you see the list of stars, followed by the names of those who helped to make the film or play (list of credits), it is often run through on a dark background. This is done by a machine rather like a mangle, which can be hand-operated or motor driven, and it is rotated horizontally or vertically, as desired. There are considerable variations in presenting these credits.

What does a set designer do?

On TV he designs and supervises the building of the sets for a programme, whether play, serial or film. Unlike a theatre set which is seen by the audience only from the front, TV sets are filmed from several angles, and the set designer has therefore to plan his sets so that they cater for cameras filming at these different angles. He must know about the light-reflecting properties of the buildings and furnishings and the sound dampening characteristics as well.

What is Eurovision?

It is the organization of the European Broadcasting Union which coordinates television and radio programmes in the Common Market countries of western Europe plus some of those that are not in the EEC. It gathers and circulates programmes from member countries to each other and to countries outside the union. It is administered from Geneva and the technical base is in Brussels, at the top of the Palais de Justice building.

When was the first official TV service in the world opened?

In March 1935 at Alexandra Palace in London. Before that, however, a number of programmes and broadcasts had been put out on a haphazard basis from various transmitters over the previous six years. Baird, the inventor of television, started outside broadcasting on BBC transmitters in 1929.

What is the IBA?
The Independent Broadcasting Authority, which originated as the Independent Television Authority in 1954 specifically to supervise the provision of an independent TV broadcasting service to the nation, and to compete with the BBC. The name was changed to IBA in 1972 to take in commercial radio.

What is audience research?
It is the process by which the BBC and IBA attempt to keep track of the opinions of their viewers and listeners, and to get their response to the programmes that are put out on national and local networks. Opinions are sought regularly by a variety of techniques, from individuals for the BBC and from family groups for IBA.

What is Teletext?
The system for displaying printed information with diagrams where needed on TV screens in the home. Two main systems are operating in Britain at present: the BBC's CEEFAX and the IBA's ORACLE.

What do CEEFAX and ORACLE stand for?
CEEFAX means Seeing Facts, and ORACLE stands for Optical Reception of Announcements by Coded Line Electronics.

How is the information conveyed?
It is made available on ordinary household TV screens by means of fitting an adapter for decoding, and specific information is called up by a small key pad hand controller. There is also a directory which lists the services that can be called (a list that is in a continuous state of growth). Information available includes weather forecasts, latest news statements, City prices, sports scores and results, etc.

What does a floor manager of a TV studio have to do?
First he has to be good at handling all kinds of people, many of whom may be on the set at one time. He has to translate commands from a director into effective orders. He has to know what is going on in the studio all the time, and to ensure that everyone else involved understands their roles too. He generally walks about with headphones on, which connect with the control room outside the studio, so that he can listen to what the control people are saying and at the same time give orders or advice to people on the set.

What is dubbing?
It is preparing certain film sequences in advance by mixing sound effects and commentary into the film to create a unified presentation of a sequence. For example, much outdoor filming of news is done in silent pictures, and so sounds have to be added in the sound effects room afterwards. This is dubbing, and it is a great skill, for it has to appear as genuine as possible.

What is video tape recording?
It is an alternative to film. A VTR apparatus receives signals directly from a TV camera and stores them on special magnetic tape. The process is similar to audio tape recording, except that the tape for video is much wider. The advantages are that the pictures can be played back instantly and they do not have to be processed.

What is Sianel Pedwar Cymru?
It is the Welsh language television service provided for Welsh speaking areas in Wales. Known for short as S4C, it also broadcasts for a number of hours on Channel 4.

Who were the Goodies?
Tim Brooke-Taylor, Graeme Garden and Bill Oddie.

What is humanism?
A term meaning belief in the idea that an honest and useful life is possible without its being geared to, or motivated by, any religious beliefs.

What, then, is Humanism?
It is the name given to the cultural movement that prevailed during the Renaissance period in Europe, which was characterized by the revival of interest in things Greek and Roman, and which enlarged the interests of people beyond the limits previously determined by the Christian religion.

What is Apartheid?
It is a policy prevailing in South Africa, and it means 'separate development' for the coloured races, on different terms from the development of the ruling white races. In practice, it means discrimination against non-European groups, to their disadvantage, even to the extent of refusing them the right to vote. As such, the policy is almost universally condemned.

Who were the Nihilists?
Nihil is the Latin for nothing, and Nihilists were a mid-to late-19th century group of Russian political activists who sometimes resorted to murder or bomb throwing in an attempt to undermine Russian society without offering anything in its place. One notable Nihilist crime was the murder of Czar Alexander II, in 1881, the first czar to alleviate the lot of the peasantry in Russia and who abolished serfdom.

What is the Bahai faith?
A religion founded in Persia in the middle of the last century by two teachers, Mirza Ali Mohammed and Mirza Husain Ali, who advocated belief in the spiritual unity of mankind and who encouraged their followers to devote their lives to the service of others.

Were the Shakers anything to do with the Quakers?
They were a small American sect of people who in the 1740s broke away from the Quakers and settled in New York State. They continued to accept most of the Quaker beliefs but added several of their own, such as that God was both man and woman, that the manifestation of man was Jesus Christ and the manifestation of woman was Mother Ann, who was a convert from England called Ann Lee. The name Shakers came from the fact that some of their rituals involved intense shaking of the body.

What is yoga?
It is an ancient Hindu philosophy which teaches the integrating of body, mind and will into a union with an Absolute Being, a state that can be achieved through a system of progressive mental and physical exercises.

What have the British Israelites to do with Israel?
Nothing strictly, but they are an English Protestant sect that believes that white Anglo-Saxon people are descendants of the lost tribes of Israel – those that were deported from Israel in the 8th century BC. This they say, makes them God's Chosen People.

Who are the Christadelphians?
An American Protestant sect, founded in 1848, who claim to practise what they say is original 1st century Christianity according to the earliest followers of Christ. They believe that only they know how to interpret the Scriptures properly.

What is the ecumenical movement?
Basically a movement among all Christians – Catholics, Protestants, Non-conformists, etc., to unite all believers. The movement was given a significant boost in 1982 when Pope John Paul II visited Britain.

EUREKA!

Who were the Levellers?
You could say they were the first English communists. They were a left wing sect of the Parliamentarians in the Civil War, whose membership was drawn from small farmers, workmen, traders, many of them serving in Parliament's New Model Army, and they campaigned for a republic with one representative assembly elected by manhood suffrage. While Cromwell had some sympathy with some of their aims, he had to suppress them in the army because of the threat they posed to good order and discipline.

Who were the Muggletonians?
This was a religious sect emerging in the Civil War in England and continuing during the Commonwealth period. It was founded by Ludovic Muggleton who issued a new interpretation of the Book of Revelations. The sect believed that it was the Father (God) not the Son (Jesus Christ) who had died on the Cross, that God himself had been in human form.

What is the transmigration of souls?
It is a belief that after death the soul enters the body of another living creature. The belief has been a tenet of several faiths, including those of some Hindu sects, of Buddhism, and it was also held by some of the ancient Greeks.

Who were the Christian Socialists?
Originally, they were a group of Christian clerical and lay leaders in the mid-19th century in Britain, who campaigned for major social reforms. They believed in the principles of socialism that were developing in Europe, but wanted to temper them with Christian teachings. They encouraged cooperative workshops, education classes for workers and other charitable activities for the benefit of the poor. They also gave support to the newly growing trade union movement.

What is anthropomorphism?
It means the attribution of human form and character to God or to gods, and also to animals or even plants. It is a tendency in most human beings at some time, instanced perhaps most obviously by regarding domestic animals as having human personalities and desires. Another form of anthropomorphism is the belief that God is some mystical human being in the sky looking down towards Earth, His creation.

What are Baptists?
They belong to a religious sect which believes in total immersion and do not approve of the baptism of infants.

What was the Oxford Movement?
This was initiated in 1833 by a group of scholars and divines at Oxford University. The movement was characterized by a desire to restore to the Church of England certain pre-Reformation principles which had been lost. Prominence was given to the Catholic character of the Church, without implying the necessity of union with Rome. When many of its leaders, notably Cardinal Newman, did become Roman Catholics the movement foundered.

Little Quiz 71
  Where are these lakes?
  1. Great Slave
  2. Van
  3. Koko-Nor
  4. Great Bear
  5. Titicaca
  6. Onega
  7. Issyk-Kul
  8. Manitoba
  9. Bala
  10. Loch Ness

Who invented the telescope?

There are various claimants, but perhaps the one with the most widely recognized claim is Hans Lippershey, a Dutch spectacle-maker who died in 1619. He is said to have invented his telescope in 1608.

Telescope

Who invented the cylinder lock?

Linus Yale (1821–1868), a locksmith who founded the Yale company.

Who invented the safety razor?

King C. Gillette (1855–1932), in 1895.

Who invented the blast furnace?

The Scottish engineer James Neilson (1792–1865), who was for nearly thirty years foreman and manager of Glasgow gasworks.

Who invented the metronome?

Johann Nepomik Maelzel (1770–1838), a German musician and instrument-maker who settled for a time in Vienna and taught music. He later moved to Paris and finally emigrated to the USA. He produced the metronome in 1816.

Who invented the mercury thermometer?

The mercury thermometer was invented in 1714. Up to then the fluid used in thermometers had been alcohol. It was Gabriel Fahrenheit (1686–1736), a German physicist who was the first to use mercury (or quicksilver) in the thermometer tube, and he fixed the freezing point at 32 degrees and the boiling point at 212 degrees.

Who invented the safety pin?

Walter Hunt (1796–1859), an American, invented the safety pin in 1844 and it was patented in 1849. He was responsible for other new ideas, including the paper collar.

Who invented the lathe?

The lathe for metal turning and screw cutting was invented by Henry Maudslay, an English engineer (1771–1831).

Who invented the gyroscope?

The distinguished French physicist Jean Bernard Léon Foucault (1819–1868), invented the gyroscope in 1852 with which he showed how the Earth rotates on its axis.

Who invented the passenger lift?

Elisha Otis (1811–1861), who was born in Halifax, Vermont. He improved his first lift of 1853 by devising a steam elevator in 1861.

Who invented the bunsen burner?

Robert Wilhelm Bunsen (1811–1899), a German physicist and chemist who became professor of chemistry at Heidelberg University in 1852.

Who invented the ophthalmoscope?

Hermann Ludwig Ferdinand von Helmholtz in 1851. An ophthalmoscope is the instrument used by doctors to examine the inside of the eye.

Who invented the spinning jenny?
James Hargreaves (1720–1788). The spinning jenny was a spinning engine which enabled a man to operate several spinning wheels at once. It was demonstrated in 1764 at Standhill in Lancashire. Hargreaves called it the jenny after his wife.

Who invented linoleum?
Frederick Walton, an English inventor, in 1860.

Who first produced the explosive mixture, nitro-glycerine?
An Italian chemist, Ascanio Sobrero in 1846.

Who invented celluloid?
The English chemist, Alexander Parkes (1813–1890). The transparent sheet was produced by the action of nitric acid on cellulose in a mixture of camphor and sulphuric acid.

Who invented the microphone?
David Edward Hughes (1831–1900), who spent several years as a music teacher in the USA and was also an experimenter with printing telegraphy. He invented the microphone in 1878.

Who invented the cotton gin?
This useful apparatus that separated the fibres from the seeds was invented in the USA by Eli Whitney in 1793. It produced a marked increase in cotton manufacture.

Who invented the flying shuttle?
This was a mechanically operated shuttle for a loom which enabled the loom to operate more quickly, and also enabled the user to make broad-cloth. It was a key invention in the Industrial Revolution, and was invented by John Kay in 1733.

Who invented the revolver?
Samuel Colt (1814–1862), in 1836. He came from Hertford in Connecticut in USA.

Who invented the flush lavatory?
Sir John Harington (1561–1612), an Elizabethan courtier, satirist and godson of the queen. During a period of banishment from court, he designed a water-closet with a reservoir and installed it in his own home near Bath in 1589. After his return to favour, two years later he constructed another for the queen herself in her palace at Richmond, Surrey. The design is to be found in his pamphlet, *The Metamorphosis of Ajax*.

Who invented nylon?
Wallace Hume Carruthers (1896–1937), an American chemist and director of research at du Pont. He invented this material which has properties similar to those of natural silk. It was moreover, the first fibre to be completely man-made.

Little Quiz 72
  Where are these waterfalls?
1. Kalambo
2. Niagara
3. Sutherland
4. Nevada
5. Victoria
6. Gersoppa
7. Kaieteur
8. Staubbach
  And these volcanoes?
9. Villarica
10. Cotopaxi
11. Erebus
12. Etna
13. Pepee
14. Nyamuragira
15. Elbrus
16. Fujiyama

What is the Pre-Cambrian era?

The first geological era in the story of the Earth, from about 4500 million years ago to about 2000 million years ago. There are three main periods in the era, Azoic, Archaeozoic and Proterozoic.

What is the Azoic period?

It is the period 4500–4000 million years ago when there was no animal life on Earth and the earliest rocks evolved.

What is the Jurassic period?

It is part of the Mesozoic Age, from about 180 million BC to about 130 million BC. It was the age of dinosaurs and other prehistoric animals, among them the earliest birds.

What is the Abbevillian period?

A period at the beginning of the Paleolithic Age (Early Stone Age). It is named after a number of finds in the estuary of the river Somme, around Abbeville in France. The finds are dated about 300,000 BC and include two-faced stone hand axes.

Where is the Olduvai Gorge?

It is in Tanzania, East Africa. Here, in the 1950s, Dr Louis Leakey and his wife Mary, found fossils of Australopithecus africanus (Southern Ape of Africa).

Who was Piltdown Man?

A remarkable forgery. Parts of a skull found at Piltdown in Sussex in 1912 by a Dr Dawson were said by him to be from a hominid, but in 1953 Professor Sir Wilfred Le Gros Clark exposed this as a scientific hoax, for the skull was from a modern man, and the associated jaw was from an orang-utan.

What is potassium-argon dating?

A method devised in 1946 for dating ancient remains. It is based on the breaking down of radioactive potassium into argon.

What was Australopithecus africanus?

It was an early ape, said for a long time to have been the ancestor of man, but now seen as an ape that lived alongside another early but slightly different ancestor of man. Australopithecus africanus wandered about East Africa between 2 and 5 million years ago.

Where is Taima-Taima, and what is it?

It is a site in Venezuela, South America, which was occupied about 12,000 to 14,000 years ago. The inhabitants produced two-faced stone axes, used scrapers and other tools, and appear also to have had some kind of horse.

Where did the first people in North America come from?

They are thought to have come from Asia by wandering across the Bering Strait in times when the strait was iced over, which was about 25,000 BC or perhaps earlier. The first men to appear in North America were hunters.

When did human beings appear in Ireland for the first time?

During the Mesolithic period in Europe, more specifically for Ireland about 7000 BC. Before that time, it is believed that Ireland was uninhabitable, even though there were early Stone Age people in almost all other parts of Europe.

What was an aurochs?

The ancestor of present-day cattle. It lived in forests in most parts of Europe, in central Asia and in China. It appears to have been domesticated as early as about 4000 BC in south-east Europe.

Is it possible to say when pottery was first made?

Pieces of pots (sherds) have been found in Anatolia (Asia Minor) which have been dated to about 7000 BC.

Who was Cro-Magnon Man?
One of the closest of our ancestors, Cro-Magnon Man lived about 30,000 years ago. Remains of this ancestor were found at Cro-Magnon in France in the late 1860s, and after that time, very similar skull and skeleton remains were found in other parts of the world.

When was Siberia colonized by man?
Probably about 20,000 years ago, especially round Lake Baikal.

What was the Jomon period?
A Japanese early culture which lasted for many thousands of years, from about 12000 to about 500 BC, in which the people hunted and fished, and made pottery, but did not know about the use of metal.

When did European peoples begin to cultivate crops in fields?
About 10,000 years ago, in the period 9000 to 8000 BC. The first crops were not native to Europe. They were brought in from Asia Minor, particularly what is now Turkey in Asia. Settlers from this area reached south-east Europe, built small mud-brick villages, kept livestock and introduced the growing of cereals.

Which was the very first ancestral ape from whom we are descended?
The African ape, Proconsul, discovered on Rusuiga Island in Lake Victoria. It lived over 30 million years ago, dwelt in trees and walked on all fours.

What was the first animal to be intentionally domesticated?
The dog, which is first reckoned to have been domesticated about 16,000 years ago. This domestication would have been the work of late Palaeolithic hunters who, as farming gradually developed, recognized the dog's value as a guard as well as a hunting companion. While the dog's immediate ancestors were wolves, it gradually lost much of the wolf's characteristic behaviour.

When did the Magdalenian culture flourish?
The Magdalenians were an advanced hunting people who occupied parts of south-western Europe, between the Alps and the Spanish Cantabrian Mountains, some time between about 15000 and 10000 BC. They were late Palaeolithic (Stone Age) people who were highly inventive and who used a variety of stone tools. They produced much cave art, notably the animals in the famous Lascaux caves in France and the Altamira caves in Spain. The Magdalenians moved into central Europe, reaching as far as Czechoslovakia, and may also have come to Britain. They hunted reindeer, fished for salmon, and made their own clothes, cutting and stitching the garments with some skill.

What was a tylosaur?
A giant, scaly reptile which flourished about 80 million years ago in what is now Kansas, USA.

Little Quiz 73
  Give the correct chemical name for these well known substances?
  1. washing soda
  2. common salt
  3. epsom salt
  4. glauber's salt
  5. heavy water
  6. caustic soda
  7. slaked lime
  8. aqua regia
  9. potash
  10. barytes

What is the correct length of a cricket pitch?
20.13 m (22 yd), and it has been so at least since the 1740s.

When did batsmen first begin to wear pads?
This is not known for certain, but one Robert 'Long Bob' Robinson, who played at Farnham in Surrey, is recorded as taking his stance in front of the wicket wearing a wooden shield round one leg. This was at the end of the 18th century.

How old is the game?
This is impossible to say for certain. There is a reference to cricket being played at a school in Guildford in the mid-16th century and another in 1654 at Eltham in Kent, for which the participants were fined. It was not until 1744 that the game was given its first proper set of rules.

What early form of cricket was played with a stone wicket?
Stonyhurst cricket, played by Roman Catholic exiles of the English College on the continent for two centuries up to 1794. This college was then set up in England as a school at Stonyhurst Hall near Preston, Lancashire, their cricket game accompanying the scholars who had been driven from *Liège*, their last refuge, by the French Revolutionary armies. Stonyhurst cricket continued to be played at the school until 1860, when it was displaced by the game played according to the MCC's regulations.

What is the origin of Lord's Cricket Ground?
One of the original members of the MCC was Thomas Lord (1755–1832), a Yorkshire born entrepreneur who leased the ground in Dorset Square to the MCC. The club moved from this ground to another nearer St John's Wood, but this was not popular among the players and

in 1814, Lord found a third site, costing £100 a year. This is the site occupied today.

What is the area of Lord's cricket ground?
About five acres, 2.025 hectares.

What is the I Zingari Cricket Club?
It is a wandering club, founded in 1845. The name is Italian for The Gypsies, and the club is still flourishing.

What is the John Player League?
A cricket league specifically played on Sundays among first class counties.

What were the first cricket rules?
They were the Laws of Cricket, drawn up in 1744 but not published nationally until 1752 when they appeared in the November issue of the New Universal Magazine. They appeared in booklet form three years later.

When was the MCC founded?
The Marylebone Cricket Club was founded in 1787, and its first headquarters was in Dorset Square, behind Baker Street in London. It cost 6d to watch one of the club's matches.

Who is still regarded as the most famous cricketer of all time?
Few would argue that it is W. G. Grace (1848–1915). William Gilbert Grace was a doctor, but his cricket career began in his teens when he made his debut at Lords and at the Oval aged only 16. During his career, Grace scored 54,896 runs in first class cricket, the highest score being 344 in the match between the MCC and Kent in 1876.

What other high score did Grace achieve?
Grace was also a top flight bowler, and in his career he took 2876 wickets in first class cricket. He captained

Gloucestershire from 1871 to 1898, and also captained 13 England test teams against Australia.

Which British test player became a Church of England bishop?
David Sheppard, Bishop of Liverpool.

What is a maiden over?
A full over during which no runs are scored by either batsman.

What is Wisden?
This is short for *Wisden's Cricketers' Almanack*. It was first published in 1864 by John Wisden (1826–1884) who played for Sussex and England. It is an annual containing well over 1000 pages with full details of all first class cricket matches of the previous year, with records, tours and so forth. From its earliest years of publication it has been accepted as the 'Bible' of cricket.

What was the Plunket Shield?
It was the leading cricket competition and trophy in New Zealand first class cricket. Originally presented in 1906 by Lord Plunket, then governor-general, it was awarded up to the 1974–75 season.

What was the body line controversy?
Harold Larwood (born in 1904), played for Nottinghamshire and England and now lives in Australia, was one of the fastest bowlers of his day. He was also one of the most accurate. In the England v Australia series in 1932–3, he concentrated on body-line bowling, that is, bowling directly at the leg stump in such a way that the ball often struck the batsman. This caused great offence in Australia, which was aggravated when the visiting team won the series.

Who is the greatest all-rounder today?
Sir Garfield (Gary) Sobers, the West Indian cricketer.

What is a 'googly'?
It is the term for a ball bowled as an off-break and sent down with a leg break action at the other end.

Who is generally regarded as the finest of all wicket-keepers?
Leslie Ames (L. E. G. Ames), born in 1905. He achieved 415 stumpings in first class cricket, which is still a world record. Ames was also a very skilled and dashing batsman.

Have any bowlers ever dismissed all eleven batsmen in a Test Match?
Yes, two: J. C. Laker for England versus Australia at Manchester in 1956; S. Venkataraghavan for India versus New Zealand at Delhi in 1964–5.

What was special about the first Australians to tour England?
These thirteen men, who toured England in 1868, were Aborigines coached by an English emigré, Charles Lawrence. Sadly, one of them, King Cole (native name Brippokei), died of tuberculosis during this tour, in which the visitors had 14 wins, 14 defeats and 19 draws. Apart from playing cricket, the tourists also gave exhibitions of their native skills, dressed in possum skins.

Little Quiz 74

What do these units of measurement measure?
1. ampère
2. hertz
3. watt
4. ohm
5. kelvin
6. joule
7. coulomb

All are names of famous scientists: which of the seven were British?

What is the sea elephant's principal diet?
The sea elephant, also known as the northern elephant seal, eats octopuses and other cephalopods such as cuttle-fish and squids.

What is a cacomistle?
It is a curious nocturnal creature, related to the raccoon, and is distinguishable by the fact that half of its yard-long body is a thick, bushy, black and white banded tail.

What is a hinny?
It is the result of a cross-breeding of stallion and she-ass.

Rhinoceroses have been dying out as a family of mammals, largely through man's insatiable urge to hunt and kill them. Only a handful of species survive. Which is the most numerous?
The black rhinoceros, in central and East Africa. This creature seldom attacks humans unless roused.

Can you tell the difference between a leopard and a panther?
There isn't one. They are the same animal, and panther is the word used in India.

Which species of fox is most commonly found in Europe?
The red fox. Its Latin name is *vulpes vulpes*.

Which animal was the standard for the Roman legions?
The eagle, which was portrayed in several forms and carried by standard bearers. One form was as a gold model on the end of a pole.

Which is the only poisonous snake left in Britain?
The adder, which is a member of the viper family.

How does the humming bird hum?
By beating its wings extremely rapidly.

Why is the hoopoe so called?
The hoopoe is an attractive bird with golden plumage flecked with black and brown, and has a longish curving beak, like a scythe blade. Its call sounds like hoop-poop-poo, and its Latin name is *upupa epops*.

What is a bush baby?
A species of lemur (mostly nocturnal and tree dwelling), about the size of a squirrel, and generally grey-brown in colour. It has paws rather like human hands, with suckers on the finger ends.

How far can the Rana dalmatina species of frog jump?
Over 1.83 m (6 ft) in one leap.

Would you be safe in the presence of a broad-fronted crocodile?
Yes. It is a small crocodile from the equatorial region of west Africa, it seldom grows beyond about 1.83 m (6 ft) long and does not attack human beings.

Eagle

What is the mongoose well known for?
Killing snakes. It is a mammal with a longish tail, and it feeds on birds, small mammals and snakes.

How far can a gibbon leap in its progress through the forest?
At least 13½ m (45 ft) in one leap from one tree to the next.

What is the largest member of the deer family?
The European elk (known in Canada and the USA as the moose).

What is an alpaca?
It is a domestic species of llama which is found in South America. Its fine long coat, black or black and white, makes excellent wool.

Which of the big cats purrs?
The cheetah, or hunting leopard (*acononyx jubatus*). This splendid creature is also the fastest animal on earth, and can run at 110 mph (70 mph).

What is a tuatara?
This is a lizard-like reptile, found in the wild only on about 20 small islands in New Zealand. It is remarkable in that it is the only surviving representative of a reptile group which lived 170 million years ago. Its peculiar features include the possession of a rudimentary third or pineal eye on top of its head, and the lowest body temperature and incubation period of any reptile. It also exhibits an incredible indifference to pain. It is believed that wild tuataras enjoy a life expectancy of a century or even more.

Which birds build the smallest nests?
The Vervain and bee hummingbirds build nests which are, respectively, about the size of half a walnut shell and the size of a thimble.

What is the world's most common bird?
The red-billed quelea, frequenting the drier regions of Africa south of the Sahara. Its population may be as high as 10,000 million, and it poses a serious threat to cereal crops. The fact that about 1000 million of these birds are killed each year appears to have no real impact on this species' overall population and range.

In what part of Britain does a species of marsupial live in the wild?
A pair of red-necked wallabies escaped from a private menagerie in Staffordshire in 1939, and their descendants still thrive in the Peak District National Park.

What was the world's most dangerous 'big cat'?
This was a tigress accorded the title of the 'Champawat man-eater' and which lived in and around Nepal in India. In the eight years prior to its being shot in 1911, it had killed 438 people.

What is the largest member of the deer family native to Britain?
This is the red deer, which is found in Scotland, the Lake District and the West Country. One killed in Scotland in 1831 weighed 238kg (525lb).

Little Quiz 75
  What are the metric equivalents of these?
  1. acre
  2. foot
  3. cwt
  4. gill
  5. fathom
  6. fluid ounce
  7. peck
  8. quart
  9. square yard
  10. pennyweight

What does a combine harvester do?
It is a large machine that plies up and
down a corn crop field and cuts the ripe
corn and threshes it, to separate the
grain from the straw.

What is a forage harvester?
This cuts, chops and blows grass into a
huge heap. The grass is fed to cows as
silage in the winter.

What is silage?
It is food for cattle, in the form of hay or
straw, stored in a silo and fermented
with the help of molasses to preserve it
throughout winter.

What is natural manure?
It is animal dung which is mixed with
straw, and this is spread over land to
fertilize the soil. The technique is as old
as civilized man.

Why do farmers grow rape?
Rape is an annual plant grown chiefly in
Europe and North America. It is grown
particularly for food for sheep and pigs. It
has a lovely yellow flower. When it is
harvested, it is crushed to extract rape oil
for a variety of uses. The residue is
mashed into what is called rape cake,
and given to the animals.

What does a baling machine do?
A baling machine (or baler) picks up the
loose straw dropped by a combine
harvester and compresses it into tight
bundles, which it then shoots out onto
the ground to be picked up and piled into
stacks. The baler is pulled by a tractor.

**What are the principal corn-growing
areas of Britain?**
East Anglia and Lincolnshire. Norfolk
produces the highest corn yields of any
British county, and has done for
centuries.

What is a harrow?
It is an iron frame containing a row of
discs or spikes in echelon which is pulled
by tractor (or in some places by horse)
over ploughed earth, to break up the
lumps into fine tilth.

**Much farm machinery these days is
huge and very expensive to buy. How
does the small farmer overcome this
problem?**
He can hire the machinery from a special
contractor who buys and maintains the
machines for this purpose, or he can pay
a contractor to bring the equipment to
his fields and do the work for him.

What are a shepherd's tasks?
Basically, to care for the flock of sheep,
building and keeping in good repair the
fences round the fields on which the
sheep graze, and seeing that the sheep do
not get caught up in thickets or tree
clumps, or fall into streams and ponds.
Shepherds also are ready to help ewes
giving birth to new lambs.

What is a cereal?
It is one or other of a number of plants of
the Graminaceae family which included
wheat, barley, oats, maize, rice and
millet. The word is used to cover types of
beans and peas as well.

Hampshire Down sheep

Which animal provides veal?
Veal is the meat from calves. Calves are taken from their mothers two or three days after birth and reared in special calf pens, being fed on nuts and hay, until it is time to slaughter them.

What is seed drilling?
The seed-drill was invented in the early 18th century by Jethro Tull (1674–1741), a Berkshire lawyer and agriculturalist, and is a machine that makes a furrow in the ground, drops seeds into it at regular intervals (which can be adjusted) and then covers up the furrow.

Where is the Royal Show held?
At Stoneleigh Park, near Kenilworth in Warwickshire.

What is ley?
This is land which is temporarily sown with grass, being ploughed after one to three years (short duration ley), or after a longer period of up to ten years (long duration ley). Ley has the same meaning as the older English word, lea.

What is a Rhode Island red?
A breed of fowl which originated in and about Rhode Island in the north-eastern USA. It is a hardy, medium-sized bird, the hens noted for their large brown eggs.

What is foot-and-mouth disease?
This is an infectious viral disease of cattle, pigs, sheep and goats. The name derives from the characteristic blisters in the mouth and on the feet. While death would not always follow this infection, in Britain all diseased animals and their contacts are slaughtered as a matter of course.

What is a gilt?
A young female pig which has not produced a litter.

What is a mixed farm?
A farm where the farmer grows crops and keeps animal stock, such as cattle, pigs, poultry, etc.

What are broilers?
They are chickens reared in a special poultry house. The birds usually number several thousand to a house and they are reared to be killed and sold off as meat.

Where is dairy farming on the whole more productive in Britain?
In the western areas, where the grass grows well on gentle rolling hills and valleys.

Little Quiz 76
   What is the feminine of?
1. gaffer
2. conductor
3. ogre
4. czar
5. wizard
6. cock-sparrow
7. man-servant
8. bridegroom
9. votary
10. testator
   and the plural of?
11. dormouse
12. louse
13. house
14. man-of-war
15. court-martial
16. grotto
17. half
18. trout
19. dozen
20. veto

355

Are local councillors paid?
They get an allowance for attending meetings, plus allowances for travel and subsistence.

What is the role of a chief executive officer of a council?
He is the head of the council's paid service and has authority over all other officers so far as is necessary for efficient management and execution of the council's functions. In effect he replaces the old town clerk or clerk to the council, but has much greater responsibilities.

Can the Press attend meetings of local councils or their committees?
Yes, except if publicity would be prejudicial to the public interest by reason of the confidential nature of the business to be transacted. This covers nearly all meetings within local authorities and their committees.

Which of the local authorities is responsible for the library?
The county council. This means that a city library, which used to be under the city council, now comes under the county council.

What are rates?
They are an annual tax on property raised locally, the amount relating to the estimated annual value of the property. Rates contribute to the ability of the county and the district to provide public services for the inhabitants of the area concerned.

What is the Rate Support Grant?
It is a grant of money by central government, paid every year to local authorities to help them meet their expenditure. If it was not paid, householders and owners of industrial premises would have to pay much higher rates every year to their local authorities.

When was London's first mayor appointed?
As far back as 1191. The title Lord Mayor was first used in 1414.

Which were the first New Towns planned for England and Wales after World War II?
Basildon, Bracknell, Crawley, Harlow, Hatfield, Hemel Hempstead, Stevenage, Welwyn Garden City, Newton Aycliffe, Peterlee, Corby and Cwmbran. The first eight were all within 30 miles of London and were intended to relieve overcrowding in the capital.

Which were the first of the new towns planned for Scotland?
Cumbernauld, East Kilbride, Glenrothes and Livingston, which were to relieve overcrowding in Glasgow.

When was the old London County Council created?
By the Local Government Act of 1888.

When was the Greater London Council (GLC) formed?
In 1963, as a result of the Local Government Act. It consists of 92 councillors. The leader of the Council is elected from the political party which has the majority of the council seats.

At which time of year are local government elections supposed to be held?
In England and Wales, on the first Thursday in May or on such other days as may be determined by the home secretary of the time.

How often do county council elections take place?
Every four years, and the whole council retires altogether. Under the old system, the elections were staggered, that is, one third of the seats were contested every three years.

What is a county council?
It is the elected body governing the local affairs of a county and is the largest of the local government units. County councils were first created in 1888.

How many county councils are there in England and Wales today?
Before the Local Government Act of 1972, there were forty-six in England and thirteen in Wales. The reorganization left England with forty-five, six of which are called metropolitan district councils, and Wales with eight county councils.

Which old counties disappeared under the 1972 Act of England?
Huntingdonshire, Westmorland, Cumberland, Rutlandshire, Middlesex.

What are the names of the new Welsh counties?
Gwynedd, Clwyd, Powys, Dyfed, Gwent, West Glamorgan, Mid-Glamorgan and South Glamorgan.

What is a community council in Wales?
Briefly, it is the replacement for the old parish council which disappeared in the 1972 reorganization of local government.

How often must a parish council meet in a year?
At least four times, including one annual meeting in which local electors are allowed to take part.

What is the principal trade union of workers in local government?
NALGO, which used to stand for the National Association of Local Government Officers and was founded in 1905 by the merger of several smaller unions serving individual trades and professions serving the councils. In 1952, to widen the membership to include people working in nationalized industries and organizations such as the health service, it became the National and Local Government Officers Association, using the same letters.

What were county boroughs?
These were large towns in England and Wales which between 1888 and 1974, or for part of that period, were for local government purposes independent of the geographical counties they lay in. Initially, county borough status was conferred upon all towns with a population of over 50,000, and upon Canterbury which was somewhat smaller. Later, towns were not accorded county borough status unless their population had reached at least 100,000.

What local government area in England has a resident population of about 4,700 and a working day population of about 340,000?
The City of London.

Where in the British Isles are islands specifically entitled bailiwicks?
In the Channel Islands: the Bailiwick of Guernsey and the Bailiwick of Jersey.

In what English county are there district councils called Dacorum and Three Rivers?
Hertfordshire.

What is the most populous of the English metropolitan counties, and what are the others in descending order of population?
The West Midlands is the largest, with a population of about 2,667,000. Then follows Greater Manchester (2,605,000), West Yorkshire (2,063,000), Merseyside (1,511,000), South Yorkshire (1,312,000), and Tyne and Wear (1,149,000). Four non-metropolitan counties have in fact populations between those of Merseyside and South Yorkshire in size: they are Hampshire, Kent, Essex and Lancashire.

Where is the crossing in a cathedral?
In a cruciform cathedral or church it is
the space where the north and south
transepts intersect with eastern and
western arms, over which is usually
raised a dome on a tower with or without
a spire.

What is the origin of the term Gothic?
It was the term used by the Italian
painter and art historian, Giorgio Vasari
(1511–1574) who so described the
architecture of the 12th to 15th
centuries, because he and his
contemporaries regarded the style as
barbaric. The Goths were barbarian
peoples who overran parts of Western
Europe in the late 4th and 5th centuries.

What is an iconostasis?
It is a screen, usually of wood and/or
stone, in an Eastern European cathedral,
on which icons are placed. It divides the
east end from the remainder of the
building. The iconostasis at St Isaacs in
Leningrad is 68 m (225 ft) wide, and is
made of gilded marble and other stones.

What is a portal?
In cathedral or church terms it is an
elaborate doorway with decoration. The
portals of the Île de France cathedrals
are almost breathtaking in their
decorative and sculptural treatment.

**Which famous sculptor wrote a book
on the cathedrals of France?**
Auguste Rodin (1840–1917). In 1877
Rodin made a tour of the French
cathedrals, but it was not until 1914 that
his book *Les Cathédrales de France* was
published.

What is a *chevet* in a cathedral?
It is a word that describes a rounded or
polygonal apse at the east end of a
cathedral, when it is flanked inside by an
ambulatory with chapels radiating from
it. (An ambulatory is a covered walkway

358

behind the high altar, used for
processions). The feature is of French
origin and is to be found in many French
Gothic cathedrals, such as Notre Dame
de Paris, Chartres and Rheims. In
England, there are chevets at Gloucester
and Norwich.

What are the Ladies of the Vale?
This is the locally known phrase
describing the three spires of Lichfield
Cathedral, in Staffordshire, which from
several angles appear all to be of the
same height.

**What famous riot took place in a
Scottish cathedral?**
In 1637, rioting broke out among the
congregation in St Giles' Cathedral in
Edinburgh, when the authorities
introduced a new service book. This had
been imposed by Charles I. The disorder
began when a parishioner, Jenny Geddes,
threw her stool at the dean.

**What are the two most interesting
facts about Salisbury Cathedral?**
It was the only English cathedral to be
built in one operation, in the 13th
century. It has the tallest spire in
England, viz 123m (404ft).

**What are the most distinctive features
of St Sophia's Cathedral at Kiev in
the USSR?**
Begun in the 11th century, this, the
oldest cathedral foundation in Russia,
has 21 domes of varying periods. Today it
is no longer used as a church but is a
museum.

**Where is there a Gothic style
cathedral that is very largely built of
structural steel and concrete?**
Grace Cathedral, in San Francisco,
USA. It is built of these materials
because of the city's liability to earth
tremors. It was begun in 1910 and
completed in 1964. (See also p 97.)

Why was Klaus Emil Julius Fuchs sentenced to 14 years' imprisonment in 1950?

Fuchs was a German-born physicist who was driven out of his native land in the 1930s when Hitler came to power. He sought refuge in Britain, and during World War II he worked with other British scientists on the atomic bomb project. For several years he was a senior figure in nuclear research, and during this time he leaked secrets about the research to agents of the USSR. He was eventually caught and sentenced to fourteen years in prison.

What were the Phoenix Park Murders?

Phoenix Park is in Dublin, Eire. Here in 1882 Irish extremists who called themselves The Invincibles, murdered Lord Frederick Cavendish, newly appointed chief secretary for Ireland, and his under-secretary, Thomas Burke, using surgical knives. The murderers were caught and hanged.

What sort of criminal was Eichmann?

Colonel Adolf Eichmann, an SS officer, was the Nazi war criminal responsible for exterminating at least two million Jewish people from various European countries who had been deported to German concentration camps as part of the Nazi programme to eliminate the Jewish race. Eichmann escaped justice after World War II and fled to South America. But in 1960 Israeli agents kidnapped him, brought him to Israel and in 1962 he was put to death after trial at Tel Aviv.

Who was Al Capone?

Alphonse Capone (1898–1947) was an American gangster who for some years dominated the criminal underworld of Chicago, but whom the police were never able to arrest and prove charges against. Then in 1931, it was found that he had

deliberately evaded paying income tax. He was brought to court, found guilty and sentenced to ten years' imprisonment.

In which gaol was Oscar Wilde imprisoned for nearly two years?

Reading Gaol.

In a celebrated and still controversial murder trial held in Edinburgh in 1857 the verdict was 'not proven'. Who was the accused?

Madeleine Smith, daughter of a Glasgow architect, was on trial for poisoning her lover with arsenic. Although it was established that she had bought arsenic on three occasions, there was insufficient evidence to prove that she had seen the man during the last days before his death.

Little Quiz 77

Of which nationality were these artists?

1. Alfred Sisley
2. Van Gogh
3. Hieronymus Bosch
4. Mantegna
5. Rubens
6. Zoffany
7. Whistler
8. Jackson Pollock
9. Edvard Munch
10. Kokoschka
11. Kandinsky
12. Juan Gris
13. Fuseli
14. Klee
15. Chagall
16. Hans Arp
17. David
18. Raeburn
19. Van Dyck
20. Gwen John

When was the first police force established in Britain?

Up to 1829, constables had been appointed by country parishes and watchmen by town councils to enforce law and order. In 1829, the Metropolitan Police Act established a regular police force for London. Borough forces were introduced in 1835 and county forces in 1856.

Why are policemen often known as 'Bobbies'?

They were nicknamed 'Bobbies' after the famous home secretary Sir Robert Peel, who was responsible for the Metropolitan Police Act. Policemen were also called 'Peelers'.

Who controls the Metropolitan Police Force?

The head of the Metropolitan Police is a commissioner, appointed by the home secretary to whom the commissioner is ultimately responsible.

Who controls the county police forces in England?

Police Committees consisting of local councillors and magistrates. The committees are often known as Watch Committees. Each county force is headed by a chief constable.

What is the principal job of a policeman or policewoman?

It is to prevent crime. The first commissioner of the Metropolitan Police, Sir Richard Mayne, stated that 'policemen should make it very difficult for anyone to commit a crime . . . within that portion of the town under their charge.' Of course, the police have numerous other duties.

What are the principal qualities needed by a police detective officer?

They are dedication to the job, a sharp eye for detail, an excellent memory, the ability to judge character, a willingness to do much painstaking and sometimes unrewarding work.

What is the role of the police at political demonstrations, strike meetings, picketing of work premises and so forth?

It is the police's task to keep the peace and to uphold existing laws about demonstrations, picketing, marches and so on. Policemen and policewomen are expected to be impartial as to the points of argument and demonstration.

Do the police carry guns?

It is a long-established custom that British police forces are not normally armed, and in fact only in exceptional circumstances does any officer carry a firearm, and firearms are only issued on the authority of a very senior official. At the same time, the police are taught to understand all about firearms and to recognize every type of weapon that could be used in committing crimes of violence, and there are occasions when specialist training on the use of firearms is given for special duties.

How can the public help the police forces to prevent crime?

The most important thing the public can do is to cooperate with the police. One good way is for members of a community to make themselves more aware of the security of each others' homes, property and persons. This means agreeing to keep an eye on the house of a neighbour who goes away with his family for a holiday, and reporting at once anything suspicious to the police.

What happens when you dial '999'?

You get through to a special switchboard manned 24 hours of the day every day, whose operators ask which service you require, Fire, Ambulance or Police. The switchboard is linked to the most convenient police stations, fire stations and hospitals, and can connect you immediately with whichever one you need.

Will the police mind if they are telephoned and the alarm turns out to be a false one?
No, not at all. They do not mind.

What are the main qualifications needed to be accepted as a recruit to the police force?
In the UK, police officers have to be ready to work shifts, must be at least 5 ft 8 ins tall (5 ft 4 ins tall if a woman), to be fit and have good eyesight, to be ready to accept discipline and responsibility, have personal integrity, be able to make decisions on their own and act quickly, be tolerant of peoples from a multitude of different backgrounds, and to work as part of a team. He or she must be a British citizen, a Commonwealth citizen whose stay in the UK is not a restricted one, or a citizen of the republic of Eire.

How long is the training?
Overall, it takes two years, during which time every recruit has to be prepared to serve in uniform as a constable. The period starts with ten weeks in residence at a police training centre (15 weeks for the Metropolitan Police, at Hendon). The candidates then return to their own force and spend another two weeks or so on a course on local procedures. Then the recruit is introduced to the 'beat', that is, the patrol of the streets, to begin with in the company of an experienced constable.

What are the ranks of the police forces in the provinces?
Upwards from the bottom, they are: constable, sergeant, inspector, chief inspector, superintendent, chief superintendent, assistant chief constable and chief constable.

Is there any difference in the ranks of the Metropolitan Police?
Yes, after the rank of chief superintendent upwards, the Metropolitan Police ranks are: commander, deputy assistant commissioner, assistant commissioner, deputy commissioner and commissioner.

How many police forces are there in England and Wales?
43, including the Metropolitan Police.

How many are there in Scotland?
Six regional forces and two combined forces.

What was the Scarman Report of 1981?
Basically, it was a report of a committee of enquiry held under the chairmanship of Lord Justice Scarman into the causes and effects of the rioting in areas such as Brixton and Toxteth in Britain in the summer of 1981, and the committee made a number of recommendations. Overall, the message was that efforts must be made for relations between police and the public to be improved, especially relations between police and immigrant communities.

Little Quiz 78
Who followed as prime minister – ?
1. Benjamin Disraeli in 1880
2. A. J. Balfour in 1905
3. Herbert Henry Asquith in 1916
4. Ramsay MacDonald in 1935
5. Winston Churchill in 1955

Who followed as president of USA?
6. John Quincy Adams in 1829
7. James Buchanan in 1861
8. William McKinley in 1901
9. Franklin D. Roosevelt in 1945
10. Lyndon B. Johnson in 1969

What does the clutch of a motor car do?

It lets the engine run without driving the wheels. It is basically two round plates between the engine and the gearbox: the engine end plate turns all the time the engine is running but the other (gearbox) end plate is stationary until you let the first plate begin to engage with it. Then, when the two are tight together, the engine is connected to the gearbox and the car can move forwards or backwards, according to which gear is selected.

What is synchromesh?

It is an arrangement of gears in the gearbox that synchronizes the driving and the driven parts before they engage, thus removing the noise and judder when the gears are engaged.

What is to double-declutch?

It is a process used in changing gear downwards when the gearbox is not fitted with synchromesh on all four gears. You have to do the matching of the gear speeds yourself, and this is done by depressing the clutch pedal twice during the movement of the gear lever from one position to the next lower gear.

How does overdrive work?

It is almost a separate gearbox providing a very high gear in addition to the others in the usual gearbox. It allows high speed cruising under easy conditions, the engine turning over at a slower rate than in normal top gear.

What is a universal joint?

It is a joint or coupling which can move in every direction.

What does the choke do?

It helps get the engine started when cold, by increasing the amount of petrol passing into the carburettor when the engine is being turned over by the starter motor.

What is the 'lollipop sign'?

This is the mandatory Stop–Children sign, carried on the end of a rod by school crossing patrols. It has black letters on a circular yellow background edged with a red border.

What is a box junction?

It is a road junction, on the road surface of which is painted a pattern of yellow criss-cross lines. The rules are that drivers must not go into the box with any part of their cars unless the way through is clear, except if you are intending to turn right in which case you may wait in the box until there is a gap in the oncoming traffic to let you through safely.

What is the differential gear?

An arrangement of gears connecting two shafts in the same line, enabling one of them to rotate at a rate faster than the other, if required. When a car turns the corner, the inner driven wheel travels for less distance than the outer wheel, and therefore slower. The differential gear in the rear axle (or front, if the car is front wheel drive) lets the two wheels turn at different speeds.

What are the advance warnings for a pedestrian crossing?

If it is uncontrolled, flashing yellow beacons. The crossing itself is also marked on the road surface by alternate black and white stripes – which explains its popular name, Zebra Crossing. There are also zig-zag white marks before the crossing on your left side, for several yards, and you should never park on these zig-zags.

What is the rule about distance between your car and the one travelling in front of you?

Leave enough space between you and the vehicle ahead, so that you can pull up safely if it slows down or stops suddenly.

What is the difference between cross-ply and radial tyres?

In crossply tyres, the cords making up the carcass run diagonally across the tyre, with alternate layers at opposite angles, forming a trellis. Radial tyres have all cords running at right angles across the tyre.

What is the hard shoulder on the left side of a motorway for?

It is for stopping in an emergency only, and not for picnicking, sight-seeing or any other non-urgent purpose.

When can a car be parked on a road without lights after lighting up time?

On roads subject to the 30 mph speed limit or lower speed limit, provided they are not parked within 15 yards of a junction.

What are disc brakes?

They are external contracting brakes where brake pads close like pincers onto a disc attached to the car wheel.

When is it illegal to use the horn?

When your car is stationary, or in motion in a built-up area between the hours of 11.30 pm and 7.00 am.

What is the MSM routine you should follow when approaching road junctions of any kind?

MSM = mirror–signal–manoeuvre: this means (i) use the mirror to see if your way ahead is not at risk from anything coming up behind and to check that you have enough time to make the next move, (ii) give the correct hand signal (or electrical signal if you have the right switches) and then (iii) move forward and turn left or right, or go straight ahead, whichever you wish, provided your path is clear.

What is a mandatory road sign?

It is a sign telling you what you must do.

Most have white symbols, with borders on a blue background.

Has there ever been a motor vehicle that could travel both on road and on rail in Britain?

The London Midland and Scottish Railway acquired a Karrier 26 seat railbus early in 1931. This was fitted with both road and rail wheels, the set not in use being locked clear. In 1931 this vehicle was used in the neighbourhood of Hemel Hempstead, Hertfordshire; in the following year it was used in and around Stratford-upon-Avon. While the wheels could be set from road to rail use or vice versa inside five minutes, the experiment was not considered worthwhile and it was abandoned before the end of 1932.

Is it true that a mail coach was once attacked by a lion in England?

What really happened to the Exeter Mail shortly after it left Salisbury one night in 1816 was that it was shadowed by an animal first thought to be a large calf. When it attacked one of the leading horses, it was discovered that it was really a lioness which had escaped from a travelling menagerie. The lioness which was being chased by its owners was caught before the horse was badly injured.

Austin 7 motorcar

363

What is First Aid?
First aid is given to sustain life and to help stop deterioration in the condition of someone who is sick or injured, until expert medical help arrives.

What is the Kiss of Life?
The simple term for mouth-to-mouth resuscitation, if an injured or collapsed person has stopped breathing. Take a deep breath, cover the person's mouth or nose with yours and blow steadily into the lungs.

How do you apply artificial respiration?
If the Kiss of Life does not produce the required result, turn the casualty so that he is lying on his stomach. Kneel at the head and lean over with your hands on his shoulder blades, throwing weight forward onto your arms. Rock backwards while holding the casualty's elbows. Raise these off the ground so that his chest expands and sucks in air, then lower the elbows again, and repeat the cycle every few seconds.

How would you stop bleeding from a wound?
Apply constant firm pressure to bleeding site or just above it with a clean pad of material such as cotton wool. The use of the tourniquet is not now regarded as advisable.

What do you do to help a child with a nose bleed?
Lift him or her onto a chair in front of a table, get a bowl and gently bend his head over the bowl, to catch the blood. Persuade him to breathe in and out through his mouth, and help him to pinch his nose, holding it at the softer, fleshy part near the nose tip for a few minutes.

If this fails, what do you do next?
If you can get some ice cubes, put a number into a handkerchief, lay the child down flat on his back, and place the pack gently on the bridge of the nose, taking it off from time to time.

What is a splint?
In first aid, a piece of wood or other rigid material for placing under or along a broken limb, to be anchored to the limb by means of handkerchiefs or lengths of string tied at intervals, though not at the actual injury site.

What action do you take if someone's clothes are on fire?
Soak the clothes in water as soon as possible, and if water is not available, roll the casualty over into a blanket or overcoat to try to smother the flames or smouldering. Don't attempt to remove the clothing once the flames are out.

What do you do if the casualty faints from the shock of an injury?
If the casualty appears to be coming back to consciousness and slipping out again, keep talking gently to him, to get him to respond, and that way he may stay conscious.

What is the normal temperature of the human body?
About 98.4 degrees F, 37°C.

What should you do about a blister?
Leave it alone until you can get to a surgery.

What should a first aid kit contain as a basic minimum?
Triangular bandages, large pieces of sticking plaster, some antiseptic cream, sterile gauze pads, antibiotic powder (a useful addition), and some safety pins. Probably a bottle of iodine would also be advisable.

What is the average pulse rate in the human being?
Anything between about 70 and 80 beats per minute is about normal.

What are the important things to remember when a person has been poisoned and you have sent for an ambulance?

You may not know what he has swallowed, and you should try to find out. It will help the medical team if you go with the patient to the hospital so that you can tell them when the poison was taken, what it was if you know, and how long the patient has been conscious or unconscious.

How does frost 'bite'?

Intense cold stops the blood circulating properly, and extremities like fingers and toes suffer skin damage. The pain is best eased by warming the whole body gently near the fire or radiator. Do not attempt to warm the frost-bitten hand or foot on its own in hot water.

What should you do if a diabetic suddenly complains of feeling faint?

He may be about to pass into a coma, in which case give him a little sugar as soon as you can; a lump or two or a boiled sweet would suffice in most cases. Then you should ring for an ambulance or get the local doctor to come as soon as possible.

What do you do to assist someone who has been injured by electric shock?

Do not touch the person if he is still in contact with the electrical appliance. Switch off the appliance, whatever it is, and remove the plug from the wall socket. Push the appliance away from the person, and then if he has been stunned, try to revive him gently with artificial respiration. You should also send at once for the doctor or ambulance.

How should you handle someone who appears to be suffering from amnesia?

There is no first aid treatment for this, which can be a serious medical problem. However, you should keep the person quiet and comfortable, then contact the police in case a reported missing person is involved.

What should you do if you find someone sleepwalking?

Do not waken the sleeper. If the person is not in danger, take him lightly by the elbow and lead him back to bed. Once in bed, the sleepwalker should be gently covered. It is then best to remain for a little while, in case he wakes and is confused.

How should you deal with someone suffering from hypothermia?

If it occurs indoors, place the patient between blankets. Allow the temperature to rise gradually, but do not force it up with hot water bottles or electric blankets. Warm sweet drinks should be given and the room warmed. If outdoors, get the person to rest in as sheltered a location as possible. Wrap in dry clothing, a sleeping bag or aluminium foil if available. Warm sweet drinks should be given if possible.

Little Quiz 79

Who wrote the novels?

1. *The Prime of Miss Jean Brodie*
2. *The Old Men at the Zoo*
3. *A Passage to India*
4. *The Go-Between*
5. *Animal Farm*

Who wrote the music for these choral works?

6. *Carmina Burana*
7. *Das Lied von der Erde* (Song of the Earth)
8. *Belshazzar's Feast*
9. *The Creation*
10. *Hiawatha*

Little Quiz Answers

Little Quiz 1, page 13

1. 1087 1100		15. 1914	
2 1589 1610		16. 1939	
3. 1888 1918		17. 1944	
4. 1558 1603		18. 1942	
5. 1306 1329		19. 1916	
6. 1001–1014		20. 1809	
7. 1556 1598		21. Hannibal	
8. 1572–1584		22. T. Q. Flamininus	
9. 1715 1774		23. Gaius Marius	
10. 1689 1725		24. Julius Caesar	
11. 1854		25. Octavian	
12. 1801		26. L. Licinius Lucullus	
13. 46BC		27. Constantine	
14. 1460		28. Charles Martel	

Little Quiz 2, page 15

1. Russian
2. Italian
3. Belgian
4. Czech
5. Austrian
6. French
7. German-French
8. Austrian (b. Bohemia)
9. English of Swedish descent
10. American

Little Quiz 3, page 17

1. Titian	20. Sir Basil Spence
2. Maclise	21. Jörn Utzon
3. Copley	22. Whitehall, London
4. Delaroche	23. Rangoon, Burma
5. Pieter Brueghel the Elder	24. Leningrad, Russia
6. David	25. Nr. Madrid, Spain
7. Munkaczy	26. Paris, France
8. West	27. Moscow, Russia
9. Bree	28. Dublin, Ireland
10. Botticelli	28. Virginia, US
11. Sir John Soane	30. Houston, Texas, US
12. Mies van der Rohe	31. Arlington, Va., US
13. James Gibbs	32. Istanbul, Turkey
14. Robert Adam	
15. Sir Edwin Lutyens	
16. Frank Lloyd Wright	
17. Inigo Jones	
18. Sir Denys Lasdun	
19. Sir Christopher Wren	

Little Quiz 4, page 27

1. Macedonia	8. Albania
2. Epirus	9. Twice
3. Russia	10. once
4. Sweden	11. four times
5. Egypt	12. twice
6. Scotland	13. twice
7. Ireland	

Little Quiz 5, page 29

1. 3	16. 1000
2. 4	17. 2240
3. 4	18. 14
4. 5	19. 1 million
5. 6	20. 4
6. 5	21. 2.54 cm
7. 6	22. 0.9144 metre
8. 3	23. 20.1168 metres
9. 12	24. 1.609 km
10. 8	25. 1.852 km
11. 36	26. 0.568 litres
12. $16\frac{1}{2}$	27. 4.546 litres
13. 1760	28. 36.368 litres
14. 4840	29. 28.35 grams
15. 640	30. 0.45 kg

Little Quiz 6, page 37

1. O	16. Aa
2. R	17. J
3. K	18. E
4. T	19. C
5. N	20. B
6. X	21. I
7. Y	22. G
8. A	23. D
9. S	24. P
10. Q	25. F
11. V	26. H
12. Z	27. L
13. W	
14. U	
15. M	

Little Quiz 7, page 61

1. Joseph	5. Daniel
2. Noah	6. Jonah
3. David	7 Naaman
4. Elijah	8. Judas Iscariot

9. Paul
10. Stephen
11. Thomas
12. Gallio
13. Judas Iscariot
14. Peter
15. the Levite
16. Genesis
17. Genesis
18. Exodus
19. Joshua
20. Judges
21. Judges
22. First Book of Samuel
23. First Book of Kings
24. Second Book of Kings
25. Exodus
26. Deuteronomy
27. First Book of Kings
28. Daniel
29. Genesis

Little Quiz 8, page 65

1. Respondez s'il vous plait (please reply)
2. Senatus Populusque Romanus (The Senate and Roman people)
3. Dame of the British Empire
4. United States of America
5. Union of Soviet Socialist Republics
6. Palestine Liberation Organization
7. Anno Domini (In the year of Our Lord)
8. Fidei Defensor (Defender of the Faith)
9. Before Christ
10. American Society of Cinematographers
11. Birmingham Small Arms
12. absent without leave
13. South East Asia Treaty Organization
14. Pre-Raphaelite Brotherhood
15. Royal New Zealand Navy
16. Royal Australian Air Force
17. United States Supreme Court
18. United Nations Educational, Scientific and Cultural Organization
19. Vertical take-off and landing
20. Fellow of the Linnaean Society
21. Fellow of the Royal Society of Literature
22. Grand Cross Knight of the Order of the Bath
23. Bachelor of Arts
24. Doctor of Philosophy
25. Imperial Chemical Industries Ltd
26. Massachusetts Institute of Technology
27. London Symphony Orchestra
28. Royal Canadian Mounted Police
29. Royal Canadian Navy (also, Royal College of Nursing)
30. New Jersey, US
31. Isle of Man
32. Irish Republican Army
33. Value Added Tax
34. United Kingdom Atomic Energy Authority
35. Associate Member of the Town Planning Institute
36. caught and bowled
37. compare (from *confer*)
38. hot and cold
39. Louisiana, US
40. Lord Chief Justice
41. died (from *obiit*)
42. care of
43. for example (from *exempli gratia*)
44. namely (from *videlicat*)
45. Teachta Dala (Deputy of Dail, the Irish Parliament), also Territorial Decoration
46. pages
47. painted it (from *pinxit*)
48. Member of the Order of Merit
49. Jesus Christ
50. Department of Health and Social Security
51. computer language used in scientific work
52. Fellow of the Royal College of Surgeons
53. Foreign and Commonwealth office
54. Standard Book Number
55. *Mitteleuropäische Zeit* (Central European Time)
56. United Nations Industrial Development Organization
57. Bachelor of Medicine
58. non-commissioned officer
59. New South Wales
60. Minnesota
61. World Health Organization
62. Unilateral Declaration of Independence
63. European Economic Community
64. Intelligence Quotient
65. International Monetary Fund
66. European Free Trade Association
67. institute
68. para-amino-salicylic acid, used in TB treatment
69. Province of Quebec
70. Regius Professor
71. Search and rescue and homing
72. *Bureau International des Poids et Mesures*, International Bureau of Weights and Measures

Little Quiz 9, page 67

1. The Cinque Ports are Hastings, New Romney, Hythe, Sandwich and Dover
2. 46
3. 8
4. 12
5. 50
6. 144
7. Mount Everest 9579 metres (29,002 feet)
8. Off the Philippines in the South Pacific
9. Nearly 12,000 metres (36,000 feet)
10. Australia
11. Atlantic
12. Pacific
13. Pacific
14. Atlantic
15. Mediterranean Sea
16. 22.8 million
17. 2.3 million
18. 13.7 million
19. 21.3 million
20. 30,000
21. 28,500
22. 214 million
23. 2 million
24. 61 million
25. 4.6 million
26. 13.6 million
27. 4.7 million
28. 52.6 million
29. 10 million
30. 218,000
31. 318,000
32. 3.7 million
33. 2.9 million
34. 108 million
35. 12 million
36. 92,000

Little Quiz 10, page 77

1. Newcastle
2. Liverpool
3. Arsenal
4. Manchester United
5. Manchester United
6. Manchester United
7. Arsenal
8. Newcastle United
9. Newcastle United
10. Manchester City
11. Wolverhampton Wanderers
12. Everton
13. Leeds United
14. Ten times (to 1977)
15. Eleven times (to 1977)
16. Once, in 1966
17. Twice, in 1908 and 1948
18. Montreal, Canada
19. Nowhere, because of the First World War
20. 1924
21. Ingmar Johannson of Sweden, in 1959
22. 1829
23. 22 yards (20.12 metres)
24. 28 inches (71.12 cm)
25. 9 inches (22.86 cm)
26. 8 feet 8 inches (2.64 metres)
27. 4¼ inches (10.8 cm)
28. It should weigh not less than 5½ ounces (156 grams) and not more than 5¾ ounces (184 grams)

Little Quiz 11, page 83

1. sow
2. cow
3. heifer
4. filly
5. bitch
6. mare
7. ewe
8. hind
9. lioness
10. wether-lamb
11. billy-goat
12. tiger
13. tom-cat
14. peacock

Little Quiz 12, page 85

1. blue
2. red
3. black
4. purple
5. green
6. silver

Little Quiz 13, page 91

1. asses
2. boxes
3. cargoes
4. potatoes
5. folios
6. pianos
7. calves
8. chiefs
9. gulfs
10. roofs
11. wharves
12. turfs
13. allies
14. alleys
15. brothers or brethren
16. oxen
17. cod
18. gross
19. score
20. species

21. brace
22. deer
23. toys

24. halos
25. cliffs

19. wizard
20. marquis
21. lad
22. bridegroom

23. sir
24. sultan
25. abbot

Little Quiz 14, page 99

1. West Germany
2. France
3. Sweden
4. Italy
5. UK
6. USSR
7. Japan
8. France
9. UK
10. Syria
11. Venezuala
12. UK (Great Britain)

13. Luxemburg
14. Morocco
15. Canada
16. Uruguay
17. Egypt
18. Ireland (Eire)
19. Burma
20. Zambia
21. Kenya
22. Chrysler
23. Ford
24. General Motors

Little Quiz 18, page 125

1. 1797
2. 1648
3. 1420
4. 1713
5. 1842
6. 1697

7. 1559
8. 1802
9. 1829
10. 1858

Little Quiz 19, page 127

1. sept
2. vingt
3. quatre-vingts
4. mille

5. zwei
6. zehn
7. fünfzig
8. hundert

Little Quiz 15, page 103

1. England
2. music
3. shoemakers
4. travellers
5. fishermen
6. Ireland
7. physicians and painters
8. Scotland
9. Wales
10. carpenters and lost causes

11. Germany
12. Spain
13. Brazil
14. Russia
15. Denmark
16. France
17. Turkey
18. India (and U.K.!)
19. New Zealand
20. Wales

Little Quiz 20, page 129

1. Nepal and Tibet
2. France
3. Switzerland
4. Nepal and India
5. Tanzania
6. Argentina
7. Alaska, US
8. Mexico
9. USSR
10. Nepal
11. Italy
12. South Pacific
13. Indonesia
14. Caucasus Mountains, USSR
15. Japan
16. New Zealand
17. Italy
18. Hawaii, US
19. Iceland
20. New Zealand
21. Asia
22. Africa
23. Africa
24. Asia
25. Africa
26. Australia
27. Canada and US
28. Australia

Little Quiz 16, page 111

1. Cain
2. Eve
3. Joseph's brothers
4. Moses
5. Delilah
6. Samuel
7. Goliath
8. David

9. Rehoboam
10. Elisha
11. Job
12. God
13. Jesus
14. Pilate
15. Agrippa

Little Quiz 17, page 113

1–5. there isn't one
6. proprietrix
7. spinster
8. countess
9. nun
10. matron
11. governess

12. patroness
13. songstress
14. traitress
15. executrix
16. hero
17. fox
18. negro

29. Canada and US
30. USSR
31. USSR
32. Chad–Niger–Nigeria
33. Baffin Land
34. Venezuela
35. Wales
36. Scotland
37. Canada and US
38. Uganda–Tanzania–Kenya
39. US
40. Northern Ireland

Little Quiz 21, page 141

1. 40,075 kilometres (24,901 miles)
2. 509,608,000 square kilometres (196,836,000 square miles)
3. 143,928,000 square kilometres (55,786,000 square miles)
4. 5,976 tonnes plus 18 noughts (5882 tons)
5. About 5,000,000,000 years
6. Nearly 148,800,000 kilometres (nearly 93,000,000 miles)
7. 382,166 kilometres (238,854 miles)
8. Six
9. Europe, Asia, Africa, two Americas, Australia and Oceania
10. Four
11. Pacific, Atlantic, Indian, Arctic
12. 4,000,000,000
13. About 6,500,000,000
14. Yes, about 3,000 quintillion, that is, 3,000,000,000,000,000,000,000
15. About 500,000,000
16. About 300,000,000
17. About 142,000,000
18. The American boxer Joe Louis
19. Louis Philippe, king of France
20. Joan Holland
21. Richard Neville, Earl of Warwick
22. The Prince Regent, later George IV, king of Great Britain and Ireland
23. Sir George Robey
24. Dr Hewlett Johnson
25. Anne, queen of Great Britain and Ireland
26. Elizabeth, queen of Bohemia, daughter of James I of England
27. Greta Garbo, Swedish film star
28. Jenny Lind, Swedish opera singer

370

29. Otto von Bismarck, Chancellor of Germany
30. Edward I, king of England
31. Lily Langtry, English actress
32. Andrew Jackson, 7th President of US
33. Napoleon I, French emperor
34. Elizabeth I, queen of England
35. Charles II, king of England
36. Oliver Cromwell, lord protector of England
37. Duchess of Marlborough
38. Personification of US government
39. Julius Caesar
40. Adolf Hitler
41. Emperor Augustus
42 Henry VIII
43. Philip II of Spain
44 Robert Schumann
45 Dauphin of France, Lord Darnley, The Earl ot Bothwell
46 Ptolemy XIII
47 Albert, Prince Consort
48. The Duke of Marlborough
49. William Shakespeare
50. Napoleon I
51. Louis XVI of France
52. She never married
53. Emperor Constantine
54. Francis of Lorraine
55. Louis VII of France, Henry II of England
56. Robert Browning
57. She never married
58. George, prince of Denmark

Little Quiz 22, page 143

The correct order is

1. New York
2. Tokyo
3. Mexico City
4. London
5. Buenos Aires
6. Moscow
7. Shanghai
8. Los Angeles
9. Chicago
10. São Paulo

Little Quiz 23, page 143

1. Hydrogen
2. Magnesium
3. Mercury
4. Lead
5. Oxygen
6. Tin
7. Silver
8. Gold
9. Uranium
10. Carbon
11. Antimony
12. Potassium
13. Sodium
14. Molybdenum

15. Barium
16. Manganese
17. Calcium
18. Chromium
19. Iodine
20. Copper
21. Radium
22. Arsenic
23. Cobalt
24. Chlorine
25. Iron
26. Fermium
27. 47
28. 8
29. 16
30. 9
31. 80
32. 13
33. 94
34. 1
35. 88
36. 30
37. 7
38. 93
39. 6
40. 92
41. 82
42. 53
43. 79
44. Chlorine, Fluorine, Iodine, Bromine
45. Neon, Helium, Argon, Xenon, Krypton
46. 11
47. 11
48. 2
49. 7
50. 21

Little Quiz 24, page 145

1. 1789–1797
2. 1801–1809
3. 1825–1829
4. 1861–1865
5. 1869–1877
6. 1875–1889 and 1893–1897
7. 1897–1901
8. 1901–1909
9. 1913–1921
10. 1929–1933
11. 1933–1945
12. 1945–1953
13. 1961–1963

Little Quiz 25, page 153

1. Schilling
2. Lev
3. Rial
4. Markka
5. Dirham
6. Yen
7. Peso
8. Escudo
9. Bolívar
10. Baht
11. Riyal
12. Rouble
13. Dollar
14. Guarani
15. Zloty
16. Pound
17. Forint
18. Kyat
19. Rupiah
20. Franc
21. Elgar
22. Delius
23. Vaughan Williams
24. Arnold Bax
25. John Ireland
26. Beethoven
27. Mozart
28. Mendelssohn
29. Bach
30. Tchaikovsky
31. violin
32. piano
33. horn
34. flute
35. cello
36. trumpet
37. organ
38. viola
39. clarinet
40. harpsichord

Little Quiz 26, page 159

1. Nelson, England
2. Agrippa, Rome
3. Rodney, England
4. Jellicoe, England
5. Togo, Japan
6. Tromp, Holland
7. Don John, Austria
8. de Tourville, France
9. Dewey, US
10. Jervis, England
11. Cassius Chaerea and Co.
12. John Wilkes Booth
13. Gavrial Prinzep
14. Balthasar Gerard
15. Ravaillac
16. Vinayak Godse
17. Lee Oswald
18. John Felton
19. John Bellingham
20. James Earl Ray

Little Quiz 27, page 177

1. Alberta, Canada
2. Wales
3. France
4. Ukraine, USSR
5. Holland
6. Virginia, US

7. Alberta, Canada
8. Spain
9. East Germany
10. Wales
11. Arizona, US
12. Australia
13. West Germany
14. Italy
15. Ireland
16. Utah, US
17. England
18. Czechoslovakia
19. An area of New York City, US
20. Peru

Little Quiz 28, page 181
1. Vincent–HRD
2. Velocette
3. BSA
4. Ariel
5. Norton

Little Quiz 29, page 183
1. herd
2. pack
3. school
4. colony
5. yoke
6. leap
7. sleuth
8. labour
9. troop
10. pack
11. cast
12. paddling
13. muster
14. nye
15. flight
16. charm
17. colony
18. gaggle
19. sedge
20. exaltation
21. 22 November
22. 31 October
23. 24 May
24. Christmas Day, 25 December
25. 8 May

26. 1 August
27. 5 November
28. 31 December
29. 1 March
30. 23 April
31. Jowett
32. Wolseley

33. Renault
34. Volkswagen
35. Rolls Royce
36. Humber
37. Riley
38. Jaguar
39. Lancia

Little Quiz 30, page 191
1. Polish
2. American
3. German
4. French
5. American
6. Russian
7. Irish
8. Irish
9. Indian, born in Trinidad
10. Scottish
11. American
12. Alexander Dumas père
13. William Thackeray
14. Herman Wouk
15. George Orwell
16. James Hilton
17. Arthur Conan Doyle
18. Katherine Winsor
19. John Buchan
20. Margaret Mitchell

21. Patrick White
22. Herman Melville
23. Boris Pasternak
24. Leo Tolstoy
25. Guy de Maupassant
26. Alan Paton
27. P. G. Wodehouse
28. Rudyard Kipling
29. Winston Churchill
30. Benjamin Disraeli
31. Feodor Dostoyevsky
32. Sweden
33. Italy
34. Germany
35. Germany
36. Greece
37. England
38. Egypt
39. Wales
40. Ireland
41. England

Little Quiz 31, page 195
1. Arthur Conan Doyle
2. Charles Dickens
3. Daniel Defoe
4. Jules Verne
5. Rider Haggard
6. 'Sapper'
7. Baroness Orczy
8. Somerset Maugham
9. Robert Louis Stevenson
10. Henry Fielding
11. Oscar Wilde

12. Alexander Dumas père
13. George Bernard Shaw
14. C. P. Snow
15. Mark Twain
16. W. E. Johns
17. F. Scott Fitzgerald
18. Henry Williamson
19. C. S. Forester
20. Thomas Hughes
21. Richard Sheridan

Little Quiz 32, page 201
1. J. M. W. Turner
2. Frans Hals
3. Thomas Gainsborough

4. Holman Hunt
5. W. P. Frith
6. Sir John Millais

7. Jean Meissonier
8. John Constable
9. Pierre Renoir
10. Leonardo da Vinci
11. French
12. Russian
13. German
14. Dutch
15. American
16. Dutch
17. French
18. Scottish
19. Swiss
20. English
21. Florence, Italy
22. Amsterdam, Holland
23. London, England
24. New York, US
25. Madrid, Spain
26. London, England
27. Leningrad, USSR
28. Tokyo, Japan
29. New York, US
30. London, England

Little Quiz 33, page 203

1. US
2. Germany
3. Japan
4. Germany
5. Switzerland
6. Peru
7. US
8. UK
9. France
10. UK
11. (1) New Zealand
    (2) Chemistry 1908
12. (1) Norway
    (2) Peace 1922
13. (1) US
    (2) Chemistry 1960
14. (1) France
    (2) Physics 1903 (with Pierre and Marie Curie)
15. (1) Germany
    (2) Physics 1921
16. (1) US
    (2) Literature 1954
17. (1) Australia
    (2) Physiology and Medicine 1960 (with Peter Medawar)
18. (1) South Africa
    (2) Peace 1960
19. (1) England
    (2) Physiology and Medicine 1929 (with Christian Eijkman)
20. (1) Ireland
    (2) Literature 1969
21. (1) US
    (2) Peace 1906
22. (1) Germany
    (2) Literature 1902
23. (1) Russia
    (2) Physiology and Medicine 1904
24. (1) Sweden
    (2) Chemistry 1903
25. (1) Italy
    (2) Physics 1909 (with C. F. Braun)
26. Dragonflies
27. Butterflies and moths
28. Beetles
29. Bugs
30. Grasshoppers, crickets
31. Fleas
32. Penguins
33. Gannets, cormorants, pelicans, etc.
34. Swans, geese and ducks
35. Pigeons, doves, etc.
36. Owls
37. Ostriches
38. Mosses
39. Ferns
40. Blue-green algae
41. Chicken
42. Fox
43. Cattle
44. The domestic cat
45. Horse
46. Bear
47. Rabbit
48. The house mouse
49. Chimpanzee
50. African elephant
51. Lemon
52. Carrot
53. Coconut
54. Black pepper
55. Maize, sweet corn
56. Cabbage
57. Oats
58. Peony
59. Sunflower
60. Buttercup

Little Quiz 34, page 207

1. 6
2. 1,000
3. 500
4. 1,427
5. 999
6. 1977

7. 85
8. 333
9. 1146
10. 19
11. Joseph Heller
12. Ernest Hemingway
13. Thomas Mann
14. Charlotte Bronte
15. Albert Camus
16. Pietro Mascagni, 1889
17. Giuseppe Verdi, 1889
18. Richard Strauss, 1912
19. Leos Janácek, 1904
20. Peter Tchaikovsky, 1879
21. Benjamin Britten, 1971
22. Hector Berlioz, 1858
23. Maurice Ravel, 1925
24. Wolfgang Amadeus Mozart, 1791
25. Jules Massenet, 1884
26. Adolphe Adam, 1841
27. Béla Bartok, 1926
28. Nikolai Rimsky-Korsakov, 1910
29. Igor Stravinsky, 1913
30. Hans Werner Henze, 1958

Little Quiz 35, page 215

3. Great Britain
7. Tonga
8. Spain
9. Sweden
11. Virginia
12. Virginia
13. Tennessee
14. South Carolina
15. Pennsylvania
16. Virginia
17. Louisiana
18. Virginia
19. Mississippi
20. Tennessee

Little Quiz 36, page 221

1. The Twelve Caesars:
   Julius Caesar (dictator, 48–44BC)
   Augustus (emperor, 27BC–14AD)
   Tiberius (14–37)
   Caligula (37–41)
   Claudius (41–54)
   Nero (54–68)
   Galba (68)
   Otho (68–9)
   Vitellius (69)
   Vespasian (69–79)
   Titus (79–81)
   Domitian (81–96)

2. English Royal Dynasties since 1066
   Normans
   Plantagenets
   Lancastrians
   Yorkists
   Tudors
   Stuarts
   Hanoverians
   Windsors
3. The Tudor monarchs
   Henry VII 1485–1509
   Henry VIII 1509–1547
   Edward VI 1547–1553
   Mary I 1553–1558
   Elizabeth I 1558–1603
4. Brian Boru
5. Kenneth McAlpine
6. Louis XIV 1643–1715
   Louis XV 1715–1774
   Louis XVI 1774–1793
7. Louis XV was the great grandson of Louis XIV; Louis XVI was the grandson of Louis XV
8. Rhodri Mawr
9. France, 1959–69
10. Poland, 1919
11. Portugal, 1928–51
12. Liberia, 1944–71
13. Finland, 1944–46
14. Egypt, 1956–70
15. Ghana, 1960–66
16. Indonesia 1945–66
17. Brazil, 1930–45 and 1951–54

Little Quiz 44, page 255

1. huit	6. tausend
2. trente	7. quaranta
3. soixante-dix	8. cinque cento
4. drei	9. otto
5. zwanzig	10. cinco

Little Quiz 45, page 259

1. Wales
2. Karakoram – India
3. India
4. USSR
5. Turkey
6. Canada
7. Greenland
8. USA
9. Ecuador
10. Japan

Little Quiz 46, page 261

1. Emperor Claudius
2. Alexander the Great
3. Prasutagus
4. Venutius
5. 1) Henry V of Germany
   2) Geoffrey of Anjou
6. Louis XIV
7. Thutmosis II
8. William III
9. Edward III
10. Richard I

Little Quiz 47, page 263

1. Texas, USA
2. India
3. New Hampshire, USA
4. France
5. France
6. West Indies
7. Switzerland
8. Germany
9. Lebanon
10. Belgium

Little Quiz 48, page 265

1. 871–900	6. 1310–1370
2. 1504–06	7. 1520–1566
3. 1740–1786	8. 1762–1796
4. 1215–1270	9. 1040–1057
5. 1016	10. 1194–1240

Little Quiz 49, page 271

1. Admiral Sturdee
2. Napoleon
3. Lord Kitchener
4. Arminius
5. Marlborough
6. Lord Wolseley
7. Ahab, king of Israel
8. Julius Caesar
9. Athelstan, king of England
10. Admiral Duncan

Little Quiz 50, page 277

1. France	6. Czechoslovakia
2. USSR	7. Holland
3. USA	8. Germany
4. Italy	9. Britain
5. Japan	10. Sweden

Little Quiz 51, page 279

1. Deoxyribonucleic acid
2. Her Majesty's Stationery Office
3. Central Intelligence Agency (USA)
4. Schutzstaffel (Nazi secret police)
5. University College Hospital (London)
6. Baronet
7. Oxford University Dramatic Society
8. Cambridge University Press
9. National Union of Students
10. Doctor of Letters (Litterarum)

Little Quiz 52, page 281

1. form
2. earth
3. nest or bike
4. hive
5. set
6. drey
7. lair or den
8. eyrie
9. web
10. warren or burrow

Little Quiz 53, page 283

1.	1627–1628	11.	1899–1900
2.	1347	12.	1689
3.	1648	13.	1453
4.	AD 70	14.	1649
5.	1807	15.	1799
6.	1191	16.	1814
7.	1868	17.	1899–1900
8.	1812	18.	212 BC
9.	1884–5	19.	52 BC
10.	1857	20.	1683

Little Quiz 54, page 289

1.	1789–1794	6.	1917–1918
2.	1857–1858	7.	1773–1781
3.	1922	8.	1642–1647
4.	AD 61	9.	49–48 BC
5.	1936–1939	10.	1911

Little Quiz 55, page 291

1.	or	6.	vert
2.	argent	7.	purpure
3.	gules	8.	tenne
4.	azure	9.	sanguine
5.	sable	10.	murrey

Little Quiz 56, page 295

1. Lothian
2. Mid-Glamorgan
3. Cornwall
4. Kent
5. Sussex
6. Lincolnshire
7. Hampshire
8. Derbyshire
9. Northumberland
10. Cheshire
11. Hertfordshire
12. Cornwall
13. Suffolk
14. Norfolk
15. Norfolk
16. Sussex
17. Berkshire
18. Clwyd
19. Dyfed
20. Strathclyde

1. France
2. Switzerland
3. Syria
4. West Germany
5. Switzerland
6. Italy
7. Syria
8. Belgium
9. France
10. Spain

Little Quiz 57, page 299

1.	West Germany	2.	Norway
3.	Denmark	7.	Sicily
4.	Sweden	8.	Portugal
5.	USSR	9.	France
6.	Turkey	10.	Hungary

Little Quiz 58, page 303

1. Spain
2. Scotland
3. Kansas, USA
4. Turkey in Europe
5. Jordan
6. Switzerland
7. Denmark
8. Mexico
9. France
10. Northern Ireland
11. Belgium
12. Sudan
13. West Germany
14. India
15. USSR
16. China
17. Argentine
18. Japan
19. England
20. Italy

Little Quiz 59, page 305

1. West Sussex
2. Essex
3. Suffolk
4. Norfolk
5. Hertfordshire
6. Cleveland
7. Humberside
8. Hampshire
9. Surrey

$2+5 \times 3-1 \div 2 = 10$

10. Derbyshire
11. Lancashire
12. West Glamorgan
13. Gwynedd
14. Mid-Glamorgan
15. Clwyd
16. Gwent
17. Dyfed
18. Powys
19. Dyfed

Little Quiz 60, page 307

1. Earl of Clarendon
2. Baron Delamere
3. Earl of Portsmouth
4. Earl of Woolton
5. Marquess of Anglesey
6. Duke of Wellington
7. Viscount Scarsdale
8. Earl of Lichfield
9. Viscount Mersey
10. Marquis of Zetland

Little Quiz 61, page 313

1. Bragging or boasting
2. Attempting to achieve or obtain the impossible
3. Making plans that will never take effect
4. Trying to find out the value of a present that someone has given you
5. Showing off
6. Resolving to improve attitudes or behaviour, and sticking to it
7. Wasting energy trying to overcome obstacles that are not there
8. Wasting time trying to get people to keep up interest in something they are no longer interested in
9. Being realistic
10. Exaggerating

Little Quiz 62, page 315

1. 1.00 pm
2. 2.00 pm
3. 7.30 pm
4. 1.00 pm
5. 7.00 pm
6. 8.00 pm

7. 10.00 pm
8. 7.00 pm
9. 9.00 am
10. midnight

Little Quiz 63, page 317

1. Cantuar
2. Ebor
3. Oxon
4. Cestr
5. Petriburg
6. Roffen
7. Carliol
8. Sarum
9. Elien
10. Exon
11. Dunelm

Little Quiz 64, page 323

1. violet
2. red
3. dark green banded
4. yellow
5. red and green
6. deep blue
7. green
8. bluey-white
9. green with red spots
10. all colours

Little Quiz 65, page 325

1. Epic Poetry
2. History
3. Astronomy
4. Song and Dance
5. Comedy
6. Lyric Poetry and Music
7. Love and Poetry and Mime
8. Tragedy
9. Sacred song

Little Quiz 66, page 327

1. skin
2. brain
3. blood
4. hardening
5. eye
6. muscle
7. mind
8. chest
9. intestine
10. joint
11. inflammation
12. cutting

13. outflow	18. kidney	
14. falling	19. ear	
15. eye	20. nose	
16. gall bladder	21. bladder	
17. liver	22. lung	

Little Quiz 67, page 331

1. second son of Adam and Eve
2. one of the 3 faithful Jews who escaped from the fiery furnace
3. youngest of Joseph's brothers
4. king who entertained Abraham
5. last king of Babylon before it fell to Cyprus, 539 BC
6. mother of John the Baptist
7. great friend of King David
8. a king of Judah
9. high priest in time of both David and Solomon
10. nephew of Abraham
11. she was turned into a pillar of salt
12. one of the main sects of Judaism in Jesus Christ's time
13. nomads defeated in battle by both Saul and David
14. the original inhabitants of Jerusalem
15. interpreters of law
16. people who lived in tents and abstained from alcohol: praised by Jeremiah
17. Gallio
18. the prodigal son
19. Mary Magdalene
20. Joseph

Little Quiz 68, page 335

1. Vitus
2. Sebastian
3. Catherine of Bologna
4. Giles
5. Dunstan
6. Stephen
7. Bernard of Clairvaux
8. Joseph
9. Nicholas of Myra – Santa Claus
10. Giles
11. Antony
12. Gerard Majella
13. Andrew
14. Luke
15. Valentine
16. Ambrose
17. Jerome
18. Antony of Padua
19. Gabriel
20. Christopher
21. James
22. Christopher
23. Brigid
24. Drogo
25. Matthew
26. Gregory the Great
27. Peter of Alcantara
28. Paula
29. Francis de Sales
30. Anne
31. Genevieve
32. David
33. Isidore the Farmer
34. Gertrude
35. Olaf
36. Severino
37. Joseph
38. Barnabas
39. Nicetas
40. George

Little Quiz 69, page 339

1. Transport and General Workers' Union
2. National Union of Journalists
3. National Union of Teachers
4. Civil and Public Services Association
5. Union of Shop, Distributive and Allied Workers
6. National Union of Public Employees
7. Confederation of Health Service Employees

8. Associated Society of Locomotive Engineers and Firemen
9. Association of Scientific, Technical and Managerial Staffs
10. National Graphical Association

Little Quiz 70, page 341
1. Kenya
2. Cyprus
3. Argentina
4. Germany
5. Poland
6. USA
7. France
8. China
9. Eire
10. Israel

Little Quiz 71, page 345
1. Canada
2. Asia Minor
3. Tibet
4. Canada
5. Bolivia and Peru
6. USSR
7. USSR
8. Canada
9. Wales
10. Scotland

Little Quiz 72, page 347
1. Tanzania
2. Canada and USA
3. New Zealand
4. USA
5. Zimbabwe-Zambia
6. India
7. Guyana
8. Switzerland
9. Chile
10. Ecuador
11. Antarctica
12. Sicily
13. Martinique
14. Congo
15. USSR
16. Japan

Little Quiz 73, page 349
1. sodium carbonate
2. sodium chloride
3. magnesium sulphate
4. sodium sulphate
5. deuterium oxide
6. sodium hydroxide
7. calcium hydroxide
8. hydrochloric acid and nitric acid mixed
9. potassium carbonate
10. barium sulphate

Little Quiz 74, page 351
1. electric current
2. frequency
3. power
4. electrical resistance
5. thermodynamic temperature
6. energy, quantity of heat
7. quantity of electricity
   Watt, Kelvin, Joule

Little Quiz 75, page 353
1. 0.4047 hectare
2. 0.3049 metre
3. 50.80 kilograms
4. 0.142 litre
5. 1.8288 metres
6. 28.4131 cubic centimetres
7. 9.0922 litres
8. 1.1365 litres
9. 0.8361 square metre
10. 1.555 grams

Little Quiz 76, page 355
1. gammer
2. conductress
3. ogress
4. czarina
5. witch
6. hen-sparrow
7. maid-servant
8. bride
9. votaress
10. testatrix
11. dormice
12. lice
13. houses
14. men-of-war

15. courts-martial
16. grottos, grottoes
17. halves
18. trout
19. dozen
20. vetoes

Little Quiz 77, page 359

1. French	11. Russian
2. Dutch	12. Spanish
3. Dutch	13. Swiss
4. Italian	14. Swiss
5. Flemish	15. Russian
6. German	16. Alsatian
7. American	17. French
8. American	18. Scottish
9. Norwegian	19. Flemish
10. Austrian	20. Welsh

Little Quiz 78, page 361

1. William Gladstone
2. Sir Henry Campbell Bannerman
3. David Lloyd George
4. Stanley Baldwin
5. Sir Anthony Eden
6. Andrew Jackson
7. Abraham Lincoln
8. Theodore Roosevelt
9. Harry S. Truman
10. Richard Nixon

Little Quiz 79, page 365

1. Muriel Spark
2. Angus Wilson
3. E. M. Forster
4. L. P. Hartley
5. George Orwell
6. Carl Orff
7. Gustav Mahler
8. William Walton
9. Franz Joseph Haydn
10. Samuel Coleridge Taylor